Ecology of Greenways

The University of Minnesota Press
gratefully acknowledges the generous assistance
provided for the publication of this book
by the Surdna Foundation.

ECOLOGY OF GREENWAYS

Daniel S. Smith &
Paul Cawood Hellmund
editors

Foreword by
Richard T. T. Forman

DESIGN AND FUNCTION OF LINEAR CONSERVATION AREAS

UNIVERSITY OF MINNESOTA PRESS   MINNEAPOLIS   LONDON

Copyright 1993 by the Regents of the University of Minnesota

All rights reserved. No part of this publication may be reproduced, stored in a retrieval system, or transmitted, in any form or by any means, electronic, mechanical, photocopying, recording, or otherwise, without the prior written permission of the publisher.

Published by the University of Minnesota Press
2037 University Avenue Southeast, Minneapolis, MN 55455-3092

Printed in the United States of America on acid-free paper
Jacket and book design by Diane Gleba Hall

Library of Congress Cataloging-in-Publication Data
Ecology of greenways : design and function of linear conservation areas / Daniel S. Smith and Paul Cawood Hellmund, editors ; foreword by Richard T. T. Forman.
    p.   cm.
    Includes bibliographical references and index.
    ISBN 0-8166-2157-8 (alk. paper)
    1. Greenways.   2. Urban ecology (Biology)
    I. Smith, Daniel S. (Daniel Somers)   II. Hellmund, Paul Cawood.

HT166.E33   1993   92-43261
304.2—dc20   CIP

The University of Minnesota is an equal-opportunity educator and employer.

Contents

Richard T. T. Forman

Foreword

Corridors, both natural and human-created, permeate the land. Rivers, roads, power lines, and hedgerows are familiar examples. Recently, worldwide interest in greenway corridors (linear open spaces or conservation areas) has increased rapidly for both recreation and conservation purposes. Thus I find this book on the ecology of greenways to be extremely useful and timely.

Greenways contribute to many ecological and societal goals. They help maintain biological diversity, protect water resources, conserve soil, support recreation, enhance community and cultural cohesion, and provide species dispersal routes during climate change. But where are the best locations for greenways? How wide should they be? How straight or curvy? How connected? This book provides practical answers to such key questions.

To understand a corridor we must see it in context, within a larger landscape. Viewing arid, forested, agricultural, or suburban land from an airplane window or on an aerial photograph, we see that every point is part of a patch, a corridor, or a background matrix. Species, energy, and materials move through corridors, through the matrix, and from patch to patch. This patch-corridor-matrix paradigm, barely a decade old, has significantly enhanced our understanding and management of both corridors and the landscape as a whole.

Large patches of natural vegetation remain the top conservation priority in most landscapes. But greenways can provide a crucial connectivity among parks and natural areas and can additionally protect waterways.

How important are hedgerows between fields, or woody plants along suburban backyards? How significant are stream corridors and remnant vegetation strips etched across a landscape? And how important are major mountain ranges or river systems that delineate the regions of a continent? Corridors at each of these ascending scales are significant and for different reasons, as elucidated in this volume.

This book is unique because for greenways it:

1. Considers wildlife and water resources together as critical elements of ecological integrity,
2. Balances ecological concerns with human use, especially recreation, and
3. Applies scientific knowledge to the challenge of design.

Planners, designers, and managers should keep this volume handy for constant reference. Teachers should place it on library reserve for their students. Researchers should address the questions it poses. Land developers should use it to create ecologically sound development patterns. Citizens should study its central themes and then send a copy to their favorite decision maker.

Harvard University
September 1992

Preface

This book is about how, when, and where to nurture connections in the landscape to allow wildlife to move freely and to protect waterways—to enhance ecological health—while finding appropriate ways to bring people into nature. This book is also about another kind of connection: bridging design and ecology so that greenways can make meaningful contributions to the well-being of both nature and people.

The need for such a bridge became apparent to one of the editors of this book several years ago when he was working for the U.S. National Park Service as a greenway planner. He was familiar with a number of promising concepts from landscape ecology and conservation biology, but he was uncertain how to apply them to real-world greenway projects. As he talked with others he discovered that his situation was not unusual: ecologically minded planners and designers typically felt there were few practical tools to help them apply ecology to the design of greenways. Through conversations with practitioners and scien-

tists across the country, it became apparent that an applied volume on greenway ecology and design could be helpful, especially given the recent surge of interest in greenways.

To create a thorough and practical volume, experts in several disciplines—landscape ecology, conservation biology, aquatic ecology, and recreation design—were invited to contribute chapters on different aspects of greenway ecology and design. Each contributor was asked to present the important ecological issues from his discipline that are germane to greenways and to propose practical solutions and guidelines for common design problems. A landscape architect experienced in conservation design was asked to review these chapters and synthesize a method for ecological greenway design based in part on the findings of the other contributors. A final chapter describes notable greenways from across the country.

Many people and organizations helped make this book possible. The writings of Richard Forman and

Larry Harris, and conversations with these far-thinking scientists, helped us understand important concepts and develop the broad themes of the book. Both of these men shared generously of their knowledge and experiences.

People from a wide range of backgrounds read and commented on drafts of the book. Jack Ahern, Christine Carlson, Richard Forman, Bill Geizentanner, and Fritz Steiner reviewed drafts of all or nearly all of the book. Their suggestions were of inestimable value in shaping and refining the book's content and presentation. Others offered valuable comments on one or several chapters: Robin DeSota, Joan Cawood Hellmund, James Karr, Geoffrey Katz, Jeff Marion, Judy Meyer, Manuel Molles, Jennifer Waite, Dennis Saunders, Michael Soulé, Carl Steinitz, Sam Stokes, Charles Tracey, Monica Turner, and Gordon Whitney.

The concept for this book was initially developed as part of a project of the U.S. National Park Service, River and Trail Conservation Assistance program and resulted in a publication titled "How Greenways Work: A Handbook on Ecology." Steve Golden of that agency was a strong supporter of the project from its inception. The Surdna Foundation, the Fanwood Foundation, and the U.S. Environmental Protection Agency (through its Wetlands Division) also contributed financially to various aspects of the project.

The Massachusetts Audubon Society and the QLF/ Atlantic Center for the Environment helped with fundraising. Chris Leahy of Massachusetts Audubon and Larry Morris of the Atlantic Center provided generous encouragement and assistance.

Several other individuals were helpful at different stages of our work: Chris Brown (National Park Service), Rupert Cutler (The River Foundation), Glenn Eugster (Environmental Protection Agency), Keith Hay (The Conservation Fund), Brent Mitchell (The Atlantic Center), and Hope Stevens (The Fanwood Foundation).

Jane Shoplick created most of the illustrations in this book and set the style for all of the drawings. We are grateful for her skill and persistence. Andrea Dzurick, Karen Gostenhofer, and Vito Vanoni created the other illustrations with help from Lara Berkley. Ferranti-Dege, Inc., helped defray the cost of photographic reproductions. Allan Dutton donated computer equipment for portions of our editorial work.

We have been extremely fortunate to work with the authors who contributed chapters to this book. We thank them for sharing their knowledge, for their dedication, and for their patience with our efforts at building a cohesive volume from diverse perspectives.

Barbara Coffin, our editor at the University of Minnesota Press, has given us strong support and invaluable assistance. We are grateful to Barbara and the rest of the staff at the Press for their expertise and guidance.

We are indebted to all of these people and organizations for making this book possible and to our families and friends for their support.

There remains much to learn about greenways and their role in the landscape. We welcome your comments on the ideas and guidelines in this book and your experiences applying them. We thank, in advance, those who will read, consider, modify, and apply concepts from this book as they take part in efforts to enhance ecological integrity through greenway design.

D.S.S.
P.C.H.

Daniel S. Smith

Introduction

Although the term *greenway* is a fairly new one, most people have had some experience with these open-space corridors. Many have hiked along a wooded trail through rolling farm country or a protected swath of land along a mountain ridge (Figure 1). Others will recall a protected river corridor (Figure 2) or a more manicured urban riverside park (Figure 3). A greenway is, in simplest terms, a linear open space. It is a corridor composed of natural vegetation or at least vegetation that is *more* natural than in surrounding areas.

The idea that greenways are "good for the environment" comes intuitively, since, like other kinds of preserves, they set aside pieces of nature, be they narrow strips or broad swaths covering thousands of acres. Professionals in planning, design, and land management have probably heard more specific benefits cited: greenways can help protect waterways from non-point source pollution, and they can decrease the impacts of habitat fragmentation by allowing animals to move between habitats that would otherwise be isolated by human activities.

Greenways can be used to create connected networks of open space that also include more traditional, nonlinear parks and natural areas. They thus offer a powerful strategy for helping to maintain ecological integrity in human-dominated landscapes, especially with regard to preserving biological diversity and maintaining high-quality water resources.

A more thorough examination of greenways reveals much variability and complexity beneath these straightforward concepts. Some greenways follow pre-existing natural corridors, like ridgelines and streams, which may also be traditional animal movement routes. Others correspond to remnant strips of upland vegetation that have been isolated by human actions, like hedgerows and trail corridors. Still others coincide with abandoned rail lines and canal towpaths. Many greenways share common characteristics simply because, by definition, they are linear and natural. However, the ecological structure and function of any given greenway will depend on its location, its shape, the types of habitat it contains, and the nature of any human

Figure 1 A protected ridgeline and hiking trail in New Hampshire's White Mountains. (Photo by George Bellerose.)

modification that has occurred within its boundaries. These and other factors will all help determine how well a greenway functions for plants, animals, water, and people.

But considering a greenway's shape and internal characteristics is only a start in trying to understand its function, which will inevitably be influenced from the outside. As greenways wind through a landscape, they come in contact with many of its elements. Along the way, they encounter a complex pattern of different kinds of vegetation and land use, a mosaic of patches that make up the landscape. Fields, streams, forests, towns, and cities, along with other types of corridors like roads and power lines, all may be skirted, straddled, or crossed. Even in seemingly simple landscapes, a diverse context will be the rule. For instance, an agricultural area that at first looks like "just fields" may consist of pasture, cropland, woodlots, wetlands, and towns; a greenway can come in contact with many and perhaps all of these parts. Because they encounter so many elements, and further still because they connect pieces of the landscape together, greenways, like other corridors, *interact* with other parts of the mosaic to a high degree. The nature of these interactions will

depend on the characteristics of the greenway itself and those of its surroundings.

In recent years, greenways have captured the attention and imagination of the open-space conservation community in the United States. Greenways, which are sometimes called environmental corridors, landscape linkages, wildlife corridors, or riparian buffers, have come to be seen as an important means of protecting natural areas and providing recreation opportunities, especially in and around cities where open land is scarce. Greenways have been promoted by land managers, landscape architects, and planners, by local communities and citizens' groups, and by local, state, and federal governments. As a result, greenways of all kinds are being designed and protected by the score— but they are not always being implemented in a way that is best ecologically.

Ecology of Greenways is an exploration of the benefits that naturally vegetated corridors offer in maintaining key ecological processes in contemporary landscapes, and of how the maintenance of these processes can best be balanced with human use, especially recreation. This book can serve both as an educational tool for those who seek to understand the ecological implications of greenways and as a practical guide for professionals and volunteers involved in greenway design and conservation.

The chapters that follow also consider the limitations of greenways. They are not a panacea; as Reed Noss points out later in this volume, "Rather they must be seen as an element of an integrated landscape management strategy necessary to maintain the values of natural environments." To be effective wildlife corridors, greenways must be connected to larger preserves. They should be complemented with careful stewardship of surrounding farmland and commercial forests. Environmentally sensitive design of human settlements is important, too, as are state-of-the-art waste disposal systems and pollution controls. Well-designed greenways add a valuable tool to the array of conservation options, but, in our enthusiasm, we should not let them overshadow other appropriate conservation strategies.

Approach and Contents of This Volume

Ecological design, especially at the landscape scale, can best be accomplished with an interdisciplinary, holistic approach because landscapes are, by definition, complex and changing systems possessing component parts that are highly interconnected. Altering one component of a landscape will invariably have an impact on other parts. Modifying these systems with an eye to a single, narrow goal is apt to be shortsighted and may result in unexpected, negative consequences in the long run.

For instance, channelizing a stream can achieve the goal of quickly removing floodwaters from a local area, thus allowing more of the stream's floodplain to be safely developed. But channelization will also destroy aquatic and wetland habitats and may cause increased flood damage farther downstream. In contrast, maintaining streams and their floodplains in their natural state can simultaneously protect wetlands that serve as natural flood storage areas, protect aquatic and terrestrial wildlife habitat, and offer people a place for relaxation. In light of the fact that natural systems are inherently interactive, *Ecology of Greenways* stresses the need to look beyond single issues and functions and to consider multiple attributes and their interactions.

A broad approach in itself is not, however, sufficient to achieve successful ecological design. Design must also be based on a clear and detailed understanding of specific ecological phenomena. Without a work-

Figure 2   Verde River Greenway, upstream from Cottonwood, Arizona. (Photo by William Whitmore.)

ing knowledge of a system's parts and how they function, designs are unlikely to work as intended. If a wildlife corridor is to be effective, it will need to include the right kind of habitat and be of appropriate dimensions for local species. Likewise, the nature of riparian buffers in a given location should reflect an understanding of site-specific conditions such as vegetation, soils, slope, and adjacent land use.

The need to consider details of particular ecological processes while simultaneously integrating multiple themes is reflected in the array of the chapters that follow, as well as in the specific contents of each.

Chapter 1, "An Overview of Greenways," outlines the development of greenways in concept and practice from both a human and an ecological perspective. It provides an overview of greenway history, definitions, and specific functions and discusses the implications of corridor design and conservation for both people and nature. The chapter introduces several key issues in ecological greenway design, as well as a series of eight case studies that are discussed at length in chapter 7.

Chapter 2, "Landscape Ecology," introduces this emerging discipline as a framework for an ecological approach to greenways. A rapidly evolving field, landscape ecology stresses a holistic approach that integrates both human and natural phenomena at the broad scale of entire landscapes. Because most greenways are, by intent, places where people and nature mix, and because they often stretch across the landscape and span multiple ecosystems (e. g., streams, wetlands, and forests), landscape ecology provides a useful perspective from which to approach greenway design.

Chapters 3, 4, and 5 address in detail the three primary themes of this book: wildlife conservation, water resources protection, and recreation design. Wildlife and water resources are the main components of natural systems that will benefit from well-designed greenways. Recreation design, in addition to offering benefits to people, can minimize the negative effects of human use on natural areas. These chapters explain the theoretical basis and empirical evidence for a variety of pertinent concepts and issues.

Chapters 3 through 5 also explore pragmatic concerns and develop guidelines for ecological greenway design. Because effective design solutions will vary greatly from one region to the next, depending on climate, vegetation, animals, and the degree of human impact on the land, the guidelines presented are, with

Figure 3 Boulder Creek Greenway, Boulder, Colorado. (Photo by D. Smith.)

few exceptions, flexible in nature. Rather than providing simple, cookbook solutions to complex and variable problems, the chapters' authors have outlined adaptable, process-oriented guidelines, most of which will need to be refined according to the conditions of particular cases. The intent is not so much to tell practitioners what to do as to help guide them in finding their own solutions.

These guidelines are arranged according to three important tasks of greenway design: *selecting alignments, setting widths,* and *preparing site designs and management plans.* In relatively undeveloped landscapes where different options for greenway location still exist, selecting a greenway alignment involves discovering the most effective route to be taken across the landscape. Once an alignment has been chosen, or if existing land uses already limit greenway location to only one possibility, guidelines focus on determining widths that will support a greenway's intended functions. Following width determination or, again, if existing circumstances have already eliminated the need for this step, emphasis shifts to within the greenway itself, where site designs and management plans are devised. Guidelines in this category apply primarily to design of recreational facilities and to restoration, enhancement, and management of streams and vegetation.

Chapter 6, "A Method for Ecological Greenway Design," develops a practical method based on hierarchical scales that can be used to apply information and guidelines from previous chapters to greenway projects of all kinds. The method invokes guidelines from chapters 3 through 5 but also stresses the need to begin the process of design by evaluating larger ecological concerns and questions at the landscape and regional scales. The chapter provides a road map of how to "put it all together." It explores ways to adapt and apply guidelines for particular situations, how to balance different greenway uses, and how to find and use sources of information such as resource inventories, maps, technical publications, and informal sources.

Finally, chapter 7 presents eight case studies from around the country that illustrate greenway functions as well as design techniques that have been applied in the field. These case studies examine, within a real-world context, many of the issues discussed in earlier chapters.

Using *Ecology of Greenways*

Although some readers may choose to read all of the chapters that follow and to do so sequentially, others may want to study particular sections as the need arises. *Ecology of Greenways* can be a reference tool for researching specific topics, or it can be used more systematically as a guide for anyone designing a greenway that involves wildlife, water, or recreation issues.

Given the rising concern over environmental degradation, preventing or reversing this degradation where possible should be a primary focus of all greenway projects. Still, it is important for readers using *Ecology of Greenways* to clearly define the goals of their own project. Is the most important goal in a particular case to protect wildlife, to enhance water quality, or to create recreational opportunities? These goals should be set carefully and with consideration for the needs of both natural systems and people. Although all three goals will often be complementary, priorities should be carefully identified case by case.

In some instances, such as an urban greenway restricted to a very narrow width, creating a beautiful space for recreation may be the primary goal. Nonetheless, the corridor's ecological function should be considered and promoted wherever possible. In other cases, where nature conservation is most important, wildlife and water issues will come to the fore; recreational facilities will need to be carefully designed, and use restrictions may be needed to avoid negative ecological impacts. Still, recreation should be included to the extent possible.

Except in areas with extremely sensitive natural

features, such as rare or endangered species, both people and nature can usually be accommodated to some degree. We would do well to move beyond the idea of inevitable conflict between natural systems and human use and search for a more appropriate synthesis of the two. By doing so, we can not only protect the integrity of natural systems but also help people learn to know and appreciate nature.

Terminology and Definitions

In any complex endeavor, clear definitions are crucial to establishing effective communication. They are especially crucial for ecological design, which draws on an expanding interdisciplinary base of concepts and information. Throughout this volume, key terms are defined, usually where the terms first appear in the text. However, a few terms that are integral to discussions throughout this volume warrant clarification at the outset.

Design: Design is used here in a manner consistent with Lyle (1985) to describe intentional change in the landscape at a variety of spatial scales. It thus refers not only to the manipulation of landscape elements at the site scale but also to manipulation of much larger areas, which is often called *planning* (e.g., ecological landscape *planning*). However, design is not used here to refer to activities also called planning that focus on organization, administration, or the development of policy.

Greenway Synonyms: As noted earlier, a greenway is a kind of corridor. There are other kinds of corridors that are partially synonymous with greenway. *Wildlife corridors* and *riparian buffers*, although by no means mutually exclusive, are specific to wildlife movement and water resource protection. Greenways intended primarily to protect natural values are sometimes called *environmental corridors* or even *ecology corridors*. Very

wide greenways (on the order of several miles wide) are often referred to as *landscape linkages*. Finally, *greenbelts* are used to encircle towns and cities with bands of open space, in part to maintain scenic quality and limit urban sprawl.

Natural: The word *natural* is seemingly straightforward and certainly important to any discussion of ecology and conservation. However, the term reinforces our cultural tendency to make arbitrary distinctions between what is human and what is natural. People have been modifying what are often considered to be natural landscapes for many thousands of years; very few places on earth remain untouched by human influence. For instance, vegetation in nearly all greenways will have been affected to some extent over time by land-use practices, air pollution, or other factors, although modification will not always be obvious. Nonetheless, the term natural remains important to our discussion as a means of distinguishing that which is *relatively* unaffected by people and their attendant complex of technology, land use, and nonnative species.

Wildlife: In common parlance, wildlife usually means wild *animal* life. As Reed Noss points out in chapter 3, a more literal definition including all non-domesticated (i.e., wild) forms of life is useful where biological diversity is concerned. Wildlife is thus used here to refer to both plants and animals that are not domesticated. Plants and animals can be further differentiated into native species, which together constitute native biological diversity, and nonnative, invasive species, which often have a negative impact on native biodiversity.

Reference

Lyle, J. H. 1985. *Design for Human Ecosystems.* Van Nostrand Reinhold Co., New York.

Daniel S. Smith

1

An Overview of Greenways

Their History, Ecological Context, and Specific Functions

Greenways can range in form from narrow urban trail corridors to winding river corridors to very wide, wilderness-like landscape linkages. They can straddle waterways, traverse ridgelines, or cut across upland areas independent of natural geomorphic features. They occur in different types of landscapes, from cities and suburbs to farmland and commercial forests.

The variety of greenways and of the contexts in which they occur stems from a number of influences. It results from the numerous kinds of natural corridors in the landscape that often form the basis for greenways, such as waterways, ridgelines, and animal movement routes. It results from various intensities of development in different landscapes, since more intense development tends to squeeze remnant natural areas into progressively smaller and more narrow spaces.

Greenway diversity also results from historical influences. In the late nineteenth and early twentieth centuries, linear open spaces were first designed as parkways, which often tied together urban park sys-

tems. During the same period, broad greenbelts were also first used to encircle cities and limit urban sprawl. In the 1960s, ecological planners and landscape architects recognized the need to protect corridors, mostly along waterways, that include a high concentration of important natural features. More recently, scientists have considered the significance of corridors for wildlife management and biodiversity protection.

All corridors have certain basic characteristics in common. But the diversity of greenway types and forms, combined with geographic differences, means that different kinds of greenways will function in different ways, both ecologically and socially. Ecologically, greenways can protect natural areas and diminish the isolating, disruptive effects of habitat fragmentation on wildlife and water resources. Their effectiveness on both of these counts, however, will vary according to their width, shape, location, context, and other factors. From a social perspective, greenways provide places for recreation and help maintain the scenic quality of landscapes. But again, not all greenways will function for people in equivalent ways.

To explain the causes and implications of this diversity and thus set the stage for subsequent chapters on ecology, recreation, and design, this chapter considers greenway history, definitions, and types, as well as the range of greenways' ecological and social functions. It also outlines the major design issues that relate to greenway ecology and briefly describes a series of case studies that are presented in more detail in chapter 7. First, the chapter defines the overarching problem that greenways can help solve: the loss and fragmentation of natural areas.

The Problem: Loss and Fragmentation of Natural Open Spaces

In many parts of the United States, there has been an unprecedented loss of open space to development in recent years, and this loss is likely to continue for the foreseeable future. In just twenty-three years, between 1959 and 1982, the total area in urban and other developed land uses in the United States increased by twenty-two million acres, or 45 percent (Heimlich and Anderson 1987). That is more than the total area of the state of Maine or roughly ten times the size of Yellowstone National Park. This trend has been under way since the first Europeans settled on American shores and began importing a new and exotic way of life and use of the land. Only recently, however, has it been widely recognized that the proliferation of intensive human activities and the loss of natural areas are leading to serious decline of ecosystems and ecological processes.

Fewer acres of open land mean less habitat and less diversity of habitat for wildlife of all sorts, including birds, mammals, reptiles, fish, and plants. This problem is especially serious for native species that are poorly adapted to human-dominated landscapes and most grave for rare or endangered species, the list of

which continues to grow. Habitat loss clearly contributes to the fact that, as of 1990, 597 species of animals and plants in the United States were listed as threatened or endangered by the U.S. Fish and Wildlife Service (U.S. Department of Interior 1990).

Development also generates contaminants like eroded soil, excess nutrients, and toxic chemicals, which reduce water quality in wetlands, streams, and aquifers. Buildings, roads, and other impermeable surfaces redirect the drainage of water that would otherwise soak into the soil. They increase the amount of surface drainage conveyed directly to waterways and can thus radically alter the hydrology of streams and rivers.

Human activity is not only reducing the size and number of remaining natural areas but also causing habitat fragmentation, which results in configurations, or arrangements, of these areas that are poorly suited to maintaining ecological function. Remaining wildlife habitats have become isolated from one another by inhospitable land uses such as agriculture, roads, suburbs, and cities (Figure 1.1, Table 1.1). As will be explained in subsequent chapters, this phenomenon of habitat fragmentation can be just as serious a problem for native wildlife as simple reductions in acreage. Small and isolated habitat areas tend to support fewer native species as well as smaller (and therefore less secure) populations of those species that do persist. Developed areas that separate habitat fragments tend to discourage dispersal of individuals between populations, thus making them more vulnerable to genetic inbreeding and localized extinctions. Finally, fragmentation encourages the spread of invasive "weedy" plants and animals that often displace or prey upon native species (Wilcove et al. 1986; Wilcox and Murphy 1985; Noss, chapter 3, this volume).

The spatial configuration of natural areas also has far-reaching effects on water resources. If arranged haphazardly within a watershed, areas of natural vegetation cannot fulfill the protective functions of continuous riparian forests. Stripped of their natural vege-

Figure 1.1 Loss and fragmentation of forested areas in Cadiz Township, Green County, Wisconsin, between 1831 and 1950. The township is 6 by 6 miles. Shaded areas represent remaining forest cover and, in the lower left, land reverting to forest from presettlement grassland. (After Curtis 1956; with permission of University of Chicago Press.)

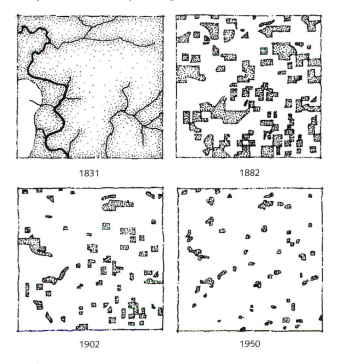

1831   1882

1902   1950

Table 1.1 Quantitative characteristics of forest loss and fragmentation in Cadiz Township, Wisconsin

	1831	1882	1902	1950
Total acres of forest	21,548	6,380	2,077	786
Number of forest patches	1	70	61	55
Average patch size in acres	21,548	91.3	34	14.3
Total edge of patches in miles	—	99	61.2	39.8
Average edge/forested acre in feet	—	80.7	152.7	276.2

Note: As the total forested area and average patch size decreased, habitat for native species was reduced. Meanwhile, the amount of edge per acre of forest increased, probably promoting the spread of invasive species.
Source: After Curtis (1956).

Biological diversity is a topic of growing public discussion. P. R. Ehrlich and E. O. Wilson (1991) suggest that there are probably between 10 million and 100 million species on Earth, although only 1.4 million species have been described scientifically. Based on current and expected human activity, they also estimate that more than one-quarter of all species may become extinct in the next fifty years, and that this rate may be significantly increased by expanded human population and economic activity worldwide.

Although the historical development of intensive agriculture greatly reduced the number of species upon which most people rely directly for sustenance, the discovery of new species and strains of organisms useful for food and medicines is likely to continue to benefit humanity (Ehrlich and Wilson 1991). Although tropical regions possess a high proportion of all species, the recent discovery of taxol, an extract of the pacific yew in North America, as a potent cancer drug suggests that temperate regions may also contain species of great value. Biological diversity also provides amenities for people, such as enjoyment and education gained through nature observation (Norton 1987). Many also argue persuasively that species have intrinsic value and should be protected on purely moral grounds (Norton 1987; Ehrlich and Wilson 1991; see the collection of essays in Engel and Engel 1990).

Even if a particular species or community is not

tation, waterways are susceptible to contamination from an array of materials moving downslope, including sediment, excess nutrients, and other pollutants (Forman and Godron 1986; Lowrance et al. 1985). Aquatic habitats and their biota become degraded by these contaminants and also suffer from decreased inputs of food and organic debris (Binford and Buchenau, chapter 4, this volume).

Diverse wildlife communities and clean water resources are both crucial to the maintenance of ecological integrity, also referred to as ecological health. Although absolute standards for acceptable or desirable levels of ecological integrity are difficult to define, the term refers in a broad sense to the degree to which ecosystems maintain natural processes and phenomena (see chapters 2 and 4 for further discussion). Ecological integrity is ultimately vital to the sustainability of both natural communities and human society.

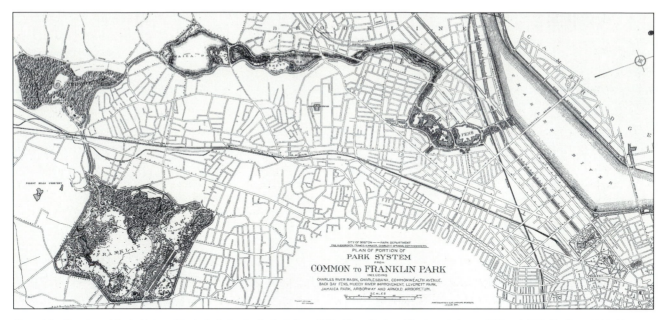

Figure 1.2 Plan view of Frederick Law Olmsted's design for Boston's Emerald Necklace. Designed in stages between 1878 and 1890, the Emerald Necklace includes a series of urban parks linked together with parkways. (Courtesy of National Park Service, Frederick Law Olmsted National Historic Site.)

threatened with complete extinction (i.e., globally), maintaining diversity at local and regional scales is an important goal of conservation. Local and regional diversity contributes to amenities like recreation, scenic beauty, and education and helps maintain the stability of "ecosystem services," like cleansing of air and water (Ehrlich and Wilson 1991).

Water resources make an often overlooked contribution to biological diversity. Although aquatic species are less visible than their terrestrial counterparts, they appear overall to be more vulnerable to extinction throughout North America (Master 1991). In a more utilitarian vein, water quality has obvious significance for human uses, including direct consumption and recreation. Clean water is consistently a major concern of public health officials, conservationists, engineers, planners, and the public in general.

Although the primary focus of this book is ecological, the indirect consequences of diminishing natural areas are significant for people too, as scenery is degraded and recreational opportunities disappear. Nature and the aesthetic, recreational, and spiritual experiences it provides are important to individuals and to our collective cultural heritage. The loss and fragmentation of open space limit what many people perceive as an already tenuous connection to the natural world. They foster a sense of alienation and decrease people's sense of place and enjoyment of the landscape.

Protecting any sort of natural area can help diminish the effects of habitat loss. In many cases, greenways can add greatly to the effectiveness of traditional preserves simply because of their linearity. They not only protect habitat but also have the potential to link other natural areas together and to straddle and protect streams and rivers. As a means of maintaining connectivity, greenways can thus help alleviate the effects of both habitat loss *and* fragmentation.

Later, this chapter will discuss some of the specific ways in which greenways can help maintain ecological integrity. First, it will consider the history of greenways, examine greenway definitions from an ecological perspective, and look at some examples of different types of greenways.

A Brief History of Greenways

Early Ideas and Their Application

The term *greenway* is relatively new, having only emerged in the late 1950s and subsequently gained wide acceptance among landscape architects, open-space planners, and conservationists (Little 1990). But the design of linear open spaces in North America predates the name by nearly a century.

As early as the 1860s, Frederick Law Olmsted recognized the great potential of linear open spaces for providing access to city parks and extending the benefits of parks into nearby neighborhoods. By designing tree-lined carriageways, which he called park ways, that linked parks to each other and to surrounding neighborhoods, Olmsted enhanced the recreational and aesthetic experience of park visitors. He first proposed these linkages in California in 1865, one in Berkeley and one running between Berkeley and Oakland (C. E. Beveridge, as cited in Little 1990). Although these first designs were never implemented, Olmsted pushed forward with the idea.

In 1866 and 1867, Olmsted and his partner, Calvert Vaux, designed Brooklyn's Prospect Park. As part of that design they proposed two connecting parkways, one leading south to Coney Island, the other linking Prospect Park with Central Park in Manhattan, which had also been designed by Olmsted and Vaux. Although the linkage to Central Park was never implemented, the parkway to Coney Island and another leading northeast to Queens, called Ocean Parkway and Eastern Parkway respectively, were later constructed (Fisher 1986; Little 1990). These parkways included broad, six-lane carriage roads and walking paths and were flanked on each side by 32-foot-wide wooded strips (Little 1990).

Olmsted and Vaux continued to use linear connections in many of their later designs, including parkways and open-space systems in Buffalo and Chicago. They emphasized social and aesthetic issues in most of their work because these were the most pressing needs of their day. However, Olmsted's design for Boston's Emerald Necklace, which he developed in stages between 1878 and 1890, also addressed problems of drainage and water quality.

Encircling the city with a ring of green that included the Back Bay Fens and the Muddy River (which flows into the tidal portion of the Charles River) as well as other parks and parkway segments, the Emerald Necklace, as it has come to be known, is one of Olmsted's most famous designs (Figure 1.2). Here, he expanded upon his earlier aesthetic focus by modifying the river to better drain surrounding neighborhoods and by reshaping the fens to provide increased flood storage (Zaitzevsky 1982; Figure 1.3). These actions were combined with the construction of sewers for human waste, which had previously run raw into the river, and flood gates to regulate periodic flooding tides. The project enhanced flood storage, improved waste disposal, and linked the area to the rest of the Emerald Necklace for recreation and transporta-

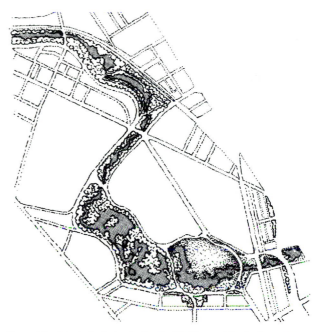

Figure 1.3 Olmsted's design for the Muddy River and the Back Bay Fens, both part of the Emerald Necklace, involved modifications that increased the flood storage capacity of the fens and helped reduce raw sewage flowing into the river.

tion. Although these modifications were more akin to modern engineering solutions than to an ecological approach, Olmsted nonetheless established an early precedent for the idea of using greenways to accommodate multiple uses.

Around the turn of the century, parkways and open-space connectors became more common in American cities as others followed Olmsted's lead. Between 1890 and the 1920s, similar linkages were designed by H. W. S. Cleveland in Minneapolis and St. Paul, by Charles Eliot in the greater Boston area, and by Jens Jensen in South Chicago (Steiner et al. 1988).

These early open-space corridors, even when fairly narrow, could usually accommodate carriage roads and walking paths while maintaining a pleasing, naturalistic setting (Little 1990). This situation changed with the advent of the automobile as a common means of transportation in the early decades of the twentieth century. With the addition of automobiles, many parkways designed after about 1920 took on a very different character, first as paved roads for pleasure driving and later as high-speed commuter routes (Newton 1971; Little 1990). Some of these later parkways were designed with wide buffers of natural land, especially those built in the 1920s and 1930s, like the Bronx River Parkway in New York and Virginia's Skyline Drive, flanked by Shenandoah National Park. Later, as cars got faster, traffic became heavier, and people traveled greater distances, these winding, leisurely roads gave way to straighter parkways designed for faster travel and eventually were made largely obsolete by today's utilitarian highways and freeways (Little 1990; E. Carr, personal communication).

An independent but somewhat related concept was developed in England at about the same time. In 1898, Ebenezer Howard proposed the design of a model "Garden City." In this idealized scheme, the inner city, mostly residential, would be encircled with a "Grand Avenue." The avenue was to be "420 feet wide, and, forming a belt of green upwards of three miles long" (Howard 1902, 24). Further out, beyond commercial

and industrial areas, Garden City was to be surrounded by extensive farms and forests (Howard 1902). Howard meant to insulate cities with belts of rural land to limit urban sprawl and to tie city and country together, thus offering the benefits of both to society. Howard's concept, including the use of greenbelts, as they came to be called, was later adapted with various degrees of success in numerous town-planning efforts in England (Newton 1971). After World War II, a greenbelt was implemented around London, mostly by means of land-use controls (Whyte 1968).

Greenbelts were later used in America in the design of several new planned communities, or "new towns." A key figure in the United States was Rexford Guy Tugwell, who proposed and headed the Resettlement Association within the U.S. Department of Agriculture during the New Deal. To provide low-income housing during the Depression, Tugwell oversaw from 1935 to 1937 the design and implementation of three new towns surrounded by greenbelts: Greenhills, Ohio; Greendale, Wisconsin; and Greenbelt, Maryland (Steiner et al. 1988; Newton 1971; Little 1990).

The greenbelt concept was further developed by the American regional planner Benton MacKaye (1928). MacKaye proposed systems of wooded open space that "would form a linear area, or belt around and through the locality" (MacKaye 1928, 179). His intent was more than just to surround cities with green space as a means of blocking urban sprawl. He also suggested bisecting settled areas with spokes of green and including recreation as a primary use of these "open ways," as he called them. MacKaye thus combined, in effect, the greenbelt concept with elements of the early parkways and urban open-space networks. MacKaye also proposed the Appalachian Trail in 1921, which he saw not just as a hiking trail, but as a large-scale version of his regional open spaces, containing the spread of development from the eastern seaboard and providing a primeval pathway for the adventurous hiker. Today, the 2,100-mile Appalachian National Scenic Trail is protected with a nearly continuous corridor of land that averages about 1,000 feet wide and also connects many larger federal and state holdings.

An Ecological Approach to Planning and Design

In the 1960s, the ideas of Olmsted, Howard, and MacKaye were followed by the emergence of a new emphasis on ecology in planning and design, which has had a major impact on the development of greenways. Early in the decade, Phillip Lewis, Jr., a professor of landscape architecture at the University of Wisconsin at Madison, stressed the importance of ecological features in guiding land conservation. By compiling and analyzing natural-resource information on transparent map overlays, Lewis found that the bulk of important resources were typically found along waterways and in areas of pronounced topography; he referred to these alignments as "environmental corridors" (Lewis 1964; Wisconsin Department of Resource Development 1962). Using this technique, Lewis systematically identified corridors in statewide studies of Wisconsin and Illinois. In Wisconsin, these corridors (Figure 1.4) formed the basis for a statewide trails plan which subsequently became a focus of state land acquisitions (Lewis 1964). Lewis's work also paved the way for successful efforts to preserve an extensive regional network of corridors in southeast Wisconsin (see case study, chapter 7).

A few years later, Ian McHarg, of the University of Pennsylvania, published his influential book *Design with Nature* (1969), in which he outlined a theoretical and technical basis for ecologically based planning and design. McHarg stressed the importance of systematic land-use planning according to the relative ecological value and sensitivity of each part of the landscape: "The distribution of open space must respond to natural process. . . . The problem lies not in absolute area but in distribution. We seek a concept that can provide an interfusion of open space and population" (McHarg 1969, 65). The idea was not so much to exclude devel-

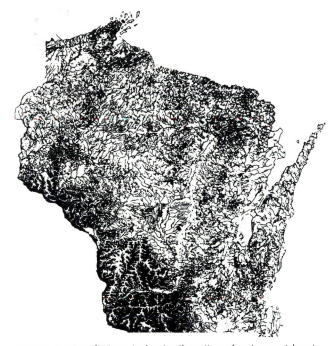

Figure 1.4 Map of Wisconsin showing the pattern of environmental corridors identified by Phillip Lewis, Jr., including waterways, wetlands, and, especially in the southwestern portion of the state, areas of pronounced topography. (Wisconsin Department of Resource Development 1962.)

opment as to distribute it in such a way as to minimize disruption of ecological processes.

McHarg's method, like Lewis's, is based on a system of transparent map overlays. Each overlay represents a different category of natural feature, such as hydrology, geology, and plant communities. For each type of feature, the more sensitive an area is to development impacts, the darker a shading it receives. (Sensitivity is determined previously through ecological inventory and analysis.) The overlays are then placed atop one another to form a composite that reveals the combined shading, and thus sensitivity, of all locations (Figure 1.5). In this way, the relative suitability of different areas for development of various kinds and intensities, or for conservation, is determined. Since stream and river corridors nearly always have important combinations of natural features—as Lewis had earlier demonstrated—this method provides an important objective rationale for corridor protection.

Although similar systems of overlays have been used since at least as early as 1912 (Steinitz et al. 1976), McHarg's development and application of the technique, together with his articulation of a comprehensive approach to ecological planning and design, mark a major step in the development of the field (Steiner 1988). Importantly, this method addresses much more than the delineation of corridors and has been used to develop spatial frameworks for both development and conservation across large, nonlinear areas (for an example, see Woodlands case study, chapter 7). Variations of the method have been adapted to computerized geographic information systems (see chapter 6 for further discussion).

It is worth noting that overlay techniques are only as useful as the ecological inventory and analysis that precede them. Many projects that use overlays look almost exclusively at the *pattern* of resource distribution, with little regard for ecological *processes*, which are less readily uncovered because they so often extend beyond the obvious boundaries of natural features. For instance, it is one thing to identify the extent of riparian vegetation, but it is quite another to determine the width of a corridor beyond (or perhaps within) this area that will effectively filter out contaminants emanating from adjacent areas or that will allow wildlife to pass unimpeded. If the nature of these processes is understood, they can be incorporated into the method.

River Conservation:
Federal, State, and Private Efforts

Although much of the historical development of greenways has been defined by planners and landscape architects, efforts in river and stream conservation have also led to the protection of many riparian greenways. Especially since the 1960s, when the problem of water pollution from sewage and industrial waste was raised in the public consciousness, restoring water quality and aquatic habitat has been a priority for government agencies and many nonprofit conservation organiza-

Figure 1.5 The map overlay process combines maps of various environmental features to create a composite map. As promoted by Ian McHarg, such overlay systems have been widely used to determine appropriate locations for different kinds of land use, including conservation.

tions. Previously strong national support for dams and other large federal water projects also came to be tempered by concerns, largely articulated by national environmental groups, about the environmental damage and lost recreational opportunities caused by damming the nation's remaining free-flowing rivers (Palmer 1986).

With passage of the National Wild and Scenic Rivers Act in 1968, protecting rivers became a component of national environmental policy. So far, this legislation has been used to protect 125 rivers or river segments, totaling 9,452 miles, from dams and impoundments (American Rivers, Inc., personal communication). Many of these designations have resulted in increased protection of riverside lands through federal land purchases, improved management of existing public lands, or increased local regulation of development and land use (P. Huffman, personal communication). Many states have implemented river protection programs that complement the federal wild and scenic system by protecting additional waterways (Palmer 1986; Stokes et al. 1989).

Another piece of federal legislation that has fostered the establishment of riparian greenways is Section 404 of the Clean Water Act, which offers significant protection to many of the nation's wetlands. Also important, although not water-related, has been the National Trails System Act, which was designed to spur the creation of a national system of hiking trails. The act has been used to purchase land along extensive stretches of the Appalachian Trail and to support planning and management efforts by numerous volunteer trail groups, who sponsor eight National Scenic Trails with a combined length of over 14,000 miles (Stokes et al. 1989).

Land-use regulations have also been used by states and municipalities systematically to protect streamside corridors across large areas. For instance, Maine's Shoreland Zoning Act requires municipalities to designate protection standards for zones 250 feet wide around lakes and ponds and 75 feet wide along streams (USDA Forest Service 1990). In similar fashion, Maryland requires towns to limit development along streams and rivers that drain into Chesapeake Bay, where reduced water quality threatens the estuary's health and productivity (Rome 1991). Although these and other regulatory programs do not usually lead to officially designated greenways, they have offered at least partial protection to thousands of miles of waterways.

Recent Developments: Greenways as a Focus of Open-Space Protection

In the 1980s, increased interest in open-space conservation converged with the growing popularity of outdoor recreation, resulting in many new greenway projects along with vigorous support across the country (Little 1990). As the loss of open space has become increasingly apparent on the national level and particularly striking in many urban areas, interest in all types of land conservation has risen to an unprecedented level. At the same time, the cost of land in many places, especially in metropolitan areas, has continued to rise while federal funding for land conservation has plummeted. Land protection has thus become increasingly difficult in many parts of the country.

Greenways are a partial solution to this problem because they often require less land than traditional, nonlinear parks, especially when recreation is the primary focus. They are often less costly and therefore more feasible to implement for local, county, or state governments or for private conservation groups. (It should be noted, however, that complex ownership patterns bisecting potential greenways may hamper acquisition and increase costs; natural features may be aligned in a linear fashion, but property boundaries rarely are.) In urban areas, where narrow streamside corridors are often the only open spaces remaining, greenways may be the last realistic option for land conservation.

Meanwhile, the increased demand for outdoor recreation of recent years has spurred on greenway initiatives. The linearity of greenways makes them well suited for trails, while their common presence along water encourages boating and fishing and makes for beautiful scenery. Recreationists therefore have a strong affinity for greenways and have become their biggest boosters among the general public, playing a significant role in greenway advocacy.

All of these trends were recognized by the President's Commission on Americans Outdoors, appointed in 1985 to study the state of open space and outdoor recreation in America (President's Commission on Americans Outdoors 1987). The commission found strong support across the country for increasing land conservation and recreation facilities and proposed a national system of greenways as a means of achieving both ends: "We have a vision for allowing every American easy access to the natural world: Greenways. Greenways are fingers of green that reach out from and around and through communities all across America, created by local action. They will connect parks and forests and scenic countrysides, public and private, in recreation corridors for hiking, jogging, wildlife movement, horse and bicycle riding" (President's Commission on Americans Outdoors 1987, 124).

One estimate put the number of greenways existing in the United States in 1989 at over 250 (Scenic Hudson, Inc. and National Park Service 1989). The actual number of greenways may be much higher, since many protected linear open spaces that lack organized management, administration, or publicity often go unrecognized. The term *greenway* can usefully be applied to many linear open spaces that have not traditionally been so named.

Dozens of greenway projects are now under way across the country in urban, suburban, and rural settings. Notable efforts with a strong recreational focus, but which also involve land protection, are taking place in San Francisco, where the Bay Trail and the Bay Area Ridge Trail trace concentric rings around San Francisco Bay; along the Chattanooga River in Chattanooga, Tennessee; from New York City to Albany and beyond along the Hudson River; and in Boston, where the Bay Circuit Trail encircles the metropolitan area much as Frederick Law Olmsted's Emerald Necklace encircled the inner city over a century ago. Several coordinated urban greenway networks are now under way that stress both recreation and conservation in cities like Boulder, Colorado; Davis, California; and Raleigh, North Carolina. The state of Maryland has launched a statewide greenways program that seeks to combine water resource and habitat protection. In Texas, the U.S. Fish and Wildlife Service is working to secure a major wildlife corridor along 250 miles of the lower Rio Grande. Other examples abound, some of which are quite important ecologically and will be discussed in chapter 7.

Greenway Definitions and Types

The term *greenway* refers to open space or natural areas that have a linear form. Charles Little offers a useful expanded definition: a greenway is a "linear open space established along either a natural corridor, such as a riverfront, stream valley, or ridgeline, or overland along a railroad right-of-way converted to recreational use, a canal, a scenic road, or other route" or, alternately, an "open space connector linking parks, nature reserves, cultural features, or historic sites, with each other and with populated areas" (Little 1990, 1).

This definition suggests a broad range of greenway types and a multiplicity of uses. Since *Ecology of Greenways* is primarily concerned with nature conservation, it focuses on corridors that are ecologically significant. Still, it is important to start with a broader understanding of greenways and the variety of forms they take, which in turn influences the functions they support.

In describing the different elements that can make up a greenway, many advocates and planners emphasize recreational corridors (which may have little ecological value) along with natural areas, both to provide for human needs and to appeal to the general public to

Figure 1.6 A recreational greenway along the Charles River in Cambridge, Massachusetts. The river is a mecca for rowers, while paths along its banks are used by walkers and joggers and by bicyclists who commute to nearby Boston. (Photo by D. Smith.)

bring diverse constituencies and resources (both land-based and financial) into greenway projects. Writing about greenways in the Hudson River valley, Karl Beard and Barry Didato speak of connecting forests and nature preserves. But they also stress human use when they write that greenways "can include such features as hiking trails, bike paths, city sidewalks, streams suitable for canoeing, abandoned railroad rights-of-way or scenic roads" (Scenic Hudson, Inc. and National Park Service 1989).

At the other end of the spectrum, conservation biologists and landscape ecologists typically describe and study, and conservationists seek to protect, wildlife corridors and streamside buffers largely from the standpoint of understanding, enhancing, or protecting ecological integrity. For example, Larry Harris defines a "faunal dispersal corridor" as "a naturally existing or restored native linear landscape feature that connects two or more larger tracts of habitat and functions as a dispersal route for native fauna and flora and for the occurrence of natural ecological processes such as fire" (Harris, personal communication). Although human beings are technically part of the native fauna of North America, this description does not include human use as a major concern.

These definitions are quite different in their emphasis, but they are not mutually exclusive. Although the functions of some existing greenways are largely limited to either recreation or nature conservation, most support some combination of the two.

Recreational greenways include trails for walking or bicycling and sometimes areas for organized sports and other group activities (Figure 1.6). Linear urban parks, often located along riversides, usually have a strong recreational focus, as do converted human-made corridors like canal towpaths or railroad rights-of-way ("rail-trails"), which often make effective routes for bicycle commuters in suburbs and cities.

Greenways devoted mostly to conservation are more likely to be established in rural areas (although such areas may undergo development in the future).

Figure 1.7 Two scenes along the Fox River in Waukesha County, Wisconsin. The first scene is an urban, recreational greenway in the city of Waukesha; the second is a wildlife sanctuary in an agricultural area south of the city. (Photos by D. Smith.)

Thus, the city of Boulder, Colorado, has designed multipurpose greenways that include walking trails, paved bike paths, and habitat for urban wildlife, while the surrounding county has designated corridors in rural areas primarily to protect elk migration routes. In a five-county area of southeastern Wisconsin, a network of "environmental corridors," mostly along waterways, has been protected in both rural and urban areas, with many of the most significant ecological corridors occurring outside of cities (Figure 1.7). (For

Figure 1.8 Wissahickon Creek in Philadelphia's Fairmount Park constitutes a major urban natural area and includes both trails and developed recreational areas. (Photo by D. Smith.)

descriptions of these examples, see chapter 7, or the case study summaries at the end of this chapter.) Because the term *greenway* has been typically associated with recreation, conservation-oriented corridors often carry different names. Nonetheless, as linear open spaces, they fit the definition of greenway.

Although the relative emphasis placed on recreation or conservation frequently shifts from urban to rural areas, most greenways incorporate both uses to some extent. Philadelphia's Fairmount Park includes a broad greenway along the Wissahickon Creek, which is both an urban natural area and a popular recreation corridor (Figure 1.8). The Appalachian Trail takes hikers on a 2,100-mile journey; it is also protected by a nearly continuous corridor of protected land that ranges from less than 1,000 feet to several miles wide (Figure 1.9). The Bay Circuit Trail, encircling the Boston metropolitan area, is billed as a recreation way for public use. It also runs through a series of natural areas and by making those areas available to the public serves as a catalyst for continued land protection along its length. Even converted rail lines, which are apt to be quite narrow, can be valuable havens for some animal and plant species if vegetation is maintained or restored.

As Jim Thorne discusses in the next chapter, greenways can also be differentiated according to the natural features they include. Ridgeline and riparian greenways trace natural physiographic corridors. Upland greenways that follow neither ridges nor waterways are usually defined by human activity on the land. Connectors can tie together other, longer greenways to provide multiple linkages and network connectivity. This typology provides useful descriptive terms that relate less to characteristics that may change over time or along a greenway's length, like recreation intensity or the type of adjacent land use, and more to primary physical and biological characteristics.

It is important to recognize that greenways of all sorts are a synthesis of both natural and cultural influences. This is true of greenways that incorporate human-engineered corridors (rail-trails or canal towpaths) that can be enhanced with native vegetation, as well as remnant natural corridors, such as riparian greenways, which have nonetheless been isolated by human actions and exist within human-modified landscapes. Similarly, a single greenway may traverse a variety of different land-use types, including both urban and rural areas.

Within the context of the preceding discussion,

Figure 1.9 Aerial photo of South Mountain, Maryland, which includes a portion of the Appalachian Trail and is important for both recreation and conservation. (Courtesy of U.S. Geological Survey.)

Ecology of Greenways concentrates on the function and design of corridors that exhibit natural characteristics and that are significant in maintaining ecological processes. Although such corridors are not purely "natural" in the sense of being pristine and unaffected by human activity, they are natural relative to their surroundings. They are distinguished spatially by adjacent lands with increased development, intensity of human land use, and disruption of ecological pattern and process. Alternatively, adjacent lands may be expected to undergo development pressure in the future. Thus, corridors that may not be currently distinguished by ecological function but that are legally protected from future development are also important from a design perspective.

Of particular interest from an ecological perspective is the question of width. Although width has not often been specifically addressed in greenway definitions, greenways are often assumed to have relatively narrow, or at least moderate, width, ranging from as little as a hundred feet to perhaps as much as a half-mile wide. Although this assumption holds true for many existing greenways, wider corridors, as much as several miles wide but nonetheless of linear shape, do indeed constitute greenways and are important to consider. Miles-wide corridors are especially valuable for wildlife because they can accommodate area-sensitive and far-ranging species. Our inquiry here need not be limited by such scale differences but rather will focus on the function of corridors across different scales.

Greenway Functions: An Overview

Ecological Functions

Like other types of preserves, greenways have a host of important ecological functions simply because they *protect* natural areas. They provide habitat for plants and animals. Riparian corridors are especially important in this respect because they can include a diversity of habitats—aquatic, riparian, and upland—within a relatively small area (Forman and Godron 1986). Greenways and other natural areas supply clean water to aquifers, wetlands, and waterways. If they occupy enough area, they can help to counteract excessive heat buildup in cities through shading and vegetative evapotranspiration, both of which cool the air (Spirn 1984). Greenway vegetation can contribute to urban air quality by filtering out particulate matter, especially pollutants emanating from adjacent roadways (Grey and Deneke 1986).

If properly designed, streamside greenways and those linked to other natural areas can also perform many functions that traditional preserves cannot. As R.T.T. Forman and M. Godron (1986) stressed in developing a conceptual framework for landscape ecology, corridors are not only structurally prominent in most landscapes but also strongly influence the flow of organisms, materials, and energy. Because greenways have the high ratio of edge to interior that characterizes all corridors, they are very much exposed to surrounding elements. They thus interact with adjacent lands—sometimes for better, sometimes for worse—to a much greater degree than nonlinear conservation areas.

This interaction between greenways and their surroundings can involve the movement of both animals and plants. Conservation biologists and landscape ecologists have suggested that naturally vegetated corridors can play a key role in allowing wildlife to move between habitat areas that would otherwise be isolated from one another (for examples, see Harris 1984; Forman and Godron 1986; Noss 1987). In recent years, this suggestion has been supported by empirical studies of animal movement, including small and large mammals in North America (Wegner and Merriam 1979; Merriam and Lanoue 1990; Maehr 1990), small mammals in Australia (Bennett 1990), and numerous birds in North America and Europe (Johnson and Adkisson 1985; Dmowski and Kozakiewicz 1990).

Providing for animal movement can have numerous benefits (Noss, chapter 3, this volume). Enhancing

Figure 1.10 Upland greenways can be used to connect habitat patches that would otherwise be isolated, thus allowing animals to avoid inhospitable areas and move in relative safety from one patch to another.

connectivity between habitat areas can increase the area available to wide-ranging species and can allow individuals to travel between different habitat types to meet daily or seasonal needs (Figure 1.10). Enhanced connectivity may also increase the long-term health of populations by increasing genetic exchange and by maintaining natural demographic processes, such as recolonization following local extinctions. Greenways can serve as movement corridors for plant species as well, allowing for recolonization of disturbed areas or for long-term genetic exchange. Finally, large-scale (both wide and long) corridors may help entire biotic communities adapt to long-term climate change, including anticipated greenhouse warming, by allowing plants and animals to migrate along latitudinal or elevational gradients. Without sufficient regional connections between habitat areas, both fauna and flora may become locked into locations whose suitability for their survival will gradually decrease.

Developing a balanced view of greenways' implications for wildlife also involves acknowledging some of their negative characteristics (Noss, chapter 3, this volume). Foremost among these is the preponderance of

edge conditions. Greenways, especially when very narrow, are greatly exposed to influences from outside their borders. Assessing these intrusions, whether they be human activity, predation by pets, or disruption of native communities by invasive species, is of prime importance. Some greenways may also have major limitations as movement corridors if they are severed by roads or lack sufficient width.

Interaction between greenways and their surroundings can also involve the movement of water, nutrients, and soil. Greenways can help maintain the quality of water resources in three important respects (Binford and Buchenau, chapter 4, this volume; Figure 1.11). Naturally vegetated riparian corridors, located between waterways and adjacent lands with intensive human use, filter excess nutrients in groundwater through vegetative uptake before they reach streams and rivers. In a similar fashion, microtopography, vegetation, and natural ground coverings such as leaves, logs, and other debris form a physical screen for materials moving downslope. Eroded sediments and associated pollutants emanating from agricultural fields, roads, construction areas, or other disturbances are thus filtered out of surface water before they have a chance to cover streambeds or fill in reservoirs. Streamside greenways, especially those containing wetlands, help maintain natural stream levels and rates of flow. By providing areas for water storage, wetlands can significantly reduce the magnitude and thus the damage of floods.

As with wildlife, edge effects can be detrimental to water as well. If a greenway is narrow and land uses along its edge impose a heavy flow of contaminants, the corridor's filtering capacity may be insufficient. If toxic chemicals are present, or if sediment loads are very high, vegetation may be damaged, further reducing the filter's effectiveness (Binford and Buchenau, chapter 4, this volume).

Protection of water quality is not only important for people but crucial to the existence of healthy aquatic organisms and communities. Riparian vegetation also helps to sustain these communities by providing shade that lowers water temperatures, by producing organic matter that feeds aquatic animals, and by helping to create diverse and dynamic stream structures such as pools, riffles, and waterfalls (Binford and Buchenau, chapter 4, this volume).

Likewise, healthy streams and aquatic communities are important to many land animals as a source of both food and water. Land and water are thus intimately connected. Larry Harris writes that "animals such as raccoons, weasels, mink and otter forage from the aquatic food chain, but spend most of their time in terrestrial habitats. Like fish, they do work by moving energy and matter up the gradient, against the gravitational field; they link the aquatic system to the adjacent upland" (Harris 1985, 4).

Social Functions

Of all the benefits greenways provide, recreation has received the most popular attention. A growing urban population with significant amounts of leisure time, combined with an overall surge in health consciousness, has led to increasing demand for outdoor pursuits such as jogging, walking, biking, and cross-country skiing.

It is no coincidence that increased demand for outdoor recreation has been simultaneous with the growing popularity of greenways, since greenways are well suited to active travel-oriented sports. Greenways lead somewhere and can connect with other greenways that go to still more places, which is exactly what bikers, runners, and walkers want to do. The fact that greenways are commonly located along streams and rivers further enhances their aesthetic and recreational appeal. Finally, greenways are often designed for recreation because it is the most immediate and tangible benefit for the public and in turn yields a strong and vocal recreation constituency.

Greenways have other social benefits that are less tangible than recreation but equally important. Like other types of parks and natural areas, they add to the aesthetic appeal of landscapes. Greenways often follow natural physiographic corridors, such as streams, rivers,

Figure 1.11 Streamside greenways can serve as buffers between waterways and adjacent land uses. Such buffers can help maintain water quality, stabilize hydrologic regimes, and maintain healthy, diverse aquatic habitat.

and ridges that have historical and cultural significance. Combined with aesthetic enhancement, this significance adds to the sense of history and culture that is so important to people's experience of a landscape and their overall sense of place. Greenways can also tie communities together by linking features such as parks, historic sites, residential areas, and shopping districts and by allowing people to travel from place to place without the noise and rush of automobiles. When designed to encircle cities and towns, green*ways* can function as green*belts* and help to maintain the distinct character of both urban and rural areas.

Environmental Ethics: Where People and Nature Meet

In addition to the specific social and ecological functions described earlier, greenways are a focal point of interactions between people and nature. Nature plays an important role in people's lives and influences society as a whole. Clearly, we are all dependent on nature for our physical survival. As organisms, we are derived from and exist as part of nature, and we are subject to its laws and processes. We must breathe air, drink water, and ingest food, and so we require healthy environments in this most basic sense.

People also have a deep psychological and spiritual need for nature as they try to balance often frenetic, stressful lives in a mechanized "human" environment by searching for serenity, beauty, and relaxation in the natural world. Summarizing numerous studies of the effects of nature on human psychology and health, Rachel and Stephen Kaplan write that "the immediate outcome of contacts with nearby nature include enjoyment, relaxation and lowered stress levels." and that "people with access to nearby-natural settings have been found to be healthier than other individuals" (Kaplan and Kaplan 1989, 173).

This relationship, however, is neither as simple nor as one-sided as it might at first seem, since what peo-

ple gain from nature in turn affects the way they treat the natural environment. Experiencing nature (Figure 1.12), whether through active, athletic recreation, passive viewing and contemplation, or more intellectual observation and study, helps people gain a sense of appreciation and respect for nature (Leopold 1949). These values can be more powerful than anything taught in a classroom or written in a book and may ultimately lead people to a more thoughtful, ethical relationship with the natural environment. In this respect greenways can have an indirect but extremely important role in efforts to protect natural resources and to maintain a healthy environment. By creating opportunities for direct contact with nature, especially in densely populated urban environments, greenways can be an important means of fostering an environmental ethic. This function has often been missing from the contemporary environmental movement, which has been based largely on more formal education and on more direct forms of intervention such as advocacy, lobbying, and ecological planning (Flink

Figure 1.12 Fly fishing in Wissahickon Creek, part of Philadelphia's Fairmount Park. The park gives city dwellers a chance to see and experience nature close to home. (Photo by D. Smith.)

1989). By providing informal opportunities for people to experience nature "close to home" on a regular basis, greenways and other forms of open space may have an important and long-lasting effect on society's environmental consciousness.

Issues in Ecological Greenway Design

The basic ecological and social functions of greenways have been outlined in this chapter. The chapters that follow will look at ecological functions in greater detail and will consider how they relate to the pragmatic task of designing greenways. The overarching aim of *Ecology of Greenways* is to illuminate the intersection of science and design and to find ways to make good use of scientific information by applying it to the art of design.

Greenway design, like any manipulation of natural systems, is a highly complex endeavor. Each case will involve unique local conditions and will present different problems to be solved. There are, however, predictable issues that are likely to come into play in many greenway projects across a wide range of settings.

From a broad perspective, because greenways must interact with surrounding lands, it is crucial to consider a greenway's context within the landscape. Understanding context may mean deciphering the ways in which animals use neighboring unprotected lands in addition to a greenway itself. Or, it may mean determining the type and magnitude of contaminants flowing toward a greenway from adjacent areas.

Understanding context also involves identifying larger habitat areas to be connected by a greenway. The location of these areas will affect the location, internal characteristics, and length of a greenway, all of which will influence the types of species that travel along its length. The size, type, and quality of these habitat areas will also determine, in part, the species that use a greenway. Thus, the conditions on either side and at either end of a greenway deserve considerable attention.

The width of a greenway can have a dramatic effect on its ability to protect both water resources and native wildlife and is thus the problem most often raised in greenway design. A greenway that is too narrow may discourage sensitive species, and it may be too permeable as a filter of stream-bound contaminants. It may also contain little area free from damaging recreation impacts, like disruption of nesting birds or trampling of vegetation that stabilizes the banks of a stream.

The width of a greenway determines, in large part, the portion of its area that will be penetrated by edge effects. Forest edge exists where physical and biological phenomena from outside the forest penetrate to various distances, sometimes tens of meters, sometimes hundreds. Most significant for wildlife is the spread of invasive species of plants and animals, which threaten many native species through competition for resources, predation, or parasitism. Although edge effects cannot be eliminated, their significance can be diminished by increasing the width of a greenway.

Connectivity—the degree of linkage of points along a greenway—is another characteristic of primary importance. For wildlife, *functional* connectivity will vary according to the needs of each species. Roads are usually the most common and prominent barriers that compromise greenway connectivity, although degraded habitat areas can have similar effects. Connectivity is also important in providing continuous protection for streams. Unprotected portions of a waterway can reduce water quality downstream and inhibit the movement of aquatic organisms. Designers can ensure connectivity by locating greenways in roadless areas, by maintaining continuous streamside vegetation, and by making use of crossing structures for wildlife like underpasses and tunnels.

Finally, the design and management of specific sites and facilities within a greenway warrant considerable attention, especially where there has been past human disturbance and where recreation has the potential to degrade natural systems. Highly modified corridors like channelized streams may need to be restored to a more functional condition. Native vegetation can be restored or maintained. Where recreation threatens soil, water, or wildlife, trails and other facilities can be located and designed to limit human impacts and to enhance visitor experience and education. Recreational use will have to be strictly limited in some situations to protect vulnerable resources; where exclusion is not necessary, facilities can be designed in a manner sensitive to natural features and processes.

These factors and others will be discussed in more detail in later chapters. Together, they will have a major impact on the functioning of a greenway and will thus play a role in deriving effective design solutions.

Case Studies

Earlier in this chapter, a number of greenways from around the country, both existing and in progress, were mentioned to illustrate the range of greenway types that occur in various environments. Many existing greenways are largely recreational in focus, and many also serve as conservation areas. However, relatively few greenways have been designed with detailed consideration of ecological functions.

In chapter 7, a variety of case studies that represent some of the most ecologically significant greenway projects in the United States are described and analyzed in detail. These eight cases are located in different parts of the country and span the continuum from urban to rural environments. They illustrate numerous problems and design solutions—some very effective, some less so—relating to wildlife, water resources, and recreation design. Although most of the examples are not based on a systematic design method, as proposed by Paul Hellmund in chapter 6, each one illustrates issues and techniques that are useful to the emerging art of greenway design.

Summaries of the same case studies are presented here to give a brief overview of the types of projects represented, their settings and characteristics, and some of the design issues faced in each case. By grounding the idea of greenways in the real world, these case studies can help place in proper perspective the technical and design-oriented discussions of the chapters that follow. Readers interested in more detail should refer directly to chapter 7.

Southeastern Wisconsin Environmental Corridors

In a seven-county area of Wisconsin, greenways (locally called environmental corridors) have been systematically identified and protected for more than twenty-five years. Efforts of the Southeastern Wisconsin Regional Planning Commission and its constituent local governments have yielded a connected network of protected open space that covers 349 square miles in urban, suburban, and rural environments:

— Resource inventory and a computerized system of map overlays are used to delineate corridors based on the locations of significant features like streams, wetlands, and wildlife habitat.

— Connectivity for animal movement is explicitly included in the corridor delineation process.

— Greenway protection is accomplished by a combination of land acquisition and land-use regulation at municipal, county, and state levels.

Florida Greenways

Because of the rapid pace of development in Florida, the state's native wildlife communities face habitat fragmentation that is increasing at an alarming rate. The state, the U.S. Forest Service, The Nature Conservancy, and other public and private organizations are responding with several efforts to maintain habitat connectivity in different parts of the state. Among these efforts are:

— The Pinhook Swamp Wildlife Corridor, which links Georgia's Okefenokee National Wildlife Refuge with Florida's Osceola National Forest.

Together, these areas cover over 600,000 acres and constitute a suitable reintroduction site for the endangered red wolf and Florida panther.

— The Suwannee River, which flows from the Okefenokee and Pinhook swamps to the Gulf of Mexico. The Suwannee River Water Management District is purchasing extensive lands along the river for habitat and water-quality protection; the river has also been proposed as a major wildlife corridor connecting coastal areas with the Okefenokee habitat complex.

— The Wekiva River Greenway, which will connect several existing state preserves on the fringes of Orlando with the Ocala National Forest to the north. On the Wekiva, black bear are the species of greatest concern.

— A series of wildlife underpasses in southern Florida along the newly constructed Interstate Route 75, which would otherwise split in two the remaining habitat of the Florida panther.

Rio Grande Valley State Park, New Mexico

This 5,000-acre state park in Albuquerque contains one of the largest intact riparian forests along the Rio Grande, one of the major rivers of the American Southwest. The park is an important reserve for birds and other wildlife and serves as a major recreation area as well. The city of Albuquerque manages the park with nature conservation as the overriding goal but is also carefully designing recreational facilities to make the park available to people without compromising natural features:

— Detailed resource inventory and analysis are used to delineate zones open to various intensities of recreational use, depending on the sensitivity of vegetation and animals.

— Reforestation of native cottonwood and willow trees is under way to return the forest to a more natural state following invasion by exotic species.

— Long-term plans call for construction of artificial wetlands to restore wildlife habitat and to biologically treat contaminated urban runoff.

Boulder Greenways, Colorado

Boulder County, Colorado, lies at the interface of the great plains and the Rocky Mountains and contains both a wealth of natural diversity and an expanding urban center. Greenways are being implemented by three complementary organizations: the county, the city of Boulder, and the Boulder County Nature Association, a private group:

— The city is implementing a series of urban riparian greenways for recreational use and water-resources protection and as habitat for urban wildlife.

— The city is acquiring an extensive greenbelt surrounding its borders to limit urban sprawl and maintain open space.

— The city has undertaken a major stream restoration project to improve water quality previously degraded by effluent from a sewage treatment plant.

— The county has identified key riparian corridors, habitat areas, and elk migration routes, which are protected through both cooperative and regulatory measures.

— The Boulder County Nature Association has delineated a more extensive network of core habitat areas, wildlife corridors, and riparian corridors and helps to protect these areas by working with private and public landowners on land management, protection, and development issues.

Santa Monica Mountains to Santa Susana Mountains Wildlife Corridors, California

To the northwest of Los Angeles, the Santa Monica Mountains, the Simi Hills, and the Santa Susana Mountains contain broad expanses of wildlife habitat and support species like mountain lion, badger, and bobcat. But habitat fragmentation, caused by high-speed freeways and urban sprawl, threatens the long-term survival of these wide-ranging species. The Santa Monica Mountains Conservancy (a state agency) and the National Park Service have designed and are working to protect greenways that will link together the core habitats of these ranges:

— Corridor design was based on studies that considered both the needs of key species and patterns of land ownership and development.

— Wildlife underpasses will be built at critical freeway crossings.

— When complete, the project will link together more than 270,000 acres of habitat. Further connected with more extensive national forest lands to the north and east, the network is expected to contain a nearly complete community of native fauna.

South Platte River, Brighton, Colorado

North of Denver, the floodplain of the South Platte River is slated to be mined for gravel over the next several decades. Traditional mining techniques would channelize the river and create deep, steep-sided ponds in the floodplain with little habitat value. An alternate scheme based on principles of landscape ecology would increase the river's value for both wildlife and people:

— Critical riparian habitats would be protected from mining, and the most sensitive areas would be protected from recreational use.

— Where possible, the river would remain unchannelized. Ponds would be shaped to create wetlands, a high degree of spatial heterogeneity, and thus a variety of habitat types.

— Vegetation would be planted to enhance spatial and temporal heterogeneity for a variety of bird species.

— Wooded corridors would connect the greenway to other nearby natural areas. Connections would also extend to adjacent residential areas to make the park environment more accessible to people.

— Trails and an interpretive center focusing on interactions between humans and the environment would make the greenway attractive and educational for people.

The Woodlands, Texas

In the early 1970s, a new town named The Woodlands was founded north of Houston and was intended to be an environmentally progressive community that would meet human needs while maintaining an aesthetically pleasing and ecologically sound environment. The firm of Wallace, McHarg, Roberts, and Todd was contracted to produce an ecological design for the town, which incorporated a system of riparian greenways:

— Streams and their floodplains were protected to maintain a natural drainage system for the town that was less costly than a traditional, engineered system and maintained wildlife habitat and recreational open space as well.

— Roads and development were concentrated on poorly drained soils, and runoff was directed to permeable soils capable of absorbing excess surface flow.

— Habitat connectivity was encouraged in the design to provide for wildlife movement.

— A series of guidelines regulated development at the site scale to protect wildlife habitat and to encourage infiltration of runoff.

Quabbin to Wachusett Wildlife Corridor Design Study, Massachusetts

Central Massachusetts is a largely forested region containing occasional small towns and dispersed patches of protected land. In 1990, the Massachusetts Audubon Society, concerned about the possibility of future habitat fragmentation, sponsored a wildlife-corridor design study by the University of Massachusetts at Amherst. Along with the design method outlined in chapter 6, this study has its origins in earlier work in the same region by Paul Hellmund. Although this well-documented study does not consider water resources or recreation, it is the most complete application to date of the kind of method described in chapter 6:

— The study used existing data bases and a geographic information system (GIS) to design corridors for two fragmentation-sensitive indicator species: fisher and river otter.

— The study used successively smaller scales to identify a large target area, habitat nodes within the target area, broad study swaths between the nodes, and specific corridor alignments within a representative swath.

— Development suitability was compared with habitat and movement corridors to examine potential conflicts between corridors and other future land uses.

— The GIS was used to test different sets of alignment criteria, one focusing on maximizing corridor suitability for wildlife, the other on minimizing disruption of private property.

Conclusion

Examples of ecologically functional greenways already exist in a variety of circumstances and can offer valuable insights for future designs. As will be discussed in detail in chapter 7, these examples also show that there is still much to learn about applying scientific knowledge to greenway design. The chapters that follow address this need by offering scientific information on corridor function as well as many ideas and suggestions for applying that information.

What becomes clear in considering the history and context of greenways is that the attempt to link environmental concerns with creative design is not entirely new. Frederick Law Olmsted's design of the Muddy River and the Back Bay Fens in Boston marked an attempt to combine water-quality maintenance and flood control with aesthetic enhancement. In the 1960s, Ian McHarg and Phillip Lewis, Jr., perceived the need for an ecological approach to landscape design and developed methods for achieving such an approach.

Today, as increasing pressures are brought to bear on the land and as understanding of the effects of these pressures increases, there is a need to look even more closely at ecological function and to develop more powerful techniques for ecological design. Toward this end, examining case studies provides important lessons from past efforts. Considering scientific information and new ideas for scientifically based design can lead to new and more effective techniques. Taken together, practical examples and more recent ideas can help conservationists, designers, and planners realize better strategies for nature conservation.

References

Bennett, A. F. 1990. Habitat corridors and the conservation of small mammals in a fragmented forest environment. *Landscape Ecology* 4:109–22.

Curtis, J. T. 1956. The modification of mid-latitude grasslands and forests by man. In W. L. Thomas, ed., *Man's Role in Changing the Face of the Earth.* University of Chicago Press, Chicago.

Dmowski, K., and M. Kozakiewicz. 1990. Influence of a shrub corridor on movements of passerine birds to a lake littoral zone. *Landscape Ecology* 4:99–108.

Ehrlich, P. R., and E. O. Wilson. 1991. Biodiversity studies: Science and policy. *Science* 253:758–61.

Engel, J. R., and J. G. Engel, eds. 1990. *Ethics of Environment and Development: Global Challenge, International Response.* University of Arizona Press, Tucson.

Fisher, I. D. 1986. *Frederick Law Olmsted and the City Planning Movement in the United States.* University of Michigan Research Press, Ann Arbor.

Flink, C. 1989. Greenways: Recreational resource versus land use ethic. In Proceedings, Third Biennial International Linear Parks Conference. Asheville, N.C. September.

Forman, R. T. T., and M. Godron. 1986. *Landscape Ecology.* John Wiley and Sons, New York.

Grey, G. W., and F. J. Deneke. 1986. *Urban Forestry,* 2d edition. John Wiley and Sons, New York.

Harris, L. D. 1985. Conservation corridors: A highway system for wildlife. *ENFO* 11:1–10. Florida Conservation Foundation, Winter Park.

Heimlich, R. E., and W. D. Anderson. 1987. Dynamics of land use change in urbanizing areas: Experience in the Economic Research Service. In W. Lockeretz, ed., *Sustaining Agriculture Near Cities.* Soil and Water Conservation Society, Ankeny, Iowa.

Howard, E. 1902. *Garden Cities of Tomorrow.* Swan Sonnenschein and Co., London. Originally printed in 1898 as *To-Morrow: A Peaceful Path to Real Reform.*

Johnson, W. C., and C. S. Adkisson. 1985. Dispersal of beech nuts by blue jays in fragmented landscapes. *American Midland Naturalist* 113:319–24.

Kaplan, R., and S. Kaplan. 1989. *The Experience of Nature: A Psychological Perspective.* Cambridge University Press, Cambridge, England.

Leopold, A. 1949. *A Sand County Almanac.* Oxford University Press, New York.

Lewis, P. H., Jr. 1964. Quality corridors for Wisconsin. *Landscape Architecture* 54 (2): 100–107.

Little, C. E. 1990. *Greenways for America.* Johns Hopkins University Press, Baltimore.

Lowrance, R., R. Leonard, and J. Sheridan. 1985. Managing riparian ecosystems to control nonpoint pollution. *Journal of Soil and Water Conservation* 40:87–92.

McHarg I. L. 1969. *Design with Nature.* Doubleday/Natural History Press, Garden City, New York.

MacKaye, B. 1928. *The New Exploration: A Philosophy of Regional Planning.* Harcourt, Brace, New York.

Maehr, D. S. 1990. The Florida panther and private lands. *Conservation Biology* 4 (2): 167–70.

Master, L. 1991. Aquatic animals: Endangerment alert. *Nature Conservancy,* April/May.

Merriam, G., and A. Lanoue. 1990. Corridor use by small mammals: Field measurement for three experimental types of *Peromyscus leucopus. Landscape Ecology* 4:123–31.

Newton, N. T. 1971. *Design on the Land: The Development of Landscape Architecture.* Belknap Press of Harvard University Press, Cambridge.

Norton, B. G. 1987. *Why Preserve Natural Variety?* Princeton University Press, Princeton.

Noss, R. F. 1987. Corridors in real landscapes: A reply to Simberloff and Cox. *Conservation Biology* 1(2): 159–64.

Palmer, T. 1986. *Endangered Rivers and the Conservation Movement.* University of California Press, Berkeley.

President's Commission on Americans Outdoors. 1987. *Americans Outdoors: The Legacy, the Challenge, with Case Studies: The Report of the President's Commission.* Island Press, Washington D.C.

Rome, A. 1991. Protecting natural areas through the planning process: The Chesapeake Bay example. *Natural Areas Journal* 11(4): 199–202.

Scenic Hudson, Inc. and National Park Service. 1989. Building greenways in the Hudson River valley: A guide for action. Privately printed report.

Spirn, A. W. 1984. *The Granite Garden: Urban Nature and Human Design.* Basic Books, New York.

Steiner, F., G. Young, and E. Zube. 1988. Ecological planning: Retrospect and prospect. *Landscape Journal* 7 (1): 31–39.

Steinitz, C., P. Parker, and L. Jordan. 1976. Hand-drawn overlays: Their history and prospective uses. *Landscape Architecture* 66 (5): 444–55.

Stokes, S. N., A. E. Watson, G. P. Keller, and J. T. Keller. 1989. *Saving America's Countryside: A Guide to Rural Conservation.* Johns Hopkins University Press, Baltimore.

U.S. Department of Agriculture Forest Service. 1990. Northern forest lands Study: A report to the Congress of the United States on the recent changes in landownership and land use in the northern forests of Maine, New Hampshire, New York and Vermont. U.S.D.A. Forest Service, Rutland, Vt. April.

U.S. Department of Interior Fish and Wildlife Service. 1990. Endangered Species Technical Bulletin 15(11).

Wegner, J. F., and G. Merriam. 1979. Movements of birds and small mammals between wood and adjoining farmland habitat. *Journal of Applied Ecology* 16:349–57.

Whyte, W. H. 1968. *The Last Landscape.* Doubleday, New York.

Wilcove, D. S., C. H. McLellan, and A. P. Dobson. 1986. Habitat fragmentation in the temperate zone. Pages 237–56 in M. E. Soulé, ed., *Conservation Biology: The Science of Scarcity and Diversity.* Sinauer Associates, Sunderland, Mass.

Wilcox, D. S., and D. D. Murphy. 1985. Conservation strategy: The effects of fragmentation on extinction. *American Naturalist* 125:879–87.

Wisconsin Department of Resource Development. 1962. Recreation in Wisconsin. Madison, Wis., 11/962.

Zaitzevsky, C. R. 1982. *Frederick Law Olmsted and the Boston Park System.* Belknap Press of the Harvard University Press, Cambridge.

James F. Thorne

Landscape Ecology

A Foundation for Greenway Design

2

Greenways are a prime opportunity to conserve a region's natural heritage, particularly in places where land development has isolated—or threatens to isolate—remaining fragments of nature in floodways, in steep-sided ravines, along rocky ridgetops, or in remnant patches of upland vegetation. In making the most of these remaining natural areas, the greenway designer is confronted with the following questions: what sizes and shapes to make wildlife habitat and movement corridors; how to account for habitat change over time; how to protect waterways by using streamside vegetation; and how to improve degraded greenways through ecological restoration. To create greenways that work well for people as well as for nature, designers must also consider recreationists' needs, such as pathways, signs, and educational features. Recreationists experience a greenway as a sequence of events and will enjoy the sequence more if it is planned to provide visual variety (both panoramic and intimate views), spots to rest, and interpretive sites.

Because a greenway is a linear sequence of habitats, simply designing isolated sites along the greenway would be inadequate; the diverse and interacting nature of the sequence must be considered. Similarly, design should reflect the fact that greenways are embedded within complex mosaics of land uses that make up entire landscapes. In much the same way that parts of a greenway are functionally linked, greenways themselves are connected to other parts of the landscape, including both human and natural elements.

Until recently in North America, a single discipline did not exist that considered the importance of linking a diversity of sites together to enhance ecological integrity in the midst of human-modified landscapes. Landscape ecology, an established discipline in Europe (Naveh and Lieberman 1984) and recently emerging in North America, does just this; it helps combine provisions for both people and nature at the broad geographic scale appropriate for greenway design. Importantly, landscape ecology includes the effects and

23

needs of people in its study of ecological phenomena.

In reviewing the field of landscape ecology as it relates to greenways, this chapter considers how landscapes operate as ecological systems: how they are structured, how they function, and how they change over time. It considers specifically how corridors function within the larger context of the landscape, as well as the role of landscape ecology in guiding the design process for greenways. The chapter concludes with a comprehensive vision for a landscape-scale greenway network, as illustrated in a case study from the Catskill Mountains in New York.

Promoting Ecological Integrity

At the outset of this discussion, it is important to define a clear goal and subsequent objectives to guide our inquiry into landscape ecology. The fundamental goal of ecological design should be to maintain ecological integrity, also referred to as ecological health. Ecological integrity is characterized by (1) natural levels of plant (primary) productivity, (2) a high level of native biological diversity, (3) natural (usually very low) rates of soil erosion and nutrient loss, and (4) clean water and healthy aquatic communities (R. Forman, personal communication).

Where natural conditions have been substantially altered by people, maintaining ecological integrity requires careful design and management of many different landscape components. For greenways, which are an especially important component, moving toward this goal involves several specific objectives, which can be summarized as follows:

1. To conserve at least a minimum amount of the full representation of a region's natural heritage. Ideally, this objective means protecting enough of all the various habitat types of an area to assure the continued survival of all plant and animal species that make up a region's biological diversity.

2. To design greenways that will function as conduits for wildlife that must move from one habitat area to another.

3. To build enough redundancy (multiple movement corridors and multiple areas of the same habitat type) into greenway design to accommodate habitat change, in recognition of the dynamic nature of landscape processes.

4. To design riparian greenways with adequate dimensions to offer optimal protection of waterways by filtering contaminants and maintaining natural hydrologic regimes.

5. To engage in ecological restoration when the existing habitat network is inadequate and to account for the technical complexities of this restoration.

6. To resolve the potential conflicts between people's aesthetic preferences and the need to maintain continuous, functional greenways.

This chapter outlines a framework for understanding how these objectives for greenway design can be achieved. Most objectives will also be discussed in further detail in subsequent chapters.

The Landscape as an Ecological Unit

In the same way that a watershed is often the most appropriate unit within which to consider issues of water quality and supply, the landscape is a particularly useful unit for understanding broad-scale issues of ecological integrity. Landscapes typically include a mixture of both human and natural features and contain numerous interacting ecosystems, such as forests, fields, waterways, and human settlements. By understanding the nature of interactions across landscapes, it is possible to address systemic ecological issues over the long term.

Most people have a strong visual response to the word *landscape*. The word may recall a broad expanse of desert enclosed by mountains with a strip of green

Figure 2.1 A desert landscape in Arizona, showing green vegetation along a stream corridor and in an irrigated human settlement, surrounded by arid uplands, with mountains in the distance. (Photo by Peter Godfrey.)

Figure 2.2 A steep-sided valley in the Canadian Rockies, with thick, coniferous forest at lower elevations giving way to alpine vegetation, scree, and bare rock above the timberline. (Photo by D. Smith.)

along the valley bottom (Figure 2.1). To others the word landscape may suggest the towering enclosure of a steep-sided valley, with bare mountaintops and a thickly forested, evergreen valley bottom (Figure 2.2). To yet others landscape may evoke a picture of rolling farmland with hedgerows and occasional patches of forest (Figure 2.3).

These images illustrate that landscapes exist within a regional context. The vegetation of a region is adapted to environmental conditions (precipitation, temperature, geology) that give it a regionally characteristic form (e.g., coniferous forest versus desert shrubland). The images also show that landscapes are heterogeneous; that is, they are composed of numerous distinct pieces, known as *landscape elements* (Forman and Godron 1986), which differ both in their appearance and in the way they influence ecological processes. In the examples described earlier, landscape elements include forests, fields, the green strip along the river, and the desert uplands. Cultural features, such as houses and roads, constitute landscape elements as well. Collectively, the arrangement of landscape elements is known as *landscape structure*.

Landscape elements receive and process energy from the sun, as well as fossil-fuel and nuclear energy when humans are present. For instance, a forest uses

Figure 2.3 An agricultural landscape in Pennsylvania, dominated by cultivated fields, and including human settlement, roads, and natural vegetation in patches and hedgerows. (Photo by D. Smith.)

solar energy to grow and function. This flow of energy in turn makes possible the movement of materials, such as water, sediment, nutrients, and living organisms. Activity caused by the flow of energy and the movement of materials (including the growth and movement of plants, animals, and humans) within landscapes is called *landscape function*. Over time, the flow of energy and consequent movement of materials in a landscape results in a new structure and new functional characteristics. This phenomenon is known as *landscape change*, which can happen slowly (as with the growth of vegetation) or very quickly (as when wildfire rages through a forest).

Landscape ecology is the study of landscape structure, function, and change at the scale of entire landscapes, as well as the application of these results to the design and management of both natural and human-dominated areas (Forman and Godron 1986).

For greenway design the most significant landscape elements to consider are *corridors,* which are defined as linear landscape elements that differ in form from their surroundings. In the landscapes described earlier, corridors would include the green strip along the river and the hedgerows and roads in the agricultural landscape. The structure, continuity, arrangement, and dimensions of such corridors are topics of intensive research in landscape ecology.

To summarize, landscapes consist of groupings of landscape elements that are different from one another and that collectively have a strong visual, structural, functional, and regional identity. Landscape ecology works with the inherent complexity and heterogeneity of real-world environments and focuses on areas of land ranging from individual landscape elements to collections of landscapes, or regions. In addition to these diverse spatial scales, landscape ecology considers landscape change at time scales ranging from minutes to hundreds of years. The discipline of landscape ecology can provide information about the proper design of corridors and networks of corridors that can serve as plant and animal habitat and movement corridors, as streamside buffers, and as places of enjoyment for people.

A Vocabulary of Landscape Form

Applying landscape ecology to the design of greenways first requires an understanding of the structural components of landscape that guide decision making. Since greenways are a kind of corridor made up of linear arrangements of naturalistic landscape, corridors are the class of landscape element that should receive primary attention.

Width, connectivity, and *quality* are the three most important variables of corridor structure. Corridor width determines how much of a corridor will be exposed to physical, human, and biological intrusions, or edge effects, from the outside. Very narrow corridors, called *line corridors,* are entirely permeated by edge effects (Forman and Godron 1986). Wider, *strip corridors* are broad enough so that a portion of their area will be free of these effects.

Connectivity is determined by the number and severity of breaks along a given stretch of corridor. Along greenways, breaks are most often caused by roads, but other land uses and even natural disturbances to vegetation can create breaks. The degree of connectivity determines the suitability of a given corridor for different uses, especially for movement of wildlife and, to a lesser degree, for movement of people. Some animal species will require a high degree of connectivity, whereas others may adapt to breaks in a corridor.

Corridor quality depends on width and connectivity but also includes consideration of the structure of vegetation within the corridor. A corridor of optimal quality will typically have good vegetation layering, a variety of plant species, and minimal presence of aggressive, weedy vegetation. Henein and Merriam (1990) note that the mere presence of a corridor of adequate dimensions may be insufficient for animal movement and habitation within hedgerows; poor corridor quality can also exclude species and prevent their movement.

By definition, a corridor is surrounded by something that differs from it. In landscape ecology, this surrounding land cover type is known as the *matrix.* The matrix is the dominant cover type of a landscape, or the one that exerts the most control over landscape processes and change. For instance, in a commercial forest, extensive stretches of managed timber constitute the matrix. Imbedded in the matrix are nonlinear

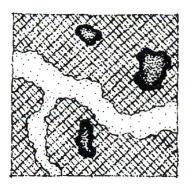

Figure 2.4 Diagrammatic representation of patches and corridors embedded in a matrix. All landscapes consist of different combinations of these three elements.

landscape elements, called *patches*, which differ from their surroundings—in this case, elements like remnant stands of old-growth forest, distinct areas of clear-cut timber, or the houses and other buildings that make up a small town. In this landscape, corridors include streams and roads.

This spatial framework of matrix-patch-corridor (Figure 2.4) is useful in describing the functional components of any landscape, ranging from urban to natural. The linkage of patches and corridors within the landscape matrix is crucial to the ecological design of greenways. Along with more site-specific considerations, this arrangement can be used to provide for habitat and human needs simultaneously.

Landscapes can be divided into five types, depending on the intensity of human influence. These divisions collectively make up the *landscape modification gradient*, which spans the continuum from pristine natural systems to areas highly modified by people (Figure 2.5; Forman and Godron 1986). At the end of the gradient representing least human influence, natural landscapes support a matrix of mostly unplanted

and unmanaged native vegetation and associated animal life. Next, the managed landscape matrix consists of planted or otherwise managed species, which may be native, nonnative, or a combination of the two. An example of a natural matrix is a forest composed of loblolly pine and other native species that colonized abandoned agricultural land in North Carolina after farming ceased in the 1930s. By contrast, an even-aged, single-species plantation forest of loblolly pine constitutes a managed landscape matrix. In the middle of the landscape modification gradient, cultivated landscapes have a matrix of agricultural lands that can be either row crops or grazing land. The suburban landscape matrix includes low- to moderate-density housing, yards, and associated commercial buildings and roads. Urban landscapes have a matrix dominated by high-density commercial and residential buildings, as well as roads and other paved surfaces. Despite their obvious differences, all of these landscape types are heterogeneous and include patches and corridors of various types.

To show the general usefulness of this vocabulary of landscape structure, two landscapes that contain elements that could be included in a greenway are illustrated in Figures 2.6 and 2.7. The first is a cultivated landscape matrix located in the Midwest, where the original vegetation would have been a mixture of prairie grasses and broadleaf herbs. Before the area was settled by Europeans, a combination of low precipitation, cold winters, and frequent fires (often set by Native Americans) limited tree growth to the riparian (adjacent to water) zone. An abandoned railroad corri-

Figure 2.5 The landscape modification gradient, characterized by decreasing intensity of human influence, is made up of urban, suburban, managed, and natural environments.

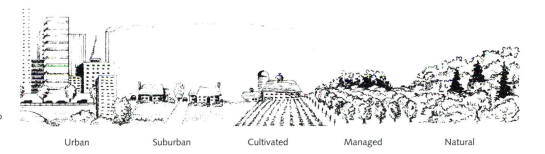

Urban   Suburban   Cultivated   Managed   Natural

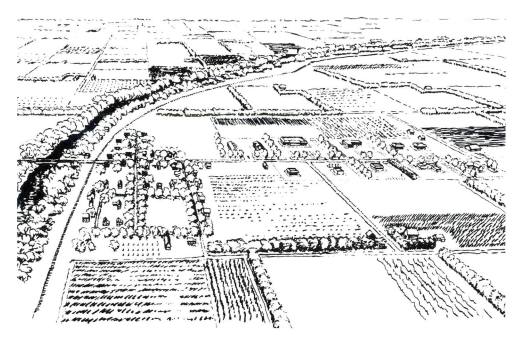

Figure 2.6 Fields of corn and soybeans in what was once a native grassland landscape in the American Midwest. The abandoned railroad corridor along the river serves as a refuge for the original prairie species. Trees are common only along the river and where planted as windbreaks.

dor runs parallel to the river; because the corridor was frequently mowed and burned in the past, it still supports native prairie plants. Between the old railroad line and the river is a riparian forest corridor. A small town (a cluster of dwelling patches) stands near the river. The dwelling patches and the railroad and riparian corridors are all set in a cultivated matrix of soybean and corn crops. This agricultural matrix is dissected by hedgerows, planted as windbreaks, which also constitute corridors.

A greenway in this landscape could include the parallel riparian and railroad corridors. The riparian forest would thus provide wildlife habitat and a protective buffer for the river. The abandoned railroad might become a bicycle trail, while also supporting native prairie plants along its margins. The greenway could also connect with selected hedgerows to provide connectivity for wildlife and trails for human access to the river. Ideally, a portion of the agricultural matrix would be restored to native prairie and linked to the greenway with a footpath. Such a design would have to consider the maintenance of the natural areas, since the conditions that originally produced these features—extensive fire and a local dominance of prairie plants as a seed source—no longer exist.

Figure 2.7 shows a suburban landscape matrix in the northeastern United States. The matrix of tract housing surrounds a remnant stream corridor, with isolated patches of forest in wet areas next to the stream and with abandoned pastures, now forested, on steeper slopes. Lower-density housing farther away from the urban center includes a patch of horse pasture and a few small patches of upland woods.

In this case the extensiveness of the suburban development would force greenway design to focus on the stream corridor and its narrow, discontinuous band of vegetation. The design could consider the needs of plants and animals likely to occupy the area if a forested corridor were restored along the length of the stream. The ability of this restored vegetation to protect the stream from contaminants and to enhance aquatic habitat would also be a primary concern. Patches of abandoned pasture in uplands could also be reforested and linked by means of a restored forest corridor to the main greenway along the stream. Because of the stream's proximity to a large number of people, construction of a nature trail would probably also be a priority.

These examples illustrate how landscape ecology and its vocabulary of landscape structure can be used to describe elements to be incorporated into greenways. In both cases, to allow movement of people as well as plants and animals, the issue of linking landscape elements to form a continuous corridor is paramount. This connectivity can be evaluated by examining the potential for movement from point A to point B. The degree to which connectivity is lacking can be expressed as the number of breaks per unit length between the two points. Landscapes that lack connectivity can be said to suffer from *fragmentation,* which results from the introduction of nonnatural land cover types and the construction of roads.

Transitions from one type of landscape element to another are an important feature of landscape structure. In humid landscapes greenways will commonly consist of a corridor of forest vegetation surrounded by a matrix of nonforested land cover. The forest *edge* forms a transition zone between forested and non-forested areas. It supports different plants and animals and appears very different from the forest away from the edge, known as the forest *interior* (Ranney et al. 1981). One reason for this difference between edge and interior is the enhanced availability of light at edges, which promotes plant growth. The edge receives light not only from above, like the forest interior, but also from the side, because of the adjacent, nonforested land. In addition to promoting plant growth, the extra light at edges results in a warmer, dryer environment. The forest edge is also exposed to higher winds gusting across open areas. In the forest interior, trees are tall and straight with foliage concentrated at the top, where light is readily available. The interior tends to have fewer low trees and shrubs than the forest edge. At the edge, trees are shorter and have wider crowns, especially toward the sunlit side. Under the trees, layers of small trees, shrubs, and herbs can produce a wall of green unless they are periodically removed. In the Northern Hemisphere, this density of plants occurs especially on south-facing edges (Wales 1972).

The various layers of a highly structured edge result in relatively high plant species diversity, which in turn gives rise to a diverse association of edge-loving animals. Wildlife species adapted to the conditions of the forest interior can only be encouraged by providing sufficient interior habitat. Because of fragmentation, extensive interior areas are rare in human-dominated landscapes. Therefore, interior species often become

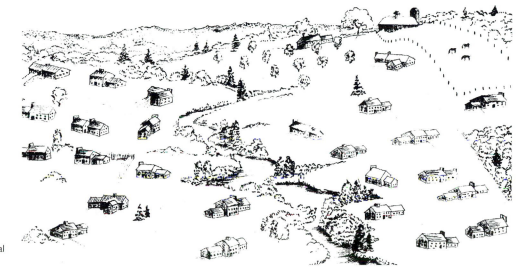

Figure 2.7 A remnant stream corridor in the suburban northeastern United States with tract housing and a partially wooded floodplain in the foreground. In the distance the stream corridor opens up some with lower-density housing and patches of forest and abandoned agricultural land surrounding the stream.

the focus of conservation biologists who are managing landscapes for biological diversity (Lovejoy and Oren 1981).

The structural conditions of edge create a variety of physical differences that affect plants, animals, and humans alike. The structure and shade created by a rich, layered edge result in a different microclimate from an edge that is not highly structured. Shading increases soil moisture and reduces ground-level temperatures. The dense layers reduce the impact of high winds, redirecting them over the canopy like an airfoil. Figure 2.8 illustrates the concepts of forest edge and interior and shows some of the physical differences between a layered, gradual edge transition and an unlayered, abrupt edge transition. In arid and semiarid landscapes, including grassland, desert, and chaparral environments, where water limits the growth of plants more than light, edges with dramatically different structure do not occur. Although edges in these environments may contain some plant and animal species not found in interior areas, the structural difference is not as visually apparent.

In all environments and at all scales, structure is a fundamental characteristic that helps determine the nature of ecological relationships. Landscape ecology provides a structural vocabulary that organizes our view of the landscape according to functionally significant components and thus helps us understand how these components interact.

The Basis of Healthy Landscape Functioning

Landscape ecology studies the arrangement and interactions of the functional units of landscape, known as *ecosystems*. Ecosystems are the combinations of plants, animals, and other organisms of a given area together with their nonliving environment. Ecosystems are not necessarily limited to any particular scale. Rather, they are defined by boundaries that make them distinct units for the processing of energy and materials. Examples of ecosystems include a suburban lawn, a pond, a remnant patch of woods, or even a much larger expanse such as an entire forest or a range of mountains. Ecosystems can thus be synonymous with landscape elements, or they can be much larger, consisting of collections of elements. Because ecosystems constitute functionally interconnected areas characterized by the processing of energy and the movement of materials, they are a useful unit for scientific study and also for design and management.

The activity caused by the flow of energy and the movement of materials (including plants and animals) in landscapes (both within and *between* ecosystems) is called landscape function. Within the landscape depicted in Figure 2.9, for example, solar energy is expended to heat the soil and the air as well as to evaporate water. This energy expenditure provides the regional growing conditions for agricultural crops, native vege-

Abrupt edge   Forest interior   Gradual edge

Figure 2.8 An abrupt, maintained edge (left) stands between the forest interior on one side and an adjacent agricultural matrix on the other. A gradual, advancing edge (right) is a more highly structured buffer between the forest interior and an abandoned field. (Edges and interior are not drawn to scale.)

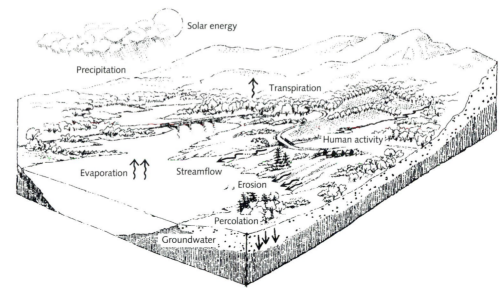

Figure 2.9 Diagram of landscape function, showing solar energy, the hydrologic cycle, erosion, and human activity. Other components of landscape function include the growth and movement of plants and animals, as well as other types of energy and material flows.

tation, and local wildlife. Evaporated water ultimately returns to the ground as rain or snow, which, when they become runoff, can then erode soil, especially on bare, steep agricultural fields or other open land. Solar energy, supplemented by fossil-fuel and nuclear energy, is also used to subsidize human activities. Overall, this flow of energy results in the cycling of water between land and earth, the washing of soil and rock to the sea (erosion), the movement and rearrangement of the earth's resources by humans (human modification), and the cycling of chemical elements essential to plant and animal growth (nutrient cycling).

Nitrogen taken up by tree roots and subsequently returned to the soil in leaf litter represents a simple example of nutrient cycling. A more complex example involves the cycling of nitrogen in agricultural fields, where nitrogen is often added as fertilizer. A portion of the nitrogen is taken up by crops and then removed when the crops are harvested. Some nitrogen may run off the surface with eroded soil or be leached into groundwater and then into streams. It is not hard to imagine, then, that the arrangement and management of the interacting ecosystems that make up landscapes (in this case, fields and streams) can strongly affect energy flow and nutrient cycling.

In particular, the arrangement of greenways can have a significant effect on landscape function, including energy flow, nutrient cycling, and the movement of materials and organisms. Greenways, like other kinds of corridors, can perform six basic functions: *habitat, conduit, barrier, filter, source,* and *sink* (Figure 2.10; Forman and Godron 1984, 1986). In different ways, these basic functions will all come into play in subsequent chapters of this book.

Habitat can be defined simply as the location where plants, animals, and people live. Ideally, greenways should include a full diversity of the natural habitat types of a region. Natural habitat diversity can include ridgetop habitats (usually very dry), upland habitats (usually with moderate levels of moisture), wetland habitats (with shallow standing water or fluctuating water level), and aquatic habitats (with deeper standing or flowing water). Habitats can be further subdivided based on local soil and climate conditions. In some situations—usually forested landscapes—these habitats can also be subdivided into edge and interior, the characteristics of which were discussed earlier.

Greenways can also act as conduits for the movement of water, plants, animals, and people. Watercourses, paths for surface water and groundwater

Figure 2.10 Six basic corridor functions: (a) habitat; (b) conduit; (c) barrier; (d) filter; (e) source; and (f) sink.

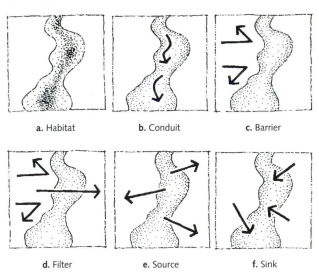

a. Habitat   **b.** Conduit   **c.** Barrier

d. Filter   **e.** Source   **f.** Sink

moving through the landscape, convey runoff and floodwaters and support aquatic and riparian habitats. As conduits for surface water and groundwater, greenways supply humans, plants, and animals with water filtered by roots and microbial organisms in the soil. As conduits for plants, animals, and humans, greenways function as distribution corridors for plant seeds, as protected movement corridors for animals, and as transportation and recreation corridors for people. Because greenways are corridors, they can connect small, dysfunctional patches of habitat into larger, functional wholes (Harris 1984; Noss 1987). The total area and proper habitat type needed for native communities of plants and animals must be considered in designing a greenway. By linking different habitat types (upland and wetland, for example) greenways can also improve habitat functioning for those animal species that require more than one habitat type. Because disturbances (e.g., fire or diseases) can also be spread by linking habitats with greenways (Simberloff and Cox 1987), the costs and benefits of any given corridor must be considered.

In contrast to functioning as conduits, greenways may also serve as barriers to movement, especially for animals. This function depends on the type of corridor and the behavior of the animal in question. Corridors can serve as barriers if the habitat provided is hostile to or inappropriate for the animal (Merriam 1984). Animals may avoid a corridor because they are too large or too small to cross the corridor. For example, a large browsing animal, such as a white-tailed deer may avoid a brushy hedgerow corridor if provided with an easier path of movement. A small animal, such as a white-footed mouse, can easily move through a hedgerow but may be blocked in its movement by a river or a road.

The filtering function of greenways can be likened to acting as a leaky barrier. As with the barrier function, filtering occurs as plants, animals, or humans try to pass through the corridor, which restricts their movement without blocking it altogether. This filtering can occur either perpendicular to the axis of the corridor or along its length. Perhaps more important than the filtering of organisms, however, is the filtration of water that occurs in riparian zones along stream corridors. Plant roots and soil microbes filter chemicals, especially fertilizers, out of soil water (Lowrance et al. 1984; Duckson 1989; Groffman et al. 1990). This filtering function is not limited to materials dissolved in water; greenways can also trap eroded soil (White and Gosz 1983) and thus prevent water pollution by soil nutrients, stream siltation, and soilborne pesticides and herbicides. Finally, riparian corridor vegetation can act as a filter by taking up groundwater, thus regulating the flow of water moving downslope toward streams and rivers.

Greenways can act as a source of species for populating adjacent areas and (as in the case of stream corridors) as a source of water. In human-dominated landscapes, little native vegetation may be left except in floodplains, on adjacent steep slopes, and on steep slopes along ridgelines. Vegetation in these relict corridors may be supplemented by vegetation in hedgerows, highway and railway rights-of-way, and other human-created corridors. The plants contained in these habitats may be an important source of native species for recolonizing abandoned land. Greenways may also function as a source of nonnative species (Noss 1987), some of which may aggressively overtake native species and thus become what ecologists call invasive species. Invasive species are generally those that are well adapted to new circumstances and have freed themselves of predators and pests from their original environment (Bazzaz 1986). Most invasives are fast-growing, resource-demanding species that thrive in fragmented and disturbed environments. Therefore, when corridors are narrow and consist mostly of edge habitat, they can be sources of undesirable species. When corridors relieve fragmentation by providing linkage and quality habitat (Henein and Merriam 1990), they can function as sources of beneficial species.

Corridors can function as sinks, as when riparian greenways filter and *retain* excessive nutrients and sediment moving toward streams. Corridors can also become mortality sinks if they entice animals into narrow areas frequented by opportunistic predators.

With a basic understanding of landscape structure and function, it becomes clear that the two realms are very much linked. Maintaining habitat that *functions* properly for native species requires the protection or restoration of certain dimensions and arrangements of natural areas (*structure*). For riparian greenways, the ability of vegetation to filter out contaminants (*function*) requires site-specific *structural* characteristics, such as corridor width and connectivity. Therefore, knowledge of landscape function is critical to informing decisions about the design of appropriate landscape structure.

Of course, both structure and function differ from one part of North America to another. The application of the principles of landscape ecology must therefore be adapted for each particular landscape to account for regional differences. Some of the regional variation in function can be attributed to differences in structure. For instance, the disappearance of pronounced edge effects when moving from forested landscapes to grasslands or desert means that specially adapted edge species of plants and animals will be less common. In these arid landscapes, the existence and management of edge habitat will be less important, and concerns about habitat will focus on the availability of water, on the size of habitat areas, and on the arrangement of habitat patches.

Also in arid areas, a seasonal or permanent lack of water often results in hard soils that retain little rainwater, leading to flash flooding during intense storms (Jenny 1980). In combination with sparse vegetation in the riparian zone (also because of low water availability), flash flooding leads to stream scouring, which in turn can stress or remove already tenuous streamside plants. This condition can be exacerbated by "flashy" urban runoff and by overgrazing of riparian vegetation, resulting in denuded riparian corridors in arid zones. Riparian denudation in arid areas can then lead to regional differences in riparian functions, such as hydrologic regulation and sediment filtration. This form of riparian degradation is less common in humid landscapes, despite the much greater total quantities of floodwater.

Overall, climate and geology are the primary regional variables affecting both structure and function. Differences in climate and geology in turn are expressed in important features like topography, soils, vegetation, drainage networks, hydrology, human modification, and land use. Understanding how these variables operate and interact is requisite to an informed approach to ecological planning and design. This knowledge establishes a necessary perspective from which to examine in further detail the site-specific parameters that will influence the design and function of a particular greenway or habitat network.

Accounting for the Inevitability of Landscape Change

From a human perspective, changes in landscape structure and function can be slow or fast, leading to

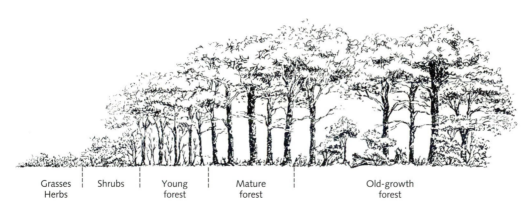

Figure 2.11 The progression of successional stages following abandonment of agricultural land in a humid climate, culminating in old-growth forest. The transition from grasses to young forest can occur over the course of a few decades, whereas several centuries are required for old-growth forest to regenerate.

Grasses | Shrubs | Young | Mature | Old-growth
Herbs | | forest | forest | forest

large differences in the significance we attach to these changes. When change is rapid and results in an obvious alteration in the soil or plant cover of a landscape element, it is referred to as a *disturbance*. Surface mining and wildfire are two examples of such quick change. Surface mining destroys the original landscape to the extent that restoring original conditions may be difficult, if not impossible. On the other hand, wildfire may be part of a natural cycle of landscape change and renewal to which plants and animals have adapted over the course of thousands of years (Albini 1984). Therefore, the definition of disturbance need not carry a connotation of negative human impact. But landscape ecologists do often distinguish between human and natural disturbances in setting baseline standards for ecological restoration. Restoration should ideally return land to a condition that includes natural cycles of disturbance, but it should also minimize those human-induced disturbances that are considered to be undesirable.

Land has a natural tendency to recover from disturbance through ecological *succession*, which involves, over the course of time, revegetation and recolonization by animals. Ecological succession (an example of slow landscape change) is the sequential change in the composition of plant and animal species of an ecosystem following a disturbance (Figure 2.11). The nature of succession and the species involved will differ according to both regional and site-specific variables like climate, the kind of disturbance, and the species available to recolonize an area.

In many forested environments, when trees reach their full maturity, succession leads to a condition where local disturbance patches are continuously formed by the death of individual trees, or sometimes groups of trees, as when a large tree falls and clears away other trees in its path. Eventually, across broad stretches of forest, these patches of vegetation will span various stages of recovery from immature to mature stages—mature patches constituting the majority—but the overall age and species composition of the ecosystem will be relatively stable. The local patches form a shifting mosaic on the landscape, but the overall condition is one of relative stability. This condition, known as the shifting-mosaic steady state, is not permanent but will eventually be disrupted by another widespread disturbance after hundreds or perhaps thousands of years, depending on local and regional variables (Bormann and Likens 1979). In forest landscapes where disturbance is especially common, steady-state conditions may never occur at all.

Slow change can also take the form of gradual landscape breakdown caused by a chronic low level of *stress*. Stress can result from natural phenomena such as cold temperatures, high winds, or drought or from human-induced phenomena such as ozone pollution, contamination of soil with toxic metals, or reduction in the size of an animal's habitat. Plants and animals generally have adapted to stresses from natural phenomena; however, novel and especially severe human-induced stresses have the potential to push change beyond the limits of resiliency. When this situation occurs, landscapes pass into a phase of *degradation*. Degradation results when the regenerative tendencies of ecological succession are overwhelmed by stress; this condition usually occurs more readily in landscapes that are naturally stressed (e.g., drought-prone, fire-prone, or extremely cold areas). For example, the applied stress of grazing animals will tend to degrade land in arid areas more readily than a comparable grazing stress in a humid environment.

Because natural successional processes are often altered by human influences, especially the introduction of exotic species and the suppression of natural fire regimes, it is necessary in many instances to actively manage successional change. A general goal for managing ecological succession should be to provide for quick transitions that support ecologically functional and aesthetically pleasing intermediate stages with minimal adverse environmental impact. Transitions and ongoing maintenance should also involve minimal monetary costs. These goals imply that we need to understand how to cleverly push ecological succession in a direction that is self-maintaining, or nearly so (Thorne and Pitz 1988).

For example, a land manager may be interested in regenerating a native mixed oak forest in the southeastern United States Piedmont on land being released from active agriculture. In this case, one concern would be the possibility that succession could be arrested by a rank growth of kudzu, an invasive vine. Kudzu is both an ecological problem because of its ability to arrest successful forest regeneration and an aesthetic problem because it quickly forms an unattractive tangled mass of vegetation. If kudzu were already established in the field, midsummer plowing could first be used to expose, dry out, and kill the kudzu roots and rhizomes. This step could be followed by planting local pines as the initial successional tree species. Once these trees had grown to a size where their bark was tough enough, low-intensity fires could be used to kill any kudzu vines that might have seeded into the field after

it was plowed. With the pines well established, temporarily stopping the burning would allow oak and hickory seedlings to become established. Once oaks and hickories were present, commercially harvesting the pines would release the hardwoods to become the new, self-replacing forest. A low brush fire could be used to suppress any regrowth of the kudzu once the bark of oaks and hickories was tough enough to withstand burning. Once established, the dense shade of the oak-hickory canopy would suppress kudzu reinvasion.

The process of manipulating ecological succession to produce a desired goal is known as ecological *restoration*. Restoration often has as its goal some other end point than the ecological state of the landscape before disturbance. In fact, to promote the full variety of successional stages, some continual form of management may be needed to create disturbances in situations where human activity has interrupted natural disturbance cycles.

Consider the role of an ecological restorationist in dealing with the aftermath of the 1988 fire in Yellowstone National Park. In this case the natural cycle of fire disturbance in the park had been interrupted for over one hundred years by intentional fire suppression. This led to excessive accumulation of litter and woody debris in the forests that eventually caused a fire of catastrophic proportion. A natural cycle of more frequent fires would burn less intensely and would spread over smaller geographic areas at any one time. The pine forests of the area have adapted over millennia to such a cycle of burning. The ecological restorationist could prescribe a program of forest restoration including planting or seeding in the most seriously damaged areas, to be followed by periodic burning of small forest areas to avoid the recurrence of such a severe conflagration as the one that occurred in 1988.

Recognition of the inherent tendency for change in nature transforms the perception of the landscape as a static, pastoral entity into a more accurate recognition of the landscape's constant dynamism. The elements of a landscape are constantly cycling between immaturity and maturity because of natural and human disturbance as well as accumulated, excessive stress. In human-dominated areas, typically widespread human disturbance is apt to result in a preponderance of immature elements (regenerating commercial forests, agricultural fields, lawns, etc.). In more natural areas, where succession proceeds uninhibited, mature elements are more likely to dominate. However, even in greenways where succession can proceed naturally, it is still important to account for landscape change by recognizing that natural disturbances, like high winds, fire, ice storms, and insect infestations, followed by succession will continuously cycle landscape elements (patches) of different sizes through various stages of development.

In designing greenways intended for wildlife movement, the spatial and temporal dynamics of the shifting-mosaic steady state, as well as the possibility of large-scale disturbances, point to the need for relatively wide corridors to maintain connectivity among mature habitats. An understanding of succession also leads to the recognition that greenways should include not only a diversity of mature habitats but also all stages of ecological succession (Harris 1984). Because some species of plants and animals are adapted to particular stages of succession, maintaining the full variety of native habitats will help ensure that native species, which together make up a region's biological diversity (biodiversity), will remain.

To summarize, in accounting for landscape change, designers and managers should (1) avoid interfering with natural cycles of disturbance and inherent stresses to which native species are adapted, (2) relieve human-induced stresses where possible, (3) facilitate change to restore landscape elements that are to become part of a planned greenway, and (4) account for the inevitability of landscape change by sizing a greenway to account for the fact that certain elements within it will change over time.

Applying Landscape Ecology to Greenway Planning and Design

A New Approach to Planning and Design

A landscape ecological approach to planning and design can readily be distinguished from a more conventional environmental planning approach. Traditionally, environmental planning has focused on regulating the supply and quality of drinking water, controlling soil erosion, and minimizing the effects of geologic catastrophes (such as landslides, earthquakes, volcanic eruption, and flooding). These problems can often be approached with standard engineering solutions. They generally do not require strict regulation of land use and are therefore more amenable to regulatory activity than maintaining biological diversity or the overall health of aquatic systems.

With this traditional approach, open space has usually been preserved without regard for its spatial configuration. Of even less concern has been the notion that lands in different stages of recovery from human use or from natural disturbance need to be represented adequately to preserve habitat diversity. A landscape ecological approach helps create more comprehensive landscape designs because it considers biodiversity conservation and because it seeks to protect water resources with ecologically sound, nonstructural (i.e., nonengineering) solutions.

Current environmental legislation, like traditional environmental planning, does not adequately address landscape ecological concerns. M. W. Dennis and colleagues (1989) have pointed out that legally mandated land-conservation activity in the United States places a heavy emphasis on wetland and coastal-zone conservation. Since species diversity depends on habitat diversity, most current conservation strategies, which lack provisions for upland and interior habitats, are limited in their ability to preserve biological diversity. When properly designed and implemented, greenways may be a partial solution to the problem of upland habitat loss. However, greenways may not fully capture habitat diversity if they are not connected to large patches of upland vegetation, since some species require very large patches or are sensitive to the edge conditions of narrow greenways.

Contextualism

From the perspective of the landscape ecologist, siting a greenway first requires an application of what landscape planners call *contextualism* (Lynch and Hack 1984). This means that design must start by examining the context within which the proposed greenway will exist. Two aspects of landscape structure are important in this regard: the pattern of elements in the landscape and the trends of the surrounding matrix.

The first aspect, element pattern, refers to the spatial (and sometimes temporal) arrangement of landscape elements with an eye toward how pattern influences the ecological integrity of the landscape. Existing element pattern may be fairly conducive to greenway design. For example, where river corridors, ridgeline corridors, and large patches of green space remain undeveloped, the landscape elements needed for greenway planning may already be in place. Element pattern can also be fairly constraining, as in a highly fragmented suburban landscape, or absolutely constraining, as in a fully developed urban landscape.

Trends in the surrounding matrix can also provide important contextual clues for greenway design. The need for corridor connectivity may vary depending on the status of the matrix. If an upland corridor is being designed to enhance connectivity for wildlife movement, the need for connectivity in this corridor will depend on whether the surrounding matrix is, for instance, managed forest or agricultural. If the matrix is managed forest, there may be less need for complete connectivity in the upland greenway, and resources might better be spent on some other aspect of the greenway project. On the other hand, in the context of an agricultural matrix, connectivity in the upland corridor may be vital. If the agricultural matrix were threatened by suburban development, the issue of connectivity for wildlife conservation might take on an even higher priority.

The ease or difficulty with which greenway planning can be accomplished, then, is correlated with the greenway's position on the landscape modification gradient. Toward the more natural end of this gradient, in natural, managed, and in some agricultural matrices, greenway planning may not be difficult. As one proceeds toward suburban and urban matrices, however, ecological greenway planning becomes progressively more constrained by landscape fragmentation and increasing development pressure.

A contextual view also suggests that traditional patterns of development can be reconsidered to promote more effective greenway design. For instance, since human activity in the late twentieth century is no longer dependent on river-based transportation networks, dense human settlement can be discouraged or minimized in the immediate vicinity of watercourses, allowing for multipurpose greenways in both the city and the countryside. Indeed, many urban riverfronts and former docklands have been restored as greenways (Little 1990). Although most of these greenways have been created primarily for recreation, they suggest the potential of realigning human settlement patterns to promote nature conservation. Redirecting development to uplands, where greenways and habitat patches can be designed as part of the development process, can provide for both human settlement needs and the preservation of upland (especially interior) habitat.

Land-cover mapping and land-ownership mapping are prerequisites for understanding the context of greenway design. These maps allow an assessment of the physical potential for linkage; the condition of the local matrix, patches, and corridors; and the feasibility of implementing a corridor design. By displaying data

Figure 2.12 A conventional planning scheme (left), which focuses on visual quality management alone and spreads houses out along a road corridor, compared with a landscape ecological planning scheme (right), which also considers habitat connectivity by clustering housing away from the movement corridor in the background. (Drawing by Donna Murphy and Fernando Fen.)

in a spatial format, maps facilitate informed decisions about the dimensions of a greenway, the need at key points for habitat restoration to improve connectivity, and the advisability of acquiring property outright versus buying easements (Thorne et al. 1991).

Including People and Aesthetics in Greenway Design

Although nature conservation is the primary focus of this chapter, landscape ecology also considers the needs of people in the landscape. Preserving the full variety of habitat types of an area, which is critical to maintaining biodiversity, is a biological conservation issue. But representation of habitat types goes beyond biology because preservation of landscape components also preserves part of our cultural heritage: that is, protecting the range of habitats also allows local examples of biological diversity to be "on display" for educational purposes and provides recreational open space for people to enjoy. Although it is possible to justify the siting of greenways on purely technical and scientific grounds, adding heritage, education, recreation, and aesthetic appeal provides reinforcing benefits in specifically human terms.

Appeals to people's appreciation of natural beauty can provide a powerful impetus for greenway establishment. However, potential conflicts between human visual preference in landscapes and ecological integrity can interfere with effective greenway design if aesthetics and ecology are not simultaneously taken into account (Steinitz 1990). Research by perceptual psychologists has shown that in naturalistic landscapes people prefer very high levels of visual complexity (Kaplan and Kaplan 1978; Kaplan 1987). The principal constraint on this preference is that the landscape be perceived as a coherent and "legible" whole (Schauman 1988), meaning that the elements of the landscape should fit into a standard mental model of a well-stewarded whole.

Fulfilling this aesthetic requirement does not necessarily mean that elements of natural vegetation will be connected or that a full diversity of habitat types will be represented. Where human aesthetic preferences are a major concern, measures to enhance visual appeal should be combined with ecological principles for landscape design. Figure 2.12 illustrates an aesthetically pleasing and complex landscape on the left that compromises wildlife corridor connectivity. On the right side of Figure 2.12 is a comparably complex and attractive landscape where upland wildlife corridor connectivity has not been fragmented by housing and agricultural fields. Both landscapes would be found attractive, but only the landscape on the right simultaneously satisfies needs for visual complexity and ecological integrity.

Creating Comprehensive Greenway Networks

When designing an open-space network across a landscape, it is helpful to break down greenways into a number of types: ridgetop, upland and stream corridors, and connectors that cross elevational gradients and link the entire system together. Riparian greenways protect both habitat and water resources, whereas ridgetop greenways often contain special dry or high-elevation habitat types. Between the two extremes, upland greenways may contain extensive areas of forest interior. Together, these three types can include the full diversity of a region's habitats. Creating multiple connectors ties the network together for people and wildlife and provides redundant connections to accommodate inevitable landscape change and disturbance (Figure 2.13).

For the full potential of such a conservation effort to be realized, habitat restoration and preservation need to take into account the functional characteristics of the landscape elements being connected. By considering (1) how corridors function as habitat, conduit, barrier, filter, source, and sink, (2) how they interact with the surrounding matrix, and (3) how they are

affected by landscape change, greenway design can account not just for ecological pattern but for the dynamic nature of ecological process as well.

The Upper Schoharie Watershed

Figure 2.14 illustrates an example of comprehensive greenway planning from the Upper Schoharie watershed, located in the Catskill Mountains in New York State (Thorne et al. 1991). The figure shows proposed areas of property acquisition and easement to provide various types of resource protection. For the conservation of biodiversity, two forest-interior mammals—fisher and black bear—were identified as most likely to be threatened by landscape fragmentation. Because of their sensitivity to fragmentation and because they are at the top of the food chain, these animals were considered to be "keystone species." It is assumed that by protecting keystone species, those species most sensitive to environmental degradation, other, less sensitive species will also be protected. The plan calls for the preservation of ridgetop corridors, ranging from about 200 to 1,000 meters (650 to 3,280 feet) in width, on steep, north-facing slopes. Connecting corridors that cross roadways are roughly 200 meters (650 feet) wide,

Figure 2.13 An integrated set of greenways including ridgetop, upland, and riparian corridors.

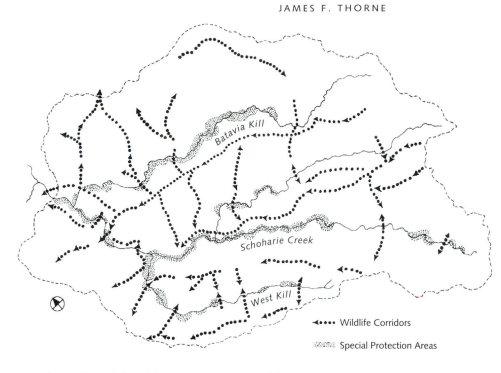

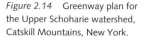
Figure 2.14 Greenway plan for the Upper Schoharie watershed, Catskill Mountains, New York.

enough to allow fisher (the more sensitive of the two species) a relatively safe passage.

Plans to protect steep, north-facing ridgetop corridors created a potential conflict with proposed development of second homes in the area. Second-home development and associated land clearing along roadways traversing the east-to-west trending ridges would disrupt ridgetop corridor connectivity if allowed to spread across entire ridges and would compromise scenic viewsheds, especially on north-facing slopes, which are highly visible from surrounding areas. However, development on moderate, south-facing slopes is not necessarily in conflict with scenic values. Therefore, both viewsheds and connectivity could be protected by purchasing conservation easements that strictly limit forest clearance on north-facing slopes. Development could still be accommodated on less steep south-facing slopes that are neither critical for wildlife movement nor in view of the highways. This aspect of the design considers the habitat and conduit functions of the ridgetops and the potential barrier function of roadside development. Landscape change is anticipated in the plan by including multiple con-

nectors across roads, which otherwise might become choke points for wildlife movement.

River valleys in the Upper Schoharie watershed are the focus of much human activity. They consist of a cultivated matrix dotted with small towns and, increasingly, an interspersion of second-home development. The most critical environmental issue in the valleys is the deterioration of water quality due to riverbank erosion and sheet erosion. The landscape ecological design for the valleys includes reforesting streambanks to improve water quality. Twenty-five-meter-wide (80 feet) greenway buffers would be restored and protected through acquisition of either full title or conservation easement, depending on the environmental significance of each buffer segment. In addition, the shading effect of the buffer strips would provide better trout habitat by cooling the water and contributing food and organic debris. The resulting greenways could serve a recreational use as well if local conservation groups wished to place paths along the riparian buffer.

The study identified cleared valley bottoms as an important aesthetic resource because they allow unrestricted views of mountain scenery, especially wooded north-facing slopes. The study also recommended purchasing easements on farmland as a way of protecting viewsheds. These purchases would not only protect scenery but also help maintain the farming community, an important component of local cultural diversity.

Finally, greenway designers must consider how such schemes might be implemented. In the case of the Upper Schoharie watershed project, funding was expected to come from a state bond act, which was voted down in a public referendum in 1990. This failure reflects a current trend of reduced availability of public funds for open-space conservation in many areas of the country. It now seems more likely that conservation in the Upper Schoharie area will come, at least in the short term, from the efforts of grass-roots organizations and local and regional land trusts.

Conclusion

This chapter has provided an outline of landscape ecology and how this discipline can provide a useful basis for greenway design that will help maintain ecological integrity while also providing for human needs. As illustrated in the Upper Schoharie case study, this goal can be achieved through carefully considering ecological structure, function, and change of landscapes and by channeling the resulting understanding toward planning solutions. To achieve this goal will entail implementing the conceptual framework provided by landscape ecology, and—as described in subsequent chapters—investigating in detail the major topics relevant to greenways, as well as combining all of this knowledge through the process of ecological design.

References

Albini, F. A. 1984. Wildland fires. *American Scientist* 72:590–97.

Bazzaz, F. A. 1986. Life history of colonizing plants: Some demographic, genetic and physiologic features. In Mooney, H. A. and J. A. Drake, eds., *Ecology of Biological Invasions of North America and Hawaii.* Springer-Verlag, New York.

Bormann, F. H., and G. E. Likens. 1979. *Pattern and Process in a Forested Ecosystem.* Springer-Verlag, New York.

Dennis, M. W., B. W. Breedlove, R. Boos, and B. H. Bauer. 1989. Disney Imagineering, Florida's natural environment and regulatory policy integrated through concepts of landscape ecology. Pages 14–15 in Fifth Annual Landscape Ecology Symposium: The Role of Landscape Ecology in Public-Policy Making and Land-Use Management. U.S. IALE Program, Miami University, Oxford, Ohio.

Duckson, D. W. 1989. Land use and water quality relationships in the Georges Creek Basin, Maryland. *Water Resources Bulletin* 25:801–7.

Forman, R. T. T., and M. Godron. 1984. Landscape ecology principles and landscape function. In Proceedings of the 1st International Seminar on Methodology in Landscape Ecological Research and Planning. Roskilde Universitets Forlag, Roskilde, Denmark, 5:4–15.

Forman, R. T. T., and M. Godron. 1986. *Landscape Ecology.* John Wiley and Sons, New York.

Groffman, P. M., A. J. Gold, T. P. Husband, R. C. Simmons, and W. R. Eddleman. 1990. *An Investigation into Multiple Uses of Vegetated Buffer Strips.* Final Report of Narragansett Bay Project, Department of Natural Resource Science, University of Rhode Island. Institution Press, Washington, D.C.

Harris, L. D. 1984. *The Fragmented Forest: Island Biogeography Theory and the Preservation of Biotic Diversity.* University of Chicago Press, Chicago.

Henein, K., and G. Merriam. 1990. The elements of connectivity where corridor quality is variable. *Landscape Ecology* 4:157–70.

Huang, C. S. 1990. *Catskill Gateway Conservation Study: A Strategy for Land Protection.* Catskill Center for Conservation and Development, Arkville, N.Y.

Jenny, H. 1980. *The Soil Resource: Origin and Behavior.* Springer-Verlag, New York.

Kaplan, R., and S. Kaplan. 1978. *Humanscape: Environments for People.* Duxbury Press, N. Scituate, Mass.

Kaplan, S. 1987. Aesthetics, affect and cognition: Environmental preference from an evolutionary perspective. *Environment and Behavior* 19:3–32.

Little, C. E. 1990. *Greenways for America.* Johns Hopkins University Press, Baltimore.

Lovejoy, T. E., and D. C. Oren. 1981. The minimum critical size of ecosystems. In R. L. Burgess and D. M. Sharpe, eds., *Forest Island Dynamics in Man-dominated Landscapes.* Springer-Verlag, New York.

Lowrance, R., R. Todd, J. Fail, Jr., O. Hendrickson, Jr., R. Leonard, and L. Asmussen. 1984. Riparian forests as nutrient filters in agricultural watersheds. *Bioscience* 34:374–77.

Lynch, K. G., and D. Hack. 1984. *Site Planning,* 3d ed. MIT Press, Cambridge.

Merriam, G. 1984. Connectivity: A fundamental ecological characteristic of landscape pattern. In Proceedings of the 1st International Seminar on Methodology in Landscape Ecological Research and Planning. Roskilde Universitets Forlag, Roskilde, Denmark, 1:5–15.

Naveh, Z., and A. S. Lieberman. 1984. *Landscape Ecology: Theory and Application.* Springer-Verlag, New York.

Noss, R. F. 1987. Corridors in real landscapes: A reply to Simberloff and Cox. *Conservation Biology* 1:159–64.

Ranney, J. W., M. C. Bruner, and J. B. Levenson. 1981. The importance of edge in the structure and dynamics of forest islands. In R. L. Burgess and D. M. Sharpe, eds., *Forest Island Dynamics in Man-dominated Landscapes.* Springer-Verlag, New York.

Robbins, C. S., D. K. Dawson, and B. A. Dowell. 1989. Habitat area requirements of breeding forest birds of the Middle Atlantic States. *Wildlife Monographs* 53:1–34.

Schauman, S. 1988. Scenic value of countryside landscape to local residents: A Whatcom County, Washington case study. *Landscape Journal* 7:40–46.

Simberloff, D., and J. Cox. 1987. Consequences and costs of conservation corridors. *Conservation Biology* 1:63–71.

Steinitz, C. 1990. Toward a sustainable landscape with high visual preference and high ecological integrity: The Loop Road in Acadia National Park. *Landscape and Urban Planning* 19:213–50.

Thorne, J. F., and D. A. Pitz. 1988. Landscape aikido—The management of succession in ecological design and planning. Pages 178–88 in Proceedings of 1988 Council of Educators in Landscape Architecture Conference.

Thorne, J. F., and C. S. Huang. 1991. Toward a landscape ecological aesthetic: Methodologies for designers and planners. *Landscape and Urban Planning* 21:61–79.

Thorne, J. F., C. S. Huang, M. T. Hatley, and A. Mathur. 1991. Applying the landscape ecological aesthetic to land acquisition planning in the Upper Schoharie Watershed, Catskill Mountains, New York. In Selected Council of Educators in Landscape Architecture Papers, 3:196–208.

Wales, B. A. 1972. Vegetation analysis of north and south edges in a mature oak-hickory forest. *Ecological Monographs* 42:451–71.

White, C. S., and J. R. Gosz. 1983. Sediment chemistry as influenced by vegetation and bedrock in the southwestern United States. *Water Resources Bulletin* 19:829–36.

Reed F. Noss

Wildlife Corridors

3

In landscapes where natural areas are increasingly fragmented by development, maintenance or restoration of habitat connectivity has become a central goal of biological conservation. Greenways have been conspicuous components of land-use plans in recent years and have the potential to improve connectivity and to function as wildlife corridors. Biological corridor issues, however, are often given little attention in greenway planning. Some of the most pressing questions that must be considered, both generically and for specific projects, include the following: What is a corridor for wildlife? Which species will benefit from a particular corridor and which will not? Is a narrow corridor, dominated by "weedy" species, better than no corridor at all? These and other issues must be addressed if we are to design greenways that contribute to broad conservation goals in addition to providing for human uses.

A few definitions at the outset will help frame these issues. *Wildlife* traditionally refers to animals, especially vertebrates, but recent definitions encompass "all forms of life that are wild" (Hunter 1990, 4) and are closely linked to the concept of biological diversity. A wildlife corridor is defined here as a swath of habitat through which nondomesticated organisms may move. Corridors can be discrete linear landscape features such as hedgerows and riparian strips, as well as broad, internally heterogeneous zones that permit dispersal of species between habitat patches, landscapes, or even regions over long periods of time (Brown and Gibson 1983). Spatial and temporal scales are important to consider in any discussion of wildlife corridors; although both are corridors, a hedgerow and the Isthmus of Panama have very different functions. I will discuss corridor functions mostly at the spatial scale at which greenways are planned (that is, within landscapes and regions) and at an ecological time scale of days to decades.

In this chapter, I review various functions of wildlife corridors, discuss potential problems and design issues, and provide recommendations for greenway planning. Biological conservation is arguably the most important potential function of greenways and of land-use planning in general. Economic, recreational, and aesthetic values of corridors are important to people and are often compatible with conservation of biodiversity. However, there will inevitably be points of conflict between people and nature, in which case human-oriented values must be considered as secondary to biodiversity. We live in a time of biological crisis; all land-use alternatives should be evaluated in light of this alarming fact.

Functions of Wildlife Corridors

Wildlife managers have long been aware of the value of movement corridors for particular game mammals and birds, such as squirrels and quail (Sumner 1936; Allen 1943; Baumgartner 1943; see Harris and Atkins 1991, for a review). Corridors have been invoked as tools for the conservation of biological diversity since the mid-1970s, when conservation biologists produced a series of influential papers on design principles for nature reserves (Willis 1974; Diamond 1975; Sullivan and Shaffer 1975; Wilson and Willis 1975; Diamond and May 1976). More recently, in North America, corridors have been a major topic of research and discussion in landscape ecology (Forman and Godron 1981, 1986; Forman 1983; Noss 1983; Thorne, chapter 2, this volume).

The design recommendations of conservation biologists for reserves in the 1970s were based largely on the equilibrium theory of island biogeography (MacArthur and Wilson 1967). Island biogeographic theory predicts that small, isolated islands (or patches of habitat that resemble islands) will experience higher extinction rates and lower immigration rates of species than large islands closer to a species source. Corridors were suggested as a means to increase species immigration to nature reserves and other habitat islands in fragmented landscapes and thus as a means to maintain species richness (Harris 1984a).

As our understanding of landscape ecology has

matured, the limitations of island biogeographic theory have become plain. Habitat patches are not truly islands in a homogenous sea. Rather, the matrix that surrounds habitat patches is a source of species (often invasive weeds) that may colonize patches, and the habitat structure of the matrix influences the ability of species to move across it. Island biogeographic theory was important because it spurred conservationists to think about patch size and isolation, but landscape ecology now takes the more realistic view of landscapes as heterogeneous mosaics.

The scientific literature on wildlife corridors has concentrated quite narrowly on how corridors function as conduits, allowing individuals of a target species to move from point A to point B. But a corridor in a real landscape will have myriad functions and will affect a large number of species. Although a particular target species may be the primary concern in some situations, the net effect of alternative corridor designs on a whole suite of species and ecological processes should be considered. The two major benefits of wildlife corridors in biological conservation are (1) providing dwelling habitat for plants and animals, and (2) serving as a conduit for movement (see chapter 2). The conduit role can be further subdivided into several functions: (a) permitting daily and seasonal movements of animals; (b) facilitating dispersal, consequent gene flow between populations, and rescue of small populations from extinction; and (c) allowing long-distance range shifts of species, such as in response to climate change.

Corridors as Habitat

Corridors, even narrow ones, provide habitat in which some kinds of organisms will live and reproduce. In many landscapes, most of the natural vegetation has been removed, and remnants are distributed either as isolated patches or as linear features between agricultural fields or along rivers, railroads, highways, power lines, or other rights-of-way. For some species, such as cottontail rabbits in a midwestern hedgerow, the value of these corridors is greater as habitat than as travel way. In fact, the habitat and conduit functions can work together for even greater benefit. It is likely that the most effective movement corridors are those that contain resident, reproducing populations of the species of interest (Bennett 1990a, 1990b; see discussion of dispersal later).

Riparian (streamside) forests are naturally linear or sinuous features with well-known habitat values for wildlife. Although riparian forests such as bottomland hardwoods have undergone significant declines (Korte and Frederickson 1977; Harris 1984b), in some landscapes they have received partial protection by default because regular flooding makes them unsuitable for development. Undammed coastal-plain rivers, such as the Suwannee and its tributaries in Florida, are often blessed with broad riparian corridors that contrast sharply with the agriculturally developed uplands. These corridors have many ecological values, including rich alluvial soils and an associated high biological productivity, microclimates moderated by the year-round presence of water, an abundance of insects and plant foods such as woody browse or acorns for vertebrates, and numerous tree cavities to serve as homes or nests for birds and mammals (Harris 1989).

Vertebrate densities are usually high in riparian forests. In Iowa, floodplain forests have been found to support an average of 506 breeding pairs of birds per 40 hectares (100 acres) compared to 339 pairs in upland forests (Stauffer and Best 1980). Many species of plants and animals are found only in riparian zones, and these areas usually contain more species than other terrestrial habitat types (Harris 1984a). Forested riparian zones also provide many benefits to adjacent aquatic communities, such as maintenance of water quality, contribution of woody debris and leaves that provide food and habitat for aquatic organisms, moderation of water temperature through shading, and moderation of floods (see chapter 4).

Riparian corridors are particularly valuable in the arid and semiarid West, where they may constitute

the only low-elevation areas with trees or tall shrubs. Southwestern riparian zones are literally "linear oases" (Johnson 1989). Some 80 percent of all vertebrate species in Arizona and New Mexico are dependent on riparian habitat for at least a portion of their life cycles (Johnson 1989). Although only about 2 percent of the Southwest was occupied by riparian ecosystems before settlement, Arizona and New Mexico are estimated to have lost 90 percent of these rare ecosystems over the last century (Johnson 1989). Thus, it is not surprising that 70 percent of Arizona's threatened vertebrates and 73 percent of New Mexico's threatened vertebrates are either closely associated with or completely dependent on riparian habitat (Figure 3.1).

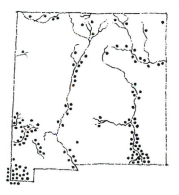

Figure 3.1 Map of New Mexico showing the distribution of rare vertebrates that occur in riparian habitats. Each dot represents a known location of a federally listed threatened or endangered species. Of ninety-four rare vertebrates in the state, sixty-nine are associated with or depend on riparian habitat. (After Johnson 1989.)

A similar affiliation of vertebrates with riparian zones occurs in less arid parts of the West. In the Blue Mountains in eastern Oregon and Washington, 285 (75 percent) of the 378 species of terrestrial vertebrates either depend on or strongly prefer riparian habitats (Thomas et al. 1979). Riparian greenways thus have the potential to support a large portion of the native biota in some landscapes. In other landscapes, however, many species are associated with upland habitats and do not occur in riparian zones; this situation is true in Florida, where upland longleaf pine and scrub communities contain many of the state's most characteristic and also most threatened species (Noss 1988). The degree to which riparian greenways can encompass the range of native species will depend on the nature of species distribution in particular landscapes.

Figure 3.2 Hedgerows may offer the only wooded habitat in many agricultural landscapes.

In agricultural landscapes, fencerows, hedgerows, shelterbelts, and even roadsides with natural vegetation stand in marked contrast to the monotony of cultivated fields (Figure 3.2). In Iowa, L. B. Best (1983) found the greatest number of bird species in fencerows with continuous trees and shrubs. Although the fencerows were considered valuable for maintaining bird populations in Iowa's agricultural landscape, the most common birds in fencerow habitats were weedy species tolerant of human habitat modification, such as the brown-headed cowbird, house sparrow, northern flicker, mourning dove, and American robin. These birds are known as edge species (in contrast to interior species) because they inhabit the interfaces between contrasting habitats, such as forest and field. Edges are generally drier and brighter than forest interiors; a fencerow or hedgerow is entirely edge habitat. Edge species often increase in abundance as landscapes are fragmented by human activity. Thus, on the one hand the value of fencerows and other narrow corridors for conservation of native species is limited. On the other hand, in landscapes where large blocks of natural habitat no longer exist, narrow corridors add biological diversity to an otherwise monotonous countryside. Some edge birds may also help control insect pests.

Farmstead shelterbelts in Minnesota, although planted primarily to protect humans and their property from high winds and snow, also provide nesting and feeding habitat for birds (Yahner 1982). Once again, however, the species that benefit are generally common edge species. Power-line corridors introduce a similar set of species into forested landscapes (Anderson et al. 1977); the greatest variety of birds is found when the power-line corridor contains a high density of shrubs such as blackberries (Kroodsma 1982). A shrubby, structurally diverse power-line right-of-way in Rhode Island, free of herbicide treatments for seven years, supported a richer bird community than a parklike residential area nearby (Geibert 1980). Although such edge-dominated corridors are not as valuable as wide greenways composed of mature vegetation, they clearly contain more biological diversity than many other land uses in urban and suburban landscapes.

Some of the best opportunities to maintain native species in linear habitats may be along railroad rights-of-way in the eastern Great Plains and Midwest. Many of the highest-quality remnants of native tallgrass prairie are along old railroad lines, since these zones were never plowed and sparks from coal-fired steam engines promoted the frequent fires that prairies require. For greenways established as part of a rails-to-trails program (Grove 1990), prairie restoration and management may be quite feasible (see chapter 2, Figure 2.6). In such cases, prescribed burning, reintroduction of extirpated prairie plants, and other restorative management should be applied (Jordan et al. 1988). Although the animal component of the prairie community can be expected to be very incomplete in narrow greenways of this sort, plant populations may thrive with diligent stewardship.

Forest-interior birds, which often avoid habitat edges, require wide forested corridors. In a study of bird use of remnant hardwood strips in pine plantations in Virginia (Tassone 1981), interior species usually occurred only in corridors at least 50 meters (165 feet) wide. Acadian flycatchers were seldom found in corridors less than 50 meters wide, hairy woodpeckers and pileated woodpeckers required minimum strip widths of 50 to 60 meters (165 to 200 feet), and the parula warbler was generally restricted to strips 80 meters (265 feet) or wider. We can assume that wider strips would be needed if the adjacent habitats were all clear-cuts rather than pine plantations, since edge effects become greater with increasing contrast between adjacent habitats (Harris 1988).

The difference in species composition between narrow and wide corridors led R. T. T. Forman and M. Godron (1981, 1986) to distinguish between line corridors, composed entirely of edge habitat, and strip corridors that contain true interior habitat, forest or otherwise (Figure 3.3). In fragmented landscapes, strip corridors are more valuable than line corridors for most native species of conservation concern. The width needed to achieve interior conditions depends on a number of complex variables and will be discussed later in this chapter.

In the wheatbelt region of Western Australia, remnants of native vegetation are confined mostly to small patches and narrow (5 to 50 meters) strips along roadways (Saunders et al. 1987). A high proportion of the region's birds use these habitats. In southeastern Australia, eighteen species of mammals, representing 78 percent of the total mammalian fauna (excluding bats), inhabit roadside strips (Bennett 1988). In Great Britain, road verges have been documented as breeding habitat for 20 of the country's 50 species of mammals, 40 of the 200 bird species, all 6 reptiles, 5 of the 6 species of amphibians, and 25 of the 60 species of butterflies (Way 1977). All of these studies point to the value of linear habitat remnants in heavily disturbed landscapes but also indicate problems associated with narrowness and associated edge effects.

Although wildlife management plans usually emphasize vertebrates, corridors may be generally more valuable as habitat to plants and invertebrates, which occur in higher densities and are therefore more likely to maintain viable populations in small (or narrow) areas. Fencerows through agricultural fields may sus-

tain populations of some plants native to the presettlement forest, although in most cases the high light levels and dry conditions of these habitats favor shade-intolerant species characteristic of forest edge rather than forest-interior species. Hence, in southeastern Wisconsin, narrow forest corridors are dominated by shade-intolerant trees such as hawthorns, oaks, hickories, yellow birch, buckthorn, willows, quaking aspen, butternut, hop-hornbeam, and black cherry. Corridors may have to exceed 100 meters (330 feet) in width to sustain populations of beech and 30 meters (100 feet) in width to sustain sugar maple, both being shade-tolerant species dependent on relatively moist conditions (Ranney et al. 1981).

North American hedgerows are typically dominated by forest-edge plants, including a number of nonnative species (Forman and Baudry 1984). E. Pol-

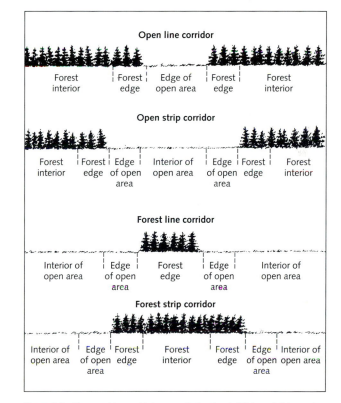

Figure 3.3 Line corridors, which are entirely edge habitat, and strip corridors, which contain both edge and interior habitat, can be either forested or open, depending on the type of surrounding matrix. (After Forman 1983.)

lard and colleagues (1974) refer to British hedgerows as woodland edges without the woods. Some 500 to 600 species of vascular plants occur in hedgerows in England, but apparently no species is limited to hedgerows. T. Lewis (1969), however, found far more species of insects in an English hedgerow than in adjacent bean fields and pastures. Thus, these narrow corridors may support species of little conservation significance at a regional or global scale of concern but are important in sustaining species diversity and a number of ecological functions in intensively managed landscapes.

In landscapes where little woodland remains, hedgerows can be important population reservoirs for some forest species (Forman and Baudry 1984). Landscape context (including the surrounding habitat matrix, the patches being connected, and the regional species pool) therefore becomes a vital consideration for appraising the conservation value of corridors (Noss and Harris 1986). Because greenways in urban and suburban landscapes will often be thin and dominated by edge habitat, ecological lessons from hedgerows and other narrow corridors will often apply to greenway design and management.

Corridors for Daily and Seasonal Movements

Another function of corridors is to allow animals to move across the landscape in relative safety to find food, water, cover, or mates, either on a daily or seasonal basis. A fox in a suburban landscape, for example, may use rows of shrubbery for nocturnal travels through its home range, whereas large mammals in a wilder setting use corridors in seasonal movements between summering and wintering areas.

Elk often make seasonal movements in response to forage conditions, especially in mountainous regions (Adams 1982). During migration, as well as on summer and winter ranges, hiding or escape cover can be important to elk (Skovlin 1982). Forested travel lanes adjacent to open meadows enable Rocky Mountain elk to make efficient use of the vegetation mosaic (Winn

1976). In the Blue Mountains in Oregon, forested corridors enable elk to cross from one canyon to another in continuous cover (Pederson and Adams 1976). Maintaining safe travel opportunities for elk is largely a matter of protecting them from human predation, often associated with road access.

Many other large herbivores make regular seasonal migrations along established routes; protecting travel corridors for such species should be a conservation priority. In southeastern Alaska, J. W. Schoen and M. D. Kirchoff (1990) recommended that old-growth forest be retained in large swaths extending from sea level to the subalpine zone in order to allow Sitka black-tailed deer to make elevational movements in response to changing snow conditions. Wide swaths of continuous natural habitat are optimal corridors for large mammals. Although developed regions no longer have this option, wildlands currently undergoing development or resource extraction should be managed to retain broad corridors.

Large predators have much to gain from preservation of secure movement corridors, since their large body size and food requirements demand that they travel widely (McNab 1963). For these wide-ranging, area-sensitive species, as for large herbivores, corridors with limited access to humans are needed to provide safe movement between large blocks of habitat. Year-round home ranges of puma (mountain lions, cougar) vary from about 12,500 to 500,000 acres, and it is not unusual for puma to travel 75 to 100 miles in linear distance (Anderson 1983). When moving between mountains and across plains and valleys, puma usually follow watercourses, seeking cover in the riparian vegetation (Young 1946). Bobcats are also known to follow natural riparian corridors in their movements, and river otters may require several miles of linear riverine and riparian habitat (which, in some cases, may constitute their entire home range). Black bears in Florida also use riparian corridors and range over an average area of 15,000 acres (Harris 1985; Harris and Gallagher 1989). Grizzly bears forage for widely dispersed food items and track seasonal changes along elevational gradients. Subadult males may disperse far out of the maternal range. Travel corridors most commonly used by grizzlies are ridgetops, saddles, and creek bottoms (LeFranc et al. 1987).

In addition to large predators and animals that make regular seasonal migrations between different habitats, many nonmigratory species depend upon multiple habitat patches in the landscape. Species that are usually considered either upland or wetland wildlife commonly require different habitats from time to time in order to fulfill dietary requirements, escape flooding, breed, or hibernate. Examples of such species include the raccoon, white-tailed deer, river otter, swamp rabbit, bobcat, gray fox, and turkey (Frederickson 1978). Many turtles inhabit aquatic habitats but require sandy upland sites, sometimes several hundred meters from a river, to lay eggs. Conversely, in times of drought, a number of upland animals move downslope to riparian areas (Brown et al. 1987); this function of corridors may be particularly critical in arid landscapes. Many vertebrates periodically depend on water sources that, at least seasonally, are some distance from their territory or nest site. In fragmented landscapes, the various habitats needed by animals on a daily or seasonal basis are often disjunct; corridors can be retained or restored to connect these patches.

Habitat for many species is dispersed in numerous patches over the landscape. For instance, the pileated woodpecker in eastern North America is no longer restricted to large tracts of mature forest but has developed the behavior of incorporating several woodlots into its home range; wooded fencerows may be important linkages followed by these woodpeckers in their movements (Merriam 1991). Large predators and large frugivores (fruit eaters) often range widely in order to meet dietary requirements. In Western Australia, Carnaby's cockatoo requires woodlands for nesting cavities and heathland or mallee for seed foraging (Saunders 1990). Broad strips of roadside vegetation help cockatoos move between vegetation patches in the landscape

(Saunders and Ingram 1987). When corridors are incomplete or of poor quality, nestling growth rates and fledging success of these birds are reduced.

Even narrow corridors of vegetation can be useful to some species for traveling about the landscape in relative safety. Blue jays, for example, may travel several kilometers in the fall to cache acorns and beechnuts for later use. When making these movements in Wisconsin, jays show a strong tendency to fly immediately above wooded fencerows. If a hawk (especially a migrating accipiter, like a sharp-shinned or Cooper's hawk) approaches, a jay dives into the cover of the fencerow (Johnson and Adkisson 1985). J. F. Wegner and G. Merriam (1979) found that several bird species flew along fencerows in preference to crossing open fields. Well-vegetated corridors probably often provide cover for escape from predators to animals that travel about the landscape.

However, human hunters and other predators may learn to concentrate their activity along animal movement routes. Thus, narrow corridors may become mortality sinks (Simberloff and Cox 1987). Greenways in developed landscapes should be designed and managed to provide adequate cover for wide-ranging species and to discourage human uses that might result in harassment. In wilder landscapes, intact roadless corridors should be maintained, and, where possible, roads should be closed to minimize conflicts between humans and wildlife.

Corridors for Dispersal

Dispersal refers to the movement of organisms away from their place of origin (Brown and Gibson 1983). A corridor can promote dispersal if individual animals or plant seeds travel from one population to another by means of the corridor, or if resident populations in the corridor allow the gradual flow of genes from one end to another (Figure 3.4; Bennett 1990a).

Natural selection exerts strong pressure on an animal or plant to disperse. Staying too near a parent can

Figure 3.4 Three ways in which corridors may facilitate dispersal of individual animals and genes between habitat patches: (a) direct, long-distance movement by a single individual; (b) periodic movement by a single animal, punctuated by pauses; and (c) gene flow through a reproducing population resident in the corridor. (From Bennett 1990a, with permission of the author.)

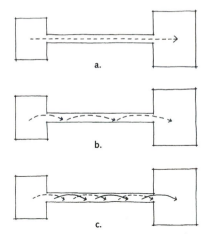

result in competition between parents and offspring, and exploring new territory is often advantageous in an ever-changing environment. Because dispersal of young birds and mammals is usually sex-biased (one sex disperses farther than the other), dispersal reduces the chances of mating between close relatives and allows genes to travel from one population to another. At regional and continental scales, dispersal helps explain how species are distributed geographically. Understanding of previous dispersal patterns allows predictions about future distributions in response to global trends such as climate change.

Dispersal is a particularly critical function in fragmented landscapes. In such landscapes, the scattered patches of natural habitat that are separated by unsuitable habitat cannot, by themselves, maintain populations of many species in the long run. A small woodlot may be mostly edge habitat and thus support only very small numbers of a forest-interior bird, such as the hooded warbler (Whitcomb et al. 1981). For interior species like this, restricted to remnant patches, movement of individuals among patches must be great enough to balance extirpation from local patches, or the regional population will eventually become extinct (Wiens 1989). Problems of population persistence in fragmented landscapes and the role of corridors in promoting persistence will be discussed in detail later.

Plants and animals have evolved many different

ways to disperse. Plants may be wind-dispersed, water-dispersed, or animal-dispersed. All of these mechanisms are passive, but the latter obviously depends on active animals. Fruits of many plants, including tick trefoil, beggar's-ticks, and ragweed, become attached to the fur of mammals, whereas fleshy fruits, such as those of cherries, blackberries, and junipers, are designed to be eaten and passed through the gut of animals. Nutty fruits of trees, such as oaks, hickories, and beech, are gathered by squirrels, jays, and other seed predators, but many of the cached nuts are never eaten and later germinate. Hence, as animals move across a landscape, the plants they carry also move.

Animal-dispersed plants benefit from corridors to the extent that their animal dispersers do. Grizzlies and black bears are among the mammals that disperse the seeds of fleshy fruits and that often use corridors such as riparian forests in their movements (LeFranc et al. 1987; Harris and Gallagher 1989). Birds are also important dispersal agents. Even in highly fragmented landscapes, beechnuts dispersed several kilometers by blue jays should be able to reach most forest patches; blue jays often follow wooded fencerows in making these movements (Johnson and Adkisson 1985). The long distances over which blue jays disperse beechnuts and acorns may explain the finding of Davis (1981) that heavy-seeded oaks and beech dispersed northward after the Pleistocene sometimes faster than trees such as spruce with light, windblown seeds. Many herbaceous forest plants, like trilliums and violets, have an oil body attached to their seeds, attracting ants that move the seed a good distance before consuming the oil body (Thompson 1981). If forest ants depend on habitat continuity for their movements, so too will these familiar wildflowers.

Movement of terrestrial animals and their plant hitchhikers may be maintained or enhanced by well-planned greenways or other corridors. Not all species depend on corridors for dispersal, however. Wind-dispersed plants, ballooning spiders, and open-country birds are obvious examples. The cabbage butterfly disperses long distances in random directions and does not detect suitable habitat patches from afar (Fahrig and Paloheimo 1988).

Some vertebrates are also random dispersers. The northern spotted owl, federally listed as a threatened species, is vulnerable to the effects of habitat fragmentation. Dispersing juvenile owls may travel from 2 to 40 miles from their place of birth (Thomas et al. 1990), a potentially dangerous journey in landscapes fragmented by logging due to the presence of edge-adapted predators such as great horned owls. Spotted owls appear to disperse freely in random directions (Miller 1989). Thin, linear corridors are unlikely to be used and could be havens for predators.

To provide for the dispersal needs of the spotted owl, an interagency scientific committee (Thomas et al. 1990) recommended that the matrix between established habitat conservation areas be managed as connecting zones with at least 50 percent of the landscape maintained in stands of timber with a mean diameter of 11 inches or more and at least 40 percent canopy closure. The idea here is that the landscape matrix itself, if managed properly, may serve as a dispersal "corridor" for spotted owls.

This discussion brings up an important point about scale and terminology. Functional connectivity (that is, the degree to which organisms or other elements are able to move across a landscape) need not depend on distinct linear corridors. At the regional scale at which the conservation of spotted owls and many other species is now being discussed, that portion of the landscape matrix that lies between two or more large habitat patches may provide functional connectivity by allowing movement of organisms between patches. As John Wiens (1989) has pointed out, the probability that dispersal can occur between fragments and forestall extinction of sensitive species on a regional scale is influenced by the configuration of the fragments and the landscape mosaic in which they are embedded. Conservationists would do well to expand their view of what constitutes connectivity for various species rather than restricting themselves to the notion of distinct linear corridors.

Another potential function of corridors in dynamic landscapes is to allow animals to escape disturbances (Noss 1987a). Landscapes are always changing because of natural and anthropogenic disturbances and subsequent succession. Disturbances in some portions of the landscape are balanced (at least in part) by regeneration elsewhere. If viewed over a sufficiently large area, some landscapes may approach a shifting-mosaic steady state of disturbance and recovery patches (Bormann and Likens 1979; see chapter 2 for further discussion). Continuity of natural habitat allows animals to adapt to these changes by moving from one area to another over time. The immediate and obvious value of connectivity is to enable animals to flee from disturbance and avoid mortality; hence, corridors may serve a "fire escape" function (Noss 1987a).

The goal of a landscape connectivity strategy should not be to encourage dispersal of all species. Indeed, there are a number of species (such as introduced weeds and diseases) whose dispersal must be actively thwarted to maintain native species composition in any given region. Whereas habitat modification by humans has imposed new barriers and has restricted movement of many species, it has facilitated movement of other species far beyond their native ranges. Introduced species are among the greatest threats to biotic integrity, both within nature reserves and across the landscape as a whole (Elton 1958; Mooney and Drake 1986; Usher 1988). The end result of the widespread mixing of faunas and floras is homogenization, where biotic regions lose their distinctive character and many endemic species are out-competed to extinction.

One common type of corridor in human-dominated landscapes—roads and roadsides—has fostered many biological invasions, including range expansions of grassland mammals (Huey 1941; Getz et al. 1978), spotted knapweed and other exotic weeds, the gypsy moth, and forest fungal diseases (Schowalter 1988). Other edge-dominated corridors, including fencerows and hedgerows, may also favor the spread of opportunistic species (both native to North America, such as the brown-headed cowbird, and exotic, such as the European starling) at the expense of sensitive species (Ambuel and Temple 1983; Simberloff and Cox 1987). In evaluating any corridor in the landscape, conservationists need to consider which species are most likely to benefit and which may potentially be harmed.

In considering the effects of corridors on species dispersal, it is important to remember the different roles corridors can play. In many instances, what is a conduit to one species is a barrier to another. A road may be a barrier to a woodland rodent trying to cross from one side to another, but the grassy roadside is a corridor to a meadow rodent. A hedgerow may facilitate movement of some animals but may have been constructed for a very different reason, such as to block the movement of livestock out of fields (Forman and Baudry 1984).

Furthermore, corridors function lengthwise not only as conduits but also as filters. Biogeographers characterize filters at large spatial scales as areas that block passage of some organisms while allowing others that tolerate the conditions of the area to migrate freely (Brown and Gibson 1983). At any scale, as the length of the corridor grows, the probability increases that individuals traveling along its length will be filtered out. Because different species will be filtered out at different rates, the net effect of any corridor will be a screening of biota; what comes out at the end will be a different set from what began. Greenways should therefore be designed with an understanding of the distance likely to be traveled by the various species of a particular landscape.

The Role of Dispersal Corridors in Population Persistence

The preceding section discussed dispersal in heterogeneous landscapes and the role of corridors of various types in promoting dispersal. This section discusses how dispersal and interchange of individuals among populations may reduce the risk of extinction, both through demographic (population process-related) and genetic effects.

Demographics

A *population* is a group of individuals of the same species living within a geographic area restricted enough so that any member of the population can potentially mate with any other member of the opposite sex. Many species are distributed as *metapopulations,* that is, as systems of local populations linked by dispersal (Levins 1970). It is the fate of local populations in these systems to "wink" off and on over time. Local extinctions may be caused by stochastic (apparently random) demographic effects, such as chance variation in sex ratios or birth and death rates in very small populations. More commonly, small local populations are eliminated by disturbances, extreme weather, or other environmental factors.

Dispersal of individuals across the landscape allows for colonization of vacated or other suitable habitats, so that the metapopulation as a whole persists despite local extinctions (Figure 3.5). If this dispersal is interrupted, as may happen when habitats are fragmented by development, the probability of persistence diminishes. The survival of metapopulations thus depends on both the rate of local extinctions in habitat patches and the rate at which organisms move among patches, which in turn is affected by connectivity between patches (den Boer 1981).

Corridors can lower the chances of extinction for small, local populations by augmenting population size and by increasing population growth rates (Merriam 1988). White-footed mouse populations in Ontario woodlots suffer high rates of overwinter extinction. Dispersal and resulting higher population growth rates in woodlots connected by fencerows assure that populations begin the winter with more individuals and have a better chance of lasting until spring (Fahrig and

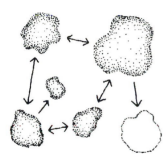

Figure 3.5 In a metapopulation, corridors may promote recolonization of patches where local extinctions have occurred.

Merriam 1985). Thus, corridors or other avenues of connectivity can provide a "rescue effect" (Brown and Kodric-Brown 1977) and allow small populations a higher probability of persistence than if they were isolated.

Corridors may also increase the likelihood that local extinctions can be reversed through recolonization of vacated patches. This, in turn, increases the chances that the entire metapopulation will survive. Decades ago, L. Baumgartner (1943) noted that fencerows in Ohio served as travel lanes for fox squirrels, allowing them to recolonize woodlots that had been "shot out" by hunters. Similarly, local extinctions of chipmunks are rapidly reversed through recolonization by individuals from other patches in Ontario landscapes where woodlots are well connected by fencerows (Henderson et al. 1985). In such landscapes, population dynamics in individual woodlots are of only local importance; one must look to the entire landscape mosaic in order to plan workable conservation strategies.

It might seem that the power of flight would free birds from any need for corridors, but, in fact, many birds have relatively poor dispersal abilities. For instance, the agricultural landscape surrounding woodlots in the Netherlands has a significant isolating effect on birds, to the point that immigration may not keep up with extinction (Opdam et al. 1985; van Dorp and Opdam 1987). The number of forest-interior bird species inhabiting woodlots is positively associated with the density of connecting corridors. A similar situation exists in Australia (Saunders and de Rebeira 1991). In

southern California, chaparral-dependent birds in patches of chaparral surrounded by development suffer high rates of extinction due to their reluctance to cross even narrow strips of unsuitable habitat. Movement corridors, even as narrow as 1 to 10 meters (3 to 33 feet) for some species, appear to offer the best prospects for maintaining populations of these species (Soulé et al. 1988).

Genetics

When considering the fate of populations over longer time spans, genetics may become as important as demographics. Small, isolated populations are prone to two kinds of detrimental genetic effects: inbreeding depression and random genetic drift.

Inbreeding depression is a result of mating between close relatives in normally outbreeding species. It occurs in isolated populations when individuals are not able to disperse and mate with individuals of other populations. By preventing the introduction of new genetic material to the population and allowing harmful recessive genes to be expressed, inbreeding can raise mortality rates (especially among juveniles) and reduce health, vigor, and fertility. The Florida panther, reduced by habitat destruction and direct killing to a small population in southern Florida, suffers from a number of inbreeding symptoms, including physical abnormalities and sperm that are more than 90 percent defective (Fergus 1991).

Random genetic drift is a change in gene frequencies in a population due to chance. In large populations, the effects of drift are insignificant. But in small populations, genetic drift leads to the loss of genetic diversity. Not only do genetically impoverished populations often show reduced viability and fertility (the effects of drift and inbreeding may be difficult to disentangle), but in the long run they will be less able to adapt to changing environmental conditions. The process of evolution itself is threatened by genetic impoverishment (Frankel and Soulé 1981; Schonewald-Cox et al. 1983).

There is little empirical evidence that immigrants contribute much to genetic variation in small populations. Indirect evidence and mathematical models, however, suggest that some level of immigration and gene flow will help populations maintain genetic diversity and will reduce the expression of harmful recessive genes through inbreeding. F. W. Allendorf (1983) predicted that an average exchange of one reproductively successful migrant between populations per generation is sufficient to avoid the loss of gene types through drift but will still allow populations to diverge as a result of adaptation to local environments through natural selection. To the extent that corridors facilitate this exchange of individuals among populations, they will help maintain genetically viable populations. A. F. Bennett (1990a, 1990b) has suggested that gene flow between populations will be enhanced if there are resident individuals of the target species within the corridor. Thus, the roles of corridors as habitat and as conduit may be complementary.

Concern has arisen about the desirability of corridor-facilitated genetic exchange and the effect it might have on genetically distinct populations (Simberloff and Cox 1987; Noss 1987a). There are essentially two forms of genetic variation within species, namely, the variety of genetic material among individuals within a population and variation between different populations. Gene flow between two populations, which occurs when individuals disperse from one population to another, will favor the retention of genetic variation within each population, but it will also make the two populations more similar genetically, reducing the between-population component of genetic variation. If enough genetic material is exchanged, the two populations may eventually become one and the same.

Some biologists maintain that the loss of genetically distinct populations within species is a problem that is at least as important as the loss of entire species (Ehrlich 1988). Local populations, particularly those near the periphery of their species' range, may have adapted through natural selection to local environmental conditions, or they may differ genetically purely as a result of random factors, such as genetic drift or mutation. A genetically distinct population may be in the early phases of speciation (formation of a new species), and increased gene flow could disrupt this process by increasing genetic similarity between populations.

D. Simberloff and J. Cox (1987) recommend that a risk analysis be undertaken before corridors are established to determine whether connection or subdivision of populations would better maintain genetic variability and population viability for a particular species. Such an approach, however, is impractical for whole communities of species that now are threatened by fragmentation in many regions (Noss 1987a). The prudent course, in the face of uncertainty, is to maintain or restore natural kinds and levels of landscape connectivity but to avoid creating artificial connections. For instance, maintaining a continuous network of forest would be sensible strategy for a region that was originally forested, whereas maintaining a continuous network of weed-dominated roadsides would not contribute to conservation goals in that same region.

Corridors for Long-Distance Range Shifts

One of the most glaring deficiencies in the conservation movement to date has been our failure to recognize and to accommodate change in nature. Conservation strategy has implicitly assumed that natural communities are unchanging, stable entities (Hunter et al. 1988). Hence, we are not prepared for change. We seek to freeze in time snapshots of scenic splendor for future generations, to "preserve" forests that naturally burn or blow down, and to maintain collections of species that have been apart for longer periods of their evolutionary histories than they have been together. Preservation is a noble idea, but we have been too concerned with static pattern and not enough with dynamic process.

Plant communities over much of North America have developed only within the last 4,000 to 8,000 years (Davis 1981; Webb 1987). Before this time, many of the species now found together were separated geographically; many of the communities we see today thus did not exist anywhere. In some regions, modern vegetation and flora have become established only over the past few centuries, for example, about 430 years ago in southwestern Wisconsin (Kline and Cottam 1979) and 300 years ago in southcentral Minnesota (Grimm 1984). Since the Pleistocene (Ice Age) ended 10,000 years ago, the ranges of many plant species have shifted by over 1000 kilometers (620 miles). Because species migrated northward at different rates and by different routes, community composition has changed continuously over space and time (Davis 1981). The response of animal species to climate change has also been individualistic, Ice-Age species associations being far different from those observed today (Graham 1986).

Our present system of isolated nature reserves is incapable of maintaining biodiversity in the face of climate change (Peters and Darling 1985; Peters 1988). Reserves that were set aside to protect a certain set of species will no longer be suitable for those species under a new climatic regime. Even natural rates of change pose significant challenges to species confined to reserves surrounded by inhospitable habitat. The increased rates of change predicted to occur with greenhouse warming may eliminate all species but the most mobile as they fail to track shifting climatic conditions. In addition to the natural barriers to migration at regional and continental scales, such as mountain ranges, desert basins, lakes, and rivers, human activities have superimposed an entirely new set of barriers in the form of cities, highways, fields, and clear-cuts. The impacts of these barriers will be cumulative, as successful long-distance dispersal becomes less likely with each additional barrier.

Can wildlife corridors function at regional and continental scales and allow species to adjust their distributions to new climates? We know that large-scale biogeographic corridors have been important during past climate changes. During the Pleistocene, several major dispersal corridors existed along North American rivers, in particular the Mississippi valley (Delcourt and Delcourt 1984). The northeast-to-southwest trending Appalachian Mountains presented no major obstacle to species moving south in advance of the glaciers and cooler climates. In Europe, however, dispersal was blocked by the east-to-west trending ranges of the Alps and Pyrenees. As a consequence of the enormous difference in migration opportunities, eastern North America is much richer today than Europe in plant species, despite the fact that the two subcontinents had similar levels of diversity before the Pleistocene. The Smoky Mountains alone contain as many species of trees as all of Europe (Whittaker 1972).

Unfortunately, historical evidence of corridor functions during past climate changes cannot assure us that corridors will provide for species migration during greenhouse warming. The rate of warming during the next half century is projected to be at least ten times greater than average rates over the last 100,000 years (Peters 1988). According to global circulation models, suitable habitat for beech could shift northward by 700 to 900 kilometers (435 to 560 miles) during the next century. Yet historical rates of beech migration averaged only 20 kilometers (12 miles) a century (but were sometimes faster, probably due to dispersal by jays). The highest migration rates known for any tree are for spruce, at 200 kilometers (124 miles) a century (Roberts 1989). Migration rates for many types of animals, such as forest invertebrates with limited dispersal abilities (Mader 1984), are also expected to be slow. Whereas other animal species may be theoretically capable of migrating quickly enough to adapt to greenhouse warming, their dependence on particular plants may prevent them from doing so. The inescapable conclusion is that, if estimated rates of global warming during the next century are accurate, north-to-south trending corridors will be of little utility for most species. The only species able to keep pace with rapid warming may be weedy plants and animals that do not require corridors of natural habitat in order to disperse—the same species that conservationists do not need to worry about protecting.

If the global warming models are overly pessimistic and the rate of warming in coming decades is similar to past climate changes, broad corridors may be effective in maintaining biodiversity. Even if the warming is faster than most past changes, corridors may work in mountainous regions, where necessary dispersal distances are much shorter (Peters 1988). A rise in temperature of 3° C translates to a latitudinal range shift of roughly 250 kilometers (155 miles) but to an elevational range shift of only 500 meters (1,640 feet) (MacArthur 1972; Peters 1988). During the warm period of the mid-Holocene, about 4,000 years ago, eastern hemlock and white pine were found 350 meters (1,150 feet) higher on mountains than they are today (Davis 1983); future responses to climate change could be facilitated by retaining upslope corridors.

Uncertainty is the dominant theme in all climatic projections. The only certainty is that climates will change, in some direction and at some rate. Maintaining habitat connectivity to allow species migration is a prudent strategy under any climate-change scenario. A general rule is that wide, continuous corridors parallel to existing climatic gradients (elevational and latitudinal) will best promote migration of species with climate change (Hobbs and Hopkins 1991).

M. L. Hunter and colleagues (1988) have suggested that a corridor of natural habitat bordering the Appalachian Trail from Georgia to Maine might facilitate range shifts for some species. Regional network designs for Florida (Figure 3.6; Noss 1987b) and the Klamath Mountains in northern California and southern Oregon (Figure 3.7; F. Pace, personal communication) were proposed in part to accommodate species migration in response to changing climate. Although the utility of corridors in conserving species in a rapidly changing climate is not proven, "their incorporation into a strategy for dealing with the effects of climate change adds an option to what is otherwise a rather sparse repertoire" (Hobbs and Hopkins 1991, 287).

Design Issues

Designing greenways that will contribute to wildlife conservation goals while providing recreational, aesthetic, and other benefits to humans is no mean task. Two broad questions are useful in framing a discussion of wildlife corridor design. First, what is the relative value of sensitive native species versus exotic or opportunistic species? Second, should corridors focus on one or several target species or on entire communities?

We cannot assume that a particular greenway will be unequivocally good for native biodiversity. Habitats represented in the greenway will meet the living and dispersal requirements of some species but not of others. In some cases, species that benefit from the greenway may be opportunistic or weedy species that prosper at the expense of more sensitive species. Corridor quality must be assessed relative to the needs of the

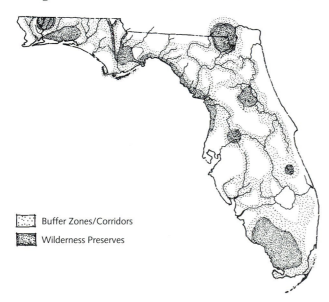

Figure 3.6 A proposed statewide conservation network for Florida, composed of large wilderness preserves (dark stipples) surrounded by multiple-use buffer zones and interconnected by miles-wide corridors (light stipples). (After Noss 1987b, with permission of *Natural Areas Journal*.)

Buffer Zones/Corridors

Wilderness Preserves

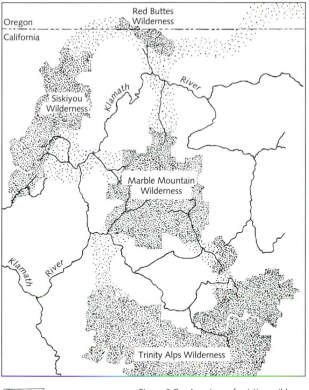

Figure 3.7 A system of existing wilderness areas in the Klamath National Forest, connected by proposed corridors. The corridors, at present, are mostly roadless and unlogged but are threatened by planned timber sales. (Redrawn with permission from a map by Felice Pace, Klamath Forest Alliance.)

latter. Vegetation in corridors may need to be managed to reduce the degree of interaction between the corridor and surrounding disturbed habitats, such as roadsides and farmland (Panetta and Hopkins 1991).

J. M. Diamond remarked that "conservation should not treat all species as equal but must focus on species and habitats threatened by human activities" (Diamond 1976, 1028). Although certainly appropriate on a global or regional scale, this rule must be considered in an appropriate context. Where it is feasible to maintain or restore large blocks of roadless, natural habitat connected by broad corridors and thus maintain large carnivores and sensitive forest-interior species, this

strategy should be pursued. But in many agricultural and urban landscapes, disturbed habitats (for example, hedgerows) and weedy species may be the only remnants of nature. Weedy remnants are preferable to a landscape where nothing "natural" remains and must be managed carefully with the goal of maintaining or restoring natural qualities.

As to the issue of focus on target species or entire communities, M. E. Soulé and M. E. Gilpin pose a narrow design criterion for planning and evaluating wildlife corridors: "Is this particular corridor . . . capable of facilitating sufficient delivery of the target species to the recipient habitat patch(es)?" (Soulé and Gilpin 1991, 3). Although appropriate for single-species management and a necessity when one is dealing with endangered species such as the Florida panther or popular game species such as elk, this criterion is insufficient for ecosystem-level management. As reviewed earlier, greenways and other corridors potentially provide a broad range of ecological services and will have quite different effects on the many species that use them. Even when a corridor is designed with a particular target species in mind, planners must consider potential effects on other species and ecological functions, or unanticipated negative impacts are likely.

In designing greenways, the two most important objectives for wildlife are to provide a high-quality corridor for native species present, especially those that are most sensitive, and to maintain enough functional connectivity along the entire length of the corridor to allow safe passage. Although many factors affect corridor quality, width is usually the most important influence. Roads and the high-speed traffic they convey present the greatest barrier to wildlife movement and thus should be a principal focus of design. These issues are addressed in detail in the following sections.

Corridor Quality and Width

Habitat quality within corridors is a fundamental consideration in any landscape and for any species. A poor-quality corridor can indeed be worse than no corridor at all if it lures animals into conditions that threaten their survival. A computer model by K. Henein and G. Merriam (1990) showed that corridors can be a drain on metapopulations of white-footed mice if they are sites of high mortality. In contrast, high-quality corridors allowed simulated metapopulations to grow and stabilize at larger sizes than at which they began. Corridors with dense, structurally complex vegetation are preferred by white-footed mice, apparently because dense cover reduces the risk that mice will be captured by predators (Merriam and Lanoue 1990).

One of the most important considerations in greenway design is width. The corridor-width issue has been troublesome because empirical studies are almost entirely lacking. When asked by planners how wide a corridor should be, conservation biologists may have little recourse but to reply "the wider, the better" (Noss 1987a; Hunter 1990). Soulé and Gilpin (1991), however, warn against wide corridors, arguing that a wide corridor will permit relatively unconstrained movement of organisms from side to side, slowing the rate of movement toward their "goal." This suggestion was based on a model assuming "stupid dispersers" with little sense of direction (M. E. Soulé, personal communication) and probably underestimates the knowledge that many vertebrates, at least, have about the landscape in which they live. Certainly, a migrating elk or dispersing bear will waste little time wandering from side to side when driven by changing seasons or flowing sex hormones. It "knows" instinctively where to go. Wide corridors offer protection to these species, not diversion.

The penetration of edge effects may be the overriding factor in considerations of corridor quality and width for many species. Narrow corridors, such as fencerows and many greenways, are entirely edge habitat and can be expected to produce high rates of mortality for sensitive species. Opportunistic mesopredators (medium-sized predators) such as jays, crows,

opossums, raccoons, foxes, skunks, and domestic dogs and cats may abound in such corridors and reduce populations of low-nesting birds (cf. Wilcove et al. 1986; Soulé et al. 1988). Many weedy species increase in edge habitat at the expense of sensitive species.

C. S. Robbins (1979) warned that corridors connecting a number of small woodlots to a larger forest might entice forest birds into the edge-dominated woodlots, where they could fail reproductively because of increased nest predation, parasitism, or competition with edge species. Conversely, narrow corridors might act as funnels, drawing opportunistic edge birds such as the common grackle (a nest predator) and brown-headed cowbird (a brood parasite) into a forest (Ambuel and Temple 1983). These suggestions raise many questions as yet unanswered by scientific research and argue, in the meantime, for careful consideration of corridor options in particular cases.

Edge effects can extend anywhere from several meters to several hundred meters, depending on the type of forest and the variables measured. Of particular importance is the difference between physical, microclimatic effects (increased light, wind, and dryness) and resulting changes in vegetation and farther-reaching penetration of opportunistic edge species of birds and mammals. Edge vegetation caused by increased light and dryness typically occupies a fairly narrow band; in Wisconsin hardwood forests, J. W. Ranney and colleagues (1981) found that significant differences in the composition and structure of vegetation extended between 10 and 30 meters (33 and 100 feet) from the forest edge. Increased frequency of blowdown typically extends 2 to 3 tree-heights into a forest (Harris 1984a). Therefore, in old-growth Douglas-fir forests in Oregon, where canopy trees are commonly 80 meters (265 feet) tall, corridors would need to be at least 520 meters (one-third of a mile) wide to maintain a modest 200-meter-wide (656 feet) interior strip. In eastern forests, most trees are less than half this tall, so corridors on the order of 350 meters (1,150 feet) wide may suffice to minimize blowdown problems.

Research in eastern deciduous forests, however, has shown that nest predation may be significantly increased up to 600 meters (2,000 feet) from a forest edge (Wilcove 1985). Since nest predation and parasitism are among the most serious threats to interior-forest bird species, a forested greenway in this environment would need to be 1.4 kilometers (0.9 miles) wide to maintain a 200-meter-wide strip of safe interior habitat (Figure 3.8).

There appears to be no practical way to fight most of the problems associated with edge effects in narrow corridors, aside from the obvious strategy of enlarging corridor width. In some cases, planting a dense buffer (such as conifers) along the edges of a corridor may ameliorate microclimatic effects and thereby discourage colonization by some edge species (cf. Ranney et al. 1981). In lieu of a more dependable solution, site-specific analysis and interpretation within the context of local, regional, and broader conservation goals will be necessary to determine whether the anticipated benefits of narrow or otherwise poor-quality corridors outweigh the potential costs. It is absolutely critical that greenway planners consult with professional ecologists about these matters.

Although larger animals may not suffer directly from physical or biological edge effects (indeed, large predators may benefit from more abundant prey), those that are shy and sensitive to human influence require wide corridors for adequate cover and seclusion. Exactly how wide depends on the habitat structure and quality within the corridor, the nature of the surrounding habitat, human use patterns, the length of the corridor, and the particular species expected to use the corridor (Noss 1987a; Bennett 1990a). Where the landscape matrix is heavily roaded and developed and

corridor edges are readily accessible to humans, corridors may need to be several miles wide to protect large mammals from human predation or harassment (Noss 1987a). If trails or other recreational facilities occur within a corridor, as they generally do within greenways, the corridor should be wide enough so that the most sensitive animals using the corridor are not disturbed by human activity.

When long corridors are used to link natural areas at a regional scale, they should ideally be wide enough to encompass resident populations of target species. Gene flow can then occur sequentially through reproducing resident populations instead of relying on individuals to make the full journey from one end of the corridor to the other (Bennett 1990a, 1990b; Figure 3.4).

L. D. Harris and J. Scheck suggested that "when the movement of entire assemblages of species is being considered, and/or when little is known about the biology of the species involved, and/or if the faunal dispersal corridor is expected to function over decades, then the appropriate width must be measured in kilometers" (Harris and Scheck 1991, 204). An example of a corridor potentially wide enough to fulfill these functions is the Pinhook Swamp corridor, purchased to link Osceola National Forest in northern Florida with Okefenokee National Wildlife Refuge in southern Georgia and to provide habitat for reintroduced Florida panthers. The Pinhook Swamp corridor is over 22,000 acres in size (Nature Conservancy 1990), about 3 to 6 miles in width, and about twice that in length (see case study, chapter 8).

One way to assure adequate corridor width is to extend corridors centered on river systems up one or both slopes so that the entire topographic gradient and

Figure 3.8 Differential penetration of edge effects in a forested environment. Light (and shade-intolerant vegetation), wind, and edge-adapted predators will penetrate progressively greater distances in forested environments.

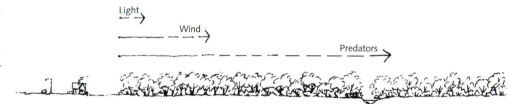

associated vegetation are encompassed. A narrow riparian corridor may not be used by many upland species and may eventually flood to the point of forcing terrestrial wildlife into unsuitable adjacent areas. R. T. T. Forman recommended that "the stream corridor should cover the floodplain, both banks, and an area of upland, at least on one side, which is wider than an edge effect" (Forman 1983, 379–80; Figure 3.9). When opportunities for wide and internally diverse corridors have been precluded by development and restoration in the short term is not likely, a network of multiple corridors may collectively encompass the range of habitat types (Figure 3.10). Networks also provide redundancy, or multiple movement pathways, and mitigate against the destruction of any single corridor by catastrophic disturbance (Forman 1983).

In recommending that a diversity of habitats be represented in corridors, I am referring to vegetation types native to the landscape (which, of course, are dynamic and constantly changing to some extent). Planting vegetation foreign to the landscape (such as exotic fruiting trees planted by wildlife managers or horticulturists) is generally not recommended because of its potential to spread and displace native vegetation, although planting foreign vegetation may be justified in emergency efforts for an endangered species. As F. L. Knopf (1986) notes, riparian vegetation that has developed along streams in the Great Plains because of interruption of the natural flood-drought

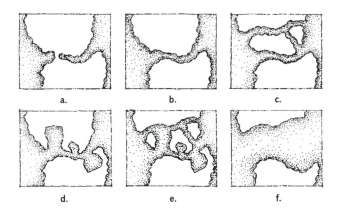

Figure 3.10 Options for corridor and network structure. The most basic concerns are avoiding breaks (a) and establishing a continuous linkage (b). Redundancy (c) provides alternative movement corridors, whereas nodes (d) provide dwelling habitat at intervals along a corridor. Redundant links and nodes can be combined to form a habitat network (e), whereas broad strip corridors (f) are the most effective at protecting habitat and movement routes.

cycle has not benefited bird species native to that region but rather has permitted the invasion of birds from eastern forests.

Roads as a Threat to Connectivity

Roads slice through many areas of otherwise contiguous habitat and may be the single most destructive element of the habitat fragmentation process. Roads and their edges are the most prominent linear features in many landscapes and thus intersect many greenways, sometimes at frequent intervals. Because roads break connectivity by acting as barriers for many species, they present special problems for the design and management of greenways. However, as mentioned earlier in this chapter, roadsides often constitute remnant natural habitat, particularly in agricultural landscapes, and therefore can have conservation value in certain cases. Roadsides also function as dispersal corridors for some species, such as grassland rodents and salt-tolerant plants (Huey 1941; Getz et al. 1978; Cusick 1984; Knowles 1985; Cale and Hobbs 1991), but the species benefited are usually weedy. Many species that disperse by means of roads are pests (Schowalter 1988; Wilcox 1989).

Figure 3.9 Riparian corridors should ideally extend upslope to include an area of upland interior habitat.

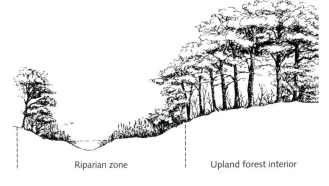

Riparian zone   Upland forest interior

Roads clearly act as dispersal barriers to many species. Animals that rarely cross roads include a number of species of forest and desert rodents and other small vertebrates and invertebrates (Oxley et al. 1974; Wilkins 1982; Garland and Bradley 1984; Mader 1984; Swihart and Slade 1984; Merriam et al. 1989). Even black bears seldom cross busy highways (Brody and Pelton 1989). Roads promote isolation of populations thus increasing chances of extinction; small populations fragmented by a network of roads are vulnerable to the demographic and genetic problems discussed earlier. A greenway interrupted by roads will fail to promote movement of many species and therefore is seriously compromised in its conservation functions.

To maintain populations of large mammals, greenways in wildland settings should be designed to minimize road density within their boundaries. Many large, mobile species, such as elk, puma, grizzly and black bears, and wolves, may learn to avoid roaded areas (Lyon 1979; McLellan and Mace 1985; Thiel 1985; Van Dyke et al. 1986; Mech et al. 1988). These animals avoid roads not because their movement is physically blocked but rather because the roads provide access to legal and illegal hunters. Although many predators follow roads as convenient travel ways (Bennett 1991), they do so at their peril. Optimal corridors for large mammals, especially carnivores, are wide roadless zones with limited access for humans.

When animals do attempt to cross roads, they risk being struck by vehicles. In areas with high traffic volumes, road kill can be a considerable or even the predominant cause of mortality. In Florida, for instance, road kill is the leading known cause of death for all large mammals, with the single exception of white-tailed deer (Harris and Gallagher 1989). (This statistic includes killing of endangered manatees by power boats as a kind of "road kill.") Equally striking is the fact that over one million vertebrates are killed each day on roads in the United States (Lalo 1987). Fortunately, greenways that cross roads can be designed to maintain connectivity and to reduce road kills by incorporating tunnels or underpasses for animal movement. In Colorado and other western states, migrating mule deer suffer considerable mortality trying to cross highways. Collisions between deer and vehicles also injure motorists. In 1970, the Colorado Division of Highways constructed a 10-by-10-foot concrete tunnel under Interstate 70 west of Vail for use by mule deer and used fences to keep deer away from the road and funnel them down to the underpass. A study by the Colorado Division of Wildlife confirmed that hundreds of migrating mule deer used the tunnel but also suggested that larger and more open underpasses would be more appealing and result in greater rates of deer movement (Reed et al. 1975).

Since the Colorado experiment, wildlife underpasses have been used successfully in many cases. Perhaps the best publicized recent experiment is the system of underpasses being constructed to facilitate movements of the endangered Florida panther under Interstate 75 in southern Florida. The road is being elevated specifically to create wildlife crossings at twenty-three locations along a 38-mile-long stretch that cuts through the core of the panthers' habitat. Each underpass provides an opening 70 feet wide and 7 feet tall. Also, thirteen planned bridges over wet areas are being expanded so that they include 40 feet of dry-land underpass for wildlife (LoBuono 1988; Harris and Gallagher 1989; see case study in chapter 8 for more detail). In another example, two mountain lions in southern California have been documented traveling beneath Interstate 91 by means of a culvert; two others that crossed nearby but did not use the culvert were struck and killed by vehicles (P. Beier, personal communication).

Other successful examples abound. In Glacier National Park, Montana, an underpass helped mountain goats get to a natural salt lick (Singer et al. 1985). In Australia, a funnel-shaped rocky corridor and two tunnels beneath a road restored natural movements of the mountain pygmy-possum (Mansergh and Scotts

1989). Small "toad tunnels" have been used in several European countries and in Amherst, Massachusetts, for years to help migrating amphibians avoid the hazards of road crossings (Langton 1989; J. Ahern, personal communication). Greenways should incorporate these various designs, tailored to the species expected to use them, when greenways intersect roads that cannot feasibly be closed.

Still, in some cases, roadsides can be managed to benefit certain species of conservation interest. To make beneficial use of highways in the southern United States, J. A. Jackson (1976) recommended that rights-of-way be maintained in mature pines to serve as dispersal corridors for the endangered red-cockaded woodpecker.

Highway departments in several states in the United States are planting native wildflowers and prairie grasses along interstate highways, often with the assistance of volunteer groups. Parkways that contain a significant land base, such as the Blue Ridge Parkway in the southern Appalachians, can be managed specifically for wildlife conservation (D. Smith, personal communication). So, although roads generally have a negative effect on wildlife, their verges can be managed to provide positive habitat and to serve as conduits, especially in regions where few other suitable corridors exist and where edge effects will not be a major problem.

Conclusions and Recommendations

Natural landscapes are dynamic, heterogeneous mosaics of differing habitat types. But, within these mosaics, most habitats are fundamentally interconnected. As humans modify a landscape, connectivity declines and natural habitats become more like islands (Godron and Forman 1983). Greenways that function as wildlife corridors are one tool that land-use planners and managers can use to maintain or restore habitat connectivity in human-modified landscapes.

Guidelines for Wildlife Corridor Design

The following recommendations, organized by spatial scale, summarize a strategy for designing and managing greenways for wildlife conservation. In any particular case, ecologists and other biologists familiar with the wildlife of the planning area should be consulted.

These first four guidelines are applicable at any scale:

1. Design and manage greenways for native biological diversity. This effort will require consideration of the needs of species sensitive to fragmentation and human disturbance over the needs of weedy, opportunistic species that tolerate or thrive in human-dominated landscapes.

2. For individual species of management concern (especially fragmentation-sensitive species), the planning unit should be the minimum area necessary to insure demographic and genetic survival of the species (Merriam 1991). The spatial scale will vary depending on the area requirements of the species and can be determined only by adequate population studies.

3. Do not allow greenways or other corridors to substitute for the protection of large, intact nature reserves. Unless disconnected greenways are very wide, they have limited conservation value.

4. Do not allow greenway establishment to divert attention from managing the landscape as a whole in an ecologically responsible manner.

Selecting Alignments

1. Link habitat patches that were connected in the presettlement landscape with greenways of similar habitat. Such patches may include nature reserves of various kinds that have become, or are in the process of becoming, spatially isolated.

2. Identify and make use of naturally existing movement corridors (such as riparian strips or traditional wildlife migration routes) in the landscape.

3. Emphasize connection of habitats (such as old-

growth forests) whose species are inherently fragmentation-sensitive due to limited dispersal abilities or other factors. Minimize connectivity of artificially disturbed habitats (for example, weedy roadsides). It is also unwise to connect edge-rich or weedy habitats with larger patches containing native wildlife communities.

4. Use wide greenways to connect habitats along elevational and latitudinal gradients to allow for long-range migration of species.

5. Avoid long stretches of greenway that lack substantial nodes of habitat at intervals suitable for species of concern, unless the greenway is very wide (1 mile or more).

6. Include a range of habitats (for instance, a topographic gradient from river to ridgetop) within a greenway, while maintaining continuity of appropriate habitat types for species of concern. Where this is not possible, include a full range of habitats in the overall greenway network. In arid landscapes, be sure to include perennial water sources.

7. Avoid roads and other potential barriers to animal movement. If possible, incorporate substantial roadless areas into the greenway network.

8. Wherever possible, manage the landscape matrix to function as a corridor for native species by providing continuity of habitats with natural vegetation structure. Matrix suitability is especially important for random dispersers, which may not use discrete linear corridors.

9. Design a network of multiple corridors linking habitat patches to provide redundancy and multiple movement pathways. Networks will be particularly important in landscapes with high rates of disturbance, such as wind or fire.

Setting Widths

1. Make greenways wide enough to minimize edge effects, and encompass as wide a swath of true interior habitat as possible. Penetration of edge effects will vary greatly depending on regional variables,

habitat structure within the greenway, and conditions in adjacent habitats.

2. Determine the necessary width of the greenway according to the needs of the most sensitive species that may use the greenway. Factors that influence species sensitivity include edge avoidance and other behaviors, vulnerability to edge-associated predators or parasites, and sensitivity to human harassment or persecution. Width should be determined in consultation with experts familiar with the habitats and species of the region.

3. The greenway interior should be wide enough to accommodate a variety of successional stages following small-scale natural disturbances.

4. Incorporate the highest-quality habitat possible for the most sensitive species within the greenway boundaries.

Preparing Site Designs and Management Plans

1. Develop a management plan to maintain or restore native vegetation within the greenway, with emphasis on habitats used by the most sensitive species. Control invasive weedy species, especially exotics, where necessary.

2. Where a greenway is intersected by roads that cannot feasibly be closed, develop designs for tunnels, underpasses, or other wildlife crossings in accordance with the behavior and needs of the most sensitive animal species using the greenway. The width of crossing required is dependent on the size of the animal. For example, 3-foot-wide tunnels may be sufficient for amphibians, whereas underpasses as much as a quarter-mile wide will work best for large mammals. Fences or other barriers can be used to funnel animals into the road crossings or simply to prevent animals from crossing elsewhere.

3. Control access and human use of corridors to protect species sensitive to human disturbance. Divert trails away from sensitive areas, such as rare plant populations or colonial water bird rookeries.

4. Seek zoning regulations or landowner agreements

that control adjacent land uses and help establish a low-impact buffer zone between the greenway and developed areas.

5. Manage narrow corridors lacking interior habitat to encourage and maintain vegetational complexity, which in turn will increase cover and corridor quality for wildlife. For instance, do not mow vegetation in corridors.

Greenways or wildlife corridors are no panacea. Rather, they must be seen as one element of an integrated landscape conservation strategy necessary to maintain the many values of natural ecosystems (Noss 1983, 1987b). Planners and environmentalists should not assume that a network of greenways across the landscape will achieve all the goals of biodiversity conservation. But if designed and managed according to the emerging principles of landscape ecology and conservation biology and if guided by an environmental ethic, greenways are an invaluable component of the overall strategy.

References

Adams, A. W. 1982. Migration. Pages 301–21 in J. W. Thomas and D. E. Toweill, eds., *Elk of North America: Ecology and Management.* Stackpole Books, Harrisburg, Pa.

Allen, D. 1943. Michigan fox squirrel management. Game Division Publication 100. Michigan Department of Conservation, Lansing.

Allendorf, F. W. 1983. Isolation, gene flow, and genetic differentiation among populations. Pages 51–65 in C. M. Schonewald-Cox, S. M. Chambers, B. MacBryde, and W. L. Thomas, eds., *Genetics and Conservation.* Benjamin/Cummings, Menlo Park, Calif.

Ambuel, B., and S. A. Temple. 1983. Area-dependent changes in the bird communities and vegetation of southern Wisconsin forests. *Ecology* 64:1057–68.

Anderson, A. E. 1983. A critical review of literature on puma (*Felis concolor*). Special Report No. 54. Colorado Division of Wildlife, Denver.

Anderson, S. H., K. Mann, and H. H. Shugart. 1977. The effect of transmission-line corridors on bird populations. *American Midland Naturalist* 97:216–21.

Baumgartner, L. 1943. Fox squirrels in Ohio. *Journal of Wildlife Management* 7:193–202.

Bennett, A. F. 1988. Roadside vegetation: A habitat for mammals at Naringal, south-western Victoria. *Victorian Naturalist* 105:106–13.

———. 1990a. *Habitat Corridors: Their Role in Wildlife Management and Conservation.* Arthur Rylah Institute for Environmental Research, Department of Conservation and Environment, Melbourne, Australia.

———. 1990b. Habitat corridors and the conservation of small mammals in a fragmented forest environment. *Landscape Ecology* 4:109–22.

———. 1991. Roads, roadsides, and wildlife conservation: A review. Pages 99–118 in D. A. Saunders and R. J. Hobbs, eds., *Nature Conservation: The Role of Corridors.* Surrey Beatty and Sons, Chipping Norton, NSW, Australia.

Best, L. B. 1983. Bird use of fencerows: Implications of contemporary fencerow management practices. *Wildlife Society Bulletin* 11:343–47.

Bormann, F. H., and G. E. Likens. 1979. *Pattern and Process in a Forested Ecosystem.* Springer-Verlag, New York.

Brody, A. J., and M. P. Pelton. 1989. Effects of roads on black bear movements in western North Carolina. *Wildlife Society Bulletin* 17:5–10.

Brown, J. H., and A. C. Gibson. 1983. *Biogeography.* C. V. Mosby, St. Louis.

Brown, J. H., and A. Kodric-Brown. 1977. Turnover rates in insular biogeography: Effect of immigration on extinction. *Ecology* 58:445–49.

Brown, M. T., J. M. Schaefer, K. H. Brandt, S. J. Doherty, C. D. Dove, J. P. Dudley, D. A. Eifler, L. D. Harris, R. F. Noss, and R. W. Wolfe. 1987. An evaluation of the applicability of upland buffers for the wetlands of the Wekiva Basin. Center for Wetlands, University of Florida, Gainesville.

Cale, P., and R. Hobbs. 1991. Condition of roadside vegetation in relation to nutrient status. Pages 353–62 in D. A. Saunders and R. J. Hobbs, eds., *Nature Conservation: The Role of Corridors.* Surrey Beatty and Sons, Chipping Norton, NSW, Australia.

Cusick, A. W. 1984. *Carex praegracilis:* A halophytic sedge naturalized in Ohio. *Michigan Botanist* 23:103–6.

Davis, M. B. 1981. Quaternary history and the stability of forest communities. Pages 132–53 in D. C. West, H. H. Shugart, and D. B. Botkin, eds., *Forest Succession.* Springer-Verlag, New York.

———. 1983. Holocene vegetational history of the eastern United States. Pages 166–81 in H. E. Wright, ed., *Late-Quaternary Environments of the United States.* Vol. 2, *The Holocene.* University of Minnesota Press, Minneapolis.

Delcourt, H. R., and P. A. Delcourt. 1984. Ice Age haven for hardwoods. *Natural History* Sept., 22–28.

den Boer, P. J. 1981. On the survival of populations in a heterogeneous and variable environment. *Oecologia* 50:39–53.

Diamond, J. M. 1975. The island dilemma: Lessons of modern biogeographic studies for the design of natural preserves. *Biological Conservation* 7:129–46.

Diamond, J. M. 1976. Island biogeography and conservation: Strategy and limitations. *Science* 193:1027–29.

Diamond, J. M., and R. M. May. 1976. Island biogeography and the design of natural reserves. Pages 163–86 in R. M. May, ed., *Theoretical Ecology: Principles and Applications.* W. B. Saunders, Philadelphia.

Ehrlich, P. R. 1988. The loss of diversity: Causes and consequences. Pages 21–27 in E. O. Wilson, ed., *Biodiversity.* National Academy Press, Washington, D. C.

Elton, C. S. 1958. *The Ecology of Invasions by Animals and Plants.* Methuen, London.

Fahrig, L., and G. Merriam. 1985. Habitat patch connectivity and population survival. *Ecology* 66:1762–68.

Fahrig, L., and J. Paloheimo. 1988. Effect of spatial arrangement of habitat patches on local population size. *Ecology* 69:468–75.

Fergus, C. 1991. The Florida panther verges on extinction. *Science* 251:1178–80.

Forman, R. T. T. 1983. Corridors in a landscape: Their ecological structure and function. *Ekologia* (CSSR) 2:375–87.

Forman, R. T. T., and J. Baudry. 1984. Hedgerows and hedgerow networks in landscape ecology. *Environmental Management* 8:495–510.

Forman, R. T. T., and M. Godron. 1981. Patches and structural components for a landscape ecology. *BioScience* 31:733–40.

———. 1986. *Landscape Ecology.* John Wiley and Sons, New York.

Frankel, O. H., and M. E. Soulé. 1981. *Conservation and Evolution.* Cambridge University Press, Cambridge, England.

Frederickson, L. H. 1978. Lowland hardwood wetlands: Current status and habitat values for wildlife. Pages 296–306 in P. E. Greeson, J. R. Clark, and J. E. Clark, eds., *Wetland Functions and Values: The State of Our Understanding.* Proceedings of the National

Symposium on Wetlands. American Water Resources Association, Minneapolis.

Garland, T., and W. G. Bradley. 1984. Effects of a highway on Mojave Desert rodent populations. *American Midland Naturalist* 111:47–56.

Geibert, E. H. 1980. Songbird diversity along an urban powerline right-of-way in Rhode Island. *Environmental Management* 4:205–13.

Getz, L. L., F. R. Cole, and D. L. Gates. 1978. Interstate roadsides as dispersal routes for *Microtus pennsylvanicus. Journal of Mammalogy* 59:208–12.

Godron, M., and R. T. T. Forman. 1983. Landscape modification and changing ecological characteristics. Pages 12–28 in H. A. Mooney and M. Godron, eds., *Disturbance and Ecosystems.* Springer-Verlag, Berlin.

Graham, R. W. 1986. Response of mammalian communities to environmental changes during the Late Quaternary. Pages 300–313 in J. Diamond and T. J. Case, eds., *Community Ecology.* Harper and Row, New York.

Grimm, E. C. 1984. Fire and other factors controlling the Big Woods vegetation of Minnesota in the mid-nineteenth century. *Ecological Monographs* 54:291–311.

Grove, N. 1990. Greenways: Paths to the future. *National Geographic* June, 77–99.

Harris, L. D. 1984a. *The Fragmented Forest.* University of Chicago Press, Chicago.

———. 1984b. Bottomland hardwoods: Valuable, vanishing, vulnerable. University of Florida Cooperative Extension Service, University of Florida Special Publication 28: 1–20.

———. 1985. Conservation corridors: A highway system for wildlife. *ENFO* Report 85–5. Florida Conservation Foundation, Winter Park.

———. 1988. Edge effects and the conservation of biotic diversity. *Conservation Biology* 2:330–32.

———. 1989. The faunal significance of fragmentation of southeastern bottomland forests. Pages 126–34 in D. D. Hook and R. Lea, eds., Proceedings of the Symposium: The Forested Wetlands of the Southern United States. General Technical Report SE–50. USDA Forest Service, Southeastern Forest Experiment Station, Asheville, N.C.

Harris, L. D., and K. Atkins. 1991. Faunal movement corridors, with emphasis on Florida. Pages 117–34 in W. Hudson, ed., *Landscape Linkages and Biodiversity: A Strategy for Survival.* Island Press, Washington, D.C.

Harris, L. D., and J. Scheck. 1991. From implications to applications: The dispersal corridor principle applied to the conservation of biological diversity. Pages 189–200 in D. A. Saunders and R. J. Hobbs, eds., *Nature Conservation: The Role of Corridors.* Surrey

Beatty and Sons, Chipping Norton, NSW, Australia.

Harris, L. D., and P. B. Gallagher. 1989. New initiatives for wildlife conservation: The need for movement corridors. Pages 11–34 in G. Mackintosh, ed., *Preserving Communities and Corridors.* Defenders of Wildlife, Washington, D.C.

Henderson, M. T., G. Merriam, and J. Wegner. 1985. Patchy environments and species survival: Chipmunks in an agricultural mosaic. *Biological Conservation* 31:95–105.

Henein, K., and G. Merriam. 1990. The elements of connectivity where corridor quality is variable. *Landscape Ecology* 4:157–70.

Hobbs, R. J., and A. J. M. Hopkins. 1991. The role of conservation corridors in a changing climate. Pages 281–90 in D. A. Saunders and R. J. Hobbs, eds., *Nature Conservation: The Role of Corridors.* Surrey Beatty and Sons, Chipping Norton, NSW, Australia.

Huey, L. M. 1941. Mammalian invasion via the highway. *Journal of Mammalogy* 22:383–85.

Hunter, M .L. 1990. *Wildlife, Forests, and Forestry.* Prentice Hall, Englewood Cliffs, N.J.

Hunter, M. L., G. L. Jacobson, and T. Webb. 1988. Paleoecology and the coarse-filter approach to maintaining biological diversity. *Conservation Biology* 2:375–85.

Jackson, J. A. 1976. Rights-of-way management for an endangered species—the red-cockaded woodpecker. Pages 247–52 in R. Tillman, ed., Proceedings of the 1st National Symposium on Environmental Concerns in Rights-of-way Management. Mississippi State University, Mississippi State.

Johnson, A. S. 1989. The thin green line: Riparian corridors and endangered species in Arizona and New Mexico. Pages 35–46 in G. Mackintosh, ed., *Preserving Communities and Corridors.* Defenders of Wildlife, Washington, D.C.

Johnson, W. C., and C. S. Adkisson. 1985. Dispersal of beechnuts by blue jays in fragmented landscapes. *American Midland Naturalist* 113: 319–24.

Jordan, W. R., R. L. Peters, and E. B. Allen. 1988. Ecological restoration as a strategy for conserving biological diversity. *Environmental Management* 12:55–72.

Kline, V. M., and G. Cottam. 1979. Vegetation response to climate and fire in the driftless area of Wisconsin. *Ecology* 60:861–68.

Knopf, F. L. 1986. Changing landscapes and cosmopolitism of the eastern Colorado avifauna. *Wildlife Society Bulletin* 14:132–42.

Knowles, C. J. 1985. Observations on prairie dog (*Cynomys ludovicianus*) dispersal in Montana, USA. *Prairie Naturalist* 17 (1): 33–39.

Korte, P. A., and L. H. Frederickson. 1977. Loss of Missouri's lowland hardwood ecosystem. *Transactions of the North American Wildlife and Natural Resources Conference* 42:31–41.

Kroodsma, R. L. 1982. Bird community ecology on power-line corridors in east Tennessee. *Biological Conservation* 23:79–94.

Lalo, J. 1987. The problem of road kill. *American Forests* Sept./Oct., 50–53, 72.

Langton, T. E. S., ed. 1989. *Amphibians and Roads.* ACO Polymer Products, Shefford, U.K.

LeFranc, M. N., M. B. Moss, K. A. Patnode, and W. C. Sugg, eds. 1987. *Grizzly Bear Compendium.* National Wildlife Federation and Interagency Grizzly Bear Committee, Washington, D. C.

Levins, R. 1970. Extinction. Pages 77–107 in M. Gerstenhaber, ed., *Some Mathematical Questions in Biology.* Lectures on Mathematics in the Life Sciences, Vol. 2. American Mathematical Society, Providence, R.I.

Lewis, T. 1969. The diversity of the insect fauna in a hedgerow and neighboring fields. *Journal of Applied Ecology* 6:453–58.

LoBuono, J. P. 1988. Alligator alley: Protecting natural habitats. *Journal of the Florida Engineering Society* Feb., 14–16.

Lynch, J. F., and D. A. Saunders. 1991. Responses of bird species to habitat fragmentation in the wheatbelt of Western Australia: Interiors, edges and corridors. Pages 143–58 in D. A. Saunders and R. J. Hobbs, eds., *Nature Conservation: The Role of Corridors.* Surrey Beatty and Sons, Chipping Norton, NSW, Australia.

Lyon, L. J. 1979. Habitat effectiveness for elk as influenced by roads. *Journal of Forestry* 77:658–60.

MacArthur, R. H. 1972. *Geographical Ecology: Patterns in the Distribution of Species.* Princeton University Press, Princeton.

MacArthur, R. H., and E. O. Wilson. 1967. *The Theory of Island Biogeography.* Princeton University Press, Princeton.

MacClintock, L., R. F. Whitcomb, and B. L. Whitcomb. 1977. Island biogeography and "habitat islands" of eastern forest. II. Evidence for the value of corridors and minimization of isolation in preservation of biotic diversity. *American Birds* 31:6–12.

McLellan, B. N., and R. D. Mace. 1985. Behavior of grizzly bears in response to roads, seismic activity, and people. British Columbia Ministry of Environment, Cranbrook, B.C.

McNab, B. K. 1963. Bioenergetics and the determination of home range size. *American Naturalist* 97:133–40.

Mader, H.-J. 1984. Animal habitat isolation by roads and agricultural fields. *Biological Conservation* 29:81–96.

Mansergh, I. M., and D. J. Scotts. 1989. Habitat continuity and social organization of the mountain pygmy-possum. *Journal of Wildlife Management* 53:701–7.

Mech, L. D., S. H. Fritts, G. L. Radde, and W. J. Paul. 1988. Wolf distribution and road density in Minnesota. *Wildlife Society Bulletin* 16:85–87.

Merriam, G. 1988. Landscape dynamics in farmland. *Trends in Ecology and Evolution* 3:16–20.

———. 1991. Corridors and connectivity: Animal populations in heterogeneous environments. Pages 133–42 in D. A. Saunders and R. J. Hobbs, eds., *Nature Conservation: The Role of Corridors.* Surrey Beatty and Sons, Chipping Norton, NSW, Australia.

Merriam, G., M. Kozakiewicz, E. Tsuchiya, and K. Hawley. 1989. Barriers as boundaries for metapopulations and demes of *Peromyscus leucopus* in farm landscapes. *Landscape Ecology* 2:227–35.

Merriam, G., and A. Lanoue. 1990. Corridor use by small mammals: Field measurement for three experimental types of *Peromyscus leucopus. Landscape Ecology* 4:123–31.

Miller, G. S. 1989. Dispersal of juvenile northern spotted owls in western Oregon. Master's thesis, Oregon State University, Corvallis.

Mooney, H. A., and J. Drake, eds. 1986. *The Ecology of Biological Invasions of North America and Hawaii.* Springer-Verlag, New York.

Nature Conservancy, The. 1990. Florida: Corporations make a trio of bargain sales. *Nature Conservancy* May/June, 25.

Noss, R. F. 1983. A regional landscape approach to maintain diversity. *BioScience* 33:700–706.

———. 1987a. Corridors in real landscapes: A reply to Simberloff and Cox. *Conservation Biology* 1:159–64.

———. 1987b. Protecting natural areas in fragmented landscapes. *Natural Areas Journal* 7:2–13.

———. 1988. The longleaf pine landscape of the Southeast: Almost gone and almost forgotten. *Endangered Species Update* 5 (5): 1–8.

Noss, R. F., and L. D. Harris. 1986. Nodes, networks, and MUMs: Preserving diversity at all scales. *Environmental Management* 10:299–309.

Opdam, P., G. Rijsdijk, and F. Hustings. 1985. Bird communities in small woods in an agricultural landscape: Effects of area and isolation. *Biological Conservation* 34:333–52.

Oxley, D. J., M. B. Fenton, and G. R. Carmody. 1974. The effects of roads on populations of small mammals. *Journal of Applied Ecology* 11:51–59.

Panetta, F. D., and A. J. M. Hopkins. 1991. Weeds in corridors: Invasion and management. Pages 341–51 in D. A. Saunders and R. J. Hobbs, eds., *Nature Conservation: The Role of Corridors.* Surrey Beatty and Sons, Chipping Norton, NSW, Australia.

Pederson, R. J., and A. W. Adams. 1976. Rocky Mountain elk research project progress report. Project No. W-70–R-6. Oregon Department of Fish and Wildlife, Portland.

Peters, R. L. 1988. Effects of global warming on species and habitats: An overview. *Endangered Species Update* 5 (7): 1–8.

Peters, R. L., and J. D. S. Darling. 1985. The greenhouse effect and nature reserves. *BioScience* 35:707–17.

Pollard, E., M. D. Hooper, and N. W. Moore. 1974. *Hedges.* W. Collins Sons, London.

Ranney, J. W., M. C. Bruner, and J. B. Levenson. 1981. The importance of edge in the structure and dynamics of forest islands. Pages 67–95 in R. L. Burgess and D. M. Sharpe, eds., *Forest Island Dynamics in Man-Dominated Landscapes.* Springer-Verlag, New York.

Reed, D. F., T. N. Woodard, and T. M. Pojar. 1975. Behavioral response of mule deer to a highway underpass. *Journal of Wildlife Management* 39:361–67.

Robbins, C. S. 1979. Effect of forest fragmentation on bird populations. Pages 198–212 in R. M. DeGraaf and K. E. Evans, eds., *Management of North Central and Northeastern Forests for Nongame Birds.* USDA Forest Service General Technical Report NC-51, Washington, D.C.

Roberts, L. 1989. How fast can trees migrate? *Science* 243:735–37.

Saunders, D. A. 1990. Problems of survival in an extensively cultivated landscape: The case of Carnaby's cockatoo (*Calyptorhynchus funereus latirostris*). *Biological Conservation* 54:111–24.

Saunders, D. A., G. W. Arnold, A. A. Burbridge, and A. J. M. Hopkins, eds. 1987. *Nature Conservation: The Role of Remnants of Native Vegetation.* Surrey Beatty and Sons, Chipping Norton, NSW, Australia.

Saunders, D. A., and C. P. de Rebeira. 1991. Values of corridors to avian populations in a fragmented landscape. Pages 221–40 in D. A. Saunders and R. J. Hobbs, eds., *Nature Conservation: The Role of Corridors.* Surrey Beatty and Sons, Chipping Norton, NSW, Australia.

Saunders, D. A., and J. A. Ingram. 1987. Factors affecting survival of breeding populations of Carnaby's cockatoo *Calyptorhynchus funereus latirostris* in remnants of native vegetation. Pages 249–58 in D. A. Saunders, G. W. Arnold, A. A. Burbridge, and A. J. M. Hopkins, eds., *Nature Conservation: The Role of Remnants of Native Vegetation.* Surrey Beatty and Sons, Chipping Norton, NSW, Australia.

Schoen, J. W., and M. D. Kirchhoff. 1990. Seasonal habitat use by Sitka black-tailed deer on Admirality Island, Alaska. *Journal of Wildlife Management* 54:371–78.

Schonewald-Cox, C. M., S. M. Chambers, B. MacBryde, and W. L. Thomas. 1983. *Genetics and Conservation: A Reference for Managing Wild Animal and Plant Populations.* Benjamin/Cummings, Menlo Park, Calif.

Schowalter, T. D. 1988. Forest pest management: A synopsis. *Northwest Environmental Journal* 4:313–18.

Simberloff, D., and J. Cox. 1987. Consequences and costs of conservation corridors. *Conservation Biology* 1:63–71.

Singer, F. J., W. L. Langlitz, and E. C. Samuelson. 1985. Design and construction of highway underpasses used by mountain goats. *Transportation Research Record* 1016:6–10.

Skovlin, J. M. 1982. Habitat requirements and evaluations.

Pages 369–413 in J. W. Thomas and D. E. Toweill, eds., *Elk of North America: Ecology and Management.* Stackpole Books, Harrisburg, Pa.

Soulé, M. E., D. T. Bolger, A. C. Alberts, J. Wright, M. Sorice, and S. Hill. 1988. Reconstructed dynamics of rapid extinctions of chaparral-requiring birds in urban habitat islands. *Conservation Biology* 2:75–92.

Soulé, M. E., and M. E. Gilpin. 1991. The theory of wildlife corridor capability. Pages 3–8 in D. A. Saunders and R. J. Hobbs, eds., *Nature Conservation: The Role of Corridors.* Surrey Beatty and Sons, Chipping Norton, NSW, Australia.

Stauffer, D. F., and L. B. Best. 1980. Habitat selection by birds of riparian communities: Evaluating effects of habitat alterations. *Journal of Wildlife Management* 44:1–15.

Sullivan, A. L., and M. L. Shaffer. 1975. Biogeography of the megazoo. *Science* 189:13–17.

Sumner, E. 1936. A life history of the California quail, with recommendations for conservation and management. California State Printing Office, Sacramento.

Swihart, R. K., and N. A. Slade. 1984. Road crossing in *Sigmodon hispidus* and *Microtus ochrogaster. Journal of Mammalogy* 65:357–60.

Tassone, J. F. 1981. Utility of hardwood leave strips for breed birds in Virginia's Central Piedmont. Master's thesis. Virginia Polytechnic Institute and State College, Blacksburg.

Thiel, R. P. 1985. Relationship between road densities and wolf habitat suitability in Wisconsin. *American Midland Naturalist* 113:404–7.

Thomas, J. W., C. Maser, and J. E. Rodiek. 1979. Riparian zones. Pages 40–47 in J. W. Thomas, ed., *Wildlife Habitats in Managed Forests: The Blue Mountains of Oregon and Washington.* USDA Forest Service Agricultural Handbook No. 553., Washington, D.C.

Thomas, J. W., E. D. Forsman, J. B. Lint, E. C. Meslow, B. R. Noon, and J. Verner. 1990. A conservation strategy for the northern spotted owl. USDA Forest Service, USDI Bureau of Land Management, USDI Fish and Wildlife Service, and USDI National Park Service, Portland, Oreg.

Thompson, J. N. 1981. Elaiosomes and fleshy fruits: Phenology and selection pressures for ant-dispersed seeds. *American Naturalist* 117:104–8.

Usher, M. B. 1988. Biological invasions of nature reserves: A search for generalizations. *Biological Conservation* 44:119–35.

van Dorp, D., and P. F. M. Opdam. 1987. Effects of patch size, isolation and regional abundance on forest bird communities. *Landscape Ecology* 1:59–73.

Van Dyke, F. G., R. H. Brocke, H. G. Shaw, B. A. Ackerman, T. H. Hemker, and F. G. Lindzey. 1986. Reactions of mountain lions to logging and human activity. *Journal of Wildlife Management* 50:95–102.

Way, J. M. 1977. Roadside verges and conservation in Britain: A review. *Biological Conservation* 12:65–74.

Webb, T., III. 1987. The appearance and disappearance of major vegetational assemblages: Long-term vegetational dynamics in eastern North America. *Vegetatio* 69:177–87.

Wegner, J. F., and G. Merriam. 1979. Movements of birds and small mammals between a wood and adjoining farmland habitat. *Journal of Applied Ecology* 16: 349–57.

Whitcomb, R. F., C. S. Robbins, J. F. Lynch, B. L. Whitcomb, K. Klimkiewicz, and D. Bystrak. 1981. Effects of forest fragmentation on avifauna of the eastern deciduous forest. Pages 125–205 in R. L. Burgess and D. M. Sharpe, eds., *Forest Island Dynamics in Man-dominated Landscapes.* Springer-Verlag, New York.

Whittaker, R. H. 1972. Evolution and measurement of species diversity. *Taxon* 21:213–51.

Wiens, J. A. 1989. *The Ecology of Bird Communities.* Vol. 2., *Processes and Variations.* Cambridge University Press, New York.

Wilcove, D. S. 1985. Forest fragmentation and the decline of migratory songbirds. Ph.D. diss., Princeton University, Princeton.

Wilcove, D. S., C. H. McLellan, and A. P. Dobson. 1986. Habitat fragmentation in the temperate zone. Pages 237–56 in M. E. Soulé, ed., *Conservation Biology: The Science of Scarcity and Diversity.* Sinauer Associates, Sunderland, Mass.

Wilcox, D. A. 1989. Migration and control of purple loosestrife (*Lythrium salicaria*) along highway corridors. *Environmental Management* 13:365–70.

Wilkins, K. T. 1982. Highways as barriers to rodent dispersal. *Southwestern Naturalist* 27:459–60.

Willis, E. O. 1974. Populations and local extinctions of birds on Barro Colorado Island, Panama. *Ecological Monographs* 44:153–69.

Wilson, E. O., and E. O. Willis. 1975. Applied biogeography. Pages 522–34 in M. L. Cody and J. M. Diamond, eds., *Ecology and Evolution of Communities.* Belknap Press of Harvard University Press, Cambridge.

Winn, D. S. 1976. Terrestrial vertebrate fauna and selected coniferous habitat types on the north slope of the Uinta Mountains. Wasatch National Forest Special Report. USDA Forest Service, Salt Lake City, Utah.

Yahner, R. H. 1982. Avian use of vertical strata and plantings in farmstead shelterbelts. *Journal of Wildlife Management* 46:50–60.

Young, S. P. 1946. History, life habits, economic status, and control, Part 1. Pages 1–173 in S. P. Young and E. A. Goldman, eds., *The puma, mysterious American cat.* The American Wildlife Institute, Washington, D.C.

Michael W. Binford &

Michael J. Buchenau

Riparian Greenways and Water Resources

4

Corridors of streamside plant communities, called riparian forests, shadow streams as they run through the landscape. These corridors with running water, moist and fertile soils, and well-developed vegetation are dynamic environments that have complex and multilayered functions. Of the many kinds of corridors in the landscape, riparian ecosystems are especially important for both conservation and human use.

The ecological integrity of a stream is largely affected by its response to sediment, nutrients, and other materials coming from uphill areas. Riparian ecosystems, which constitute the interface between land and water, intercept these materials from above. They also supply vital materials to streams, including food and organic debris. Therefore, natural areas located between a stream and degraded sections of the landscape can lessen the effects of upland disturbances and maintain healthy aquatic processes.

Riparian corridors also moderate in-stream flow and thereby influence water availability and the magnitude of floods. Streamside vegetation reduces bank and floodplain erosion by slowing the stream and reducing its erosive energy. Trees and shrubs produce shade and control water temperature, which can be a critical variable for many aquatic organisms. The capability of riparian systems to stabilize, buffer, or control all of these processes, and in turn to improve water quality, is essential for healthy landscape function. Finally, riparian vegetation is vitally important to wildlife (both aquatic and terrestrial), which is typically most abundant and most diverse in these habitats.

Riparian corridors are very attractive for a variety of human uses. They are often used for transportation and agriculture. Many waterways are used for disposal of municipal and industrial waste or channelized and dammed for flood control and power production. Water is diverted for agricultural and urban needs, resulting in the decline of riparian forests and aquatic habitat. Streamside environments are also highly valued recreational areas.

When human uses extend to the edge of a stream, they cause fragmentation of the riparian corridor and can thus diminish its function as a connecting element within the landscape. Some animals may not cross gaps in streamside vegetation. Aquatic ecosystems are also degraded along and downstream from bare stretches. Water quality at a given location may be only as good as the most degraded reaches upstream. Thus, the health of a particular stream segment is dependent on the integrity of the entire riparian network.

Protecting and restoring streamside vegetation are increasingly used as strategies for maintaining or improving water quality. The challenge for planning and design professionals is to use specific knowledge of the characteristics of riparian ecosystems to create greenways that help achieve water-quality goals. Although the same basic ecological processes operate everywhere, the details of each ecosystem are unique. Factors that control nutrient and sediment flow, hydrologic regime, and wildlife use for a given riparian system must be understood in detail in order to establish effective greenway designs. This understanding will also show that riparian corridors are rarely a complete buffer between upland development and streams. Each system has its own limitations, which must be respected by designing and managing upland activities and developments so that they will not overtax streamside corridors.

This chapter describes how riparian greenways help maintain high-quality water resources and discusses how these corridors can be designed, managed, or restored. We describe the ecological structure, function, and context of riparian corridors in some detail because these complex systems must be understood before they can be modified or managed properly. We then discuss specific design issues and suggest guidelines for the design, management, and restoration of riparian greenways.

Structure of Riparian Corridors and Their Associated Watersheds

Riparian corridors are ecosystems: they consist of interacting living and nonliving components in an area defined in space and time. All ecosystems have functional connections with neighboring ecosystems, are elements of the landscape, and are comprised of smaller ecosystems. This hierarchical and interconnected organization requires that the larger system of which riparian corridors are a part be understood and considered if greenway design is to be successful. This section provides an overview of watershed geomorphology and stream processes. We define several widely used terms and describe the processes that control stream and watershed shape and ecological function.

Watersheds and Stream Networks

A watershed, called a catchment in Europe, is an area of landscape that provides runoff to and sustains flow in a main stream and its tributaries (Gregory and Walling 1973); a watershed is the next ecosystem larger than a riparian corridor. Topographic divides form the boundaries between watersheds (in Europe, it is these divides that are called watersheds) (Figure 4.1). The amount, movement, and characteristics of many substances and phenomena can be measured and described within this unit, including energy, water, nutrients, biomass, patterns of biological diversity, human activities, and habitat patches and corridors. Watershed ecosystems are therefore useful for ecological study and for landscape design and management. (Unfortunately, basin divides seldom coincide with political boundaries. Streams usually mark political divisions, and their basins are typically divided between two or more jurisdictions. For design or management to be successful in a basin, political coordination is often crucial.)

Although every watershed is unique in detail, geologists have defined a set of general, quantitative char-

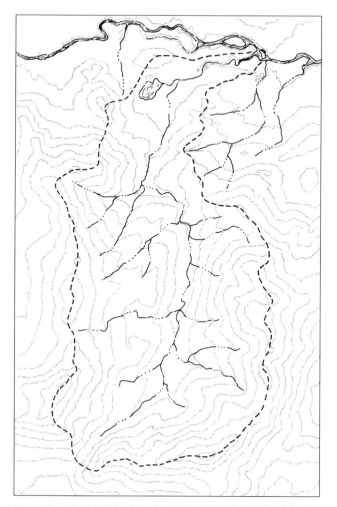

Figure 4.1. Map of Hubbard Brook watershed in the White Mountains in New Hampshire, showing the watershed's topographic boundaries and stream network. As part of the Hubbard Brook Experimental Forest, several of the subwatersheds shown have been sites of long-term ecosystem studies for over twenty-five years.

Table 4.1 Morphological characteristics of watersheds and stream channels

Characteristic	Units	Relationships
Watersheds		
Area (A)	m²	measured (map scale dependent)
Perimeter (p)	km	measured (map scale dependent)
Watershed length		
Channel length (CL)	km	measured (map scale dependent)
Valley length (VL)	km	measured (midvalley line)
Air length (air)	km	measured (shortest distance between mouth and source of stream)
Total Length of all channels in watershed (L)	km	measured (map scale dependent)
Elevation (e)	m	measured (map resolution dependent)
Relief (R)	m	$e_{high} - e_{low}$
Slope (between point x and point y)	m/m	$(e_x - e_y) / CL_{x-y}$
Shape		
Form factor (F)	dimensionless	A / L^2
Watershed circularity	dimensionless	$4 \pi A / p^2$
Watershed elongation (E)	dimensionless	$2 \sqrt{(A/\pi)} / CL$
Channel density (D_d)	m m⁻²	L / A
Storage area (lakes and wetlands)	m²	measured
Stream Channels		
Channel length (L)	km	measured (map scale dependent)
Channel area (A_c)	m²	measured cross section (field study)
Channel volume (V_c)	m³	$L A_c$
Channel sinuosity*		
Total sinuosity (CI)	dimensionless	CL / Air
Topographic sinuosity (VI)	dimensionless	VL / Air
Hydraulic Sinuosity (HSI)	%	(CI - VI) / (CI - 1) x 100%

Note: All measured variables are scale dependent, which means that they vary depending on the scale of measurement. For example, watershed perimeter would be less if measured at 1:25,000 than if measured at 1:200 because more curves are visible at the larger scale. It should be obvious then that any variable derived from these measurements is also dependent on the scale. The variables are useful for comparisons between watersheds or between different times in the same watershed.

*Note that sinuosity can also be described qualitatively. Schumm (1963) has defined five categories to describe increasing sinuosity: straight, transitional, regular, irregular, and tortuous.

Source: From Gregory and Walling (1973).

acteristics useful for describing and comparing characteristics of watershed shape (Table 4.1). These characteristics are related to one another, and each affects functional aspects of the system (Gregory and Walling 1973). For example, within a given climatic and topographic region, streams in larger watersheds have greater length and sinuosity, higher discharge, and more channel cross-sectional area than streams in smaller watersheds, but have lower average slope. The amounts of water and sediment that come from a watershed are controlled by area, length, shape, and relief. Large, flat watersheds produce a smaller output of sediment and water per square mile than do small, steep watersheds because there is more area with mild slope for deposition before sediment is delivered to the stream. Sediment yields are influenced further by existing vegetation and land uses.

The evolution of the shape of watersheds is a natural process governed by physical, chemical, and biological factors. Climate and bedrock are the master controls, and interactions between precipitation and temperature on the one hand and soils and vegetation on the other determine the form of all watersheds. A dynamic balance is established between rock weathering, soil erosion, and the subsequent transport and deposition of eroded material. Sediment moves downslope through floodplains and channels and eventually into ponds, lakes, reservoirs, and the ocean. Along the way, the stream channel meanders by eroding material on the outside of bends and depositing it on the inside of downstream bends (Figure 4.2).

Within a watershed, stream discharge varies throughout the year, and the periods of high and low flows are different in different regions of North America (Poff and Ward 1989). In Rocky Mountain snow-

melt streams and eastern perennial streams, discharge is usually highest in spring and lowest in early to mid-autumn. On the West Coast, discharge is highest during wet seasons that extend from fall through spring and is lowest in summer. In the southwestern part of the United States, high discharges can occur in virtually any season, depending on the elevation and geographical location of the watershed. In desert watersheds, however, summer is often the season of highest discharge. Periods of high discharge are also periods of maximum erosion, and much sediment can be deposited on the floodplain during floods.

The relative size of streams and watersheds can be described with a stream order classification. According to the leading scheme, headwaters with no tributaries are first-order streams (Strahler 1964). Where two first-order streams join, a second-order stream is formed, and so on (Figure 4.3). Higher-order streams are formed only by the joining of two streams of the same lower order. Thus, a second-order stream that joins a first-order stream does not make a third-order stream, but two converging second-order streams do. Cascading mountain streams are usually first- or second-order streams. Large, navigable rivers, like the Hudson or the Missouri, are likely to be sixth-, seventh-, or eighth-order waterways. Stream order designations are not as useful for larger, navigable streams and major rivers because the differences between adjacent orders are not so pronounced. For example, although there are important hydrological and ecological differences between first- and second-order streams, ninth- and tenth-order streams are usually quite similar.

All of the characteristics in Table 4.1 are correlated with stream order. Higher-order streams have watersheds with larger areas, longer lengths, wider and deeper channels, greater relief, and less slope. Some variables, like stream network density and relative relief, vary inversely with stream order and consequently with watershed area (Gregory and Walling 1973).

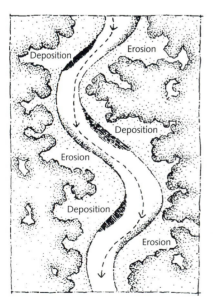

Figure 4.2 Bank erosion and sediment deposition, caused by different speed and direction of flow in different parts of a stream channel, result in a dynamic and changing stream environment.

Figure 4.3 Stream order designation after Strahler (1964). Two first-order streams join to form a second-order stream, two second-order streams join to form a third-order stream, and so on.

.... First order
- - - - - - Second order
- - - - Third order
——— Fourth order

Physical gradients (gradual changes in physical characteristics) along streams and rivers from headwaters to lower reaches result in a continuum of structural and functional characteristics of biotic communities. A description of stream ecology based on these gradients, known as the river continuum concept (RCC), is a useful way to view both the structure and function of waterways (Vannote et al. 1980; Cummins et al. 1984).

The continuum concept indicates that headwaters have fast-moving water, steep slopes, shaded channels, low temperature, and minimal organic matter stored in sediments. Since water temperature is low and dissolved oxygen concentrations are usually high, oxygen-dependent species such as trout can thrive. Stream-water chemistry is determined predominantly by the chemistry of rainfall and bedrock. Stream organisms use energy from organic material produced outside the stream, usually coarse particulate leaf litter from riparian vegetation.

At the other end of the continuum, large lowland rivers have sluggish flow, mild slopes, channels open to the sky, and a large proportion of organic-rich sediments. These sediments are produced both by upstream biological processing of terrestrial litter (shredding by insects, etc.) and by primary production of aquatic algae and higher plants. Dissolved oxygen concentration is lower because large water bodies have relatively less surface exposure to atmospheric oxygen and because abundant plants and animals use more oxygen than the aquatic plants produce. Intermediate stream reaches have intermediate characteristics, depending on the relative position between headwaters and mouth.

Of course, this simple description is a generalization that will differ from case to case. The manner by which the system changes along the gradient depends on regional and local climate, geology, and the nature of tributaries and long-term human activities (Minshall et al. 1985). For example, one of the basic premises of the continuum concept is that the overall influence of the riparian zone decreases as the stream becomes larger and therefore as the volume of water relative to the area covered by riparian forest becomes larger. For greenway design, this premise suggests that, in general, a high level of protection for lower-order streams will yield the greatest benefits for the stream network as a whole.

However, this generalization does not hold true universally. For instance, along rivers that have broad floodplains in their lower reaches, riparian forests can be a major source of dissolved organic matter, which is critical to the stream's metabolism. This effect has been documented on the Ogeechee River in the coastal plain of Georgia, where the influence of the riparian forest on metabolic processes increases along downstream reaches (Meyer and Edwards 1990). Thus, designers and managers who wish to compare a specific stream with the generalized predictions of the RCC should understand where their case fits into the original theory, as modified by more recent research on specific stream types.

Riparian Corridors

Defining the precise extent of a riparian corridor is not a simple procedure. Each stream system is the result of a combination of many physical, climatic, geological, and biological processes, and no two cases exist in which all the variables are identical. Nor are all variables likely to coincide exactly for a given system; there are no simple lines to be drawn. General principles must be adapted to individual situations in order to develop accurate and dependable descriptions of the systems and to allow formulation of valid design and management proposals.

Defining riparian corridors begins with identifying

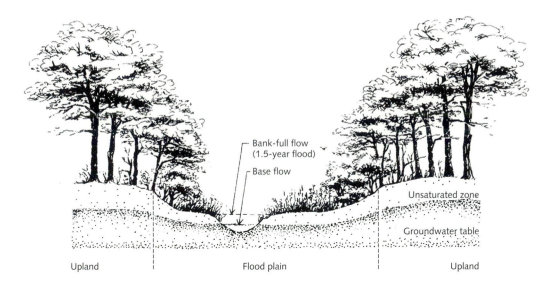

Figure 4.4 Cross section of a typical riparian forest, showing characteristics of the stream channel, floodplain, and uplands.

the corridor's basic geological unit, the floodplain. The floodplain is the area adjacent to the stream channel that is periodically inundated with water (Figure 4.4). Although this definition seems simple, there are at least three ways that floodplains are defined in the United States. First, the geomorphic floodplain is the area within which a stream meanders over decades to centuries and is limited by uplands or terraces on either side of the stream. Second, the recurrence-interval floodplain can be defined as the area covered by floods of a certain magnitude likely to recur over the course of a given interval of time (e.g., the 100-year floodplain). Third, a legal floodplain is defined arbitrarily by experience, law, custom, or insurance companies as a riparian area that might be flooded. This last designation may or may not coincide with either geomorphic or recurrence-interval floodplains. The geomorphic definition of floodplain is the most appropriate for designers and environmental managers because it describes the physical extent of the channel, and any structures built in the geomorphic floodplain risk eventual loss (over periods of decades to centuries) due to river meandering.

At the least, the riparian environment extends from the stream and the floodplain in which it meanders, up the banks of the floodplain where shallow aquatic veg-

etation grades into a terrestrial plant community, and to the transitional area where upland slopes and the riparian ecosystem meet. Riparian ecosystems have two essential characteristics: laterally flowing water that rises and falls at least once within a growing season and a high degree of connectedness with aquatic and upland ecosystems (Ewel 1978). The common combination of rich alluvial soils deposited in the riparian zone by floodwaters and a readily available water supply explains the existence of rich vegetation typical of the margins of rivers and streams. Riparian ecosystems are subject to constant physical changes as the stream meanders in response to cycles of water flow, bank erosion, and sediment deposition. Not coincidentally, streamside trees have historically provided productive stands for harvesting fuel wood, especially in arid regions where they might be the only trees in the landscape.

Riparian corridors usually include wetlands, which have characteristic hydrological properties and vegetation. Because geomorphic floodplains have saturated soils at least part of the year, wetlands tend to form along stream channels. Water and other materials moving from the uplands must traverse these wetlands before entering the stream. True wetlands exist along a moisture gradient from shallow ponds to seasonal standing water to wetland forests that lack standing water but have high water tables (Mitsch and Gosselink 1986). All riparian wetlands carry out the functions described for riparian corridors in the next section to some extent, and all are valuable for maintaining the quality of stream resources.

Riparian Corridor Functions

Defining Water Quality

Water quality is a description of the suitability of water for its intended use, whether by biological communities or by people. It can be expressed quantitatively by physical variables (temperature, velocity, flow regime), chemical variables (dissolved materials including nutrients and nonnutrient elements, pH, and alkalinity), and biological variables (diversity, abundance and health of organisms, biological productivity, and the presence of pathogenic organisms). The amount, concentration, or magnitude of each variable helps determine overall water quality. Historically, water quality has been defined strictly by physical and chemical characteristics. Although these are important descriptors, they are insufficient to fully describe and understand the ability of water resources to support living systems, including humans. For many purposes, especially biological ones, high-quality water resources are characterized by stable and natural temperature, high oxygen but low nutrient concentrations, pH within a natural range determined by bedrock and soil weathering, and diverse biological communities including abundant organisms with narrow environmental tolerances (i.e., pollution-sensitive species). Each of these properties is influenced by riparian corridors, which moderate the influence of external factors.

This section outlines the major functions of riparian greenways that relate directly or indirectly to water quality, including hydrologic regulation, filtration of sediment and dissolved nutrients, stabilization of stream structure, and regulation of water temperature.

Hydrologic Regulation

Hydrologic regimes—the quantity and timing of stream flow—are largely dependent on climate and precipitation patterns (Figure 4.5). Vegetation also helps control hydrology in several ways. Vegetation throughout a watershed passes moisture to the atmosphere through transpiration. Wetlands and floodplains also provide natural floodwater storage, and their vegetation physically slows the velocity of floodwaters (Stabler 1985).

Figure 4.5 Within a riparian corridor and beyond, the hydrologic relationship between streams and groundwater depends largely on climate. In humid regions or during wet seasons (a) groundwater recharges streams and maintains base flow. In arid environments or during dry seasons (b) stream flow recharges groundwater.

The litter and soil characteristics associated with riparian vegetation act as a sponge to hold water for slow release, creating a stable water supply and aquatic environment. Vegetation retards runoff and increases the rate at which water infiltrates soil. Water then seeps slowly through the soil to the stream to maintain base flow (stream flow during the driest time of the year). This process moderates both floods and droughts and is especially important in arid regions where base flow may depend completely on water stored in the soil profile (Lowrance et al. 1985). The magnitude of moderating effects is directly related to the proportion of watershed covered by, and consequently to the width of, the riparian corridor.

Riparian wetlands perform an especially important and effective role in reducing flood flows because they allow floodwater to spread horizontally, to infiltrate soils, and to be released slowly. After a devastating flood in the greater Boston area in 1968, the U.S. Army Corps of Engineers declared that wetlands in the Charles River watershed in Massachusetts should

Figure 4.6 Wetlands along the Charles River during (top) a period of normal stream flow and (bottom) after spring flooding. The wetlands were found to be highly effective for flood storage. (Photos courtesy of U.S. Army Corps of Engineers.)

be protected as a nonstructural flood-control alternative (Figure 4.6; U.S. Army Corps of Engineers 1968). According to the corps' calculations, if 40 percent of the watershed's wetlands were drained, dikes and dams costing as much as $100 million would have to be built to protect Boston, Cambridge, and other towns along the lower reaches of the Charles (U.S. Army Corps of Engineers 1976). Buying or otherwise protecting the wetlands was estimated to be much less expensive.

Flow in a stream with a riparian forest is more constant but may have lower total annual discharge than in

one without, because some soil moisture is taken up by vegetation and transpired to the atmosphere. By retarding flow, vegetation and the litter layer also allow for a higher proportion of the water to evaporate than if the runoff were to enter the stream directly.

All of these effects differ greatly between humid and arid areas. In arid landscapes, elimination of woody riparian vegetation and debris may result in the eventual loss of summer stream flow because the water storage capacity of soils is reduced (Stabler 1985). The age of riparian vegetation can affect hydrological characteristics of streams in arid areas. Recent studies in Utah have shown that whereas young trees with shallower roots use water that would otherwise support stream flow, mature trees use water from below the active stream-flow zone (Dawson and Ehleringer 1991). If this observation holds true in general, newly restored riparian corridors may temporarily reduce stream discharge, but as the vegetation matures, discharge should not only return to the higher levels but also be more constant seasonally because of improved litter and soil conditions.

In humid areas, widespread deforestation around intermittent streams can cause them to become perennial because of the increased water yield during growing seasons and thus can increase sediment transport (Corbett and Lynch 1985). Greenways in humid regions, however, may have minimal effects on the overall amount of water reaching a stream because riparian vegetation transpires a small percentage of the total groundwater flow. In drier climates, where there is much less groundwater, vegetation along a stream may have a significant effect, even though arid-region plants use little water per unit of biomass (Forman and Godron 1986).

Sediment and Nutrient Filtration

In many instances, the greatest threats to water quality are excessive inputs of sediment and nutrients from adjacent lands. These and other contaminants can be filtered by vegetative buffers, which can also help to stabilize and reduce erosion of stream banks.

Although all stream segments will benefit from such buffers, protecting greenways along low-order streams may offer the greatest benefits for the stream network as a whole. Human activity in headwaters has a disproportionate influence on downstream areas for several reasons. Because networks of first- to third-order streams comprise about 85 percent of the total length of running waters, they obviously make up the bulk of the stream miles in a given watershed (Leopold et al. 1964). Because riparian corridors are narrower along headwater streams, upland disturbances are usually closer to the stream. Consequently, the input of contaminants per unit area of the corridor is apt to be greater than in higher-order streams. When contaminated headwater drainage moves downstream, it will inevitably affect lower reaches. If pollutants can be filtered out along headwaters, water-quality benefits for the network as a whole will be substantial.

Erosion and Sediment Control

Upland erosion occurs naturally, but in an undisturbed landscape equilibrium is established between sediment production on the one hand and sediment transport to streams and out of the watershed on the other hand. When upland disturbances cause an excessive amount of material to enter a stream network, sediment can carry excess nutrients to the waterway and smother rocky or gravelly streambeds with silt. Excessive sedimentation blankets the gravel beds in which eggs and young fish develop and destroys habitats for aquatic invertebrates such as insects, crustaceans, and shellfish. Sediment deposited in lakes and reservoirs can degrade water quality and decrease water storage capacity.

Riparian vegetation often filters out upland sediment moving toward streams. The amount of material trapped in the riparian zone can be substantial. For example, the riparian forest of the Little River in Georgia trapped nearly all of the annual sediment yield from an agricultural watershed (Lowrance et al. 1985).

As a sediment sink, riparian vegetation can be effective for a very long time. In another watershed on the coastal plain of Georgia, the riparian zone has trapped all the sediment eroded from adjacent agricultural fields, plus additional sediment derived from upstream areas, since 1880 (Lowrance et al. 1986).

Although riparian wetlands trap sediment, they may retain this material on a time scale of only decades or less (Phillips 1989). Trapped sediment may eventually be added to streams when floodplains are eroded by moving floodwater, in which case the sediment will be deposited downstream in riparian areas when floods recede. Over tens or hundreds of years, sediment trapped by wetlands is thus removed by the stream at a rate specific to the channel's shape and meander pattern and the stream's discharge and flooding characteristics.

Filtration efficiency increases with greater width and decreased slope of the vegetated corridor, with greater density of vegetation and litter cover, and with larger size and greater concentration of particles in suspension (Karr and Schlosser 1978). Erosion and sedimentation are directly controlled by runoff velocity, which is a function of slope and surface roughness. Faster runoff has higher erosive energy and carries more sediment; a wider buffer is therefore required to effectively filter the runoff.

The overland distance required for sediment to be deposited from runoff varies according to particle-size distribution. As water velocity slows, larger particles drop from suspension before smaller particles. Consequently, narrow riparian corridors may be able to trap sand but not silts or clays. Floodplain swamps provide the best opportunity for clay deposition because water velocity slows to nearly zero and water is resident in the swamp long enough for the fine clay particles to settle out of suspension (Cooper et al. 1987).

Filtration efficiency also varies with the type of vegetation. Vegetation reduces flow velocity and therefore enhances sediment filtration as long as the vegetation is tall enough not to be submerged or bent in the current (Karr and Schlosser 1977). Riparian areas can be effective sediment filters over long periods of time because of natural changes in the plant community from year to year. For example, in experimental riparian areas in the White Mountains in New Hampshire, sediments do not clog loose surface litter, nor do they decrease filtration efficiency, because leaf fall forms a fresh litter surface annually (Gosz et al. 1972).

Filtration and storage capacity of riparian corridors is greatest where runoff is spread evenly in sheet flow. Most surface runoff (and sediment), however, is routed through swales, gullies, and rills where flow is concentrated during rainstorms (Dunne and Leopold 1978). Flow concentration is even more likely in arid regions and in rough terrain where uncommon but severe storms are the norm and where the landscape is especially susceptible to uneven erosional patterns (Ruhe 1975).

Bank erosion and channel scour (erosion from the stream bottom) are minor sources of sediment when the stream is stable, but they can be important sediment sources where the stream's bottom or banks are unstable (Schlosser and Karr 1981). Maintaining stability is largely a matter of maintaining streamside vegetation, of which roots, stems, and foliage are important. Stems and foliage reduce flow velocity, and roots and rhizomes reinforce the soil, particularly the nutrient-rich clays commonly found along stream banks (Bache and Macaskill 1981; Forman and Godron 1986). Riparian vegetation and debris also increase channel roughness and thereby reduce flow velocity and potential energy during periods of elevated discharge (Schlosser and Karr 1981).

Nutrient Removal

To understand how riparian vegetation filters out excess nutrients, it is first important to consider the ways in which nutrients move through biological systems, known as nutrient cycling. Six elements—carbon, hydrogen, oxygen, nitrogen, phosphorus, and sulfur—comprise about 95 percent of all living biomass and as

such are essential nutrients for life. Because they are so important and occur in such large quantities, they are called macronutrients. Many other elements, including calcium, potassium, and iron, are also essential for life processes but are needed in smaller amounts; these are called micronutrients.

All nutrient elements cycle through living and nonliving components of ecosystems. Inorganic, mineral forms are necessary for plant growth and are used to create organic compounds that are the basis for all living tissue in plants and animals. Nutrients in excreted organic waste and dead organic matter must be converted back to mineral forms (mineralized) before they are available again to plants. Microorganisms execute the important chemical transformations of decomposition and mineralization, converting biologically unavailable forms of nutrients to available forms. If there is an inadequate supply of any one of these essential elements for a particular organism, its growth and health will be limited. Thus, the biological production of entire ecosystems, beginning with photosynthetic plants, can be limited by the lack of availability of a specific element. The manipulation of ecosystem production by controlling production-limiting elements is often an objective of environmental management. If the goal is to preserve clean water, then biological production should be maintained at natural levels by restricting the artificial input of limiting nutrients. The natural rate of production, and its controls, can be determined by research on each system that is subject to management.

For example, cultural eutrophication is a common problem marked by the enrichment of water bodies by increased nutrient input from human activities. Eutrophication causes unfavorable changes of the composition of aquatic plant communities, reduction of the diversity of the aquatic biota, unpleasant odors and tastes, and even human health problems. Eutrophication is usually the result of excessive phosphorus (and sometimes nitrogen) input from sewage disposal, agricultural fertilizers, or erosion. To reduce cultural eutrophication, nutrient input to the water body must be limited.

In particular, the availability of nitrogen and phosphorus has been shown to limit primary production in most ecosystems. Phosphorus is often a limiting nutrient in freshwater systems in northern temperate areas, and both phosphorus and nitrogen limit production in terrestrial and marine ecosystems. Many freshwater systems in midlatitude and subtropical areas, in more arid regions such as prairies and deserts, and at high altitudes are nitrogen limited, at least for part of the year (Brenner et al. 1990; Goldman 1981). Phosphorus is generally the least available of all the macronutrients because it has no gaseous component in its cycle but is added to ecosystems only from rock and soil weathering or from human sources. Phosphorus control is also less expensive than nitrogen control and has been the focus of most eutrophication modeling and abatement planning (Reckhow and Chapra 1981).

Nutrient elements occur in both particulate and dissolved forms. Inorganic silt and clay particles have large surface areas on which nutrient molecules attach, and water is a strong solvent for many nutrient-bearing compounds. Nutrients can enter streams directly, accumulate in the soil in the riparian corridor and eventually be flushed into a stream or lake, or be incorporated into riparian vegetation as biomass.

In most cases where careful measurements have been made, nearly all phosphorus and much nitrogen in surface runoff are attached to sediment, especially clays (Karr and Schlosser 1977; Delwiche and Haith 1983; Cooper et al. 1987). Substantial amounts of nutrients in surface runoff can therefore be removed by trapping sediments in runoff in riparian vegetation. Likewise, dissolved nutrients in both surface runoff and soil water can be removed by plant uptake and subsurface microorganisms in the riparian forest. Vegetation and soil can filter as much as 99 percent of total phosphorus mass and from 10 to 60 percent of total nitrogen (Karr and Schlosser 1977). Nitrogen removal by microbial organisms, called denitrification, and sub-

sequent loss of gaseous nitrogen to the atmosphere are also important mechanisms for nutrient filtering that can increase the total percentage of nitrogen removed from groundwater (Lowrance et al. 1985). This process requires anaerobic conditions (i.e., a lack of free, molecular oxygen) and occurs most efficiently in soils that undergo periodic flooding and drying, such as in riparian areas (Patrick and Reddy 1976).

Riparian vegetation, especially woody trees and shrubs, also removes nutrients from shallow groundwater flow (Lowrance et al. 1984a, 1985). Nitrogen dissolved in groundwater can be a major input to streams (Peterjohn and Correll 1984). Nitrogen can be controlled either by reducing inputs from upland sources or by maintaining riparian vegetation. Uptake by vegetation is especially important in watersheds that have permeable soils overlying impermeable material (subsoil or bedrock) because groundwater will remain in or near the zone where roots can absorb nutrients. This situation existed in the Little River in Georgia (Lowrance et al. 1985), where woody vegetation removed six times as much nitrogen as was exported to the stream.

In a coastal-plain agricultural watershed in Maryland, 61 percent of the nitrogen input to a riparian forest was via groundwater (Peterjohn and Correll 1984). Eighty-nine percent of the groundwater nitrogen (54 percent of the total input) was removed by the riparian forest. One-third of this amount was retained by vegetation, and two-thirds was lost to the atmosphere by denitrification. Because most phosphorus occurs in particulate form, 94 percent of the phosphorus input to the forest was through surface runoff, of which the riparian vegetation retained 80 percent (or 75 percent of the total input). Other studies in the coastal plain of the southeastern United States have demonstrated that similar proportions of nutrients leaving cropland areas were removed in riparian areas (Yates and Sheridan 1983).

Wetlands can also filter out excess nutrients but are much more variable in this respect than riparian

79

forests. Although wetlands almost always function as sediment sinks, at least over fairly short time scales (years or decades), they can serve as either sources or sinks of nitrogen, phosphorus, and other nutrients. Even when soil-bound phosphorus is retained in wetland sediments, it may later be released in soluble forms. The filtration capacity of wetlands will depend on their particular hydrological, chemical, and biological characteristics; determinations should therefore be made case by case.

Riparian forests retain other nutrients and contaminants such as calcium, potassium, magnesium, and lead (Lowrance et al. 1985). For example, field studies in northern Virginia showed that 85 to 95 percent of the lead in nonpoint (dispersed) urban runoff is trapped with bulk sediment in riparian zones (Hartigan et al. 1979). Riparian vegetation can also filter oils and other pollutants such as insecticides and herbicides, although the magnitudes of removal are not well documented (Bottom et al. 1983; Lowrance et al. 1985). The movement of pesticides into streams is highly variable and is determined for each separate compound by the chemical characteristics that control its persistence in the environment.

Seasonal growth patterns of riparian vegetation in the temperate zone can control the timing, composition, and concentration of the input of excessive nutrients and sediment to waterways. Nitrogen is taken up by riparian forests in summer and released in the fall and early spring (Kibby 1978), rather than during the peak summer growing season. In addition to any net retention of nutrients, the release of nutrients after the growing season means that primary production in the stream may not increase appreciably. Instead, excess nutrients flow downstream and will thus affect receiving water bodies, but not the stream segment in question.

Although the information in this section is complex, it is clear that riparian forests can be effective filters for most sediment and nutrients that flow from uphill land uses. The filtration capacity is determined by both the slope and width of the floodplain and by the nature of the riparian vegetation, including density, successional stage, and seasonal variation of growth and senescence. Wider, denser riparian forests filter better than narrow, sparse ones, and fast-growing, early successional vegetation will absorb more nutrients than mature forests.

Factors That May Diminish the Effectiveness of Greenways for Contaminant Filtration

The vegetation that traps contaminants before they reach streams may eventually be compromised by its own effectiveness if too great a quantity of contaminants accumulates. The most obvious problem is that riparian vegetation may be damaged by sediment that contains salts, heavy metals, and other hazardous chemicals. The effects of pollutants on the growth of riparian vegetation are not well documented, although it is likely that plants are harmed, biological productivity is impaired, and trapping efficiency is consequently reduced in areas where pollutant concentrations are high.

In some cases, the capacity of riparian corridors to filter nutrients may be a short-term phenomenon. When forest succession reaches steady state, there is usually little or no net accumulation of nutrients (Gorham et al. 1979; Bormann and Likens 1979). With no net uptake, as much nutrient mass leaves the riparian corridor as enters. Over many years, intercepted nutrients eventually find their way into the stream through groundwater or are washed downstream by bank erosion (Omernik et al. 1981). Much of this nutrient input, however, will be in the form of organic debris, which serves as food for many aquatic organisms like animals, bacteria, and fungi and is less likely to cause eutrophication than dissolved inorganic nutrients, which are readily available to plants.

Riparian forests may also be seasonally ineffective at filtering materials when plant growth does not coincide with pulses of runoff-borne pollution. For example, road salting occurs in northern temperate climates in the winter and contributes significant material to streams. When combined with snowmelt, large storm events result in elevated runoff and stream discharges in early spring before riparian forests have begun to take up nutrients. As noted previously, although early spring discharge does not coincide with periods of aquatic growth, these nutrients could still affect downstream reaches later in the season.

Some of these problems can be solved by management strategies designed to remove accumulated materials. Selective tree harvesting and sediment removal in areas of concentrated deposition have effectively mitigated these problems in several cases, mostly in the southeastern United States (Lowrance et al. 1985). These practices removed nutrients in several watersheds in the Atlantic coastal plain for at least twenty-three years of similar land use and cropping patterns (Yates and Sheridan 1983). Harvesting should be carefully timed and executed to avoid adverse effect on the riparian zone's capability to control non–point source pollution. Only mature trees should be harvested, and this should be done during dry periods to minimize soil disturbance. If vegetation remains in an active growth phase and the composition of the trapped sediment is not toxic, then the riparian forest should be a sustainable, effective nutrient and sediment filter.

Regulating Water Temperature

Temperature is an important water-quality characteristic. Higher water temperature reduces the capacity of water to carry oxygen and, in turn, to decompose organic material and waste and to support aquatic organisms. Many desirable game fish, especially most species of trout, require cool water temperatures and are excluded from streams that are too warm. Higher temperatures also increase the release rate of nutrients from accumulated sediment. For example, slight increases in temperature above $15°C$ produce substantial increases in the release of sedimentary phosphorus (Karr and Schlosser 1978).

Riparian vegetation, especially when directly adjacent to the stream channel, prevents temperature extremes by shading the water surface in summer (Figure 4.7). Thus, in the northern hemisphere, vegetation on the southern bank of a stream is more important for this purpose than vegetation on the northern bank (Budd et al. 1987). Within and beyond the riparian corridor, vegetation also increases infiltration and the water storage capacity of soils, which help keep water temperature in streams lower in warm seasons. Because of their increased infiltration and storage capacity, wider greenways will usually maintain lower water temperatures than narrower corridors. When groundwater input forms a significant amount of stream discharge, water temperatures will be more stable because groundwater temperature is often constant and equal to the annual mean air temperature (Budd et al. 1987).

Figure 4.7 Streamside forests help maintain low water temperatures by producing shade. (Photo by D. Smith.)

81

This temperature stability may be especially present in small streams, whose lowest flows are sustained solely by groundwater (base flow). In all streams, the distance that a protected corridor extends upstream will have a major influence on water temperature at a particular location.

Because of their low water volume, temperatures of small headwater streams are also greatly influenced by changes in solar radiation (Brown and Krygier 1970). Headwater temperatures are thus easy to control with streamside vegetation (Karr and Schlosser 1978). Larger, wider streams, although they have proportionally smaller shaded areas, are usually less affected by solar radiation because greater water flow and volume offset surface temperature increases (Everest et al. 1982). Low-gradient streams are exceptions to this generalization because water residence time in the channel is longer and the daily variation of water temperature can be substantial (J. Meyer, personal communication).

For very small streams, the density of vegetation, and thus its ability to produce shade, is the only characteristic of the riparian vegetation important in its ability to control temperature (Karr and Schlosser 1978). In these cases only, the overall width of riparian corridors is not important for temperature control as long as the density of vegetation is high.

The results of more recent studies point out that these conclusions are only applicable to very small streams. Along larger streams (second- and third-order) near Toronto, Ontario, both the length and width of riparian corridors influenced summer water temperature to the extent that important fish species were excluded from streams with narrow or fragmented corridors (Barton et al. 1985). Brook, brown, and rainbow trout do not occur in the Ontario streams with an average summer temperature higher than 22° C. Thus, maintenance of low water temperature is an important management objective. Figure 4.8a, a contour plot of stream temperatures derived from empirical data, indicates that narrower buffers must

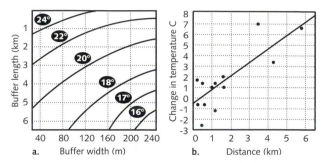

Figure 4.8 (a) Relationships between buffer width, buffer length, and stream water temperature from empirical model based on data from southern Ontario streams. (b) Relationship between stream water temperature and distance below intact riparian forest. (Reprinted from Barton et al. 1985, with permission of American Fisheries Society.)

extend farther upstream to maintain stream water temperature at a desired level. As Figure 4.8b shows, where downstream areas are exposed, water temperature rises about 1.5° C per kilometer downstream from the end of the riparian forest. When width and extension upstream are considered together, a linear extrapolation of stream water temperature may present a guide for determining the minimum width of a riparian forest: "An unbroken buffer extending 3 km upstream of a site need only be 10 m wide to produce a maximum weekly temperature of less than 22° C" (Barton et al. 1985, 376).

The authors of this study caution that the extrapolation may not be appropriate beyond their study site or to other environments and that it is valid only if stream water temperature less than 22° C is the sole management objective. Furthermore, fish distribution in other parts of the world may be constrained by temperatures that are lower or higher than 22°. Nonetheless, this study indicates the sort of useful guidelines that can be derived from local or regional research programs.

Riparian Corridors and Aquatic Habitat

Many structural, hydrologic, and water-quality processes that are influenced by riparian vegetation have, in turn, a direct influence on stream organisms and communities. Streamside vegetation is essential to aquatic life because, in addition to the functions described earlier, it stabilizes and contributes to the diversity of stream habitat. Fallen trees, branches, and root masses that come from the riparian area establish pools, waterfalls, and riffles (Figure 4.9), and standing trees stabilize banks (Budd et al. 1987). Diverse habitats produced by the debris give rise to greater diversity of aquatic organisms (Benke et al. 1984; Angermeier and Karr 1984). Material that falls into streams and vegetation along the bank provide a diversity of cover. Most aquatic insects are directly or indirectly dependent on riparian vegetation at some stage in their life cycles (Erman 1981). In addition, the more a stream meanders, the more diverse are the aquatic habitats available to stream organisms (Karr and Schlosser 1977). As the diversity of bottom types, water depths, and water velocity increases, fish diversity increases (Gorman and Karr 1977).

Forests adjacent to streams are also a major source of food energy for aquatic organisms. In forested watersheds, over 99 percent of the energy in the stream food web may originate in the forest adjacent to streams (Budd et al. 1987; Likens et al. 1970; Bormann and Likens 1969). Along headwater streams, riparian veg-

etation is especially critical as an energy source. Large, woody debris from riparian forests also forms dams that impede downstream movement of organic matter in both headwater and higher-order streams, thereby providing a reliable, year-round food supply (Angermeier and Karr 1984).

A rich and diverse population of aquatic organisms develops when there is a diversity of food sources in the riparian vegetation (Meehan et al. 1977). Herbaceous ground cover is high in nutrient content and is consumed by organisms as soon as it falls into the stream. Leaves from deciduous shrubs and trees are higher in fiber content and take 60 to 90 days after entering the stream to be utilized fully by the organisms. Coniferous leaves take 180 to 200 days to be processed. Stems and trunks that enter the stream constitute a long-term nutrient reserve for a stream's food chain. Healthy and diverse riparian vegetation thus provides a dependable supply of food throughout the year.

Habitat fragmentation, the focus of much attention for terrestrial species, can also be a major threat to the integrity of aquatic ecosystems. Through the impacts described earlier, excessive alteration of uplands and riparian vegetation can reduce the movement of fish and other aquatic organisms upstream and downstream. Extreme changes in water quality caused by urban and agricultural development have been shown to isolate populations in stream networks (Vannote et al 1980). Like terrestrial animals, some aquatic species cannot tolerate these changes, whereas others can. In addition to providing habitat, intact and continuous riparian corridors maintain connectivity and movement pathways for aquatic organisms.

Effects of Human Activities on Riparian Corridors

Waterways and riparian ecosystems have been a critical resource for nearly every culture in the world, past and present (Toth 1990). Just as predictable as the location

Figure 4.9 Pools and riffles created by fallen trees are crucial to establishing diverse aquatic habitats. (Photo by D. Smith.)

of human activity along rivers have been the effects of this activity on aquatic ecosystems. The major human activities that affect water quality and the ecological integrity of riparian corridors are agriculture, urbanization, forestry, transportation, recreation, flood control, and withdrawals for water supply. Each activity has a characteristic set of negative consequences, some of which may be ameliorated by maintaining or restoring natural riparian vegetation.

The flow of materials into streams can either be concentrated at a single spot (point source) or be spread across a wide area (non–point source). Discharges from sewage treatment plants, storm sewers, and waste pipes are examples of the former. These point sources of contaminants can be controlled with engineering solutions, but riparian vegetation does not have much effect on them. Some authorities believe that half of the pollution of surface waters in the United States comes from point sources (Smith et al. 1987).

Most human activities also provide non–point sources of contaminants. These sources are much more difficult to control because there are no single points at which they enter streams. The best method of non–point source control is to eliminate contaminants at their source through effective land-use planning in upland areas. But where the sources do exist, a buffer of intact riparian vegetation can be a very effective second line of defense.

Agriculture

The federal Clean Water Act of 1972, along with more recent versions, has resulted in enormous investments in cleaning up the nation's waterways. Most of the effort has been spent on controlling municipal and industrial effluents, which are usually point sources. These programs have success stories, such as the restoration of Lake Erie (Makarewicz and Bertram 1991) and Lake Washington in Seattle (Lehman 1986). But despite two decades of action, most of the surface

waters of the nation have continued to suffer water-quality degradation. Although atmospheric deposition, deforestation, and increasing human and domestic animal populations all contribute to non–point nutrient loading of aquatic systems, agriculture probably has the greatest influence of all human activities (Smith et al. 1987).

Agricultural practices remove natural vegetation, manipulate and transport soils, introduce fertilizers and toxic chemicals as insecticides and herbicides, and generally change the structure and processes of both terrestrial and aquatic communities. Nutrients in fertilizers applied to the land and not taken up by crops eventually end up in surface-water runoff or in groundwater. Moist and fertile soil conditions have made riparian corridors productive areas for agriculture. Consequently, once continuous corridors are often fragmented by croplands. When bottomland areas are converted to agriculture, a twofold detrimental impact occurs downstream. Sediment and nutrient inputs from the surrounding landscape are increased, and the filtering capability of the remaining riparian forest is diminished because of clearing (Cooper et al. 1987).

Livestock

In the arid West, riparian corridors often provide the only oases for livestock in an otherwise inhospitable landscape. They offer a reliable supply of water, plentiful vegetation, and more shelter than surrounding dry areas. However, livestock congregate in riparian areas for extended periods, trampling streambanks and often eating most of the vegetation (U.S. Government Accounting Office 1988).

Stream banks and floodplains erode rapidly when trampled and stripped of vegetation, and this erosion in turn degrades the stream's ecological integrity by the processes described earlier. Degraded riparian vegetation is unable to trap sediments and nutrients in runoff and is unable to diffuse flood energy, which leads to still more erosion. The stream then deposits more sediment into receiving lakes and reservoirs. Lacking healthy vegetation and stream structure, the corridor loses its capacity to hold water, and the local water table is lowered. In arid areas, a stream may then change from perennial to intermittent, and the stream may dry completely in the summer months. Livestock in both arid and humid regions also add additional waste and thus excess nutrients to the stream. The composite effect can be devastating to the stream, its water quality, biota, and terrestrial wildlife as well as to ecosystems and land uses downstream (Platts and Rinne 1985).

Channelization

Flood-control programs during the past century resulted in the channelization (straightening and deepening) of many streams in the United States, with the objective of facilitating runoff and lowering groundwater levels. The question of whether channelization has yielded flood-control benefits is controversial, but the consensus among biologists is that channelization is an ecological disaster (Goudie 1990; Karr and Schlosser 1978). Channelization reduces the length of streams and the area covered by riparian vegetation. The effects of upstream channelization can ultimately neutralize many efforts to filter sediment, showing the importance of comprehensive watershed management.

One of the best documented examples of channelization effects is Florida's Kissimmee River. J. R. Karr (1988) described the primary effects of channelization as follows:
— Transformation of the river from a 103-mile meandering channel to 56 miles of wide, deep channel that is almost useless as a biological system.
— Lowering of the water table because of increased drainage and the consequent loss of water to most of the floodplain wetlands.
— Degradation of the remaining wetlands because seasonal flow no longer floods previously wet areas.

— Alteration of high and low seasonal flow patterns so that during periods of low flow the channelized system acts more like a reservoir than a river.
— Reduced complexity of both terrestrial and wetland plant communities and thus diminished habitat for both terrestrial animals and fish.

Stream channelization, including the removal of riparian forests, has potent effects on non–point source pollution. Nitrogen and phosphorus levels in a channelized stream in a North Carolina coastal-plain watershed were significantly higher than in undisturbed streams (Yarbro et al. 1984). Nitrogen inputs increased because lowered groundwater levels allowed riparian wetlands, which previously trapped nutrients, to be converted to agriculture. Lowering the level of groundwater also reduced groundwater discharge to the river so that flow from upstream areas, which contained a significant concentration of nitrogen, made up the bulk of stream flow. Phosphorus concentrations also increased as a result of greater erosion in the cropland and on steepened channel banks.

Diversion and Groundwater Extraction

Streams, reservoirs, and groundwater are all used as water sources. In each case, water quality and the integrity of riparian vegetation can be degraded. D. C. Erman and E. M. Hawthorne (1976) showed that lowered water levels caused by headwater diversion are especially devastating to fish that use these waters for spawning and as hatcheries because of diminished discharge. Decreased in-stream flow also degrades water quality by concentrating contaminants.

As in many other riparian corridors across the West, groundwater extraction lowered the water table in the Carmel River valley in California and caused the decline of riparian vegetation and subsequent increases in bank erosion (Groeneveld and Griepentrog 1985). This conflict between groundwater extraction and maintaining the water table often exists because soils in floodplain aquifers are generally excellent sources of groundwater, especially in arid areas (Lowrance et al. 1984b).

Transportation and Utility Corridors

The corridors that rivers and streams have carved into the landscape often provide convenient locations for transportation and utility facilities because they have gentle topography and easily worked soils. Roads, especially, can have a major impact on stream environments. When lead, salt, and other chemicals from roads are washed into the system, vegetation can be damaged and the ability of the riparian corridor to trap these pollutants can be overwhelmed. Erosion is also accelerated by increased runoff from impermeable surfaces of roads, buildings, and parking lots.

Recreation

In recent years, riparian corridors have become magnets for recreational use. This attraction is a result of the variety of recreational opportunities and settings that riparian corridors provide and of the affinity people have for running waters. Effects of recreation on riparian corridors can include the loss of vegetation and litter layer from trampling, compaction, and reduced soil permeability and subsequent increases in runoff, erosion, and sedimentation (Manning 1979). The presence of human beings and their pets disturbs animals that use the corridor. This topic is discussed at much greater length by David Cole in chapter 5.

Urbanization

When urbanization covers the landscape with impermeable surfaces, water cannot infiltrate the soil and so runs off much more rapidly than it would otherwise. Drainage is altered, and contaminants enter streams readily and in more concentrated forms. This situation is especially likely during construction because freshly disturbed and devegetated soils are highly susceptible to erosion.

Much of the runoff from urban systems goes into storm drains, through storm sewers, and then into receiving streams. Storm-sewer effluent contains high concentrations of sediment, nutrients, and toxic materials that are washed off roads and parking lots. Sometimes, storm runoff is conducted through on-site retention or detention basins (Ferguson and Debo 1987), which permit sedimentation. Riparian vegetation usually has little influence on these point sources. In some cases, however, point sources have been diverted to constructed wetlands where filtration can occur (see Boulder case study, chapter 8).

Most sanitary sewage from urban areas in the United States and Canada is now treated to some degree at central facilities and thus becomes a point source that flows directly into waterways. In suburban and rural areas, however, sewage is commonly disposed of in septic systems and community leaching fields. These practices add contaminants, mostly nutrients, to groundwater, which can then be taken up by vegetation.

Applications in Design and Management

There is little doubt that intact, healthy riparian corridors protect water quality and aquatic habitat. Conversely, altering or removing riparian vegetation from the margins of streams can set off a chain reaction of undesirable results. In many greenway projects, however, a disproportionate effort goes to the process of land acquisition rather than to the design of the most appropriate corridor dimensions and configuration. As many of the examples discussed earlier illustrate, simply protecting an arbitrary swath of land is unlikely to be the most effective course; the specific design of a corridor will largely determine how well a greenway functions. This section examines the principal issues in the ecological design of riparian greenways for the purpose of maintaining high-quality water resources. The section explains the need for measuring ecological health and understanding the context of riparian corridors and discusses specific issues such as corridor width, the elements that should be included in a greenway, ecological restoration, and corridor management.

It is also important to recognize that research on the specific capacities and limitations of riparian corridors is in early stages. Very little is known about the more complex ways that many processes work in riparian corridors and about how these ecosystems interact with uplands and streams. Although the trend toward maintaining riparian corridors as greenways is encouraging, there is a danger that riparian corridors might be considered a panacea for protecting water resources. The solution is clearly not that simple.

Leaving a strip of riparian vegetation to mitigate the effects of a forest clear-cut or an urbanizing upland is not an adequate measure on its own, since too much pressure from upland activities can overwhelm and degrade the riparian ecosystem. Although riparian forests play a vital role in ameliorating the effects of erosion, both the health and growth rates of riparian vegetation can change because of increased inputs of sediment, associated nutrients, and toxic chemicals (Lowrance et al. 1984b). How these changes ultimately manifest themselves is unknown. Care must be taken to design agricultural, suburban, and urban development so that greenway functions will not be compromised by upland disturbances.

Measuring Ecological Health

Although maintaining ecological health or integrity is the objective of much environmental legislation, the concept has not often been well defined. According to one recent definition, a healthy biological system is one that realizes its inherent potential, is stable, has the capacity for self-repair when perturbed, and requires minimal maintenance (Karr et al. 1986). Included in

the idea of inherent potential is a biotic community that possesses healthy individuals and community structure, a high level of native biodiversity, and natural levels of productivity.

Since change is an inherent condition in nature even where human disturbance is minimal, it is unlikely that strictly defined baseline conditions representing ecological health can be identified for a given ecosystem. Still, it is possible to identify and measure generalized conditions that indicate the degree of ecological integrity for a given system.

For designers and managers, identifying healthy conditions when they exist—or predicting their potential when they are degraded—will often be crucial in setting objectives for maintaining or restoring the quality of water resources. Measurement will also be important in gauging the relative success of a project over time. Although ecological health can be estimated qualitatively in a very rough way, a scientific approach is more effective and provides an objective description of healthy conditions. This section outlines one such approach, the Index of Biotic Integrity, which is a method for assessing the ecological health of streams through direct sampling of aquatic communities.

The Index of Biotic Integrity

The Index of Biotic Integrity (IBI) is a relatively simple and easily learned method for assessing the ecological health of aquatic systems based on the diversity, productivity, and health of fish communities (Karr 1991). For a given site, the IBI is the sum of scores assigned to twelve different biological characteristics (determined by sampling the aquatic community) compared with the sum of scores for a similar site in an undisturbed condition. Although the specific characteristics studied may differ from region to region, they include measurements of species richness and composition (total number of species, number and kind of sensitive bottom-dwelling species, water-column species, long-lived species, pollution-intolerant species, and pollution-tolerant species), trophic composition (percentages of omnivores, insectivores, and top carnivores), and the abundance and condition of individuals (for example, the total number of individual fish in samples at a site, the percentage of hybrid individuals, and the percentage of diseased or deformed individuals).

Each characteristic is checked against the same characteristic at a similar but undisturbed site. The degree of correspondence with values expected at undisturbed sites determines the score for a given characteristic, each of which is assigned a score of 1 for poor, 3 for moderate, and 5 for good correspondence. A perfect score of 60 (5 multiplied by the 12 characteristics) defines an undisturbed site, whereas lower scores indicate some degree of ecological degradation.

Of particular importance is the fact that the potential scores for criteria of this index are scaled regionally. For example, streams in the coastal drainages of the middle-Atlantic states naturally have higher fish species diversity than Rocky Mountain streams. Thus, the index values for total number of fish species are scaled relative to a local, undisturbed situation.

The costs of measuring the IBI were reported in 1989 to be $740 per sample for the fish community, and $824 for the macroinvertebrate community (insects, crustaceans, and shellfish). Each sample is used to measure the twelve characteristics. These costs were provided to Karr (1991) by the Ohio Environmental Protection Agency and may be different in other parts of the country. Also, the number of samples needed and the frequency of sampling will depend on careful specification of the objectives of the study and on the size and extent of the area in question. It is therefore impossible here to accurately estimate the cost of the IBI. However, an investment of $10,000 to $50,000 would probably be sufficient for determining the IBI of a typical stream or stream segment in most cases.

The significance of the IBI as a method of measuring ecological health becomes evident when one compares watersheds with different levels of urbanization and riparian forests. IBI scores for ten watersheds in southern Ontario were very strongly related to the pro-

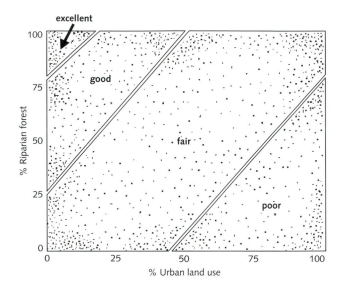

Figure 4.10   Contour plot of Index of Biotic Integrity (IBI) ratings in southern Ontario streams as a function of urbanization and riparian forest. IBI is expressed qualitatively within regions that have given proportions of urban land and of remaining riparian forest. For example, if 25 percent of a watershed is in urban land use, then at least 50 percent of the riparian forest should be preserved along the stream to maintain a "good" IBI. (From Steedman 1988, with permission of *Canadian Journal of Fisheries and Aquatic Science.*)

portion of urban land use and the percentage of remaining riparian forest (Steedman 1988; Figure 4.10). These watersheds were near Toronto, where climate, stream ecology, and human activities are similar to those in the upper midwestern and northeastern United States.

Understanding the Context of the Riparian Ecosystem

When designing a greenway for a portion of a riparian network, understanding how that portion functions within the network is essential. The location of the corridor, for instance, in the headwaters or middle reaches of the network, and its condition in comparison to the other reaches should be factors in design and management practices. Recall that removing riparian vegetation alters headwater streams more than high-order streams and that a corridor's width, length, and extension upstream from a site are important for maintenance of water temperature. On the one hand, within a relatively healthy network, a stretch that stands out as degraded might be a priority for restoration and protection. On the other hand, if a watershed is highly industrialized, maintaining the health of a few undisturbed headwater segments may be a more realistic goal and will prevent further degradation of water that will eventually affect downstream reaches.

Special emphasis should be given to greenways that connect a variety of habitats and thus aid in the preservation of biodiversity over a broad area. For example, riparian greenways often include areas where two or more streams converge. These sites are nodes in the larger network, and they connect numerous areas that would otherwise be separated. If a break in a greenway occurs at a node, then the loss of greenway function may be more than doubled compared to the loss from a break in a single section, because at least two corridors are interrupted by one disturbance. A break at a node prevents organisms that use the greenway from moving between the various segments and may also allow material that would otherwise be filtered to pass into two channels. Thus, nodes should be recognized and protected both by increasing the width of the corridor and by restricting use of the banks (Figure 4.11).

It is also important to understand a corridor within the context of its surroundings. Through what sort of landscape does a river flow, and how does the corridor function in relation to the other components of the landscape (i.e., adjacent upland forest, grassland, agriculture, or suburbs; Figure 4.12)? Is the corridor important for wildlife movement? How does the corridor segment affect, and how is it affected by, other

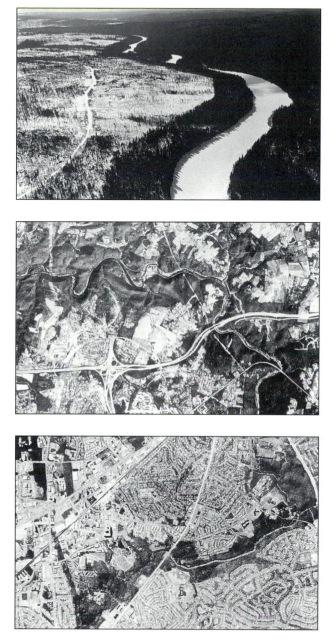

Figure 4.12 A riparian corridor's context within the landscape will be crucial to its design and the way it functions. (top) The Allagash Wilderness Waterway in northern Maine is separated from adjacent managed forest by a state-owned buffer of several hundred feet. (Photo by Chris Ayres.) (center) The Patapsco River Greenway extends from the riparian ecosystem into forested uplands in a mixed landscape of farms and suburbs outside of Baltimore. (Photo courtesy of U.S. Geological Survey.) (bottom) Rock Creek Park is a narrower, urban greenway in Washington, D.C. (Photo courtesy of U.S. Geological Survey.) In each of these settings, greenways will have different design requirements and functions.

Figure 4.11 Nodes in a riparian network, formed where two streams join, should receive special attention and ideally be protected with a wider corridor.

Table 4.2 Tasks and budget for preimplementation study of riparian greenway with objective of preserving water quality in the stream.

Measurements	Method	Estimated cost (1990 dollars)
Bulk precipitation	Continuous gauge (tipping bucket)	5,000 (installation)
Stream discharge	Gauging station with continuous stage recorder, established rating curve	5,000 (installation), 5,000 per year (monitoring)
Groundwater discharge	Well nests, peizometers	20,000 (installation)
Water and sediment chemistry (precipitation, runoff, stream, and groundwater)	Precipitation collector, flow-weighted sampler, grab samples, sampling from wells	10,000 (installation), 5,000 per year (sampling)
Laboratory analyses	NO_3, total Kjeldahl N, ammonium-N, total-P, orthophosphate-P, organic matter conc., exchangeable ammonium-N, total Kjeldahl-N, exchangeable orthophosphate-P, total-P, total suspended particulate, and organic matter concentrations as biochemical oxygen demand (BOD).	15,000 per year (about $1.00 per analysis per sample)
Vegetation	Point-quarter, quadrat, or other technique for trees. Increment cores in trees for standing biomass and age distribution analysis.	10,000 (first year only)
Upland land uses: crops, suburbs, golf courses, etc.	Data on fertilizer applications from farmers, homeowners, greenskeepers, etc.	5,000 per year
Data analysis, computer modeling, etc.	Mass-balance description of system, analyzed as mass of nutrient or other material per m^2 per year input, output, change in storage in each component of ecosystem.	10,000 per year
Total cost	**First Year**	**100,000**
	Second and subsequent years	**40,000**

Note: The objective of the study is to measure the movements and transformation of waterborne nutrients (N, P, and C) as they move into an ecosystem, then through the watershed to the stream in surface runoff and shallow groundwater. The measurements result in quantitative estimates for the mass of nutrients imported by precipitation and from upland areas, the rates of nutrient uptake and loss in riparian vegetation, and the amount of material that is transported to the stream under different riparian conditions.

Ideally, the study should last for a minimum of two years before implementing the greenway. Subsequent years of monitoring should give information about the influence of variable weather, changes of land use, and so on. These costs assume that the stream is first- through fourth-order with a watershed of less than 100 km^2 (40 sq. miles) or that the proposed greenway extends less than 10 km (6 miles) along a higher-order stream.
Source: After Peterjohn and Correll (1984).

segments upstream and downstream? The condition of the surrounding landscape should be surveyed, including the extent to which it has been modified by human activities and the character of the non–point source pollution entering the riparian corridor. This assessment includes defining the mixture, intensity, and configuration of the land use adjacent to the stream and understanding how various land uses—forestry, agriculture, suburbs, or urban development—influence the corridor.

Designers and planners can gain an understanding of the ecological characteristics of the greenway and its surroundings by consulting with local ecologists, agronomists, foresters, or other land-use experts. Many

components and processes should be investigated, including soils, nutrient cycles, vegetation and animal communities, the physical structure of the stream, the nature and frequency of natural disturbances, and changes in the stream and its corridor over time. The hydrologic regime—flood stages and frequencies, low-flow characteristics, groundwater discharge and recharge periods, and stream water velocity—must be determined. Government agencies, like local offices of the U.S. Geological Survey or state water-resources agencies, often have data or empirical models useful for predicting stream flow. Stream ecologists affiliated with universities or environmental consulting firms can provide data and expert opinions if asked the right questions, which should be possible after one has carefully read this chapter.

Ideally, these questions should be investigated through original, site-specific research. A sample design for a preimplementation study followed by monitoring during management is given in Table 4.2. The study measures sediment and nutrient fluxes (via surface runoff and shallow groundwater) from upland areas to the riparian zone and to the stream itself, as well as nutrient cycling processes within the riparian forest. Such a study is quite comprehensive and should cost about $100,000 in the first year and $40,000 per year thereafter for monitoring. Proposed greenways with more modest objectives than complete nutrient and sediment control will be less expensive because the full range of variables will not require measurement. Depending on the particular case, a useful study might be accomplished for much less than these amounts.

Other materials such as pesticides, heavy metals, or road salt could also be measured with the same field methods at some increase of laboratory expense. Observation stations, including wells and discharge gauges, can be maintained for long-term monitoring. A study of temperature regulation modeled after the Ontario streams work by D. R. Barton and colleagues (1985) mentioned earlier could be accomplished even more cheaply.

Riparian and stream ecosystems are different at each location. Such differences should provide the basis for formulating greenway designs and should thus be thoroughly investigated. A proper study may seem expensive, and some organizations will simply not have the resources to pay for one. However, to put it in a different light, a description of a riparian ecosystem sufficient for design and management purposes can be established in two to three years, whereas greenway management may occur for the next century or more. A moderate investment at the beginning of a project followed by relatively inexpensive monitoring is likely to be a sound, long-term investment. If funding is not available, knowledge from local experts and con-

sultants may have to suffice. Part of the job for designers and managers is to advise decision makers about the information requirements for certain decisions; advocacy of ecosystem studies or other consultations is often an important part of that advice.

We wish to point out the similarities between product research and development carried out by industry and these preimplementation studies, as well as the similarities between quality-assessment and quality-control programs in manufacturing and monitoring during environmental management. Industries allocate a certain portion of their resources to both activities, and we believe that environmental management programs deserve the same sort of investment.

Corridor Design

Although a riparian greenway may have many intended uses, protection of water resources and environmental integrity should always be a primary goal. Toward this end, several core components should always be included in a greenway: the geomorphic, hydrological, and vegetational components of the original, natural riparian zone. At a minimum, the greenway should contain the following features (note that there is often a great deal of spatial overlap among these components):

1. the natural meandering span of the stream, which we have defined as its geomorphic floodplain;
2. the riparian forest; and
3. the area over the stream's shallow groundwater system including any significant groundwater recharge areas in uplands outside the floodplain and riparian forest (the water table near streams is both a source and a sink for stream water, depending on the time of year and recent weather).

Together, these elements make up the riparian ecosystem and are thus essential to its healthy functioning. Beyond these core components, additional area should usually be added to the greenway if it is to function optimally. Two questions about the physical form of the greenway must be answered. First, what will be the most effective width at various locations along the greenway? Second, what additional critical areas beyond this width should be included in the corridor, and what critical areas within the boundaries should receive special management attention?

These questions can be answered and the core components defined most effectively by using the information from the studies described in the previous section and by consulting with local experts. Appropriate greenway dimensions and configuration differ regionally according to climate and physiography, as well as locally between the streams of a watershed, along stretches of a particular stream, and according to land use and other variables. The structure and function of the landscape through which the stream passes therefore provide the most appropriate guide to designing the greenway.

Determining Width

Along a greenway, variable widths will often be needed for filtering sediments and nutrients, to help maintain natural flow regimes, and to protect significant natural features. The width of a riparian corridor should not be defined arbitrarily. The fixed widths typically set by statute as part of stream protection programs are straightforward and easily measurable for making and implementing policy. However, an arbitrary distance from the stream typically results from compromises between ecological, economic, and political interests. In most cases, an arbitrary width will not reflect the highly variable circumstances found along the length of any given corridor. A set width may be too narrow in some places and unnecessarily wide in others (Figure 4.13).

Numerous studies and regulations have tried to set single effective widths for a wide variety of stream types, but no consensus or magic number has emerged. For example, in the Pacific Northwest of the United States, a minimum recommended buffer of 30 meters

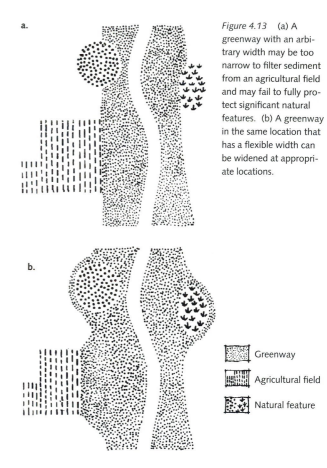

Figure 4.13 (a) A greenway with an arbitrary width may be too narrow to filter sediment from an agricultural field and may fail to fully protect significant natural features. (b) A greenway in the same location that has a flexible width can be widened at appropriate locations.

Greenway

Agricultural field

Natural feature

(100 feet) on each side of streams is cited often in the papers reviewed by W. W. Budd and colleagues (1987). E. S. Corbett and colleagues (1978) also suggest that a 30-meter strip of riparian vegetation protects stream ecosystems from the effects of logging in the eastern United States. In numerous northern California streams, J. D. Newbold and colleagues (1980) showed that most or all of the logging impacts on invertebrate life were prevented by buffer strips of 30 meters or more. The Washington State Shorelines Management Act protects land within 60 meters (200 feet) of a creek, within the 100-year floodplain, or within the creek's associated wetlands, whichever is greater (Morrison 1988). The plan includes an ostensibly inviolate 15-meter (50-foot) buffer adjacent to the stream or wetland, although previously existing land

uses are exempt and observers report that the law is not well enforced. In Maryland, the Chesapeake Bay Critical Area Commission designated land within 300 meters (1,000 feet) of the bay as critical area, and requires intensive review of proposed development (Davis 1987). For all regions, R. E. Toth (1990) recommends that activities within a zone of 150 meters (500 feet) on both sides of riparian corridors be subject to agency and public review for their effects on the stream.

According to recent research, some of these widths may be insufficient for stream protection. For example, most sediment eroded from cultivated fields in a coastal-plain watershed in Maryland was deposited in the forested buffer strip, but significant deposition extended 80 meters (265 feet) from the forest-field edge (Lowrance et al. 1988). A much smaller amount of sediment was deposited closer to the stream, suggesting that 80 meters would constitute an effective buffer in this case. The surface drainage area of the field was only about 4.63 hectares (11.4 acres) with an average slope of 2 to 5 percent, and the field was managed with moderate erosion-reduction practices. In a similar study on the coastal plain of North Carolina, slopes of cultivated fields varied from 0 to 7 percent, and slopes of an uncultivated upland buffer adjacent to the floodplain ranged up to 20 percent. In this case, slightly more than 50 percent of the total sediment was deposited within 100 meters (330 feet) of the field-forest boundary (Cooper et al. 1987). Another 25 percent of the sediment was deposited in a floodplain swamp lateral to the stream channel at various distances from the field-forest boundary. These two studies indicate that 80 to 100 meters would be a reasonable minimum range of buffer widths in these and similar systems if the objective were to reduce sediment load by 50 to 75 percent; wider corridors would be necessary for greater sediment removal. In cases with more intensive erosion, steeper slopes, or less effective erosion-control practices, the distance within which sediment is deposited is likely to be even greater.

The width of a riparian buffer should increase in direct proportion to (1) the size of the area contributing runoff, sediment, and nutrients; (2) the steepnesses of both the adjacent slope and the riparian zone; and (3) the intensity of cultural activities and disturbances in the uplands, such as agriculture, forestry, or suburban or urban development. Less width may be needed when there is greater complexity, density, and roughness of corridor vegetation and microtopography (Cooper et al. 1987).

Again, width should ideally be determined after thorough scientific studies have been completed. As an alternative, Budd and colleagues (1987) have developed a practical method for subjectively determining stream-corridor width by using simple field survey methods on selected reaches of a stream. With this method, a riparian corridor's potential for sediment filtration and temperature control is assessed qualitatively, as are terrestrial and aquatic habitat and vegetation's contribution to stream structure. Characteristics surveyed include stream type, slope of the streambed, soil class, runoff and erosion potential, water capacity of the soil, vegetation cover, temperature control, stream structure, sedimentation control, and wildlife habitat. All these factors are used by the evaluator to estimate necessary corridor width, an estimate based as much on intuition and experience as on objective criteria. In a study of a stream in King County, Washington, all corridor widths were recommended to be 15 meters (50 feet) wide or less. Those determinations are probably significant underestimates that were based more on existing land use than on any ecological principles.

This approach may be appropriate where no resources are available to support the studies that help determine corridor widths objectively. Nonetheless, it is problematic on several counts. First, being qualitative, the approach is subjective and not replicable and is therefore hard to defend in legal or scientific terms. If several different evaluators, each with a different bias, were to examine the streams, they would probably recommend several different widths, and a commission or judge would still not know with any certainty which width would be adequate. One particular perspective, whether that of developers, foresters, environmentalists, or some other interested party, could prevail without respect to ecosystem properties. Second, this particular method is unclear and incomplete as described. The authors do not state how soils, slopes, vegetation, and other characteristics are to be used in the determination but only state that they are important criteria. Third, the method depends on having relatively undisturbed reaches of the stream available for analyses. If no segment of the stream remains undisturbed, then a recommendation cannot be made. Nonetheless, this or other qualitative methods, if conducted by well-trained, experienced, and disinterested resource professionals, are likely to be the next best alternatives when complete scientific studies cannot be undertaken.

Critical Areas to Include

Several types of critical areas, both adjacent to and beyond the main corridor, should also be included as part of a greenway and given special management attention. Intermittent tributaries, gullies, and swales draining into the stream are critical areas because large quantities of sediment and runoff collect in them before entering the stream. The physical structure and natural vegetation in and along the side slopes of these minor drainages should be maintained. Vegetation in these areas has naturally dense growth because of good soil and moisture conditions and thus provides excellent sediment and nutrient filtration capacity. Natural vegetation left in minor and intermittent drainage ways promotes channel stability in the main stream by slowing flow during storms and decreasing erosion in swales (Cooper et al. 1987). Keeping these areas undisturbed and vegetated is very important, especially in arid lands where most watercourses are intermittent.

Another kind of critical area includes potential and actual areas of erosion or deposition in contact with the stream. These areas include steep slopes, unstable soil areas, lateral wetlands, undercut banks (especially on the outside of bends), bridge crossings, path or boat-ramp accesses, and other locations vulnerable to increased disturbance and erosion or having potential to act as sediment sinks (Schlosser and Karr 1981; Budd et al. 1987).

Other critical areas that may or may not be in direct contact with a stream have an important influence on sediment input and must be considered when designating a protected riparian corridor. Development sites, areas of intensive forest cutting, pastures or paddocks subject to overgrazing, and cultivated fields near streams are examples of critical watershed areas (Cooper et al. 1987; Toth 1990). The existence of such areas requires wider riparian corridors because of the need to sequester a greater volume of eroded sediment.

Aquifer recharge or discharge zones that help maintain year-round stream flow should also be protected. These areas are not often easily discovered by simple, qualitative field methods; only hydrogeological studies are capable of proving that an area is a discharge or recharge zone. Some simple rules of thumb, however, can be applied to indicate whether further studies are necessary. If a wetland or seasonally wet soils occur uphill from a stream, then they are probably groundwater recharge areas. Outcrops of bedrock known to be aquifers are also important recharge areas. Springs laterally uphill from streams are discharge areas for the aquifer and may be recharge areas for the stream. Finally, nearly all of the geomorphic floodplain is either a recharge or discharge area for stream water.

One last critical area is the zone just above the point of topographic leveling of floodplain banks, or the shoulder of the hill (Figure 4.14). If this zone remains undisturbed, it can be a highly effective sediment filter because of its gradual slope compared to the banks below. This upland area will also be a stable, long-term sink for sediment and nutrients, whereas wetlands and riparian areas may eventually be disturbed by bank erosion and stream-channel meander.

Figure 4.14 Agricultural fields along a segment of the Willamette River in Oregon extend to the point of topographic levelling, or to the shoulder of the hill. In this case, if natural vegetation extended beyond the top of the river's banks, it would probably be a better, long-term sediment filter. (Courtesy of the Oregon Department of Parks and Recreation.)

The edge of some floodplains consists of multiple terraces caused by very large floods in the past that deposited huge amounts of sediment. In these cases, the protected corridor should ideally extend beyond the last terrace, because this marks the point beyond which the stream is unlikely to meander in the future.

Site Design, Vegetation Management, and Alternative Planting

Once a greenway's boundaries have been determined, there remains the task of designing elements within the corridor itself at the site scale. The most important areas for attention are along the greenway's edges where intensive land uses such as agriculture or urbanization are immediately adjacent to the riparian buffer. If the disturbance is severe and sediment inputs are great, additional efforts may be required to prevent contaminants from overwhelming the riparian corridor. For example, detention or retention basins are required below developments in many states as best management practices, and a large literature describing the function of these structures has been published

(e.g., Hartigan et al. 1979; Hartigan and Quasebarth 1985). Alternatively, a combination of berms and dense vegetation at the forest edge may be necessary to provide additional barriers to the agricultural runoff (Cooper et al. 1987).

After a greenway has been designed and implemented, riparian forests must often be managed on an ongoing basis so their function of protecting water resources can be maintained. As described earlier in this chapter, selective harvesting of trees will remove accumulated nutrients from the riparian system and promote continued nutrient uptake and forest growth. In areas with very high levels of sediment deposition, periodically removing sediment can prevent the corridor vegetation from being damaged over the long term.

Native vegetation is usually the most effective for maintaining water quality and requires little or no maintenance. A diverse vertical stratification with trees, a shrub layer, and herbaceous ground cover should be encouraged within the corridor.

Alder, which is a native species in many riparian communities, can be effective for long-term bank protection because its roots are water tolerant and support the bank by penetrating deeply into the soil (Kite 1980). However, alder roots bear nodules that contain nitrogen-fixing microorganisms and may supply biologically available nitrogen compounds to the stream (Bormann and Gordon 1984). If nitrogen is a limiting nutrient for the stream, alders may increase productivity and contribute to eutrophication, although the significance of this effect is not well studied. Where excess nitrogen is not a concern, alder should make an excellent stream-bank planting. Even where nitrogen is a problem, alder may safely be used in a limited way to stabilize streams at points where banks are particularly vulnerable. Other native species, like willow and cottonwood, will also be effective in specific situations and should be identified by consulting with local botanists or horticulturalists.

However, if human activities make natural vegetation impossible to maintain, alternative plantings may be more durable and quite effective. In one instance, a 300-meter (1,000-foot) strip of planted coastal Bermuda grass removed 99 percent of the sediment from runoff with an initial concentration of 5,000 parts per million—a moderately high level (Karr and Schlosser 1977). Although this species will not be appropriate in many landscapes, other plants may function in a similar manner. In general, plants used for sediment filtration should have deep and vigorous root systems to resist scouring in swift currents, dense, well-branched top growth, and an ability to recover after being inundated with sediment. Agressive plants that might spread to other areas and compete with native vegetation should be avoided.

Riparian greenways with trails are sometimes landscaped with closely cut grass (Figure 4.15). When grasses are clipped and flow rates are high enough to submerge the sod, filtering efficiency can be lost entirely (Karr and Schlosser 1977). Therefore, mowing streamside vegetation should be discouraged, especially during periods when storms or high flows are likely.

Corridor Restoration

Restoring stream corridors can be a cost-effective means of controlling non–point source pollution (Lowrance et al. 1985). As we have emphasized, the primary objective of stream restoration should be to re-create the natural habitat, not just to plant a species that is hardy, attractive, or easy to maintain (Baird 1989). Restoration efforts should therefore be guided by the structure of the original riparian vegetation as well as by the original structure of the stream and its hydrologic processes. Restoration should establish an appropriate structure within which natural processes can operate so that the system can be sustainable and capable of recovery following natural disturbances.

The first requirement in a restoration project is to restore the stream's original flow regime because naturally fluctuating flows are essential to riparian communities. The second step is to restore the stream's ability to attain its appropriate meander pattern and riffle-pool structure (the alteration of still pools and faster flowing riffles) by removing dams and channel levees

Figure 4.15 Mowed grass or other low vegetation will usually make a poor filter of sediments carried by surface water and should thus be avoided. (Photo by D. Smith.)

(Decamps et al. 1988). These actions may be the ones needed if seed sources of the original riparian vegetation exist nearby or upstream. In this case revegetation and physical changes to the stream channel will occur by themselves over time. Restoring the meander pattern by moving earth or redirecting flow may speed the process but can be very expensive.

In one of the best contemporary examples of stream restoration, degraded areas along the Kissimmee River in southern Florida have recovered dramatically following the diversion of channelized flow back into the old river course (Karr 1988). In only a few years, habitat complexity and diversity have increased. Connections between the stream and riparian habitat have been enhanced, resulting in increased input of insects to the river and its food chain, flushing of floating plants and sediment that had accumulated in the channel, and growth of fish and waterfowl populations (Figure 4.16).

If the stream's channel or hydrology has been irreversibly altered, complete restoration may not be possible (Decamps et al. 1988). The most common examples of permanent changes are large dams, which prevent flooding downstream, and flood-control levies that protect towns and cities by restricting floodwaters. In such cases, expectations will have to be lowered. Instead of full restoration, other important objectives, such as maintenance of clean water or special kinds of fisheries, may be attainable.

Riparian ecosystems damaged by livestock often recover naturally if grazing is eliminated or restricted (Platts and Rinne 1985; Winegar 1977; Behnke and Raleigh 1978; Apple 1985). Cottonwood, alder, sycamore, and willow grow prolifically after livestock exclusion, assuming there are no other ongoing stresses to the system (Davis 1977; U.S. General Accounting Office 1988). Successful solutions depend both on the specific characteristics of the degraded corridor and on the alternatives for modifying ranching operations. For example, in the Coronado Forest in southern Arizona, completely fencing out livestock was the only method

Figure 4.16   A segment of the Kissimmee River, before (top) and after (bottom) restoration. Returning diverted flow to the original river course has helped flush out accumulated sediments and aquatic growth and has enhanced wildlife habitat and fisheries. (Courtesy of Southwest Florida Water Management District.)

that ensured adequate protection and improvement of riparian systems (Ames 1977). But complete exclusion may not be necessary in other cases. In a damaged riparian zone in the Rocky Mountains a combination of seasonal exclusion and lowering the number of grazing animals resulted in intermediate levels of stream protection (Platts and Rinne 1985). Whether complete or partial exclusion is needed will depend on many local variables, including the type and health of vegetation and soils, the degree of aridity, and rainfall patterns.

A restoration technique that holds promise for some areas is the reintroduction of beaver. In Wyoming, a combination of livestock exclusion and beaver reintroduction was instrumental in improving degraded riparian corridors (Apple 1985). Beaver dams reduced stream flow velocities, erosive potential, and capacity to carry sediment and increased both sediment deposition and the level of the corridor's water table. The combination of beaver activity and livestock exclusion allowed willows to become reestablished, and the riparian plant community became self-sustaining after three years. Beaver introductions may cause problems in some situations because new ponds and wetlands may not be appreciated by landowners and ornamental plants are often considered delicacies by hungry beavers. In these cases the maintenance of at least a partially natural habitat by adjacent landowners may be essential but not always easy to achieve. Educational programs, original development covenants or compensation for conservation easements, and clever landscape design (Nassauer 1990) can all help create the essential goodwill.

Finally, several technical problems are common in any restoration or enhancement project and must be avoided (Baird 1989). Water ponding and damage to some plants are a consequence of clayey soils often found in subsoils or fill material. Exotic weeds colonize newly created riparian habitat to the detriment of intended plantings. Groundwater depth determines whether planted riparian vegetation survives and should be a key issue in selecting enhancement sites. In addition, soil microorganisms important for nutrient uptake by newly planted vegetation should be introduced by spreading leaf litter collected from nearby mature riparian communities following planting.

This list is not exhaustive and actually only begins to describe all the issues and problems that might be encountered with restoration projects. Designers and managers should recognize that scientists understand ecosystems in a general way but do not usually know enough about the structure and function of specific riparian ecosystems to specify effective management or restoration methods without detailed investigations.

Guidelines for Riparian Greenway Design

The following guidelines are based on the preceding discussion and are divided into three sections: selecting alignments, setting widths, and preparing site designs and management plans. (Note that for riparian greenways, potential alignments are already defined by the existing stream network; the key task here is *evaluating* and *prioritizing* alignments within a given network to determine which stream segments are most in need of protection.)

We stress that the most important guideline for any project is that objectives for design and planning be made explicit and be understood by all parties. Only then can options for achieving the objectives be discussed. We cannot define realistic and achievable objectives for specific cases in this chapter. They must be discussed and decided on by local participants with the consultation of experts.

Selecting Alignments

1. Include waterways and adjacent lands within greenways and make them as continuous along the waterways as possible. Cover both sides of the waterway.
2. In evaluating potential alignments, identify the location of the stream segment in question within the stream network and understand its relationship to upstream and downstream areas by answering the following questions:
   a. Is the reach in the headwaters, the middle sections, or near the mouth of the stream? According to the River Continuum Concept, riparian forests along each section have different functions.
   b. How significant are upstream gaps in the riparian forest? If they are large, then restoration of upstream forest may be necessary for the stream at the site to function properly.

3. If possible, include all tributaries of a watershed in the greenway system because protecting headwaters will offer the greatest water-quality benefits for the network as a whole. If it is not possible to include all tributaries, they should be ranked in importance according to the existing or potential impact of adjacent land uses.

4. Place a high priority on areas with a high potential for erosion, such as areas with steep slopes or erodible soils, and on areas with high levels of biodiversity or rare species.

5. Place a high priority on protecting nodes, that is, the confluence of two or more streams or areas where upland greenways cross the stream. Nodes are critical links in stream networks, especially for animal movement.

Setting Widths

1. Before setting widths, identify and understand the impact of surrounding land uses on the integrity of stream communities and riparian corridors. This understanding should ideally be gained through comprehensive study of sediment and nutrient flows, hydrology, and local biotic integrity but can be obtained by referring to existing information and by consulting with local experts. This information should form the basis for the greenway design.

2. Include within a riparian greenway, at minimum, the stream's geomorphic floodplain, the riparian forest, wetlands, and the stream's shallow groundwater system. These areas are the most critical to riparian ecosystem function.

3. Also include other critical areas such as intermittent tributaries, gullies and swales, aquifer recharge and discharge areas, adjacent slopes beyond the point of topographic leveling, and potential and actual areas of erosion (steep slopes, unstable soil areas). All of these areas can have a major impact on the riparian ecosystem.

4. Set corridor widths that vary in proportion to the impacts of adjacent land uses. Forest clear-cutting, intensive agriculture, and dense housing development require wider corridors. Determining widths should involve consultations with local experts and, ideally, a comprehensive study of sediment and nutrient flows and biotic integrity.

Preparing Site Designs and Management Plans

1. Maintain or restore the natural stream channel and flow regime to maintain or restore natural communities and stream processes.

2. If a greenway is located along a very small (first-order) stream and if maintenance of low temperature is the *only* objective of a management plan, maintain natural vegetation a minimum of one tree height from the stream bank and of sufficient density to shade the stream surface.

3. Where vegetation management is necessary, maintain a diverse vertical stratification of vegetation with special attention to the ground layer for purposes of sediment filtration. This management will be especially important along minor or intermittent tributaries where sediment can be most effectively filtered.

4. Do not mow streamside vegetation, since this will decrease its filtering effectiveness and decrease its habitat value for animals.

5. If nonnative species are necessary for restoration, choose those with high filtering capacity, but in nitrogen-limited systems, be careful of nitrogen-fixing plants such as alder. Avoid exotic species that may spread and overtake native vegetation.

6. Where sediment inputs to the riparian ecosystem are likely to be high and corridor width is insufficient for sediment filtration, design retention basins or berms with dense plantings of vegetation to trap sediment.

7. Where nutrient filtering is an important greenway function, a long-range plan for selective tree har-

vesting to maintain forest productivity and thus nutrient uptake may be advisable. This planning should be done in consultation with local foresters and nutrient-cycling experts. (Keep in mind that the stream can process large masses of leaf material, thus exporting nutrients from the forest, without negative impacts. Therefore, such harvesting will usually be more important for maintaining nutrient uptake than for preventing the flux of organic matter to the aquatic system. In many cases harvesting may not be necessary.)

8. Exclude livestock from riparian vegetation where possible. If livestock access is necessary, it should be limited to short segments on only one side of the stream. This guideline is especially important in arid regions.

9. Maintain or reintroduce beavers where human density and development of adjacent lands allow. This program may require additional education and management to allow happy coexistence between beavers and people.

Conclusions

These guidelines will be most effective when designers, planners, and managers have gained a thorough knowledge of the ecosystem in question and its context in the landscape. Occasionally, this knowledge may already exist in sufficiently detailed form. But in most cases, original research will be well advised. A comprehensive study can answer most if not all of the pertinent design questions. However, it may not always be within a project's budget. Fortunately, there are alternatives that, although much less effective, are more affordable. Many scientists in colleges, universities, or environmental consulting firms have experience with local stream systems and may be willing to work with designers and managers to establish more specific recommendations for corridor configuration and composition.

For example, the Index of Biotic Integrity (IBI) depends on a knowledge of regional fish ecology. Universities with an ichthyologist on the faculty probably have collections of samples from local streams and lakes, some of which may be considered undisturbed localities for baseline determinations and others of which may be the streams of interest to the designer or manager. A reasonable estimate of the IBI can be determined from archived collections or unpublished data with the assistance of the biologist. If recent maps or aerial photographs are available, the spatial relationships between land use, riparian forests, and stream water quality can easily be determined. In any event, local ecological knowledge will always be useful. It is the designers' and managers' responsibility to be educated sufficiently to ask the right questions of scientists and the scientists' responsibility to answer the questions in ways that are useful to designers and managers.

If we as a society believe that protecting clean water and biological diversity is important, the preservation or restoration of riparian vegetation can go far toward achieving this goal. Ecosystem and environmental scientists must study sediment and nutrient flows from uplands through riparian zones to streams. Stream ecologists must collaborate with terrestrial ecologists to understand the relationships between land use, the configuration and composition of riparian vegetation, and stream water quality and biotic integrity. Environmental designers, planners, and managers must become educated about the ecological function of these systems, must learn how to ask appropriate questions of scientists and consultants, and then must understand their answers well enough to implement effective programs. Perhaps even more important, ecologists should become more involved in applying their knowledge to the practical problems and be willing to help practitioners ask appropriate questions, to argue strongly for suitable studies, and to provide useful answers.

References

Ames, C. R. 1977. Wildlife conflicts in riparian management: Grazing. Pages 49–57 in R. R. Johnson and D. A. Jones, eds., *Importance, Preservation and Management of Riparian Habitat: A Symposium*. USDA Forest Service, General Technical Report RM–43.

Angermeier, P. L., and J. R. Karr. 1984. Relationships between woody debris and fish habitat in a small warmwater stream. *Transactions of the American Fisheries Society* 113:716–26.

Apple, L. L. 1985. Riparian habitat restoration and beavers. Pages 489–90 in R. R. Johnson, C. D. Ziebell, D. R. Patton, P. F. Ffolliott, and R. H. Hamre, eds., *Riparian Ecosystems and Their Management: Reconciling Conflicting Uses*. First North American Riparian Conference. USDA Forest Service, General Technical Report RM–120.

Bache, D. H., and I. A. Macaskill. 1981. Vegetation in coastal and stream-bank protection. *Landscape Planning* 8:363–85.

Baird, K. 1989. High quality restoration of riparian ecosystems. *Restoration and Management Notes* 7:60–64.

Barlow, T. J. 1982. Why streams need trees. *Garden Magazine* 6:2–6.

Barton, D. R., W. D. Taylor, and R. M. Biette. 1985. Dimensions of riparian buffer strips required to maintain trout habitat in southern Ontario streams. *North American Journal of Fisheries Management* 5:364–78.

Behnke, R. J., and R. F. Raleigh. 1978. Grazing and the riparian zone: Impact and management perspectives. Pages 263–67 in *Strategies for Protection and Management of Floodplain Wetlands and Other Riparian Ecosystems: Proceedings of the Symposium*. Forest Service General Technical Report WO–12, Washington, D.C., U.S. Government Printing Office.

Benke, A. C. 1985. Importance of the snag habitat for annual production in a southeastern stream. *Fisheries* 10:8–13.

Benke, A. C., T. C. Van Arsdall, Jr., D. M. Gillespie, and F. K. Parrish. 1984. Invertebrate productivity in a subtropical blackwater river: The importance of habitat and life history. *Ecological Monographs* 54:25-63.

Bormann, B. T., and J. C. Gordon. 1984. Stand density effects in young red alder plantations: Productivity, photosynthate partitioning and nitrogen fixation. *Ecology* 65:394–402.

Bormann, F. H., and G. E. Likens. 1969. The watershed: Ecosystem concept and studies of nutrient cycles. In G. M. Van Dyne, ed., *The Ecosystem Concept in Natural Resource Management*. Academic Press, New York.

Bormann, F. H., and G. E. Likens. 1979. *Pattern and Process in a Forested Ecosystem*. Springer-Verlag, New York.

Bottom, D. L., P. J. Howell, and J. D. Rodger. 1983. Final report: Fish research project Oregon, salmonid habitat restoration. Oregon Department of Fish and Wildlife, Portland.

Brenner, M., M. W. Binford, and E. S. Deevey. 1990. Lakes. Pages 364–91 in R. L. Myers and J. J. Ewel, eds., *Ecosystems of Florida*. University of Florida Press, Gainesville.

Brown, G. W., and J. T. Krygier. 1970. Effects of clear-cutting on stream temperature. *Water Resources Research* 6:1133–39.

Budd, W. W., P. L. Cohen, P. R. Saunders, and F. R. Steiner. 1987. Stream corridor management in the Pacific northwest: I. Determination of stream corridor widths. *Environmental Management* 11:587–97.

Burns, J. W. 1972. Some effects of logging and associated road construction on northern California stream. *Transactions of the American Fisheries Society* 101:1–17.

Cooper, J. R., J. W. Gilliam, R. B. Daniels, and W. P. Robarge. 1987. Riparian areas as filters for agricultural sediment. *Soil Science Society of America Journal* 51:416–20.

Corbett, E. S., J. A. Lynch, and W. E. Sopper. 1978. Timber harvesting practices and water quality in the eastern United States. *Journal of Forestry* 76:484–88.

Corbett, E. S., and J. A. Lynch. 1985. Management of streamside zones on municipal watersheds. Pages 187–90 in R. R. Johnson, C. D. Ziebell, D. R. Patton, P. F. Ffolliott, and R. H. Hamre, eds., *Riparian Ecosystems and Their Management: Reconciling Conflicting Uses*. First North American Riparian Conference. USDA Forest Service, General Technical Report RM–120.

Cummins, K. W. 1974. Structure and function of stream ecosystems. *BioScience* 24:631–41.

Cummins, K. W., G. W. Minshall, J. R. Sedell, C. E. Cushing, and R. C. Petersen. 1984. Stream ecosystem theory. *Verh. Internat. Verein. Limnol.* 22:1818–27.

Davis, G. A. 1977. Management alternatives for the riparian habitat in the Southwest. Pages 59–66 in R. R. Johnson and D. A. Jones, eds., *Importance, Preservation and Management of Riparian Habitat: A Symposium*. USDA Forest Service, General Technical Report RM–43.

Davis, C. A. 1987. A strategy to save the Chesapeake shoreline. *Journal of Soil and Water Conservation* 42:72–75.

Dawson, T. E., and J. R. Ehleringer. 1991. Streamside trees that do not use stream water. *Nature* 350:335–37.

Decamps, H., M. Fortune, F. Gazelle, and G. Pautou. 1988. Historical influence of man on the riparian dynamics of a fluvial landscape. *Landscape Ecology* 1:163–73.

Delwiche, L. L. D., and D. A. Haith. 1983. Loading functions for predicting nutrient losses from complex watersheds. *Water Resources Bulletin* 19:951–59.

Dunne, T., and L. B. Leopold. 1978. Water in Environmental Planning. W. H. Freeman, New York.

Erman, N. A. 1981. The use of riparian systems by aquatic insects. Pages 177–82 in A. Sands, ed., *Riparian Forests in California: Their Ecology and Conservation.* Institute of Ecology Publication No. 15., University of California, Davis.

Erman, D. C., and V. M. Hawthorne. 1976. The quantitative importance of an intermittent stream in the spawning of rainbow trout. *Transactions of the American Fisheries Society* 105:675–81.

Everest, F. H., N. B. Armantrout, S. M. Keller, W. D. Parante, J. R. Sedell, T. E. Nickelson, J. M. Johnston, and G. N. Haugen. 1982. *Salmonids Westside Forest—Wildlife Habitat Relationship Handbook.* U.S. Forest Service, Pacific Northwest Forest and Range Experiment Station, Portland, Oreg.

Ewel, K. C. 1978. Riparian ecosystems: Conservation of their unique characteristics. Pages 56–62 in *Strategies for Protection and Management of Floodplain Wetlands and Other Riparian Ecosystems: Proceedings of the Symposium.* Forest Service General Technical Report WO–12. Washington, D.C., Government Printing Office.

Ferguson, B. K., and T. N. Debo. 1987. *On-site Stormwater Management: Applications for Landscape and Engineering.* PDA Publishers, Mesa, Ariz.

Forman, R. T. T., and M. Godron 1986. *Landscape Ecology.* John Wiley and Sons, New York.

Goldman, C. R. 1981. Lake Tahoe: Two decades of change in a nitrogen-deficient oligotrophic lake. *Verh. Internat. Verein. Limnol.* 21:45–70.

Gorham, E., P. M. Vitousek, and W. A. Reiners. 1979. The regulation of chemical budgets over the course of terrestrial ecosystem succession. *Annual Review of Ecology and Systematics* 10:53–84.

Gorman, O. T., and J. R. Karr. 1977. Habitat structure and stream fish communities. *Ecology* 59:507–15.

Gosz, J. R., G. E. Likens, and F. H. Bormann. 1972. Nutrient content of litter fall on the Hubbard Brook Experimental Forest, New Hampshire. *Ecology* 53:769–84.

Goudie, A. 1990. *The Human Impact on the Natural Environment.* 3d ed. MIT Press, Cambridge, Mass.

Gregory, K. J., and D. E. Walling. 1973. *Watershed Form and Process.* Halstead Press of John Wiley and Sons, New York.

Groeneveld, D. P., and T. E. Griepentrog. 1985. Interdependence of groundwater, riparian vegetation, and streambank stability: A case study. Pages 44–48 in R. R. Johnson, C. D. Ziebell, D. R. Patton, P. F. Ffolliott, and R. H. Hamre, eds., *Riparian Ecosystems and Their Management: Reconciling Conflicting Uses.* First North American Riparian Conference. USDA Forest Service, General Technical Report RM–120.

Hartigan, J. P., B. Douglas, D. J. Biggers, T. J. Wessel, and D. Stroh. 1979. Areawide and local frameworks for urban nonpoint pollution management in northern Virginia. Proceedings of National Conference on Stormwater Management Alternatives, Wilmington, Del., 3–5 October.

Hartigan, J. P., and T. F. Quasebarth. 1985. Urban nonpoint pollution management for water supply protection: Regional versus onsite BMP plans. International Symposium on Urban Hydrology, Hydraulic Infrastructures and Water Quality Control, University of Kentucky, Lexington, 23–25 July.

Karr, J. R. 1988. Kissimmee River: Restoration of degraded resources. Proceedings Kissimmee River Restoration Symposium, South Florida Water Management District, West Palm Beach, Fla., October.

Karr, J. 1991. Biological integrity: A long-neglected aspect of water resource management. *Ecological Applications* 1:66–84.

Karr, J., K. Fausch, P. L. Angermeier, P. R. Yant, and I. J. Schlosser. 1986. Assessing biological integrity in running waters: A method and its rationale. Illinois Natural History Survey, Special Publication #5, Champaign, Ill.

Karr, J. R., and I. J. Schlosser. 1977. Impact of nearstream vegetation and stream morphology on water quality and stream biota. U.S. Environmental Protection Agency, Ecological Research Series. EPA–600/3–77–097.

Karr, J. R., and I. J. Schlosser. 1978. Water resources and the land-water interface. *Science* 201:229–34.

Kibby, H. V. 1978. Effects of wetlands on water quality. Pages 289–97 in *Strategies for Protection and Management of Floodplain Wetlands and Other Riparian Ecosystems: Proceedings of the Symposium.* Forest Service General Technical Report WO–12, Washington, D.C., Government Printing Office.

Kite, D. J. 1980. Water courses—Open drains or sylvan streams? In Trees at Risk, Tree Council Annual Conference, London, March. (available from the Tree Council, London.)

Lehman, J. T. 1986. Control of eutrophication in Lake Washington. Pages 301–16 in *National Research Council. Ecological Knowledge and Environmental Problem Solving: Concepts and Case Studies.* National Academy Press, Washington, D.C.

Leopold, L. B., M. G. Wolman, and J. P. Miller. 1964. *Fluvial Processes in Geomorphology.* Freeman, San Francisco.

Likens, G. E., F. H. Bormann, N. M. Johnson, D. W. Fisher, and R. S. Pierce. 1970. Effects of forest cutting and herbicide treatment on nutrient budgets in the Hubbard Brook watershed-ecosystem. *Ecological Monographs* 40:23–47.

Lowrance, R. R., R. L. Todd, and L. E. Asmussen. 1984a. Nutrient cycling in an agricultural watershed: I. Phreatic movement. *Journal of Environmental Quality* 13:22–32.

Lowrance, R., R. Todd, J. Fail, O. Hendrickson, R. Leonard, and L. Asmussen. 1984b. Riparian forests as nutrient filters in agricultural watersheds. *BioScience* 34:374–77.

Lowrance, R., R. Leonard, and J. Sheridan. 1985. Managing riparian ecosystems to control nonpoint pollution. *Journal of Soil and Water Conservation* 40:87–92.

Lowrance, R., J. K. Sharpe, and J. M. Sheridan. 1986. Long-term sediment deposition in the riparian zone of a coastal plain watershed. *Journal of Soil and Water Conservation* 41:266–71.

Lowrance, R., S. McIntyre, and C. Lance. 1988. Erosion and deposition in a field/forest system estimated using cesium-137 activity. *Journal of Soil and Water Conservation* 43:195–99.

Makarewicz, J. C., and P. Bertram. 1991. Evidence for the restoration of the Lake Erie ecosystem. *BioScience* 41:216–23.

Manning, R. E. 1979. Impacts of recreation on riparian soils and vegetation. *Water Resources Bulletin* 15:30–43.

Meehan, W. R., F. J. Swanson, and J. R. Sedell. 1977. Influences of riparian vegetation on aquatic ecosystems with particular reference to salmonid fishes and their food supply. Pages 137–45 in R. R. Johnson and D. A. Jones, eds. *Importance, Preservation and Management of Riparian Habitat: A Symposium.* USDA Forest Service, General Technical Report RM–43.

Meyer, J. L., and R. T. Edwards. 1990. Ecosystem metabolism and turnover of organic carbon along a blackwater river continuum. *Ecology* 71:668–77.

Minshall, G. W., K. W. Cummins, R. C. Petersen, C. E. Cushing, D. A. Bruns, J. R. Sedell, and R. L. Vannote. 1985. Developments in stream ecosystem theory. *Canadian Journal of Fisheries and Aquatic Science* 42:1045-55.

Mitsch, W. J., and J. G. Gosselink. 1986. *Wetlands.* Van Nostrand Reinhold, New York.

Moring, J. R., and R. L. Lantz. 1975. The Alsea watershed study: Effects of logging on the aquatic resources of three headwater streams of the Alsea River, Oregon. Part I - Biological Studies. Fishery Research Report No. 9, Oregon Department of Fish and Wildlife, Corvallis.

Moring, J. R., G. C. Garman, and D. M. Mullen. 1985. The value of riparian zones for protecting aquatic systems: General concerns and recent studies in Maine. Pages 315–19 in R. R. Johnson, C. D. Ziebell, D. R. Patton, P. F. Ffolliott, and R. H. Hamre, eds., *Riparian Ecosystems and Their Management: Reconciling Conflicting Uses.* First North American Riparian Conference. USDA Forest Service, General Technical Report RM–120.

Morrison, S. W. 1988. The Percival Creek corridor plan. *Journal of Soil and Water Conservation* 43:465–67.

Nassauer, J. I. 1990. The appearance of ecological systems as a matter of policy. Paper presented at the fifth annual Landscape Ecology Symposium, Miami University, Oxford, Ohio, 21–24 March.

Newbold, J. D., D. C. Erman, and K. B. Roby. 1980. Effects of logging on macroinvertebrates in streams with and without buffer strips. *Canadian Journal of Fisheries and Aquatic Sciences* 37:1076–85.

Omernik, J. M., A. R. Abernathy, and L. M. Male. 1981. Stream nutrient levels and proximity of agricultural and forest land to streams: Some relationships. *Journal of Soil and Water Conservation* 36:227–31.

Patrick, W. H., Jr., and K. R. Reddy. 1976. Nitrification-denitrification reactions in flooded soils and water bottoms: Dependence on oxygen supply and ammonium diffusion. *Journal of Environmental Quality* 5:469–72.

Peterjohn, W. T., and D. L. Correll. 1984. Nutrient dynamics in an agricultural watershed: Observations on the role of a riparian forest. *Ecology* 65:1466–75.

Phillips, J. D. 1989. Fluvial sediment storage in wetlands. *Water Resources Bulletin* 25:867–73.

Platts, W. S., and J. N. Rinne. 1985. Riparian and stream enhancement management and research in the Rocky Mountains. *North American Journal of Fisheries Management* 5:115–25.

Poff, N. L., and J. V. Ward. 1989. Implications of streamflow variability and predictability for lotic community structure: A regional analysis of streamflow patterns. *Canadian Journal of Fisheries and Aquatic Sciences* 46:1805–18.

Reckhow, K. H., and S. C. Chapra. 1981. *Engineering Approaches for Lake Management.* Vol. 1: *Data Analysis and Empirical Modeling.* Ann Arbor Science.

Ruhe, R. V. 1975. *Geomorphology: Geomorphic Processes and Surficial Geology.* Houghton Mifflin, Boston.

Schlosser, I. J., and J. R. Karr. 1981. Riparian vegetation and channel morphology impact on spatial patterns of water quality in agricultural watersheds. *Environmental Management* 5:233–43.

Schlosser, I. J., and J. R. Karr. 1981. Water quality in agricultural watersheds: Impact of riparian vegetation during base flow. *Water Resources Bulletin* 17:233–40.

Schumm, S. A. 1963. A tentative classification of river channels. U.S. Geological Survey Circular 477.

Smith, R. A., R. B. Alexander, and M. G. Wolman. 1987. Water-quality trends in the nation's rivers. *Science* 235:1607–10.

Stabler, F. 1985. Increasing summer flow in small streams through management of riparian areas and adjacent vegetation: A synthesis. Pages 206–10 in R. R. Johnson, C. D. Ziebell, D. R. Patton, P. F. Ffolliott, and R. H. Hamre, eds., *Riparian Ecosystems and Their Management: Reconciling Conflicting Uses.* First North American Riparian Conference. USDA Forest Service, General Technical Report RM–120.

Steedman, R. J. 1988. Modification and assessment of an Index of Biotic Integrity to quantify stream quality in southern Ontario. *Canadian Journal of Fisheries and Aquatic Science* 45:492–501.

Strahler, A. N. 1964. Quantitative geomorphology of watersheds and channel networks. Section 4-2 in Ven te Chow, ed.,

Handbook of Applied Hydrology. McGraw-Hill, New York.

Thompson, K. 1977. Riparian forests of the Sacramento valley, California. Pages 35–38 in A. Sands, ed., *Riparian Forests in California: Their Ecology and Conservation.* Institute of Ecology Publication No. 15. University of California, Davis.

Toth, R. E. 1990. Hydrologic and riparian systems: The foundation network for landscape planning. Paper presented at International Conference on Landscape Planning, University of Hannover, Federal Republic of Germany, 6–8 June.

Triska, F. J. 1984. Role of wood debris in modifying channel geomorphology and riparian areas of a large lowland river under pristine conditions: A historical case study. *Verh. Internat. Ver. Limnol.* 22:1876–92.

U.S. Army Corps of Engineers, New England Division. 1968. Charles River watershed study: Summary of the fourth meeting of the coordinating committee for the Charles River watershed. USACOE, Waltham, Mass. 15 February.

U.S. Army Corps of Engineers, New England Division. 1976.

Natural valley storage: A partnership with nature. Public Information Fact Sheet, USACOE, Waltham, Mass.

U.S. General Accounting Office. 1988. Public rangelands: Some riparian areas restored but widespread improvement will be slow. Report to Congressional Requesters. GAO/RCED-99–105.

Vannote, R. L., G. W. Minshall, K. W. Cummins, J. R. Sedell, and C. E. Cushing. 1980. The river continuum concept. *Canadian Journal of Fisheries and Aquatic Sciences* 37:130–37.

Wineger, H. H. 1977. Camp Creek fencing—Plant, wildlife, soil and water responses. *Rangemans Journal* 4:10–12.

Yarbro, L. A., E. J. Kuenzler, P. J. Mulholland, and R. P. Sniffen. 1984. Effects of stream channelization on exports of nitrogen and phosphorus from North Carolina coastal plain watersheds. *Environmental Management* 8:151–60.

Yates, P., and J. M. Sheridan. 1983. Estimating the effectiveness of vegetated floodplains/wetlands as nitrate-nitrite and orthophosphorus filters. *Agriculture, Ecosystems and Environment* 9:303–14.

David N. Cole

Minimizing Conflict between Recreation and Nature Conservation

5

Most greenways are created with multiple goals in mind. Two of the foremost are providing recreational opportunities and conserving nature. Although these two goals frequently enhance each other, sometimes pursuing both simultaneously can result in conflicts. In some cases, recreational use can so severely degrade an area that not only is the environment damaged but the quality of the recreational experience itself is diminished.

This chapter explores various ways of reducing the conflict between recreational use and nature conservation. The chapter begins with an overview of the impacts of recreation on natural environments and the factors that influence the severity of these impacts. These factors—whether characteristics of recreational use or of the environment—suggest a number of alternative design strategies for managing impacts. A case study illustrates how a range of design and management strategies have been adapted to a specific situa-

tion. Finally, practical guidelines for design and management of greenways are proposed.

Ecological Impacts of Recreation

Greenways are used for a variety of recreational activities. Most greenways support nonconsumptive activities such as walking, jogging, picnicking, nature study, and photography; others permit consumptive uses such as fishing and hunting. Some are used for specialized recreational activities, like rock climbing, bicycling, and horseback riding. Each of these uses has a slightly different impact on the environment, which in turn calls for different design or management practices.

For the sake of clarity the following discussion is divided into sections corresponding to the four major landscape components that are affected by recreation: soil, vegetation, wildlife, and water. Important linkages, however, exist between each of these components and should not be overlooked. For example, if hikers trample an area and the soil becomes compacted, plant growth may decline because of less favorable growing conditions, erosion may be accelerated due to the sparser vegetative cover, eroding sediments may increase the siltation of nearby water courses, and the silty water may reduce stream quality for fish habitat. A single recreational activity can set in motion events that can cause impacts to all four of the major components of the landscape.

Clearly, impacts are not isolated occurrences. Instead, they occur in combination and can exacerbate or compensate for each other. Therefore, it is important for designers and managers to look comprehensively at ecosystems and at their design and management programs rather than to focus narrowly on individual places, recreational activities, or types of impact.

Impacts on Soils

Trampling by humans causes most of the impact that recreation has on soils and vegetation (Figure 5.1; Figure 5.2). Although all five of the typical components of soil—mineral matter, air, water, dead organic matter, and living organisms—are disturbed by trampling, it is the impact on the latter four that is most detrimental to the various forms of life that the soil supports.

Most of the dead organic material in soil is concentrated in the upper layers, particularly in a surface layer that usually consists primarily of organic matter. This layer, called the organic horizon, is critical to the health of a soil because of the important role it plays in the soil's biological activity. The organic horizon also promotes good water relations by increasing the absorptive capacity of the soil, decreasing runoff, and increasing moisture retention. It is a source of nutrients critical to plant growth and can effectively cushion underlying mineral soil horizons, which are more vulnerable to the compacting and eroding effects of rain-

fall and recreation. Organic horizons are generally less vulnerable to erosion than mineral soil, but if organic matter is pulverized by trampling, they too can be eroded away, exposing the mineral soil beneath.

When trampling compacts the mineral soil, which lacks the physical resiliency of organic matter, particles are squeezed together tightly, drastically reducing the amount of pore space between particles. The larger pores—those that promote good soil drainage and are normally occupied by air—can be nearly eliminated (Monti and Mackintosh 1979). Their elimination can reduce aeration and water availability and make it difficult for plant roots to penetrate the soil. These changes can reduce both germination success and the vigor of established plants and can be detrimental to soil-dwelling organisms. The loss of soil-dwelling biota can cause further impacts on soil and vegetation because these organisms are important agents in promoting the development of soil structure and are criti-

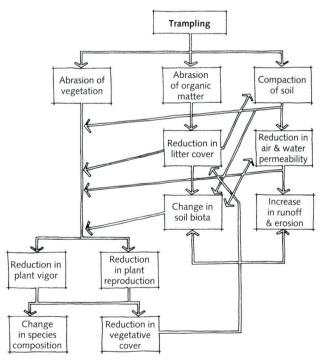

Figure 5.1 A conceptual model of trampling effects on vegetation and soil. (Based partly on Liddle 1975 and Manning 1979.)

Figure 5.2 An example of vegetation loss and soil erosion caused by trampling along a trail ascending the banks of the Verde River, Arizona. (Photo by D. Smith.)

cal to the process of nutrient cycling. In addition, compacted soils lose much of their infiltration capacity, leading to an increase in surface runoff following rains or other precipitation. This runoff often results in increased soil erosion wherever soils have been compacted, on trails, at picnic sites, at vista points, and along river banks. Soil compaction is reversed, however, by the effects of biotic and frost action in the soil.

Impacts on Vegetation

Recreation's impacts on vegetation are generally more obvious than impacts on soils. Places that receive heavy recreational use often become crisscrossed by informal trail networks, and in the process, large areas may become completely devoid of vegetation. Damage can also result when shrubs and trees are cut for firewood, to make tent poles, or to create clearings. Hack marks and initials are frequently found on woody vegetation, and sometimes recreationists cut vegetation for no apparent reason.

Trampling can crush, bruise, shear off, and uproot vegetation. Plants in trampled places may have reduced height, stem length, leaf area, flower and seed produc-

tion, and carbohydrate reserves (Liddle 1975; Speight 1973). All of these changes lead to reduced vigor and less successful reproduction. Sometimes they lead to a plant's death. Consequently, vegetation in trampled places generally has less biomass, sparser cover, different structure (generally shorter stature), and different species than in undisturbed places.

Species differ in their tolerance of trampling, and these differences are reflected in the mix of plant species—the floristic composition—found in an area. Tolerant species are apt to thrive with increased recreational use because they face reduced competition from intolerant species that are weakened or killed by trampling. Also favored are those plants that can take advantage of the changes in microclimate—such as increased light and temperature—that result from trampling (Liddle and Moore 1974; Dale and Weaver 1974). Some species may be injured by trampling but survive nonetheless because they have adaptive characteristics, such as flexible stems or leaves.

Recreation sometimes plays a role in the introduction of exotic species, some of which have had serious impacts in areas of North America. Seeds of exotic species can be carried into greenways by recreationists, dogs, horses, or straying livestock, or they can be introduced by birds, water, or wind. Once in an area disturbed by recreation, exotic species often thrive because they favor the environmental conditions found there. The significance of this problem depends on the importance placed on maintaining strictly natural conditions as well as on the competitiveness of the exotic species. As Reed Noss notes in chapter 3, narrow greenways with abundant edge habitat are particularly vulnerable to invasion by exotics.

Although some of the impacts of trampling on vegetation are inevitable with recreational use, the felling and mutilation of large shrubs and trees is largely needless. Most damage to these plants is caused by activities that are either malicious (e.g., hacking tree trunks) or unnecessary (e.g., cutting trees for firewood). A substantial amount of impact to vegetation also occurs in the construction of recreational facilities, such as the creation of trails and picnic areas.

The conceptual model in Figure 5.1 summarizes the various ways in which trampling affects soils and vegetation. As the figure shows, significant reciprocal and cyclic relationships exist between soil and vegetation impacts. For example, reductions in litter cover make the soil more susceptible to erosion; with increased erosion, more litter cover is lost, which increases susceptibility to erosion, and so on. A particularly important cyclic relationship involves vegetation, litter cover, and soil biota. As vegetative cover diminishes, a prime source of organic litter is lost. With diminished inputs of organic matter to the soil, the density of soil biota declines. Changes in soil biota reduce the availability of nutrients to plants, which in turn can cause further loss of vegetation. Once this sequence is under way, many of the damaged components will need to be repaired before the system can be restored.

An important characteristic of both soil and vegetation impacts is their highly concentrated nature. Most impact is confined to the specific place where recreation occurs, such as around recreational facilities and along connecting travel paths (Manning 1979). A few yards from totally denuded and eroded trails or vista points, soils and vegetation may be completely unaffected by recreational use (McEwen and Tocher 1976). As will be discussed later, designers and managers can use this fact to their advantage in planning for recreational use and impact.

Impacts on Animals

Because animals disturbed at one place can remember the experience and respond differently as they move to other locations, recreational impacts on animals can have more far-reaching effects than those on plants. Moreover, because animals are capable of teaching their offspring, reactions to disturbance can be passed from generation to generation. In contrast to vegeta-tion impacts, impacts on animals are not usually obvious to people, they are difficult to study, and they are poorly understood.

As the conceptual model in Figure 5.3 outlines, there are four general ways in which recreational activities can affect wild animals: harvest, habitat modification, pollution, and direct disturbance:

1. Animals can be harvested through hunting or fishing.

2. Their habitats can be modified, either intentionally or unintentionally. Creating trails, for instance, can have pronounced impacts on populations of small mammals, birds, reptiles, amphibians, and invertebrates in localized areas.

3. Animals can suffer from pollutants, litter or food, left by recreationists. Discarded plastic six-pack rings or fishing line, for instance, can entangle birds. Less obvious, but more common, is the disturbance that results when animals are fed by recreationists or when animals eat food or garbage left behind. The significance of this problem is hard to assess. It has certainly been detrimental to bears in national parks. As bears become habituated to human foods, contact between bears and humans increases, and the bears often must be destroyed to avoid dangerous encounters.

4. Direct disturbance may result when recreationists come too close to animals. This disturbance, sometimes called harassment although it is usually unintentional, is probably the primary means by which recreationists affect larger vertebrates—birds and mammals. It can reduce the effective size and habitat quality of an area and even destroy a greenway's value as a migration corridor. The significance of harassment varies from place to place and from species to species. Unfortunately, our understanding of the problem is limited.

Although an animal may respond to recreational disturbance by changing its behavior and thereby reducing or avoiding the disturbance, the animal may be

Figure 5.3   A conceptual model of the impacts of recreational use on animals.

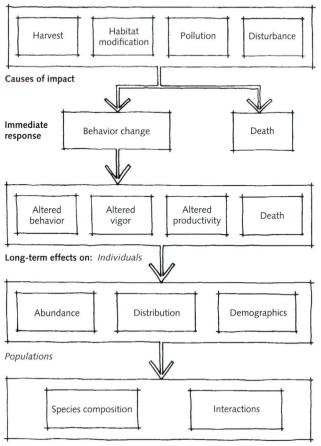

increase the populations of generalist species—those that are capable of capitalizing on human food sources and of crowding out species of greater ecological significance.

— Unintentional harassment by recreationists can lead to diverse behavioral responses such as interruption of feeding by bald eagles, abandonment of nests by golden plovers, increased heart rates in bighorn sheep, and flight of elk and moose.

Many of these immediate responses to disturbance are short term. For example, deer typically return within hours to areas they have left after being disturbed by snowmobiles (Dorrance et al. 1975). Even short-term effects, however, can have a major impact on animals living in stressful conditions, like deer trying to survive in deep snow and cold. Unfortunately, we know little about the long-term effects of recreational disturbance on the energy balance or survival rate of individuals or on entire populations and communities of wildlife.

Reed Noss has noted in chapter 3 that greenways should ideally function both as habitat and as conduits for movement. The long-term impacts that might reduce the habitat value of greenways include (1) the displacement from an area of individuals or entire populations of wildlife species, (2) decreased productivity due to disturbance of birthing sites, and (3) the loss of native species displaced by disturbance-loving species.

Abandoning disturbed places in favor of undisturbed places has been documented for a number of large mammals, including caribou and bighorn sheep (Geist 1978). Sensitive bird species may be displaced in a similar manner.

Birds have been the focus of most of the work showing decreased productivity due to disturbance from recreation. For example, in the Boundary Waters Canoe Area in Minnesota, loons experiencing fewer human contacts produced significantly more surviving young (Titus and Van Druff 1981). In Illinois, generalist bird species, such as blue jay, robin, and cowbird, were attracted to a nature trail in a forested area, where

unable to do so; if the disturbance is severe enough, the animal may not survive. Of course, death is the intended result of hunting and other forms of harvesting. But nonconsumptive activities can also kill animals, although such impacts are generally localized and confined to small, inconspicuous animals such as invertebrates. Consequently, these impacts are often ignored.

Behavioral changes by animals can be a serious concern in greenway design and management, as the following examples show:

— Habitat modification can cause valued bird species to seek out alternative places to nest.

— Improper disposal of food and garbage may

through competition, predation, and nest parasitism they may displace forest-interior, area-sensitive species, like veery and scarlet tanager (Hickman 1990)

There is little available evidence that recreational use interferes with the utility of a greenway as a conduit for animal movement. There are a number of situations, however, where interference is likely to occur. For example, even low levels of recreational use can reduce the movement in greenways of large, wide-ranging mammals, like bear and mountain lion, that are intolerant of people. Greenways that receive heavy recreational use and that are invaded by exotic plants may no longer provide suitable habitats for migrating birds or smaller mammals. Clearly, there is much to learn about the impacts of recreation on animal populations, their habitats, and their movements.

Impacts on Water

The effects of recreational use on water are also poorly understood. A number of studies have examined the impacts on water of motorboating, shoreline housing developments, and sewage disposal. However, little study has been made of the effects on water of the nonmotorized, casual types of recreation typical of most greenways.

In wild settings where camping is common, contamination of drinking water by human waste is a pressing concern, as are the increased nutrient inputs that may result (King and Mace 1974). For example, an exceptionally high level of phosphorus was recorded at a semiwilderness lake in Canada that had experienced a twentyfold increase in recreational use (Dickman and Dorais 1977). Some greenways such as those in developed landscapes may receive enough contamination from other upstream sources that local recreational impact is rendered inconsequential.

The most significant effects of recreation on water, however, are likely to occur indirectly, through disturbance of soils and vegetation. As discussed earlier, recreational use tends to lead to the loss of vegetative cover and soil organic horizons and contributes to the compaction of mineral soils. These impacts result in increased overland runoff, erosion, and deposition of sediments in waterways. Unfortunately, these impacts tend to be exacerbated by the attraction of recreationists to water. Because of heavy use, vegetation loss and soil erosion on trails and in trampled areas are often most severe along the banks of watercourses—the very places where these impacts are most harmful. Such impacts can reduce the overall filtration and erosion-control functions of greenways. The tendency for the height, cover, and diversity of vegetation to be reduced by recreational use also limits the capability of vegetation to buffer water temperatures and to provide habitat and food for animals.

Factors That Influence the Amount of Impact

Some degree of environmental impact is inevitable wherever recreation occurs. Since it is rarely desirable to preclude all opportunities for recreational use, the challenge for the designer or manager is to keep recreational impacts within acceptable limits. Strategies for minimizing impact become clearer with an understanding of the factors that influence the amount of impact. For example, if motorcycles are damaging an area, then an obvious strategy is to restrict such use. But if disturbance is occurring in an especially fragile site, then the strategy should probably be to exclude all recreational use of that site regardless of the type of recreation. Thus, design and management efforts should be focused on those factors that have the greatest potential to affect a site.

Recreational impact occurs when there is interaction between recreational users and an environment that is vulnerable to disturbance. Therefore, the amount of impact is a function of both use and environmental characteristics. The amount is also influenced by the design of the site and the intensity of management. (For example, the inherent vulnerability of a site can be reduced by paving a trail.)

Use Characteristics

Many characteristics of recreation determine its impact on an environment. The most significant are (1) the amount of use, (2) the type of recreational activity, (3) the behavior of recreationists, (4) the spatial distribution of use, and (5) the temporal distribution of use.

The relationship between the amount of use and the resulting amount of impact has been studied intensively. Most studies report that this relationship is asymptotic; that is, differences in the amount of use influence the amount of impact most when levels of use are relatively low (Figure 5.4). (The difference in impact between an unused and a lightly used place will tend to be greater than the difference between a place that is heavily used and one that is very heavily used.) Accordingly, the amount of impact increases rapidly with initial increases in the amount of use; at higher use levels, however, large increases in use may result in very small increases in impact. For example, once trampling exceeds relatively low threshold levels, vegetation loss and soil compaction are pronounced regardless of the amount of use (Cole 1987a). Similarly, a study of the effects of cross-country skiers on moose and elk in a park in central Alberta found that although the animals moved away from trails with the onset of skiing, they did not move any additional distance as the number of skiers increased (Ferguson and Keith 1982).

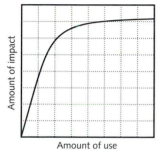

Figure 5.4 A generalized model of the asymptotic relationship between the amount of use and the amount of impact. Where use levels are low, incremental increases in the amount of use have a pronounced effect on the amount of impact. Where use levels are moderate to high, incremental increases in the amount of use have little effect on the amount of impact.

The implications of these studies are profound because they support the strategy of minimizing impact by concentrating use as much as possible. Increasing use levels in places that are already heavily used will probably have few negative effects; however, minimizing use levels in undisturbed places may have tremendous positive effects. When allocating land for greenways, it is imperative to define the boundaries so that the greenway is wide enough to accommodate both high-impact corridors as well as zones that are virtually undisturbed. Then it is incumbent upon greenway managers to see that undisturbed zones remain that way.

Impacts can differ greatly with the type of recreational activity. For example, consider the obvious difference in impact that hunting and photography have on animals. In a controlled experiment on a grassland in Montana (with a 15-degree slope), 200 passes by a motorcycle removed twice as much vegetation as the same number of passes by a horse and 9 times as much vegetation as 200 hikers (Weaver and Dale 1978). Although there are exceptions, motorized uses will usually cause more impact than nonmotorized uses, horses will cause more impact than hikers, and overnight users will cause more impact than day users.

The behavior of recreationists, whether alone or in groups, is also highly significant in determining the impacts of recreation. A disproportionate amount of the total impact received by an area comes from people who engage in malicious acts or vandalism, although they may be unaware of the full effects of their activities. The felling of trees is an obvious problem. More subtle and pervasive are the impacts caused through ignorance, for example, nest abandonment caused by bird-watchers getting too close to nesting birds. People with dogs usually disturb wildlife more than those without, particularly if the dogs are unleashed (MacArthur et al. 1982).

The way recreational use is distributed spatially influences both the overall amount and the distribution of the resulting impacts. Concentrated use—the norm in many greenways—results in pronounced disturbance of a few places with little impact elsewhere (McEwen and Tocher 1976). Where use is widely dispersed, more of an area is disturbed. Unless use levels are quite low, dispersal may not dilute impacts; it may merely result in more widespread damage. This conclusion follows from the research findings, mentioned previously, about the asymptotic relationship between the amount of use and the amount of impact. Concentrating use may be particularly effective in greenways because they are often narrow. Only by concentrating use will it be possible to maintain other portions of the greenway in a near-natural condition.

The way recreational use is distributed over time is the final influential use characteristic to be discussed here. Soils, for example, are particularly vulnerable to impact during the times of the year when they are water saturated. Hikers attempting to get around seasonally boggy places on trails can create wide mud holes and multiple trails that disrupt drainage. Also, some animals are particularly vulnerable to disturbance at certain times of the year, such as when they are nesting or stressed by winter conditions, or at certain times of the day, such as at the time when animals are accustomed to visiting water sources to drink.

Environmental Characteristics

The amount of impact an area receives is also influenced by the inherent vulnerability of the soils, vegetation, animals, and water in the area and by its topographic characteristics. For example, in trampling experiments, 40 passes by hikers in a year eliminated half of the vegetation under a closed-canopy forest, whereas 10 times as much use—400 passes per year— was needed to eliminate half the vegetation in an open grassland (Cole 1987a).

Although there are no absolute rules regarding these issues, most studies have found that mature trees and grasslike plants are usually resistant to trampling, whereas mosses are neither highly resistant nor highly

sensitive. Shrubs vary from being quite resistant to moderately sensitive, forbs vary from moderately resistant to highly sensitive, and lichens and tree seedlings are generally quite sensitive (Cole 1987b). Although these broad categories are useful as general indicators, the vulnerability of specific vegetation needs to be assessed site by site.

The likely resistance of vegetation can also be predicted by evaluating the morphological and physiological characteristics of plants. Characteristics that individually or in combination make a plant tolerant of trampling include (1) being either very small or very large, (2) growing either flat along the ground or in dense tufts, and (3) having leaves and stems that are tough or flexible. Characteristics that make a plant susceptible to damage include (1) growing to a moderate stature, (2) having an erect growth form, and (3) having woody, brittle, or delicate stems and leaves (Figure 5.5). Since most plant associations are made up of both tolerant and vulnerable species, trampling effects can be decreased by locating trails and other improvements in places that have a preponderance of tolerant species.

The vulnerability of soils varies with a large number of factors, including characteristics both of the soil itself and of the site. Some broad generalizations about relationships between soil properties and vulnerability are listed in Table 5.1. In most cases, vulnerability is lowest when the soil properties listed in the table are at

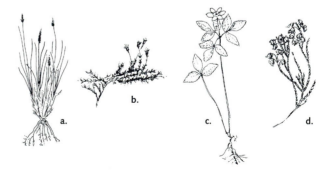

Figure 5.5 Plants that are (a) tufted and wiry or (b) prostrate and matted are generally resistant to trampling damage; plants with (c) erect herbaceous and leafy stems or (d) brittle woody stems are generally sensitive.

Table 5.1   Relationships between soil characteristics and site vulnerability

	Level of Vulnerability		
Soil Property	Low	Moderate	High
Texture	Medium (loam)	Coarse (sand)	Fine (clay)
Organic content	Moderate	Low	High
Soil moisture	Moderate	Low	High
Fertility	Moderate	High	Low
Soil depth	None	Deep	Shallow

moderate levels. For instance, soils with low moisture levels are unable to support dense vegetation and are therefore susceptible to erosion. Soils with high levels of soil moisture, however, are even more fragile, because they are readily deformed when subjected to stress. Water-saturated soils quickly degenerate into quagmires when trampled. In most cases, soils with moderate moisture levels have the lowest vulnerability to recreational impact.

The vulnerability of wild animals is complex and poorly understood. Much of the complexity results, as mentioned earlier, from the ability of animals to learn from experience and thereby adapt to recreational disturbance. Several studies suggest that animals subjected to predictable, nonthreatening disturbances can become habituated to and tolerant of those disturbances. For example, mountain goats in Glacier National Park have learned to tolerate frequent contact with park visitors (Singer 1978). Conversely, animals are likely to respond to frequent and predictable negative encounters by avoiding them, as has been demonstrated in comparisons of hunted and nonhunted wildlife populations (King and Workman 1986). Since this behavior is largely learned, two individuals of the same species may differ greatly in their vulnerability to the same disturbance. These differences make anticipating impacts on wildlife all the more challenging.

The vulnerability of water to pollutants (such as sediments and nutrients) from recreational activities is likely to be determined by characteristics of both the water and the surrounding land. If the surrounding

land has vegetation, soils, and topography that make it highly vulnerable to erosion, then erosion is likely to result and water quality to decline. If, for instance, a trail is constructed along a stream on steep slopes with highly erodible soils, then a considerable amount of sediment will probably find its way into the water. Thus, adjacent land-use practices can have a major impact on vulnerability.

Waterways are more susceptible to contamination if they are not frequently flushed out by large quantities of water and if they lack chemical properties capable of buffering pollutants. Thus, small water bodies and streams with low flows have a greater vulnerability than larger ones with higher flows.

Topographic characteristics influence the likelihood that facilities, such as trails, will deteriorate. For example, a trail's potential for erosion is influenced by the degree of slope of the trail, both along and across it, and by the trail's position (whether the trail is close to the top or to the bottom of the slope). Trails that run uphill readily channel water and are more subject to erosion than trails oriented perpendicular to the slope (Bratton et al. 1979). Trails located high on slopes have smaller areas draining into them and are therefore less likely to erode than trails located lower on slopes.

It is dangerous to draw sweeping generalizations about the relative vulnerability of landscapes. There will almost always be certain characteristics that make one environment more vulnerable than another and other characteristics that make it less vulnerable. The greenway designer has the difficult job of carefully evaluating the vulnerability of many critical parameters, deciding on the relative importance of each, and basing an ultimate evaluation of vulnerability on this analysis.

Design Strategies and Practical Tools

Many of the factors that influence the extent and intensity of an impact can be manipulated to reduce that

Table 5.2 Factors that influence recreational impacts and management strategies and examples of tools for minimizing impacts.

Factor	Strategy	Tool
Use characteristics		
Amount of use	Limit amount of use	Limit number of entrants Limit size of parking lot
Type of activity	Limit destructive activities	Prohibit certain activities Zone by activity type
Visitor behavior	Influence behaviors	Low-impact education Prohibit certain behavior
Use distribution		
Spatial	Concentrate use	Concentrate use at facilities such as trails
Temporal	Control timing of use	Close areas at certain times
Vulnerability	Control location of use	Locate facilities on durable sites Close fragile areas
	Harden sites	Surface trails
	Shield the site from use	Bridge vulnerable places Install toilets

impact. For example, how use is distributed spatially can be changed by rerouting trails or changing access points. Or the inherent vulnerability of a site can be decreased through management intervention. Thus strategies for minimizing impact should respond to the combination of use and environmental characteristics that determine the type and level of impacts in an area. This section explores such strategies and some practical tools for controlling impacts on greenways (Table 5.2).

Understanding Use Characteristics

In most situations, limiting the amount of recreational use an area receives is the simplest strategy for reducing recreational impacts. As mentioned earlier, this strategy will be most useful in places that are not heavily used or disturbed. In places that are already highly used and disturbed, limiting use by itself may have little effect on impact levels. Even where there is a need

to limit use, there are often more subtle options besides placing a strict quota on the number of visitors. Parking can be restricted to established lots, and the number of parking spaces can be limited. The location of access points, the types of facilities that are provided, and the amount of advertising that the area receives can all be controlled to limit use. These subtle means of influencing both the amount and distribution of use can be key to managing greenways without resorting to strict regulations.

Prohibiting or limiting specific activities that are particularly destructive can be another effective strategy. Using motorized vehicles, bicycling, horseback riding, hunting, and walking dogs can all be particularly destructive and in many locations have been prohibited. Sometimes it is possible to implement a zoning strategy in which these uses are allowed in carefully selected areas of the greenway and prohibited elsewhere (Figure 5.6). This strategy of concentrating use is discussed later. Barriers may be needed to exclude or limit certain activities, such as off-road vehicle use. But, it also may be possible to discourage some of these activities in subtle ways. For example, if horse-unloading ramps are not provided, some riders will decide not to use an area.

Figure 5.6 Horses are excluded from the floodplain of the Verde River in Arizona because of the fragile nature of the floodplain and its banks. (Photo by D. Smith.)

Influencing behavior through education and interpretation is one of the strategies with the greatest potential for long-term success. Certain types of impacts, like hacking of trees, can sometimes be eliminated completely by educating recreationists. Other impacts, such as trampling of vegetation, cannot be totally eliminated but can be reduced if there are shifts in people's behavior. Many conservation agencies have produced signs, displays, videotapes, brochures, and even radio and television spots that are designed to teach recreationists how to minimize their impact on the land (Martin and Taylor 1981; Hampton and Cole 1988).

There are several key points to remember in utilizing education and interpretation: (1) make people aware of the link between inappropriate behavior and specific ecological problems, (2) clearly demonstrate appropriate ways for visitors to behave so that problems can be avoided, and (3) encourage a sense of commitment in people to do something about these problems. Traditional methods of persuasive communication include trailhead bulletin boards and brochures explaining to recreationists how to reduce their impacts. Messages about reducing impacts can also be included in interpretive displays along greenways. For example, a display on nesting birds could include a message about the importance of visitors' not getting too close to nesting sites because of the serious consequences of nest abandonment.

Controlling the spatial distribution of recreational use is usually attempted by confining recreationists to trails and other facilities. Two points are crucial: (1) people should be encouraged to stay on planned traffic routes and at activity centers, and (2) these facilities should be located on durable sites. To convince people to use trails, paths must lead where people want to go, and people have to be aware that the trails do so.

Controlling where people go in a greenway requires knowledge about what motivates them, what kinds of behavior are compatible with a particular setting, what an appropriate trail surface is, and how to design and locate signs when destinations cannot be seen from the start of a trail. One technique to use before going to the expense of trail development is first to observe how recreationists use an area, including the informal trail network they develop, and then to design the formal trail system based on the observations.

A common problem is that people often take shortcuts at trail switchbacks, causing unsightly, easily eroded paths. Although shortcutting can be reduced by prohibiting it and by educating people about the problems it creates, the ultimate solution is to make it inconvenient to shortcut the trail or at least to make it appear so (Figure 5.7). This solution can be achieved

Figure 5.7 Properly designed switchbacks that run perpendicular to the direction of water flow are an effective way of preventing trail erosion on steep slopes. (Courtesy of Appalachian Mountain Club.)

by varying the layout of switchbacks, hiding the view of one switchback from another, maintaining a steep grade between switchbacks, and using barriers such as rock outcrops, brush, or boulders.

Barriers are also an effective means of keeping people on surfaces designed for recreational use. The word *barrier* usually brings to mind something obtrusive like a fence, and such a strong barrier may be needed in certain places. More often, however, barriers of native materials, such as large rocks or logs, can be used to define the edges of trails, parking lots, or other areas. In the case of a trail, something as subtle as dense undergrowth may keep people from straying from the tread way. More obtrusive are the scree walls built along the high-altitude trails in the White Mountains in northern New Hampshire. The walls keep people from trampling the adjacent alpine vegetation.

Controlling when all or selected parts of a greenway may be used can be an especially important strategy for minimizing impact on wildlife and soils. Areas can be closed during certain seasons when wildlife are particularly vulnerable, such as when birds are nesting. Also, use can be limited during seasons when soils are water saturated and prone to disturbance. For example, the Long Trail in the Green Mountains in Vermont is closed during the spring mud season, when melting snow saturates high-altitude organic soils. Such strategies can be implemented through regulations, educational and interpretive programs, or a combination of both. Strategies range from prohibiting use and fining violators to attempting to persuade recreationists to avoid certain places at critical times. In Vermont, television stations have broadcast public service announcements explaining the seasonal closing of the Long Trail.

Reducing Site Vulnerability

Site vulnerability can be reduced by locating greenway facilities in more durable areas. Careful attention to the location of trails and other improvements will reduce costs associated with overcoming site limitations or with remedial measures that become necessary after damage occurs. For example, for the reasons discussed earlier, trails should avoid places with wet soils and steep slopes. Wet soils can be bridged, and steep slopes can be negotiated by using switchbacks and drainage devices, but these are costly solutions that require ongoing maintenance.

The location of ecologically sensitive and valuable places also needs to be considered when locating facilities. Sensitive areas that are not especially attractive to recreationists should simply be bypassed. Sensitive

areas, such as stream banks or alpine meadows, that attract recreationists are more problematic. Recreational disturbance can be minimized at these sites by limiting access to spur trails (Figure 5.8) so that only those willing to make the extra effort required to get

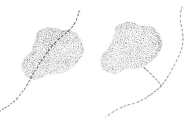

Figure 5.8 Since most people will stay on the main trail, limiting access to sensitive areas to a spur trail may reduce the number of visitors to the sensitive area.

there will go to these special places. The majority of people will stay on the main trail and bypass the sensitive site. Ideally, providing a well-defined system of trails and other improvements is all that is needed to keep visitors away from sensitive areas. In some cases, however, it may be necessary to close highly sensitive areas that would be damaged by even slight use.

A second strategy to deal with sensitive areas is to place natural mulching materials such as wood chips, gravel, and crushed rock on the surface of trails and other places that receive concentrated trampling. In places with very heavy use the surface may have to be paved with asphalt or concrete.

When surfacing trails, it is important to allow for proper drainage of any runoff in such a way that natural drainage systems are not disrupted and erosion is not increased. For this reason permeable materials, such as wood mulch, are often the best choice because they allow water to drain into the soil below. Constructing water bars (Figure 5.9) and other drainage devices or more elaborate systems of ditches and culverts can also help remove water from trails before it gathers enough force to cause significant erosion.

A third option is to shield the site from use by physically separating people from vulnerable elements. Bridges over standing water and elevated walkways over wet soils are good examples of shielding (Figure 5.10). The actual vulnerability of the soil is not

Figure 5.9 Water bars are simple devices commonly used to divert water off the trail surface, which is highly erodible. (Courtesy of Appalachian Mountain Club.)

changed, but the amount of impact is reduced because the soils are no longer being trampled. Providing toilets or outhouses so that human waste is kept to one place and away from water is another way of separating users from the environment. This strategy can be very effective, especially where use is heavy. However, it has several potential drawbacks. Where naturalness is a management objective, a structure such as a toilet may be seen as an intrusion on visitors' recreational experience. The shielding approach also has a high initial cost and usually requires periodic maintenance. On the other hand, this strategy can result in a more comfortable experience for the recreationist and can be a very effective way to protect resources.

Treating Symptoms

A final strategy, rehabilitating sites, involves treating symptoms rather than changing or eliminating root causes. Problems are only addressed once they appear and are in need of attention. This strategy is reactive management rather than proactive design. For example, picnic sites that have lost their vegetation and are eroding can be closed to use, soil can be brought in, and new vegetation can be planted. This solution might be effective in the short term, but if the site is

ever opened to use again, the same problems are likely to reappear. Rehabilitation is most effective when used in concert with actions designed to attack the underlying causes of problems.

Combining Strategies

These design and management strategies and tools range from those that are highly regulatory and restrictive to those that are subtle and do little to hamper the recreationist. Where recreational use is heavy and produces considerable impact on highly valued resources, there may be little alternative but to restrict use. For instance, if the overriding goal of a greenway is to preserve nature, it may be necessary to tightly restrict or perhaps even prohibit recreational use. Where more subtle techniques are likely to be effective, they are preferable because they are less restrictive of the freedom and spontaneity that is important to people's enjoyment of nature.

Although the preceding strategies and tools were discussed one by one, that is not the best way to apply them. There are usually several possible approaches for dealing with a specific problem, and the likelihood of success will increase if a combination of approaches is

Figure 5.10 This elevated walkway separates hikers from the boggy soils underneath. (Photo by D. Cole.)

adopted. A range of potential solutions should be evaluated, and a suite of the most promising should be tried.

Balancing Recreation and Conservation at Craggy Pinnacle

A good example of how these strategies can be adapted to specific situations is the design for Craggy Pinnacle along the Blue Ridge Parkway in North Carolina. Craggy Pinnacle offers some of the finest views and rhododendron displays in the southern Appalachian

Figure 5.11 (top) Craggy Pinnacle is easily reached from the Blue Ridge Parkway. (Courtesy of the National Park Service.) (bottom) With its rock outcrops, the summit is an almost irresistible spot for viewing the surrounding mountains. (Courtesy of Bart Johnson.)

Mountains (Figure 5.11). Visitors hike a half-mile-long trail to the summit where they can enjoy panoramic vistas that are framed by the numerous rock outcrops that encircle the peak. These rock outcrops enhance visitor experiences by offering extensive views, privacy, flat ledges for informal seating, and intriguing places to explore (Johnson 1989a). They also harbor six rare or endangered plant species that account for nearly 90 percent of the vascular plant coverage on the rock outcrops. Uncontrolled visitor use of the area over the years has resulted in a system of informal trails that converge—along with the official trail—at the summit, where trampling of the rare flora is a serious problem.

Confronted with the problems of informal trail development and damage of rare plants, researchers from the National Park Service carried out a trial management program in an attempt to solve these problems. They surveyed visitor use and the distribution of rare plants and assessed the microhabitat needs of the rare plants. Parkway administrators closed unofficial trails with brush and signs and monitored the effectiveness of the closures (Johnson 1989a).

They found that visitor use was as high as 484 people per day during the height of the fall foliage season and that as many as 50 percent of those users arrived at the summit by way of unofficial trails. Use at the peak was concentrated in an area of just 1000 square feet, of which 750 are rock outcrops with rare plant habitat. The plant survey found conditions that ranged from areas that were relatively untrampled to completely decimated places where up to a foot of soil had been eroded, leaving bare rock exposed (Johnson 1989b).

Initial attempts to close trails with brush were not very successful. Over a two-month period, ten of the eleven brush barriers were either destroyed or rendered ineffective. In another attempt small signs that read "Fragile Habitat — Area Closed" were placed in front of the brush. The signs helped dramatically—only one brush barrier was rendered ineffective in two months, and the number of ineffective barriers increased to only three after the fall season. Managers concluded that

Figure 5.12 Design of an overlook for Craggy Pinnacle that will (1) concentrate use in a designated area, (2) protect rare plants from trampling, and (3) provide an attractive place for people to view the surrounding mountains. (Redrawn with permission from plan by Bart Johnson.)

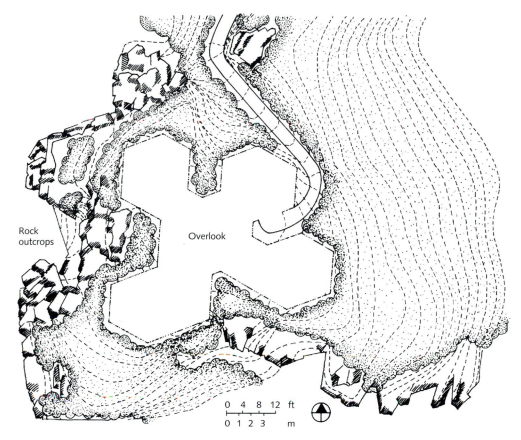

Rock outcrops

Overlook

0 4 8 12 ft
0 1 2 3 m

the small interpretive signs were critical to keeping people on official trails, but that the signs and brush barriers were still only a partial solution to the problem (Johnson 1989c).

From observing visitor behavior came the idea for a larger overlook platform that will concentrate use, shield the rare plants from visitors, and retain most of the desired aesthetic attributes of the rock outcroppings. Once constructed, the stone-walled overlook will provide views and ledges to sit on (Figure 5.12). Alcoves in the overlook will give visitors a greater sense of privacy than before, as well as interesting nooks to explore. Interpretive displays will both enhance visitor enjoyment and, by explaining the fragility of the site, increase the likelihood that visitors will stay within the walls of the overlook while they are at the summit of Craggy Pinnacle (Johnson 1989a).

With visitor use better controlled and the underlying cause of the problem solved, the final step will be restoring the damaged plant communities. Experiments with propagating and reestablishing the rare plants are being conducted. In addition, the microhabitat assessment is helping to identify the habitat needs of each species, making it more likely that a self-sustaining community can eventually be reestablished (Johnson 1989b).

Craggy Pinnacle offers a number of important lessons for greenway design and management. This example shows how site research and experimentation can be used effectively to identify and respond to the specific underlying problems faced by an area. In this case, both visitor behavior and environmental conditions were analyzed to help identify the root cause of the problems. A variety of strategies are being used to

119

deal with the conflicts: visitor use is being concentrated in a smaller space, vulnerable sites are being shielded from visitor use, certain areas are being closed with barriers, education and interpretation are being used to change destructive visitor behavior, and damaged sites are being rehabilitated. None of these techniques by itself would have the likelihood of success that this combination does.

Conclusions and Guidelines

Where greenways have the twin goals of providing recreational opportunities and preserving nature, managers are challenged to maximize the synergism that exists between these goals while minimizing the conflict. The key to the latter is to develop an understanding of both the recreational visitors and the environmental constraints. Successful recreation design and management avoid fighting against what people want to do; rather, they channel recreationists' desires in ways that will have less impact on the environment. Designers and managers may also have to increase the durability of sites to withstand use, and in some cases they may have to shield the site from intensive recreational use.

The following suggestions, organized by spatial scale, should help guide the design and management of greenways:

Selecting Alignments

1. Select places for recreation that offer settings and recreational opportunities that are scarce in the surrounding region so that unique recreational areas are protected.
2. Select places that offer a diversity of settings so that a variety of areas are protected.
3. Design networks of greenways so that there are opportunities for both short and extended recreational visits.

Setting Widths

1. Set boundaries so that greenways are wide enough to provide both high-impact corridors of concentrated recreational use (if there is to be any recreation) and zones that are virtually undisturbed. This action will provide a balance between recreational opportunities and nature preservation by separating the potentially conflicting uses.
2. Increase greenway width as the sensitivity of the natural resources within them increases, as the importance of ecological values increases, and as the quantity and destructiveness of recreationists increase. Wider greenways provide greater opportunities for separating uses through zoning and for channeling use toward durable areas and away from sensitive places.

Preparing Site Designs and Management Plans

1. Locate and design facilities (trails, access points, picnic areas, visitor centers, etc.) to enhance recreational experiences as well as minimize environmental impact.
2. Concentrate visitor use on surfaces that separate users from the environment wherever levels of recreational use are high. Alternately, channel use to ground surfaces that are either inherently durable or that have been modified to be more durable.
3. Locate and design facilities to account for both the sensitivity of ecosystems and the type and amount of recreational use anticipated.
4. Use interpretation and education to reduce impact. Visitors should be made aware of (a) the value of sensitive natural resources, (b) the problems that certain types of behavior cause, and (c) how they can behave to minimize impact.
5. Use subtle means of encouraging appropriate behavior from visitors instead of restricting or eliminating access. Restrictions, closures, and law

enforcement, however, become more important with the increasing value and vulnerability of the resources needing protection.

6. Establish a system of zones—based on the capability of the landscape—that allows certain activities only in designated zones. These zones will provide a diversity of recreational activities while separating particularly destructive types of recreation from sensitive areas.

7. Discourage off-trail use by (a) creating, when appropriate, trails that go where people want to go, (b) making certain that people know the trail goes there, and (c) providing a well-defined trail of adequate width with an appropriate surface for walking. Maintaining dense vegetation, placing logs and rocks along a trail, and routing a trail through rough terrain can all help to keep people on a trail. Fences and signs should be used as last resorts.

8. Avoid wet soils and steep slopes when routing trails. Where wet soils are unavoidable, they should be bridged, taking care not to disrupt the natural drainage. Erosion of short steep stretches of trail can be minimized by using steps or strategically placed water bars. Longer stretches should incorporate carefully designed switchbacks. Damage to switchbacks will be minimized if they have tight turns and are well drained and if shortcutting is discouraged by placing the turn in heavy forest or by taking advantage of rock outcrops, cliffs, and boulders.

9. If heavily used trails are to be surfaced, choose a material based on user requirements, aesthetic considerations, impact potential, and the cost of construction and maintenance. Permeable surfaces should be used when possible because they function similarly to the natural cover by allowing water to permeate the soil. If an impervious material is used, special attention must be paid to drainage and the potential for erosion.

10. Minimize trail width and clearing in forest interiors to reduce the attractiveness of trails to edge-oriented species of wildlife that could displace more sensitive interior-forest species.

11. Design spur trails off of primary trails to provide access to ecologically sensitive areas, rather than routing a primary trail through or along a sensitive area.

12. Locate centers of activity, such as parking lots, picnic areas, and visitor centers, at the edge or outside of a greenway. Locate them in environments that are common in the area and durable.

13. Keep the number of travel routes within centers of activity to a minimum, clearly delineate them, and, if necessary, harden them. Barriers may be needed to confine and direct traffic. Subtle barriers, such as vegetation or grade variations, should be used as much as possible.

14. Use several management strategies and actions when attacking a specific problem. Most often a combination of approaches will increase the likelihood of success.

15. Consider all the likely consequences of any course of action. An action undertaken in one place to attack one problem may cause changes in other areas or create other problems.

Sources of Additional Information

This chapter has dealt with a wide variety of material in only a few pages. For more information on recreational impacts on the environment see *Wildland Recreation: Ecology and Management* by W. E. Hammitt and D. N. Cole (1987) and *Visitor Impact Management: A review of Research* by F. R. Kuss et al. (1990). An excellent annotated bibliography on recreational impacts on wildlife, titled *Nonconsumptive Outdoor Recreation: An Annotated Bibliography of Human-Wildlife Interactions,* was prepared by Boyle and Samson (1983). Unfortunately, few books are available that offer much detail on management strategies and tools. However, a good source for trail design and management is *Trail Building and Maintenance* by Proudman and Rajala (1981).

References

Albuquerque Parks and Recreation Department, Open Space Division. 1987. Rio Grande Valley State Park management plan. Albuquerque, N. Mex.

Boyle, S. A., and F. B. Samson. 1983. Nonconsumptive outdoor recreation: An annotated bibliography of human-wildlife interactions. USDI Fish and Wildlife Service Special Scientific Report—Wildlife No. 252, Washington, D.C.

Bratton, S. P., M. G. Hickler, and J. H. Graves. 1979. Trail erosion patterns in Great Smoky Mountains National Park. *Environmental Management* 3:431–45.

Cole, D. N. 1987a. Effects of three seasons of experimental trampling on five montane forest communities and a grassland in western Montana, USA. *Biological Conservation* 40:219–44.

———. 1987b. Research on soil and vegetation in wilderness: A state-of-knowledge review. Pages 135–77 in R. C. Lucas, comp., *Proceedings, National Wilderness Research Conference: Issues, State-of-knowledge, Future Directions*. USDA Forest Service General Technical Report INT–220, Ogden, Utah.

Dale, D. R., and T. Weaver. 1974. Trampling effects on vegetation of the trail corridors of North Rocky Mountain forests. *Journal of Applied Ecology* 11:761–72.

Dickman, M., and M. Dorais. 1977. The impact of human trampling on phosphorus loading to a small lake in Gatineau Park, Quebec, Canada. *Journal of Environmental Management* 5:335–44.

Dorrance, M. J., P. J. Savage, and D. E. Huff. 1975. Effects of snowmobiles on white-tailed deer. *Journal of Wildlife Management* 39:563–69.

Ferguson, M. S. D., and L. B. Keith. 1982. Influence of nordic skiing on distribution of moose and elk in Elk Island National Park, Alberta. *Canadian Field-Naturalist* 96:69–78.

Geist, V. 1978. Behavior. Pages 283–96 in J. L. Schmidt and D. L. Gilbert, eds., *Big Game of North America: Ecology and Management*. Stackpole Books, Harrisburg, Pa.

Hammitt, W. E., and D. N. Cole. 1987. *Wildland Recreation: Ecology and Management*. John Wiley and Sons, New York.

Hampton, B., and D. Cole. 1988. *Soft Paths: How to Enjoy the Wilderness Without Harming It*. Stackpole Books, Harrisburg, Pa.

Hickman, S. 1990. Evidence of edge species attraction to nature trails within deciduous forest. *Natural Areas Journal* 10 (1): 3–5.

Johnson, B. R. 1989a. Footprints on rare plants: Habitat protection through design, interpretation and restoration. *Georgia Landscape*, Spring, 11–13.

———. 1989b. Detailed microhabitat assessment accompanies restoration of rare plants, rock outcrop communities. *Restoration and Management Notes* 7 (2): 97–98.

———. 1989c. Interpretive signs increase effectiveness of brush-pile barriers. *Restoration and Management Notes* 7 (2): 103.

King, J. G., and A. C. Mace, Jr. 1974. Effects of recreation on water quality. *Journal of the Water Pollution Control Federation* 46:2453–59.

King, M. M., and G. W. Workman. 1986. Responses of desert bighorn sheep to human harassment: Management implications. *Transactions of the North American Wildlife and Natural Resources Conference* 51:74–85.

Kuss, F. R., A. R. Graefe, and J. J. Vaske. 1990. Visitor impact management: A review of research. National Parks and Conservation Association, Washington, D. C.

Liddle, M. J. 1975. A selective review of the ecological effects of human trampling on natural ecosystems. *Biological Conservation* 7:17–36.

Liddle, M. J., and K. G. Moore. 1974. The microclimate of sand dune tracks: The relative contribution of vegetation removal and soil compression. *Journal of Applied Ecology* 11:1057–68.

MacArthur, R. A., V. Geist, and R. H. Johnston. 1982. Cardiac and behavioral responses of mountain sheep to human disturbance. *Journal of Wildlife Management* 46:351–58.

McEwen, D., and S. R. Tocher. 1976. Zone management: Key to controlling recreational impact in developed campsites. *Journal of Forestry* 74:90–93.

Manning, R. E. 1979. Impacts of recreation on riparian soils and vegetation. *Water Resources Bulletin* 15:30–43.

Martin, B. H., and D. T. Taylor. 1981. *Informing Backcountry Visitors: A Catalog of Techniques*. Appalachian Mountain Club, Boston.

Monti, P., and E. E. Mackintosh. 1979. Effects of camping on surface soil properties in the boreal forest region of northwestern Ontario, Canada. *Soil Science Society of America Journal* 43:1024–29.

Proudman, R. D., and R. Rajala. 1981. *Trail Building and Maintenance*. 2d ed. Appalachian Mountain Club, Boston.

Singer, F. J. 1978. Behavior of mountain goats in relation to U.S. Highway 2, Glacier National Park, Montana. *Journal of Wildlife Management* 42:591–97.

Speight, M. C. D. 1973. Outdoor recreation and its ecological effects: A bibliography and review. Discussion Paper in Conservation 4, University College, London, England.

Titus, J. R., and L. W. VanDruff. 1981. Response of the common loon to recreational pressure in the Boundary Waters Canoe Area, northeastern Minnesota. Wildlife Monograph 79, The Wildlife Society, Bethesda, Md.

Weaver, T., and D. Dale. 1978. Trampling effects of hikers, motorcycles and horses in meadows and forests. *Journal of Applied Ecology* 15:451–58.

Paul Cawood Hellmund

A Method for Ecological Greenway Design

6

Greenway designers who hope to create greenways that reach their full potential to protect natural processes may need to reexamine long-held conceptions about how to create a design. As readers of the preceding chapters may surmise, there is no simple checklist for designing a greenway. This is especially true when the greenway is expected to perform such ambitious functions as maintaining or enhancing biodiversity and water resources and providing people the opportunity to be in nature. With fewer and fewer opportunities to conserve nature, it is incumbent upon us to pursue multiple goals for almost every greenway, no matter how small or how urban it may be.

Some models and methods of design, particularly those that cannot accommodate the changes that are inevitably part of landscapes, are not well suited to ecological design. For example, one of the traditional concerns of landscape architects has been preserving or enhancing views. But, narrowly pursuing visual goals by trying to capture or re-create a static image can have

tremendous costs, both financial (in trying to maintain that picture) and ecological (in the loss of ecological health that comes with attempts to block or ignore landscape change).

This chapter presents a method for ecological greenway design. The method is intended for use by anyone wanting to design a greenway based on ecological principles. Professional designers, planners, foresters, and scientists may find it useful, as may volunteer groups who selectively rely on experts. In this chapter the term *designer* is not meant to refer solely to professional designers such as landscape architects but more broadly to anyone who undertakes the design of a greenway. This is not to say that in most situations an ecologically sensitive greenway can be designed without expert advice. Scientists of many kinds are indispensable in explaining the ecology of the landscapes under study, and landscape architects, planners, and other experts can help create designs based on that understanding.

The method is flexible and can be used for many different kinds of greenway projects. It is divided into four stages that are based on successively finer scales, although some projects will not go through each stage. The four stages correspond to the scales into which the guidelines of the previous chapters were grouped so that at each stage one is guided through decision making based on ecological knowledge. The method is intended to bridge the gap between scientific knowledge, such as that presented in earlier chapters, and the practical design of greenways. It should help elucidate the ecological context of greenway design and show how to consider ecological integrity at each design stage. This chapter should make clear that the method itself does not provide any direct answers. Instead it identifies important questions and suggests ways to go about answering them for the specific landscapes of a particular greenway project.

Experiences with the Blue Ridge Parkway illustrate some of the special concerns of designing linear conservation areas. Of utmost importance in the design of the parkway, which snakes along ridgetops of the Appalachian Mountains in Virginia and North Carolina

for 469 miles, were the dramatic panoramas of the area's ridges and valleys (Jolley 1969; Figure 6.1). At places the boundaries of the parkway are barely wider than the two-lane roadway at its center (Figure 6.2). This tight fit did not matter much in the early years after construction began in 1935 because there was little neighboring development to compromise the dramatic views. (In many segments of the parkway the topography is severe enough that development will probably never threaten the views.) But on lands adjacent to the parkway where suburbs or other kinds of development have been built, visitors now see very unparklike scenes.

Views from the parkway differ widely from season to season. A gas station that in summer is screened by deciduous vegetation becomes at other times of the year part of the parkway scenery. Segments of the parkway that are sylvan tunnels of emerald green in summer offer expansive panoramic vistas of brown and gray in leafless winter. Thus, the visual experience of visitors differs not only from year to year as new development encroaches but also from season to season as the changing vegetation redefines the perception of dis-

Figure 6.1 The Blue Ridge Parkway was built, starting in 1935, to capture dramatic panoramic views of the southern Appalachian Mountains. Although it was not created with strictly ecological goals, the parkway offers many lessons about the challenges of linear conservation. (Historic photograph courtesy of the U.S. National Park Service, 1950.)

Figure 6.2 In some locales the Blue Ridge Parkway is barely wider than its roadway, making its scenery vulnerable to intrusions from neighboring properties. (Historic photograph courtesy of the U.S. National Park Service, 1950.)

124

tance and the visual dominance of landscape elements.

These themes—landscape change and the impacts of neighbors on narrow conservation areas—are two of the main concerns faced when trying to integrate a greenway's design into an area's ecology. Frequently greenways are narrow strips optimistically designed to protect dynamic and potentially wide-ranging phenomena. In many ways fixing greenway boundaries is like trying to hit a moving target: the ecological processes that boundaries are meant to contain may shift frequently.

Of course, there are significant differences between designing a road that will offer motorists a sequence of beautiful vistas and designing a greenway that will accommodate migrating wildlife and help maintain the quality of stream water. A few discordant views along the Blue Ridge Parkway may not be what the typical tourist comes to these mountains to see, but they alone probably would not cause a visitor to suddenly stop, turn around, and go back the other way. Wildlife, however, react differently. Depending on the sensitivity of the species, one disruption can make a greenway entirely useless as a wildlife corridor. Similarly, pollutants entering a stream at even one point can have a devastating effect on water quality and riparian life for a great distance downstream. (Pollution can cause effects upstream as well, as is pointed out in chapter 4, when it blocks organisms from moving in that direction.)

These observations about the Blue Ridge Parkway and the differences between static design and design that embodies landscape change point to the need for a greenway design process that recognizes the *dynamics* of landscapes. The susceptibility of the parkway to visual intrusions hints at the high degree of interaction between greenways and their neighbors. This interaction underlines the need to fully consider *context* when creating a greenway design. This chapter develops a framework and method for such an approach, an approach that encourages the ecological design of greenways.

An Ecological Greenway Design Method

The ecological greenway design method is one designer's attempt to integrate the concepts of the earlier chapters and to suggest how these concepts can be put to work in creating greenways of all sorts. The method has been drawn from many other sources in addition to the previous chapters of this book, including findings in the sciences (especially landscape ecology), interviews with people from across North America who have designed or managed greenways, the literatures of ecological planning and design, and the author's academic and professional design experience. A detailed listing of the method may be found in the appendix at the end of this chapter. Because it is not easy to get an overview of the method simply by scanning the table, the process is summarized in Figure 6.3 and characterized in the following discussion. The balance of the chapter details the four design stages and discusses the background of the method.

The method is not an attempt to present *the* definitive, universal procedure for ecological greenway design according to some rigidly defined recipe of guidelines (although it may be tempting to use the book's guidelines in this way). Rather, it is a framework that seeks to raise important ecological issues of greenway design through a careful sequence of questions and to suggest ways of answering those questions. It is the job of the project designer to tailor the design process to local conditions and requirements. The method should be augmented by posing and answering questions about issues specific to the project.

Each of the method's four stages corresponds to a different scale in the process of greenway design. At each stage the designer is presented with one or more broad questions and, most often, several more specific, subsidiary questions. By systematically answering these questions, project-specific goals, objectives, and actions can be identified. Also associated with each stage are design guidelines that can be used, along with relevant guidelines from the earlier chapters of this book, for

Figure 6.3 Summary of the four-stage ecological greenway design method. The questions posed at each stage help narrow the possible greenway solutions in the region. Stage 1: Reviewing the region to understand its opportunities and constraints for creating a greenway. Stage 2: Selecting project goals and key uses for the greenway and defining a study swath within the region with good potential for a greenway. Stage 3: Selecting and evaluating alternative alignments for a greenway and then locally setting widths that respond to local ecological conditions. Stage 4: Creating and implementing site designs to locate uses and facilities within the greenway and preparing and carrying out management plans.

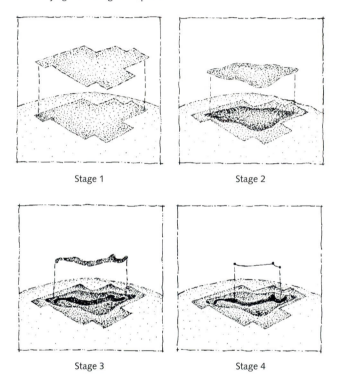

Stage 1   Stage 2

Stage 3   Stage 4

guidance in answering the questions. Further assistance in answering the questions is offered by the more specific steps or actions suggested with each subsidiary question. In this manner, at each stage options are evaluated and alternatives narrowed.

Put another way, the greenway design method is a process of subtracting, that is, of using the best knowledge available at each stage to remove from consideration those areas of the landscape that do not meet the goals of the project. It is a process similar to the way a sculptor might approach her work. At the start she may have a somewhat vague idea of the sculpture that she wants to create. She goes in search of a block of

marble that seems suited to the project. If she finds something that looks like a match she buys it. (In searching, however, the artist may discover a piece of stone that inspires her to consider a project totally different from the one that launched her search.)

Back in her studio, the artist begins investigating the slab she has selected by making a few cuts here and there and watching what happens to the stone. From then on, as she chips away at the marble, her thinking constantly goes back and forth between the image she has in mind, which is evolving and becoming more distinct, and what she sees being uncovered in the stone. Early in her work the artist may decide that what she is discovering in the stone is better suited to some other image, which she has the option of pursuing. But before long her chipping away will leave few options. At that point the sculptor is limited to two choices. She can continue pursuing the original image with this piece of stone, or she can leave it for another that might be better suited to her project.

This process of repeatedly exploring and evaluating and then deciding to go forward or not is the same as the one used in the greenway design method. In trying to develop greenways that live up to their full ecological potential, designers are trying to implement very ambitious goals for what greenways should be and do. At any given time these goals are being considered and evaluated within the framework of what is known about a particular landscape at that moment. It is clear that more will be learned about that landscape in subsequent stages, but at each stage, before more of the area being studied is removed from consideration (chipped away), it is important to reassess how well the goals of the design process are being realized. The design method formalizes and gives structure to these cycles of decision making by creating four stages of investigation. (The sculptor, in contrast, using a personal, intuitive process of design, does not face many of the requirements typical of greenway design: working with groups of decision makers, having to explain the design process including its goals, objectives, values, and methods to the public, and creating a product that is dynamic.)

Because the design process is divided into distinct stages, issues are addressed at the most relevant scale or scales. Many greenway concerns are scale dependent. Problems can result if a concern is investigated at an inappropriate scale. It is the same for the sculptor and her stone. Early on as she is roughing out the form of the sculpture, she knows it is inappropriate to be concerned with finishing detailed parts of the sculpture that now are rightfully very rough blocky shapes.

Early on in the greenway design method (Stage 2), designers are asked to identify potential nodes. But because this identification is part of identifying a broad study swath and not the selection of specific greenway alignments, there is no detailed analysis of the nodes. That analysis comes in Stage 3, when the entire swath is carefully evaluated for nodes. Even though at Stage 3 the earlier assessment of nodes is disregarded, this does not mean that the earlier steps are unnecessary. Those earlier steps, somewhat crude and quick, prepare the way for later refinement.

Aldo Leopold advised readers of his book on wildlife management that the techniques given in his book "represent examples of how to think, observe, deduce, and experiment, rather than specifications of what to do" (Leopold 1933, xxxii). It is in a similar spirit that the suggested steps are offered at each stage of the greenway design process: they are offered not as strict fail-safe procedures but as examples of how to think through the questions. Designers should not view the method as rigid nor be afraid to pursue alternative questions and make improvements appropriate to their own project.

Greenway projects typically *start* with assumptions about where the greenway should be located and perhaps about what its functions should fulfill. The greenway design method, however, asks project designers to take a broader perspective. It calls not only for examining the status and prospects of all kinds of conservation throughout the region but also for considering multiple-

function goals. Also, designers of those greenways intended primarily for recreation might feel the method is too detailed for what they see primarily as a simple task of laying out trails. The discussion here attempts to show that the design method with its parallel structures for addressing biodiversity, water, *and* recreational issues can help ensure that ecological issues are effectively addressed even when the main focus is recreation.

The method, which is intended for designing individual greenways, can also be adapted for creating networks of greenways. But, greenways are only one form of protection in the conservation palette, and they cannot usually be planned without simultaneously thinking about the other ways of protecting nature, especially through extensive protected areas. Often these extensive areas form the intermediate and end nodes that greenways connect.

Project Goals and Characteristics of the Method

It is always important to keep a project true to its goals and to know why a specific design or research activity is being carried out. In this method goals lead to broad questions, broad questions are answered by researching subsidiary questions, and subsidiary questions are answered with the help of suggested steps and guidelines. This lineage means that every action should be traceable back to one or more project goals; if this tracing cannot be done, then an action is probably not directly supporting the project. This accountability not only keeps the design true to original intent but also helps explain the rationale and development of the project to the public or to officials.

Several goals are integrated directly into the method: protecting water resources, protecting biological diversity, and providing recreation (as long as recreation does not compromise the other two goals). Protecting ecological integrity is a fundamental concern of the design method because of the current assault on the natural world. (See chapters 2 and 4 for discussions of ecological integrity.) Recreation is also included as a goal because the long-term sustainability of protected areas will depend on public support and understanding of them. Certainly many greenways have been and will continue to be created principally for recreation, but this purpose does not relieve designers of the responsibility to protect ecological integrity. Nor should greenway projects devoted primarily to protecting plants, animals, and water automatically dismiss recreation if compatible forms of recreation can be accommodated.

James Thorne's goals and objectives for maintaining ecological integrity (see chapter 2) were critical in creating the method. Other goals, complementary to

Thorne's, also influenced the design method (Table 6.1). Also shown in Table 6.1 are practical techniques that have been integrated into the method in support of each goal. These techniques are presented in more detail in a later discussion of the four stages of the design method.

Integrating an understanding of a landscape's ecology into the design of greenways—as challenging as it may be—is crucial to the success of the greenway. Greenway ecology differs significantly from the ecology of other, typically nonlinear, conservation areas. This difference is primarily due to the fact that a typical greenway abuts many elements along its path. Also, because of their long, narrow shape, greenways have a high edge-to-area ratio and usually many more neighbors than a typical squarish park of the same size (Figure 6.4). This narrowness can make desirable greenway functions, such as wildlife movement, water purification, or recreation, more vulnerable to influence by adjacent land uses than these functions would be in other parks of similar area. Along with more neighbors, there are proportionally more areas within the greenway that are penetrated by edge effects, including potential intruders (pets, pollutants, people, etc.). (See discussions in earlier chapters, especially chapters 2, 3, and 4.)

One characteristic of the design method deserves special note. The ability to make decisions with limited information is vital because in many situations there will be no means of getting other than rudimentary data about a place. Being able to move forward in the design process with less than complete data is a key characteristic. This capability, however, should not be used as an excuse to avoid thorough inventorying when it is possible and needed.

Sometimes more detailed information may surface at a later point. With the method's open structure and use of guidelines as a mechanism for recording how decisions are made, it is a straightforward matter to trace through the process and make adjustments in the design based on new discoveries. Or, even if it is too

Table 6.1 Goals of the greenway design method

The design method should be:	Techniques to achieve the goals
adaptable so that the process can be adjusted for the uniqueness of local ecological conditions.	Questions are raised about *local ecological conditions* and their spatial and temporal patterns.
heuristic to keep track of issues that are raised at one point in the design process and need attention later.	Throughout the process whenever important ecological issues are raised that will affect later decisions, the issues are *recorded and carried forward.*
scale sensitive so that ecological issues are addressed at an appropriate scale or scales.	Careful distinction is made for the *scale* at which decisions are made.
driven by *specific* rather than generic or vague values.	*Key uses* serve as lenses through which to view the landscape and with which to make design decisions.
systemic, in order to look at the landscape as an interrelated whole, not as isolated pieces.	The process is grounded in concepts from landscape ecology and ecological landscape planning that recognize the *dynamic interrelated nature of landscapes.*
frugal and *flexible in its use of data,* so that even with limited data the method makes good use of what are available and can be updated as better information becomes available.	Many of the *suggested steps* of the design method can be carried out with whatever resolution data are available and then rerun when better data are available.

128

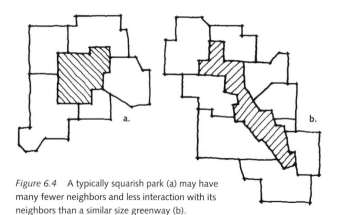

Figure 6.4 A typically squarish park (a) may have many fewer neighbors and less interaction with its neighbors than a similar size greenway (b).

late to make changes to the earliest parts of the greenway, unimplemented portions of the design may be corrected.

Several issues that may be relevant to the design of some greenways are not discussed in this chapter. Important, related subjects outside the focus of this book, such as economics and community participation, for example, are touched on only briefly or not at all. In most cases, such topics are rightfully part of greenway design, and it is the designer's responsibility to incorporate them as appropriate.

The design method provides the most detailed help through the point in Stage 3 where greenway boundaries are set. The method offers more general help for site design and management, the final stage, because the variability of project goals and site ecology make it nearly impossible to outline design steps without knowledge of project specifics.

The Role of Guidelines

Guidelines play an important and varied role in the method and that is why most of the chapters in this book conclude with guidelines. In general, these guidelines suggest how to decide what conditions contribute most to maintaining or enhancing ecological health under particular circumstances. For each stage of the method, several additional guidelines are included in the Appendix. Other guidelines will be cre-

ated in the process of carrying out the design method, for example, through interviewing scientists, through reading articles in scientific journals, or through discoveries in the process of design or management. (See the case studies of the Santa Monica Mountains and The Woodlands in chapter 7 for examples of how guidelines have been used.)

At its best, an *ecological* guideline encapsulates what is central to an ecological issue and brings that knowledge into the design process with as little misrepresentation as possible. An ecological guideline thus serves as a bridge between scientific knowledge and greenway design. The confidence with which a guideline can be applied will depend on how well understood its particular subject is. Recording well-studied and well-explained ecological phenomena, such as an aspect of the surface flow of water, may be straightforward. Other guidelines, however, may be closer to rules of thumb, garnered from practical experience and viewed as best guesses under the circumstances. Although all of the guidelines can contribute to greenway design, the source of each guideline and some sense of its reliability should be recorded and reviewed before the guideline is applied.

Most of the guidelines in this book are too general to be applied directly to the specifics of a given project. They are intended as *guidelines* and not hard and fast rules. The expertise of ecologists and other kinds of scientists who know about local conditions will be needed to adapt most guidelines to local conditions. For example, a guideline from chapter 4 states that areas with a high potential for erosion, such as bridge crossings or steep slopes, should have a high priority for protection. This guideline warns that areas with high erosion potential can have a major effect on water quality within a riparian corridor and thus should be carefully considered. The guideline directs the designer to investigate specific soil types, slope, and erosion potential, and, perhaps with the assistance of a soil scientist, to determine what local combinations of such factors may contribute to a high erosion potential.

Uses of the Method

The design method's open structure allows the design process to be customized to local conditions. Thus, designers of greenway projects of all sizes and situations should find the method useful. Projects may be in landscapes where many options exist for greenways, in locales where the basic orientation of the greenway is already established by set end points or the location of a river or former railroad line, or in landscapes where development severely limits greenways to very specific boundaries. In other words, projects may be in landscapes of any type along the landscape modification gradient (Figure 6.5), although the four stages of the design method may be somewhat curtailed in more developed landscapes (see chapter 2 for a discussion of the gradient).

Designers in many urban landscapes, for instance, may find fewer of the method's suggested steps applicable because of the dominance of urban land uses over natural spaces. With a superabundance of pavement and buildings, greenway boundaries may be all but set, and there may be no opportunity to encourage wildlife movement except that of less desirable, opportunistic species, such as raccoons. Or, with little plantable, undeveloped space there may be limited opportunity to buffer urban streams from non–point source pollution by restoring native vegetation. Yet, the portions of greenways that pass through urban settings can have a significant effect on flood control, and they provide, even if only with nonnative vegetation, some green to inspire people. (See Anne Whiston Spirn's book *The Granite Garden: Urban Nature and Human Design* (1984), for a discussion of the challenge of nurturing urban nature.)

Community Participation

There are many reasons why community members need to be involved in greenway design. For some public projects the law may require community involvement. But more importantly, involving people can help sustain a greenway over the long term. Because greenways' abundant edges can make intrusion easy (by people, pets, livestock, exotic plants, etc.), they can be difficult to manage. If the public, especially owners of property adjacent to the greenway, understand and are supportive of the greenway and its goals, then they may help monitor the greenway and notify managers when there are problems. In some cases, greenways may not be publicly owned lands but legally or even informally designated thoroughfares across private lands. Instituting such a greenway requires a great deal of public understanding and cooperation; maintaining it can require even more.

Members of the public can play important roles throughout the design and management of a greenway. They can help identify project goals and can provide volunteer services ranging from resource inventorying to site construction and maintenance. If members of the public play a part in developing a greenway plan, they are more apt to understand the needs of the greenway and to support it. The design process can help educate the public about what it takes to sustain a

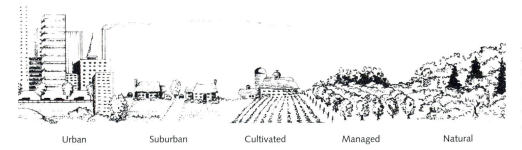

Urban   Suburban   Cultivated   Managed   Natural

Figure 6.5 The general characterisics of a greenway will in large degree depend on where it is located along the landscape modification gradient. The greenway design method can be adjusted for projects at different places along the gradient.

greenway and how they will benefit from the greenway. An advisory committee made up of members of the public, government officials, scientists, other technical experts, and representatives of interested organizations may be a helpful addition to the design process.

Involving the public is important even if the greenway will have little or no recreational component. The involvement will help develop support for the greenway. Allowing people to enter a greenway whose purpose is to protect sensitive biodiversity or water resources may be possible at carefully controlled points, such as overlooks. These points can be used for educating the public about how the greenway functions and why people are excluded.

The Four Stages of Greenway Design

Discussed below are the questions and steps for the four stages of the design method (from appendix) and the major concepts important at each stage.

Stage 1: Understanding Regional Context

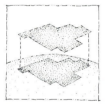 The first stage of the method is intended to help designers step back from a greenway project and look beyond what may already seem to be obvious solutions based on local perceptions. Starting a project with a greenway alignment or firm project goals already in mind may cause designers to overlook a better alignment or neglect a conservation need that may be more urgent.

The start of a project "is a time for letting impressions sink in, for listening to people, not telling them, for questions, not answers, for dabbling and generally messing about within shadows that only slowly take form," says landscape architect John Lyle (1985, 136). He warns designers to avoid reaching premature conclusions that may seem all too obvious at the start of a project. Getting a general sense of the region within which a greenway is being considered and becoming

familiar with the ecology of the landscapes found there are appropriate beginnings. (Forman and Godron define a region as "an area, usually containing a number of landscapes, that is determined by a complex of climatic, physiographic, biological, economic, social, and cultural characteristics" [Forman and Godron 1986, 598].) Because of the high degree of interaction between greenways and their surroundings, the significance of understanding the region and its landscapes—which will be the context for the greenway—cannot be overemphasized.

Greenways are effective when they maintain or enhance natural features and processes; otherwise they would hardly be worth the effort it takes to create them. Hence the crucial questions at the first stage aim to determine to what extent linear conservation zones can be useful in protecting important landscape features and processes in the region. Furthermore, since most greenways make connections, the nodes that a greenway might connect must also be examined.

Existing protected areas should not automatically be assumed to be effective conservation nodes simply because they have been given an official designation. They may be degraded or otherwise incompatible with greenway functions. The locations and sizes of these "free" (i.e., already protected) lands should influence the alignment of a greenway only if they have qualities and uses that are compatible with the goals of the greenway. For instance, if a heavily used recreational area is planned as a significant intermediate node in a wildlife greenway, then that area may act more as a barrier, interrupting the flow of wildlife.

Work at this stage is focused more on determining the overall importance of the region's features and the potential means for protecting them than on determining precisely where they are within the region. Maps, such as of publicly owned lands, zoning, or general vegetation types, may be collected and used at this stage. But, mapping is generally broadbrush and probably not computerized because of the expense it would entail.

(Broad question) 1.1. *Are there significant unprotected biological, water, recreational, or other features in the region that could be maintained or enhanced by a greenway or network of greenways?*

— **(Subsidiary question) 1.1a.** *What are the characteristics of greenways that successfully maintain or enhance natural features and processes?*

Before it is possible to identify which of a region's natural features could be protected by a greenway, it is necessary to understand what a greenway is good at protecting and what it is not good at protecting. Other chapters in this book, other books on greenways, as well as articles in conservation journals can help describe the characteristics of successful greenways. Two organizations, one part of the federal government and the other private, may be of assistance: the U.S. National Park Service's River, Trail, and Conservation Assistance program and the Conservation Fund's American Greenways program.

— **1.1b.** *Are there significant opportunities for maintaining or enhancing biological diversity in the region? What are the constraints?*

— **1.1c.** *Are there significant opportunities for maintaining or enhancing water resources in the region? What are the constraints?*

— **1.1d.** *Are there significant opportunities for maintaining or enhancing outdoor recreation in the region? What are the constraints?*

— **1.1e.** *Are there other significant opportunities for greenway development in the region? Are there any other constraints?*

Determining how significant natural features and processes are is not usually an easy matter. Although judging local significance may be easy because a locale may be well known by many people, judging significance within successively larger areas is progressively harder because fewer and fewer people know the areas from personal experience. Winter deer yards that may

be common in an area under study may be the only ones for miles around. Personal experience alone often is not enough to assess the significance of a local occurrence of a species or a landscape feature. This assessment is a task for public and private organizations that look specifically at the issues being evaluated. For example, the Natural Heritage Program of most states can help determine the relative significance of plant and animal species and communities in a state. If national, state, or local government agencies or private conservation organizations have been working in an area, there may be an extensive understanding of its ecology and conservation needs. If there has been little or no ecological investigation, creating the groundwork needed for the project can take considerable effort. (Several other possible steps to determine the significance of a region's natural features are listed in Stage 1 of the appendix.)

Another important early activity is reviewing the possible means of securing ownership or access to a greenway. The ways that a greenway can be protected may range widely and can affect decisions at every stage of the design process. Natural features can be protected from development by federal, state, or local laws that regulate the use of such land wherever it may be found; by protection of a specific area, as when a forest or park is set aside from development; by the lack or expense of technology to overcome physical site limitations, such as poor soil drainage; by the decision of a landowner to keep an area free from development; or by the lack of demand for development on a property. Accordingly, the degree of protection given to an area and its permanence can vary widely.

Attention should be paid not only to the conservation opportunities present in the region but also to the existing or potential development of the landscape that could threaten the region's ecological features. Scanning the region's landscape types will tell the existing range according to the landscape modification gradient and suggest some of the possible conflicts with ecological systems typical of different types (see chapter 2).

Talking to realtors and planning officials can help identify development trends that also may be threats to conservation. Special note should be made of linear forms of development—infrastructure such as roads, canals, and power, telephone, and gas lines—because they are likely to cause breaks in any greenway. The presence of environmental problems, such as water pollution, soil erosion, flooding, and sedimentation of streams and lakes, may indicate areas that could greatly benefit from a greenway or other form of conservation.

1.2. *With the knowledge gained from the contextual study, should the greenway project go forward?*

After reviewing the relative significance of the region's ecological features and functions, the degree to which they are protected, and the threats to the region's ecological integrity, it is important to ask whether creating a greenway should be a conservation priority for the region. These early investigations may lead to some other conclusion: perhaps the greatest need is not for a linear conservation area but instead for protection of an extensive area of wildlife habitat or an entire watershed. By the end of this stage if nothing has been uncovered to suggest some other conclusion, then the project can go forward.

Stage 2: Selecting Project Goals and a Study Swath

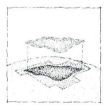

Through the first stage there may have been no definite project goals or study boundaries. Most often this lack is an advantage that prevents conclusions from being reached too early. To go much farther, however, a project needs direction. There must be a basis for decision making. Thus the purpose of the second stage of the method is to select goals to guide the development of the project and to identify a preliminary geographic area of study.

2.1. *What are the goals of the project?*

— **2.1a.** *Which ecological or recreational issues of the region discovered in Stage 1 should be addressed by the goals of a greenway?*
— **2.1b.** *What are workable objectives for each of the goals?*

Locating boundaries and making other decisions about a greenway cannot be accomplished effectively without some means of evaluating the many alternatives that must be considered. To do this evaluation requires *goals* that define what it is hoped the greenway will be and what purposes it will serve. The better articulated these goals are the better they can aid in making decisions.

Because of declining opportunities for protecting biodiversity, for preserving water quality, and for providing recreational opportunities in natural areas, single-goal greenways are hard to defend and should only rarely be proposed. Therefore, the design method presupposes that every greenway project will at least *begin* with goals related to biodiversity, water, and recreation. These goals are a reasonable starting point because most wildlife corridors also help preserve water quality, and many can accommodate at least some recreation without adverse impact on wildlife and water quality. Also, greenways created for recreation frequently maintain and enhance biodiversity and water quality.

Goals are not just for getting projects started; they influence the entire design and management processes. It is the project goals and their supporting objectives that can be turned to when choices must be made between alternative swaths, alignments, widths, network schemes, site designs, management plans, or any other aspects of a greenway.

Not every project goal will be obvious from the start. Some will only become apparent as the design process goes forward. Others may be set early but become focused only as the study goes forward. Still others may have to be abandoned if ecological or sociopolitical conditions are not right to support them.

Given the complexity of greenway design—involving myriad spatially and temporally changing landscape characteristics, numerous landowners, and (most likely) a public approval process—if goals do not get translated into workable objectives, major difficulties or even project failure can result.

The public can play an important role in identifying goals for a greenway project through discussions at public meetings, by comments solicited through local newspapers, organizational newsletters, surveys, or questionnaires, or through interviews with knowledgeable individuals such as local officials. Such contact not only helps to develop goals, but is also likely to uncover the concerns that people may have about the prospect of a greenway. At the same time looking for members of the community that share these goals may help identify an ongoing constituency for the greenway.

Goals formulated at the start of a project should clarify priorities. When there is a conflict between demand for recreation and protection of biodiversity, there must be a very strong case for resolving the situation in favor of anything other than the protection of biological diversity, because, as Reed Noss reminds us in chapter 3, we live in a time of biological crisis.

2.2. *What are the key uses of the greenway?*
— **2.2a.** *What will be the most important uses of the greenway?*
— **2.2b.** *What are the ecological conditions needed to maintain and enhance each use?*

Designing a greenway (or anything for that matter) involves making choices about things large and small. This book argues that these choices should be made on an ecological basis. But, it is not often clear how to apply general ecological principles or more specific guidelines to particular problems. Specific criteria are needed to make decisions. For this reason the design method identifies *key uses* for each greenway. Carefully selected key uses will have specific, documented needs that can guide goal setting and decision making.

The key use concept is very broad. It can help integrate into a design the movement and habitat requirements of individual species or groups of plants or animals, the criteria associated with types of recreation (such as hiking or bird watching) or other human activities, and the criteria for protecting water quality or providing flood control.

Any prospective greenway use for which criteria can be identified may serve as a key use. For example, for the South Platte River project, near Denver, Colorado, the use by humans (primarily bird-watchers) and six species of birds was considered key in the design process. Although most of the bird species are rare or locally in decline, two of the species were selected because they are popular with bird-watchers (see the case study discussion in chapter 7). Use by humans was included as key because of the area's potential for bird watching and other forms of recreation. Criteria for what it would take to accommodate these uses on the site were used to make design decisions.

Key uses are similar to but distinct from the concept of indicator species, which has been heavily criticized. Because of the similarity between the two ideas and because of the possible pitfalls of considering plant or animal species to be indicators of entire communities, it may be helpful to review the indicator species concept and its shortcomings.

To use the indicator species concept, a handful of plants or animal species are monitored as an indication of the general health of a larger group of plants or animals or both (Verner 1984). The use of indicator species grew out of the desire to reduce the costs of conducting environmental assessments or monitoring natural communities on federal lands. For example, a handful of species are selected for monitoring because they are readily observable and because they are believed to be present in an area only if there are sufficient populations of other desirable species. The careful study of the indicator species is thought to give an adequate indication of the community's health without monitoring all species.

The concept is attractive because with it great ecological complexity is viewed through a manageable number of species, usually species whose life histories are reasonably well understood and that can be readily monitored. The indicator species concept has been faulted by Verner (1984), who points out that the members of the group (e.g., a community) from which one or a few species have been selected as indicators may be affected differently by certain habitat changes. Also, because of interspecific competition, the presence of one species (the indicator) may *prevent* the establishment of other members of the same group rather than indicate their presence. Because of these flaws, Verner sees the monitoring of entire guilds to be a more promising way to suggest the "capability of habitat zones to support populations of wildlife species" (Verner 1984, 1).

Guilds are "groups of species that exploit the same class of environmental resources in a similar way" (Root 1967, 335). Since guilds are investigator-defined units, there can be considerable variety in how species are grouped (Verner 1984). Various techniques, ranging from mathematical to intuitive, have been developed for structuring guilds (see for examples, Thomas et al. 1979; Severinghaus 1981; Short and Burnham 1982; Short 1983). What all members of a guild have in common is the use of the same resources for a particular activity or activities, such as nesting, feeding, or a combination of the two. The criteria describing these resource needs can be used as design criteria, as long as it is not assumed that if the criteria are met, *all* of the guild members will be present (for the reasons described earlier, as given by Verner). Instead, it is more reasonable to assume that any member of the guild *may* be present.

None of this is to say that the requirements of individual species should never be used in greenway design, only that the validity of doing so is often questionable if that species is meant to be a surrogate for a larger group. For example, in designing movement corridors and highway underpasses for Florida panthers (see case study in chapter 7), it is clearly important to design for this species. The panther gets close attention because it is very rare, wide-ranging, and vulnerable to road kill.

Selecting key uses for a project deserves careful consideration. Sometimes there will be obvious candidates, other times there will not. Selecting key uses should grow out of the project goals. For a recreation goal, ask what kind of recreation is intended. For biodiversity protection, ask what species or guilds of plants and animals are intended to use the greenway. For water protection, ask if the issue is controlling floods, maintaining water quality, or a combination of issues. Since greenways have the potential to counteract some of the effects of habitat fragmentation, it may be useful to include a fragmentation-sensitive species as a key use. This was done in the Quabbin to Wachusett corridor study described in chapter 7. Because of the tremendous influence key uses have in the design process, their selection warrants advice from experts.

Key uses should be selected that are researched well enough to have adequate information available for identifying the needs of each. There may be a temptation to select many key uses, and certainly too few would not give a complete picture of greenway needs. But, too many key uses can make the method unwieldy. The South Platte River project, which had as its two main goals protecting wildlife habitat and providing recreation, used people (bird-watchers) and six birds to represent the key uses. The wildlife corridor component of the Quabbin to Wachusett corridor study used two: river otter for riparian corridors and fisher for upland areas.

Specifying key uses can be a great aid to the design process because instead of attempting to satisfy a very general design objective—like maximize opportunities for wildlife movement—the designer has a number of fairly specific criteria based on the requirements of a particular species or groups of species. The criteria identified for key uses can be recorded as project-specific guidelines and used with other guidelines. For example, a scientific journal article may report that a certain species (one selected as a key user of the greenway) strictly avoids open areas. This information can be made into a guideline for use in designing the greenway. The more specific the guideline the better. For instance, is the species of interest never found any closer than a certain distance from the edge of a forest? If so, that fact would be very helpful in the guideline. When measurements, especially of distance, are reliably known, they should be incorporated into guidelines because they will be needed in mapping useful habitat and movement requirements.

Ranking the key uses will help during the design process if there are conflicts between the needs of different uses.

2.3. *Where is the most promising study swath?*

Once goals and potential greenway uses are identified (or at least initially identified), it may be possible to reduce the area under study to something smaller than the entire region. (How much smaller will depend on the region being studied and the greenway goals.) In this stage the study area goes from what may be a loosely defined region to a broad but clearly delineated study area or *swath.* Further study is confined to the swath, which is selected so that it includes areas with strong potential for a greenway and no insurmountable barriers.

More than one viable swath may be identified. If so, the one that appears to hold the *greatest* potential for supporting the key uses could be selected for study. Or, several could be carried forward to create a greenway network. It may be helpful to investigate one swath at a time, however, and to design a greenway in that swath before moving on to the next swath. In that way the lessons learned from study of one of the swaths can be applied to the others.

Reviewing old maps and other historical documents may reveal the locations of areas in the region

that are degraded today but were formerly corridors or part of the matrix of a landscape that had high levels of connectivity. If such lost links are restored ecologically, they may serve as wildlife corridors in the greenway network. With the uncertainties about genetic variability and population viability associated with creating connections in the landscape, restoring former connectivity or maintaining existing connectivity is the prudent course, according to Reed Noss. But he warns *against* creating artificial or very narrow connections that may compromise conservation goals by encouraging weedy species (see chapter 3).

Answering the following subsidiary questions will help select a swath.

— **2.3a.** *Which areas within the region have the qualities needed to serve as nodes for a greenway?*

Most greenways connect areas to each other. Hiking trails connect one park to another. Wildlife corridors connect nature preserves. Riparian corridors connect ponds, lakes, and wetlands. For wildlife and recreation, there may be many choices of which areas to connect. For recreation and especially for wildlife, it is highly important to identify and connect areas of high quality. For water there is usually no choice of what to connect; topography determines the paths of existing streams and rivers and the locations of ponds, lakes, and wetlands to and from which they flow.

As mentioned earlier, it is unwise to assume that all protected lands can serve as end points or intermediate nodes in a greenway system. Existing lands may have been set aside (and used) for activities that are not compatible with the greenway's purpose. Nodes need to serve the key uses and not merely make a connection on a map.

Successful nodes for wildlife will be areas that provide habitat for species that have been identified as key users of the greenway. Although the focus of this method and book is on linear conservation zones, unless they are very wide, greenways alone will not be very useful for wildlife conservation if the large areas they lead to cannot support viable populations of plants and animals. For a review of the ecological design issues of protected areas for wildlife, see Craig Shafer's *Nature Reserves: Island Theory and Conservation Practice* (1990), especially the sections "Conservation guidance" and "A Nature Reserve Strategy."

Mapping at this second stage, as at the first, will probably be very broad. But, because general locations are now important, maps will probably be overlaid or combined in some fashion. Most likely hand-drawn maps, such as might be drawn as overlays to or directly on U. S. Geologic Survey topographic maps, will be sufficient, but computer mapping may be used if data are readily available. At this stage, boundary locations are not as important as they will be later; they should be drawn very wide and inclusive rather than exclusive.

— **2.3b.** *Which areas are already managed for biological diversity, water resource protection, or recreation?*

When areas are managed in ways that are compatible with greenway goals and the areas are already protected, then they may be especially effective as intermediate or end nodes or as part of the corridor itself.

— **2.3c.** *Where are there linear landscape elements, such as abandoned rail lines or hedgerows, that might form the spine of a greenway (even though they may not connect significant nodes)?*

Not all greenways are created to connect places, especially if they are primarily intended for recreational use, such as for providing a bicycling path along a former railroad right-of-way. The value of a greenway may be greatly enhanced if it connects with another greenway or with significant nodes, but a "freestanding" greenway may help protect ecological integrity. According to one report there are 120,000 miles of abandoned railroad rights-of-way potentially available nationwide (President's Commission on Americans

Outdoors 1987). If such opportunities exist in the region and they are consistent with the project goals, the areas should be included in the study swath.

This question pertains to human-created linear elements; streams and other natural elements should automatically be included in the swath because of the way that swath boundaries are drawn (i.e., according to watershed boundaries).

— **2.3d.** *What areas can easily be eliminated from consideration because they present significant constraints and no opportunities for a greenway with the given goals?*

Areas can be removed from consideration if they obviously cannot meet greenway goals. If the greenway is primarily intended to protect wildlife, the swath should probably not encompass a nearby downtown urban center. And, a study to protect a riparian corridor does not need to investigate areas that are outside the stream's drainage basin. The kinds of areas that can be reasonably ignored, that is, left outside the swath, will depend on the scope of the intended greenway network and its goals. It may be easy to eliminate areas as unimportant if the project is attempting, say, to create a short greenway segment. But if the intent is to design an intricate regional network of greenways with very diverse goals, then the swath and the region may be one and the same.

— **2.3e.** *What general areas are suitable for some form of development (housing, agriculture, etc.) that might compete for land with greenways?*

Given the choice and depending on the greenway's goals, it may be better to locate the greenway in a part of a region or landscape that has little or no potential for development rather than where land has such potential. This location is preferable because of the possible negative effect on the greenway of future adjacent development and because, perhaps more significantly, antagonism may be created toward a project

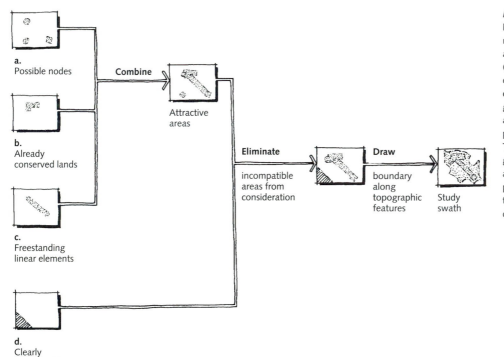

Figure 6.6 Adding together the locations of (a) potential greenway nodes, (b) lands already protected, and (c) freestanding linear elements (such as abandoned rail corridors) creates a map of some of the region's elements that are attractive for a greenway. Areas in the region that are incompatible with the greenway project goals (d) can be taken away. To identify a study swath, draw a generous boundary around the attractive areas, avoiding the incompatible areas, but extending out to a topographic feature, such as the divide between drainage basins.

if a region's sparse developable land is proposed for conservation.

Predicting the future certainly is not easy, but there are ways to make guesses about future development. One way is to anticipate development in areas with soils that are capable of supporting it and where local zoning allows it. Local planners or realtors can temper this projection with their knowledge of the likely demand for development.

By combining the maps that result from answering the earlier questions (2.3a–d), a composite map (Figure 6.6) can be created that shows, if they exist in the region, (2.3a) potential end nodes for a greenway, (2.3b) areas already managed for conservation, (2.3c) freestanding linear features such as streams or rail corridors, and (2.3d) areas that can automatically be eliminated from consideration because they cannot meet project goals. The first three elements (2.3a, b, and c) are added to the map to show places that may be attractive for a greenway. The fourth (2.3d) shows areas that must be taken out of consideration even if

there are overlaps with the first three. For example, an entire railroad corridor might show as a desirable element in the composite of the first three categories. But, the part of the rail corridor that runs through an area that cannot meet project goals would be eliminated when the fourth component is considered. A possible fifth component (2.3e) could show areas that are likely to be developed. Such areas would not automatically be treated as ecologically undesirable but should be carefully considered because of possible edge effects and socioeconomic repercussions.

The areas of interest on the map that result from these steps form a core or a skeleton that can be fleshed out to define the study swath. The swath should be a broad zone that covers the skeleton and then extends out to a natural boundary such as the limits of a watershed or some other topographic feature (Figure 6.6). This is a way of defining a study area for the next stage that is large enough to include both natural features attractive for conservation and the areas around them that will play a part in the analysis. The areas that are filled in around the skeleton will include candidates for connecting corridors such as streams and ridges.

2.4. *With the knowledge gained to this point should the project go forward?*

The investigation at this stage may reveal that a greenway project is not appropriate or possible. The reason might be that no swath could be located that would potentially meet the proposed goals. At such a point the project may be dropped, or it may be possible to review and reconsider the project's goals by returning to the start of this stage.

The steps of Stage 2 culminate in one of the following decisions: (1) there is an appropriate study swath and the greenway process should continue with the current goals, (2) the project should be dropped, or (3) the project should be started over again with new or revised goals.

Part of the design process at this stage includes the identification of possible nodes within the study swath. If any of these nodes are currently unprotected and they eventually become part of the greenway network that comes out of this project, then separate steps must be taken to acquire, design, and manage these areas. Other than identifying where they are and how they relate to the greenway, the method does not contain steps to aid in their design.

Stage 3: Defining Greenway Boundaries

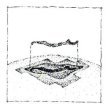 In the third stage the boundaries of the greenway are determined. This activity is divided into two general parts: (1) finding greenway alignments that will serve the needs of the key uses, and (2) setting widths along the alignments. This stage involves more intensive mapping than the previous stages.

3.1. *Where within the swath is the best general alignment for the greenway?*

Because of the potential complexity of determining the precise boundaries of a greenway, it is helpful first to select from within the swath a general alignment for the greenway without setting definite widths. Alignments are selected for *each* key use one at a time. This procedure helps keep the criteria separate and insures that the alignments that are meant to serve a key use will serve it. If uses are grouped, it can be harder to verify that the separate sets of criteria are being met for each use. Later, all of the alignments are examined in composite.

But first a background question should be researched:

— **3.1a.** *What are the disturbance characteristics of the swath that might affect either greenway alignment or width setting?*

Particular note should be made of those landscape disturbances—both human-caused and natural—that occur in the region. Determining the range in size of these disturbance patches will help in setting greenway widths. If, for example, large, wind-caused gaps are common in a forested landscape, then greenway width should be set so that functions within the greenway will not be disrupted if the width is narrowed by such a gap. A similar analysis could be undertaken in landscapes where fires are common. Ecologists and other scientists familiar with the region will be aware of the kinds of disturbances that could potentially disrupt greenway function. Long-term studies of ecosystem dynamics in areas similar to the swath should help determine the range of sizes of disturbance patches. In some situations aerial photographs may help make measurements of such patches.

Given that many kinds of landscape disturbance, such as those resulting from wind or fire, occur naturally, some readers may wonder why the design of a greenway should be adjusted for such natural phenomena. In many landscapes dominated by development, natural corridors are few in number. The loss in such a landscape of one corridor even if due to natural disturbance could have a disastrous effect on connectivity. The effect would be far different than the loss of a corridor in a landscape without development or where the overall level of functional connectivity is high.

— **3.1b.** *Where are the best alignments for the key biological uses?*
— **3.1c.** *Where are the best alignments for the key water resource uses?*
— **3.1d.** *Where are the best alignments for the key recreational uses?*

The best alignment for a key use is one that has good functional connectivity for that use, especially when it is wildlife. The alignment may be a corridor that presently exists or one that reinstates historical connectivity. Artificially increasing connectivity by making connections where there have been none should only be undertaken after very careful consideration and review by experts (see chapter 3, for discussion).

Functional connectivity is the measure of the continuity along the corridor's length that is needed for some use, such as the movement needs of an animal species, the pollution-buffering ability of streamside vegetation, or the required path conditions for a bicyclist (see Figure 6.7). Like the proverbial chain, for many ecological concerns a greenway is only as strong (i.e., as effective) as its weakest link. For some species of wildlife even a subtle break—subtle to humans, that is—can have serious ecological consequences. As

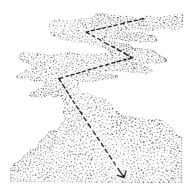

Figure 6.7 Functional connectivity is the measure of the continuity along a corridor's length of conditions needed for some key use.

David Cole explains in chapter 5, these breaks in effectiveness can be caused by locating even a small facility such as a trail in a sensitive place or by the occasional, but poorly timed, use of an area by recreationists.

Subtle breaks can be especially hard to anticipate in greenway design because, although much is known about habitat needs of plants and animals, relatively little is known about species' movement requirements (see chapter 3). Typically this uncertainty is compounded when there is little choice but to rely on generalized information for predicting where inhospitable zones are encountered.

A large, wide-ranging carnivore may move through a corridor in a matter of minutes or hours and a small mammal in several days, but a small invertebrate or a plant species may take years and many generations to make the journey. Very long greenways intended as wildlife movement corridors must have intermediate habitat nodes appropriately spaced along their lengths if some species are to use the corridor successfully. Without these nodes the longer the corridor, the more it will function as a filter along its length and the fewer the species that will successfully use it (Noss, chapter 3, this volume).

It is probably no great surprise that some of the greatest and most frequent disrupters of greenway networks are the networks of infrastructure that humans build, especially roads. Both greenway and human networks tend to share a high degree of connectivity as a fundamental goal. Hence they frequently are in conflict. Rarely have wildlife and water quality been better off because of such conflict, as evidenced by the staggering estimates of wildlife road kill in this country and the substantial amounts of contaminants reaching streams from roads. Where intersections of the two types of networks cannot be avoided—total separation is certainly an ideal solution—structural separators, such as underpasses, may be needed. (See the case studies of the southern Florida panther underpasses and the Santa Monica and Santa Susana mountains wildlife corridors, chapter 7.)

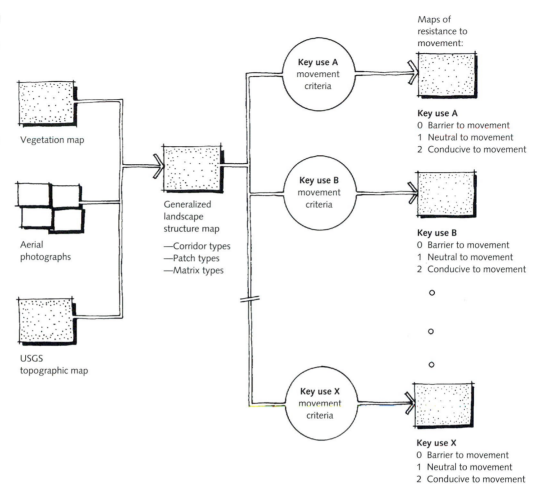

Figure 6.8 The generalized landscape structure of the study swath is mapped from vegetation maps or aerial photographs. This structure map is interpreted using criteria of individual key uses to form maps for each use, showing resistance to movement for each key use.

Vegetation map

Aerial photographs

USGS topographic map

Generalized landscape structure map
—Corridor types
—Patch types
—Matrix types

Key use A movement criteria

Key use B movement criteria

Key use X movement criteria

Maps of resistance to movement:

Key use A
0 Barrier to movement
1 Neutral to movement
2 Conducive to movement

Key use B
0 Barrier to movement
1 Neutral to movement
2 Conducive to movement

Key use X
0 Barrier to movement
1 Neutral to movement
2 Conducive to movement

In traditional parks or in very wide greenways, animals can often avoid barriers or undesirable, degraded areas simply by choosing alternative travel routes. Within the more restrictive boundaries of a typical greenway, however, there may be no alternative routes. This situation makes greenways somewhat like "parks without padding." Greenways may sometimes lack the extra space that would provide, for example, choices to elk moving from summer to winter range. Ideally then, greenway alignments and widths should be set to preserve very high-quality wildlife corridors because in the future these corridors may be the only hospitable travel paths wildlife have in an area. Another step to protect connectivity for a key use is to have redundant links so that one break to the system does not make the entire network useless.

Key uses, selected in the previous stage of the method, are applied here individually to help interpret the landscape and select alignments. The following is a technique for selecting alignments. It is intended primarily for key wildlife uses but may be helpful with some forms of recreation uses. Because the nodes and connectors of riparian systems usually are existing lakes, wetlands, and streams, the issues of selecting alignments, but not widths, for riparian greenways are usually simple.

Ideally field measurement should be used to determine landscape structure for the entire swath. Given

141

the likelihood that sufficient time or resources are unavailable for such an undertaking, existing maps and aerial photographs can be used. The landscape structure of the swath is mapped by delineating its matrix, patches, and corridors as they appear on a map of vegetation types or aerial photographs (Figure 6.8). Less desirable, but still useful, is to use U. S. Geologic Survey topographic maps. This landscape structure map is then analyzed for likely use based on the requirements of individual nonwater key uses. (The surface movement of water can almost always be readily located on existing maps.)

The landscape structure map is then examined with the movement needs of each key use in mind. A new map is created to show the resistance to movement of every area on the former map for each individual key use. Those areas conducive to movement for a key use are not necessarily linear landscape elements; they may be patches or part of the matrix. (Resistance to movement might be evaluated in broad categories, such as 0 = barriers, 1 = strong resistance to movement, 2 = some resistance to movement, 3 = little or no resistance.)

In a separate analysis a series of maps are created that evaluate the suitability of all areas in the swath to serve as end or intermediate greenway nodes according to the requirements of individual key uses (Figure 6.9). As mentioned earlier, nodes were identified in Stage 2, as part of the process of selecting boundaries for the study swath. Those nodes were only generally located and were selected without detailed study. The node analysis in Stage 3 should be more thorough, being based on key-use criteria.

For wildlife, suitability analysis is an evaluation of existing habitat (not movement) suitability. If degraded areas have the potential for being restored, they too may be designated as possible nodes. The evaluation for recreation consists of finding existing or potential areas that are suitable for nonlinear forms of recreation that are compatible with project goals, such as lakes for swimming, meadows for bird watching, athletic fields for organized sports, or tent sites for camping. Large-area nodes may not be as important for recreation as they are for wildlife because spending time along a greenway may be all that recreationists desire.

Those areas of sufficient size and quality, as defined by the criteria for key uses or uses compatible with them, are potential nodes in a greenway system. Each node on each of the node suitability maps should be rated as to how well it is suited to its use. (Node suit-

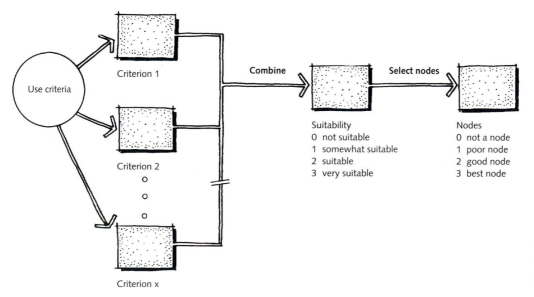

Suitability
0 not suitable
1 somewhat suitable
2 suitable
3 very suitable

Nodes
0 not a node
1 poor node
2 good node
3 best node

Figure 6.9 Key use criteria are used to identify and evaluate nodes for individual key uses.

ability might be ranked, for example, on a scale of four: 0 = not suitable as a node, 1 = poor node suitability, 2 = moderate node suitability, and 3 = good node suitability.) These ratings will be useful later in selecting between alternatives. It is possible that all of a swath might be at least somewhat suitable for the intended use. In such a case the areas of highest suitability might be considered node centers. The size of a node depends on the requirements of its intended use. Areas that have the potential to be good-quality nodes and that are already protected may be viewed as especially attractive points to include in the greenway alignment. Also attractive might be large, single-owner properties, which might be easier to acquire for an easement or partial purchase than areas with many owners of small properties.

The next step is somewhat like playing connect the dots. With the locations of the best nodes overlaid on the resistance-to-movement map, nodes are connected along paths of least resistance (Figure 6.10). The paths of least resistance for wildlife are those lines along which there are suitable conditions for movement. For recreation, the paths are those that provide the highest recreational experiences as defined by the key uses. What results is a map for each key use showing the network of possible nodes and links. Each of these links, along with the nodes it connects, can be considered an alignment. No widths have yet been determined for the alignments, other than the sizes of the nodes. Width-setting comes only after the best alignments are selected for each use and after the separate alignments from each use are combined and reconciled.

Each alignment should be ranked for how well its nodes and links meet the criteria of the key uses they are intended to serve. (A four-scale ranking might be used: 0 = areas on the map that are not alignments, 1 = low-quality alignments, 2 = moderate-quality alignments, 3 = high-quality alignments.) Depending on the criteria of the key uses, this evaluation may be complex and lengthy and may necessitate field work by experts. Field work may especially be necessary for

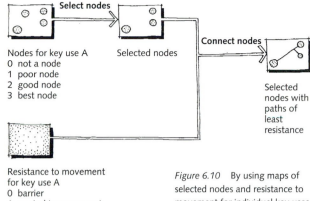

Nodes for key use A
0 not a node
1 poor node
2 good node
3 best node

Selected nodes

Selected nodes with paths of least resistance

Resistance to movement for key use A
0 barrier
1 neutral to movement
2 conducive to movement

Figure 6.10 By using maps of selected nodes and resistance to movement for individual key uses, alternative alignments are created.

wildlife, whose use of the landscape may be in response to conditions that are only poorly represented on maps and whose life histories may not be well understood. Field work might include searching for evidence of existing use by the key biological users and surveying the habitat conditions along the alignment.

Although identifying the alignments of riparian corridors is generally easy because of the availability of good mapping, assessing water quality along alignments can rarely be done without field investigations. Michael Binford and Michael Buchenau discuss various ways of carrying out such investigations in chapter 4.

For recreational uses the evaluation should be simpler because the criteria are generally straightforward. Field checking might be accomplished by hiking alternative alignments and reviewing important aspects such as slopes, views, and vegetation conditions that might be important in testing conclusions drawn largely from maps.

Depending on the acquisition strategies selected for the project—whether greenway lands are to be acquired fee simple, by easement, or by some other means—and depending on the particular configuration of property lines and sizes, landownership may have to be mapped early in this stage so that it can influence the selection of alignments. One of the scenarios developed for the Quabbin to Wachusett corridor study (see chapter 7) favored alignments along property lines so that easements might be more easily acquired. If the mapping of property ownership can be postponed until later in Stage 3, at the point where widths are being determined for specific alignments, then there will be fewer areas to map.

— **3.1e.** *How are the best alignments to be combined into a single unified greenway system?*

Depending on how many key uses and nodes there are, this step of the process can become very complex. For this reason it is important to record which key use each node and link is intended to serve.

Once alignments are found separately for all of the uses, they can be combined to check for overlap or near overlap (Figure 6.11). If an alignment or one of its links can serve more than one use, then that segment may be an especially useful part of the greenway as long as the uses do not conflict. Often alignments that nearly coincide can be accommodated in one corridor if widths are carefully set (in a later step in the method). Even if an alignment serves only one key use, it must remain part of the greenway if that link is required for that use.

If all of the key uses are to be accommodated by a single greenway, then every link must serve each of the key uses. If, however, because of its sensitivity, an alignment cannot accommodate the needs of all the key uses, it may be necessary to select the most signifi-

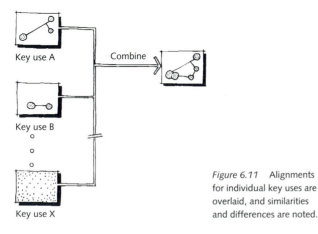

Key use A

Combine

Key use B

Key use X

Figure 6.11 Alignments for individual key uses are overlaid, and similarities and differences are noted.

cant use and accommodate it. In such cases the uses that are left out will require different alignments or possibly will have to be dropped from the project.

When looking at what may be a tangle of routes, the designer should try to identify a single alignment that serves all of the uses. This can be considered the core alignment, and it has the highest priority for further study. Additional links should be added if they provide qualities that support the key uses. Including redundant connections for wildlife, for example, is a good way to reduce the impact of future breaks to the system.

3.2. *Where should the boundaries for the greenway be set?*

Whether greenway boundaries get drawn on paper or staked in the field, one of the strongest determinants of where the lines are drawn is typically the location of existing property boundaries. Existing patterns of ownership and the availability for purchase or donation of individual properties usually have a tremendous effect on the configuration of a greenway. (Exceptions occur in new towns, such as The Woodlands, Texas, which is described in chapter 7, or in planned unit developments, where all the land uses, including open space, are planned simultaneously.) A frequent strategy for creating a greenway is to identify an approximate alignment for the greenway and then, working within the confines of existing property boundaries, to try to secure the minimum amount of property to make a continuous greenway. Sometimes a minimum greenway width is used, based upon some vague sense of ecological conditions. Yet given the heterogeneity of most landscapes, it is hard to imagine that a constant width can be trusted, unless it has been very liberally set (Figure 6.12).

An alternative approach—the one proposed here and supported in earlier chapters—is to adjust greenway widths in response to locally varying ecological conditions. With this approach the greenway is less

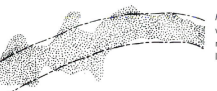

Figure 6.12 Constant-width boundaries may not correspond to landscape functions.

likely to be too narrow to accommodate its intended uses, and a potential route will not have to be rejected because in one place it was restricted to a width that did not meet the arbitrary minimum even though it could support the greenway functions at that point.

Having responsive widths may make acquisition more challenging and costly, but it is worthwhile to the degree that it assures the ecological integrity of the greenway. For example, consider a greenway project that has as a major goal protecting a movement corridor wide enough for a species that avoids open areas and requires continuous interior-forest conditions. Using a constant width along the greenway does not recognize that the parts of the greenway near high-impact land uses may have edge effects that extend considerably farther into the greenway than they do elsewhere. Depending on how generously the width was set, the greenway may be compromised for that species.

A similar situation may exist when a set-width greenway is intended to protect water quality. If the greenway has the same width adjacent to a farm that uses heavy applications of fertilizers and pesticides as it does next to an area of selectively logged forest, the constant width may not be sufficient to buffer the stream next to the farm. Greenway function is better protected when width responds to the specific characteristics of adjacent uses.

The ownership and management of lands within the swath play an important part in setting widths. Ideally each property adjacent to the greenway should be inventoried for ownership, management agency (if any), current use, general condition, recreation potential, development potential, current public access, zoning, and degree of protection (Massachusetts Division of Conservation Services 1990).

— **3.2a.** *How can widths be set locally along the greenway alignment in response to the needs of key uses?*

At each link the requirements of each of the key uses that are intended for that segment are applied locally to determine the needed widths. Specifying greenway widths that vary with local ecological conditions is no simple task. The designer has to read the landscape very carefully to discern what the relevant ecological factors are at each given point, how they vary along the greenway, and how they are likely to change over time. Using a set width is easier and faster, and in landscapes with little variability, it may give satisfactory results.

Local conditions change not only over space but also over time, as the example of the Blue Ridge Parkway illustrated. The effective width and functional connectivity of a greenway may change from season to season (Figure 6.13) (for example, before and after leaf

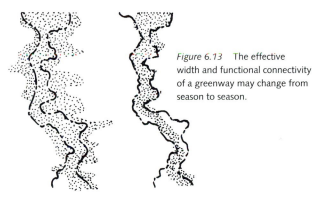

Figure 6.13 The effective width and functional connectivity of a greenway may change from season to season.

fall along an upland corridor or with winter application of road salts along a stream) and even from day to day (with and without high levels of weekend visitors) or from hour to hour (during daylight and after). Also, as years pass, development surrounding a greenway may change dramatically and with it the kinds and intensities of inputs to the greenway. A greenway's dimensions have to accommodate all of these changes if the greenway is to be consistently effective.

A common response to these many unknowns is to add extra width where possible along the greenway. This response may be the best way to deal with a complex situation, but it works best if it comes only after careful examination of the present and (likely) future factors affecting width. Such an approach is analogous to the way financial projections are often made: first all the known costs and revenues are estimated as carefully as possible, then an additional amount—a contingency—is added for whatever may have been overlooked or unanticipated. Similarly, deciding on the most appropriate width for a greenway at a particular location means identifying and quantifying (even if only approximating) the factors affecting width at that location and then adding a contingency to compensate for anything that may have been overlooked.

For example, if the size of an aquifer recharge area along a proposed riparian greenway is uncertain, then a best guess of the extent of the recharge area could be used and, depending on the degree of confidence in the estimate, an additional distance could be added to supplement the greenway width at that point.

The miles-wide approach to setting widths that is sometimes suggested for wildlife movement and habitat corridors may partially be in response to the potentially confounding complexity of variable width setting and the need for adding a contingency. But even with an approach that sets a very liberal width, there needs to be a constant reading of landscape changes along the greenway. These kinds of readings not only help direct or evaluate dimension setting but also flag potential management problems that may need to be monitored. For instance, during width setting it may be noticed that extensive erosion is taking place on adjacent property. Ongoing monitoring of the situation may be necessary to detect threats to the greenway.

Computer programs—specifically geographic information systems (GISs)—can facilitate setting widths that respond to local ecological conditions. Using techniques of combining maps called cartographic modeling (Tomlin 1990), appropriately detailed data, and carefully developed criteria, a GIS can set widths at intervals along the length of a greenway. The success of this process depends, among other

things, on how well articulated the criteria are and how detailed the supporting data are. Completely automating the process of width setting would most likely take very sophisticated cartographic modeling, but even partially computerizing the process can be very helpful.

One simple cartographic modeling technique that can be useful in setting greenway widths is to establish a buffer (or spread) around those landscape elements that could potentially harm greenway function. The width of the buffer depends on the extensiveness of the impacts. These buffers and the elements they surround are avoided when the greenway alignment is identified.

A computerized approach, however, can be data intensive and beyond the technical abilities or finances of some small greenway projects if the GIS is only intended for the design phase. But, if the GIS will be used for both design and management, such as is the case at Rio Grande Valley State Park (see case study, chapter 7), then its expense and usefulness are spread over a greater length of time. Technical assistance for using a GIS and for cartographic modeling may be found at landscape architecture, geography, forestry, and other university departments.

— **3.2b.** *What is the priority for acquiring and implementing each segment of the greenway?*

The significance of each segment of the greenway should be ranked according to its contribution to greenway functions, the degree and immediacy of threat from development, the number of landowners, and any other important project-specific criteria. This ranking helps determine which segments to acquire and complete first.

3.3. *With the knowledge gained to this point should the project go forward?*

Once widths have been assigned it is important to determine how well the entire system serves the key uses and if there are any trouble spots in the greenway.

This kind of reexamination, much of which might take place in the field, should be carried out as if the greenway design were being come upon for the first time. Any shortcomings of the greenway in meeting the project goals and accommodating the key uses should be carefully noted. If significant problems are identified that cannot be corrected by adjusting widths or alignments, then there will have to be a looping back in the design process. How far back in the process the project will have to go will depend on the kind of problems discovered and whether they are concerned with the goals, uses, and criteria identified for the project or with data quality.

Another consideration is whether the funds necessary to implement the greenway could be more usefully applied to protecting large areas rather than connectors. Although it will probably be very difficult to undertake any formal cost-benefit analysis to evaluate such trade-offs in a particular region, the matter nevertheless deserves careful consideration. It would be a disservice to the conservation movement if greenways were allowed to become a fad pursued at the expense of other important work.

Stage 4: Creating and Implementing Site Designs and Management Schemes

The last broad stage of the design method includes  creating site designs to show where trails and other facilities go and formulating plans to specify how a greenway is to be managed. In a real sense this last stage of design never actually ends because it includes managing the greenway.

It is difficult to predetermine the design steps for this final phase of the work because of the site-specific nature and wide range of the activities. Identifying the type of facilities that will be needed and their locations has to be in response to specific site conditions and in support of specific project goals. Accordingly, this stage of the greenway design method provides fewer specific steps than previous stages and is more dependent on the designer's ability to read and understand the landscape in the field. The discussions and guidelines in earlier chapters of this book, especially David Cole's, provide helpful site-scale design guidance. Specialized texts on specific topics, such as ecological restoration and environmental management, should also be consulted.

4.1. *What is the design program for the greenway?*

With the familiarity of the greenway and its key uses gained in the previous stages of the design process, a preliminary list can be composed of the kinds of facilities that will likely be built in the greenway. These facilities, such as trails, wildlife underpasses, and check dams, are the items, large and small, that are needed to support the key uses of the greenway. Collectively they are the design program. Even as it is important to be able to trace every step in the design process back to one or more goals, so every element constructed in a greenway should be tied to at least one goal.

The scope of the design program will depend on the intensity of the key uses and the sensitivity of the greenway's sites. For some greenways, such as those that have little or no recreational use and are primarily for wildlife and water protection, only modest construction may be needed to facilitate the greenway goals. Other greenways, especially those that are recreational, may have abundant facilities to serve recreationists, such as trails and toilets. Still other facilities, such as barriers and bridges, may be needed to protect the greenway's natural features and processes from overuse by recreationists.

To maintain ecological integrity the design of every facility should be as ecologically sensitive as the other phases of greenway planning. Particular care should be given in designing and siting facilities so that these elements do not interrupt connectivity for a key use. Also, the materials and means used in constructing the facilities must be carefully selected so that they do not introduce elements into the greenway that will compromise its ecological integrity.

Greenway facilities need to be designed to respond to the dynamic natural processes of the greenway. If the greenway is susceptible to seasonal flooding, for instance, then this must be considered when designing trails and wildlife underpasses.

4.2. *Where should facilities (such as trails, wildlife underpasses, bridges, etc.) be sited and how should they be implemented?*

Site design should be a continuation of the previous stages of the design method. Frequently, however, site design is done by someone other than the designers who carried the project to this point. When this is the case, it is vital that the lessons that have been learned in the process be passed on to the site designer. It may be convenient, for instance, to communicate such lessons as guidelines suitable for informing design.

Facilities should be sited in such a way that they complement the key uses of the greenway. If use by wildlife is the highest priority, then trails should be sited so that they meet recreational goals without interfering with the wildlife functions of the greenway. Thus, facilities constructed in support of one key use cannot disrupt another key use if both uses are intended for the same segment of the greenway.

Dividing the greenway into distinct zones that reflect each area's intended uses can be a good way to avoid treating the entire greenway as if it were a homogeneous unit. (See the case study of the Rio Grande Valley State Park in chapter 7, for example.) With such zoning, facilities and uses are allowed only in zones where they will not be ecologically disruptive. The type and intensity of allowable recreation, for example, might be limited to those zones that can accommodate them. This same system of zoning can also function in greenway management.

Siting facilities requires field work and, most often, careful, extensive mapping since specific directions of

where and how to construct the facilities must be developed for the construction to take place. Some facilities, such as trails, may be laid out directly in the field.

4.3. *How should ecological restoration be accomplished where it is needed?*

Some degraded areas will likely be included within the greenway that need to be restored ecologically if they are to support greenway functions. Plans should be formulated to carry out this restoration in consultation with restoration experts. For a discussion of ecological restoration, see *Environmental Restoration* (Berger 1990), *Restoration Ecology: A Synthetic Approach to Ecological Research* (Jordan et al. 1987), and *Rehabilitating Damaged Ecosystems* (Cairns 1988).

4.4. *How should the greenway be managed?*

Designing and implementing the greenway may seem lengthy, but that time is short in comparison with what is spent maintaining the greenway. Ideally greenway management philosophy and practice grow directly out of the project goals set early in the design process and out of all of the lessons learned during that process. The same goals given for the design process (Table 6.1) also apply to management, since both greenway design and management are concerned with the same natural phenomena. It would not make sense, for instance, after giving biodiversity or water quality very close attention during the design process to allow maintenance vehicles to frighten wildlife or to pollute water.

The key uses selected for design decisions can play a role in managing the greenway. Such uses can be monitored to assess design and management success, and the criteria identified for each use should be reviewed before making management decisions. The maps developed for greenway design, especially geographic information systems, can also be extremely useful in managing that greenway. At the Rio Grande

Valley State Park in Albuquerque, a GIS is used for monitoring wildlife and vegetation communities (see chapter 7).

There may be a tendency to believe that since greenways are natural corridors, once they have been created they can be left without management. There is too much interaction between greenways and their neighbors, however, for this to be true. Depending on the greenway's uses and ecology and on what surrounds it, the greenway may require more maintenance than similar acreage in a typical nonlinear protected area.

Process Overview:
The Importance of Scale

From stage to stage, there is variability in the design process, especially regarding how much specific direction is given to the designer. The first stage of the process is very general as the designer searches for the basis of a future greenway project. The second and third stages have much more structure and give considerable advice for decision making, whereas the last stage depends more on the designer to determine the questions and answers. Although generalities are useful early on, as the greenway becomes more defined, the decisions to be made call for questions and answers specific to the project area.

Separating design decisions into discrete phases does more than ensure that issues are dealt with at the most relevant scale or scales. Moving methodically through the four stages and making the evaluations and decisions associated with each stage can also provide the opportunity to reduce the geographic area of study. In this process the area given attention begins with a region, shifts to a broad swath large enough to include a number of greenway alignment options, narrows to the greenway boundaries, and finally focuses inside the greenway on site design and management. By successively reducing the extent of the area under study, significant savings in time and money can result

because as more detailed data must be gathered there is less area for which data must be collected.

An area that illustrates this potential savings is land ownership. Gathering detailed property maps for an entire region or even for a very broad swath within it can be a major task. With the approach described in this chapter, when investigating a region or picking a swath, only general land ownership patterns are examined (such as the pattern of private and public ownership or the typical size of parcels). It is usually not until the point of drawing greenway boundaries that the locations of specific parcel boundaries are significant.

Considering water quality in the design process is another factor that is simplified by examining successively smaller areas. At the broadest scale the questions are more qualitative and general, such as where the major breaks are in riparian vegetation or where land uses are that are obvious polluters. When making decisions on greenway width and site design, more detail will be needed to deal with such things as the levels and timing of human-induced nutrient inputs and variations in water temperature.

With greenway design, a successively smaller area is identified as worth further study until a greenway alignment is located. Certainly the process is not as automatic as this description makes it sound. Knowing what is worthy of further consideration at each greenway design stage can be hard intellectual work. Distinctions must be made between sometimes subtle differences to determine what is worth further study and what is not.

There may be a tendency to start a project by amassing as many maps and other documents as can be found, even if there is no clear sense of how the maps are to be used. Then, anticipating some kind of overlay process, each map is carefully redrawn to a consistent scale. The designer is next faced with the monumental task of making sense of these map "resources." But without a specific goal this task can resemble an effort at alchemy—turning piles of paper into a meaningful design. With the design method, however, detailed information is gathered only when its use is known and then only with the detail that is necessary to a particular scale or stage of work. This approach recognizes that gathering and analyzing data can be very time consuming and costly.

Furthermore, different techniques for analyzing maps may be appropriate at different stages. Cruder, more general mapping approaches, such as the steps in Stage 2, may be all that are necessary early on.

Beginning a project with a comprehensive resource inventory can therefore be a big mistake. How can appropriately scaled and classified maps be gathered before the questions have been articulated? An overview of maps, however, a kind of environmental scan, is helpful; it can, in fact, be crucial to understanding a project's setting (Frederick Steiner, personal communication). But it is generally best not to start mapping without a clear reason, not to skip what Lyle calls "a time for letting impressions sink in. . . for questions, not answers" (Lyle 1985, 136).

Ideally a greenway project starts with a broad-scale analysis (Stage 1) and then progresses systematically toward the site scale, but not every project will progress this way. Many times—especially with sites that are at the urban end of the landscape modification gradient—the kinds of decisions a greenway designer might make at the broadest scale have already been preempted by existing development. For example, the only potential alignment for a greenway in an existing suburban neighborhood might be the scant open space that is left between the back fences of house lots, along a steep slope. The only question the designer may be able to pose is, Will the little land that is available here support our greenway goals or not?

In other situations important early decisions, such as project goals, will limit the investigation at a given scale. For instance, if protecting water quality in a particular stream is a project goal, that stream and its headwaters will most likely become the spine of the greenway. Or, if an abandoned railroad bed is being considered for conversion to a bicycle path, then the

analysis would start with the right-of-way (or the rail bed) as the centerline of the greenway. In both cases, the process of selecting the greenway's alignment is truncated because there is a strong determinant for the project's location: the stream in the first example and the rail bed in the second.

There can be other reasons why the design process may not go through progressively tighter scales of investigation, or if it does, some of the stages may be greatly abbreviated due to ecological, economic, or sociopolitical determinants. For instance, it may be useful to complete a small test segment of the greenway before designing the rest. In Boulder, Colorado, the Boulder Creek greenway was completed as a showpiece of what the rest of the system would be like as it extended into other parts of the city (see chapter 7). As Little (1990) points out, such a demonstration area can engender public enthusiasm and support for the larger project. With such an approach the test segment passes through all of the stages before the rest of the greenway.

Completing some segments early can also be a way of testing ecological assumptions made in the design or management processes or of testing construction materials or techniques. Depending on the results observed by monitoring these trial areas, changes may be made in the design or management of uncompleted areas along the greenway. This same process of monitoring the entire greenway and adjusting (redesigning) as necessary should be part of its ongoing management.

Geographically the design method is very much a top-down approach, the early considerations are regional (or possibly larger), and at each stage the scope becomes smaller. Some projects, however, will get started because outstanding local features, such as wildlife corridors or streams, make people wonder if perhaps a greenway is a viable form of conservation. Such a project might be approached bottom-up, by using the special features as a starting point. Another approach would be to follow the design method given here, keeping track of what happens to the landscape feature that instigated the project and comparing its conservation potential to that of other features in the region.

At any stage of the process problems may arise that cannot be fully resolved at that point. By carefully recording these issues they can be recalled and resolved at a future stage. In general, the earlier a problem can be resolved, the better, especially if doing so prevents the issue from becoming an ongoing management problem. For example, not running a greenway adjacent to a land use that is particularly disruptive of greenway function may be best, but if such a neighbor cannot be avoided in setting the general alignment of the greenway, then perhaps extra width can be allocated at that point. If that is not possible, then perhaps the design of site features—say the configuration of a footpath—can reduce the impact of the neighbor. In the absence of that possibility, the problem may be left to management.

Sources of Data and Help

The design method relies on a gradual inventory of natural and social features. Inventorying is not one of the stages of the method; it is something that happens throughout the method.

It may be tempting for greenway designers to rely on books such as popular field guides to answer ecological questions about an area. These books, however, need to be used very carefully and only to respond to

Table 6.2 Professionals involved in greenway design, their location, and journals to which they contribute

Professionals	Locations	Journals
Wildlife (plants and animals)		
Wildlife biologists, ecologists, landscape ecologists, biologists, botanists, conservation biologists, fisheries biologists	Departments of biology at universities and colleges, departments of fisheries and wildlife in state and federal governments, private consultants, state Natural Heritage programs, private nonprofit conservation organizations	*Conservation Biology, Biological Conservation, Journal of Biogeography, Ecology, Journal of Applied Ecology, Environmental Management, Wildlife Monographs, Wildlife Management Bulletin, Wildlife Resources News, Wildlife Abstracts, Wildlife Review, Journal of Mammalogy, Ark, Condor, Wilson Bulletin, Landscape Ecology, Landscape Journal, Habitat Suitability Models of the U.S. Fish and Wildlife Service, Natural Areas Journal, Journal of Wildlife Management*
Water Resources		
Water resources specialists, hydrologists, limnologists, aquatic ecologists, landscape ecologists, environmental engineers, agricultural engineers, physical geographers, environmental scientists, agronomists	Departments of ecology, agricultural engineering, and geography at universities and colleges, Departments of soil and water conservation in state and federal governments, private consultants, private nonprofit conservation organizations, U.S. Environmental Protection Agency, private land trusts	*Ecology, Environmental Management, Journal of Soil and Water Conservation, Environmental Science and Technology, Environmental Conservation, Ecological Applications, BioScience, Ecological Engineering, Journal of Environmental Quality*
Design		
Landscape architects, landscape planners, recreation planners, regional planners, ecological planners, environmental planners, community planners	Departments of landscape architecture and planning at colleges and universities, National Park Service, local, regional, and state outdoor recreation commissions, USDA National Forest Service	*Landscape Architecture, Landscape Journal, Landscape and Urban Planning*
Outdoor Recreation		
Outdoor recreation planners, foresters, landscape architects	Departments of outdoor recreation at colleges and universities, National Park Service, local, regional, and state outdoor recreation commissions, USDA National Forest Service	*Biological Conservation, Journal of Applied Ecology, Journal of Environmental Management, Journal of Wildlife Management, Natural Areas Journal, Restoration and Management Notes, Journal of Forestry*

very general questions because they are, for the most part, generalized discussions of regions, not detailed descriptions of smaller areas.

Since few greenway designers are conversant in all the ecological topics needed to complete a project, professional help with ecological questions will usually be needed. Many kinds of professionals devote themselves to the study of the issues related to greenway creation and may be useful as consultants on a project. In addition, the journals these professionals read and write for may have articles that can help greenway designers. (See Table 6.2 for a list of some of the relevant fields and their journals.) Some of these professionals, especially those at universities or local, state, or federal agencies, may offer their services at little or no charge.

Natural Heritage programs, collaboratives of The Nature Conservancy and state conservation agencies, use a standard approach to evaluate the presence of threatened and endangered species or critical natural communities (Pearsall et al. 1986). Although the program may not tell the exact location of a project's key species, generalized maps of the locations of federally and state-listed species and important communities can be supplied.

As mentioned earlier, general assistance in creating greenways may also be obtained from the National Park Service's River, Trail, and Conservation Assistance program or from the American Greenways program of the Conservation Fund in Arlington, Virginia, which has embarked on several statewide greenway efforts.

There are also many informal sources of information that may prove useful in designing greenways. Experienced naturalists, hunters, trappers, and other people who spend considerable time outdoors often have firsthand experience with a landscape over many years. Specific soil characteristics, other than what is given in county soil surveys, are sometimes difficult to discover without fieldwork, but farmers and others may be able to help because of their highly developed abilities to read a landscape's soil conditions. Possible

future development patterns can sometimes be obtained from realtors, developers, private land planners, government planners, or others that are abreast of an area's development trends. Road maintenance departments may have records of where the most frequent automobile accidents occur with wildlife. Such locations may indicate the presence of important wildlife movement pathways.

Finding and Using Maps

There is no such thing as a standard list of maps needed for greenway planning. But, as one identifies goals and objectives and carries out the steps of the design method including identifying key uses, it will be clearer what kinds of maps will be needed. Some sources of map data are given in Table 6.3.

As mentioned earlier, it is important not to *start* a greenway planning project with map making. Although it may be convenient to gather all kinds of maps, they should not be redrawn or otherwise prepared until they are needed and the scale at which they

Table 6.3 Sources of map data

Type of Map	Sources
Topography	U. S. Geologic Survey topographic quadrangle maps
Land use	U. S. Geologic Survey, state or local government planning agencies
Vegetation	Aerial photographs from state highway departments or planning departments
Ownership	U. S. Geologic Survey topographic quadrangle maps (for many public lands), tax assessor's maps (for detailed ownership)
Zoning	City, town, or county planning office
Soils	U. S. Department of Agriculture Soil Conservation Service county surveys
Floodplains	U.S. Department of Housing and Urban Development (National Flood Insurance Program)
Property boundaries	Tax maps

will be used is known. Given the nature of greenway planning there will probably be a need to use, reuse, and modify maps, so flexibility is important. There are effective ways of working with maps by hand and computer. The project budget, the expertise of the project team, and the cost and availability of maps will all help determine which route to take.

There are affordable and capable computer mapping and analysis programs available for personal computers. For larger or more complex projects these or programs for larger computers may be of inestimable aid. One thing to keep in mind in pricing such systems is that usually the greatest expense and time commitment of creating a geographic information system is getting the maps into a form that is useful in the computer (Starr and Estes 1990). This process—called digitizing—can take a great deal of time, although more and more often today some map data can be purchased in a digital form.

The advantage of using a computer and digitized data is the ability to test many alternative schemes quickly. This ability can be especially valuable in greenway design because of the large number of contingencies involved. Computer systems also make available analysis techniques that are almost impossible by hand. These techniques enable one to perform complex or extensive searches around points on a map and to find locations that have specific combinations of characteristics from many maps.

A geographic information system is being used to determine the location of the trails and other facilities at the Rio Grande Valley State Park (see chapter 7). The park's GIS is also used for ongoing monitoring and management of animals and vegetation. There is a continuous updating of bird and mammal populations and habitat, human use patterns (trails, illegal camp sites, and dumping sites), adjacent land uses, and burned areas.

When maps are not available, aerial photographs can be used to create base maps, such as was done for the southeastern Wisconsin environmental corridors

(see case study, chapter 7). Much of their GIS was based on interpretation of aerial photos updated every five years.

There are flexible ways of managing maps even without a computer. One approach is to transfer the areas of useful characteristics from a map onto an acetate overlay. Then appropriate overlays from many maps can be combined on a light table (or a window) and analyzed visually for those areas that have specific good characteristics and lack undesirable characteristics.

A useful variation on this process developed by Steinitz and colleagues (1976) involves reducing all maps to a relatively small and manageable size (e.g., 8½ by 11 inches), with separate overlays for each category from a map. (This approach is sometimes known as a data sandwich.) For example, a single slope map might become six separate slope-class maps, one showing slopes from 0 to 3 percent, one for 3 to 6 percent and so on. Then, in an analysis that includes consideration of slope, each of the overlays for the slope classes to be considered is included. To give extra weight to a factor in an analysis, such as slope, additional copies of the same overlay are included, giving those areas a darker appearance. The sandwich is flexible and can easily be recomposed with different layers representing different criteria.

It is quite an art to find ways to get combinations of maps to reveal answers to questions that arise in the design process. Fundamental to the process is clearly articulating the criteria that are to be used to make evaluations.

If in overlaying maps—either by hand or with a computer—most of the study area meets the preset criteria, the designer may have to decide if additional criteria are needed to distinguish the good areas from the even better ones. If, however, there are few or no areas that meet the criteria, it may be necessary to look more closely at the criteria and the limitations they impose. It may be possible that the limitations can be overcome at the site scale. For example, if slopes are consistently too steep or soils are too wet for a bike path, can switchbacks or bridges be built? Or, it may be that there are few options in the area for the kind of greenway envisioned.

Conclusions

As the preceding presentation of the design method makes clear, much attention and care are required in the process of designing greenways if they are to fulfill their ecological potential. The design method is a flexible, working hypothesis. It says that if an effort is made to discover and understand the ecological workings of a landscape and this information is applied to greenway design, then greenways can do much to protect ecological integrity. The results of testing this hypothesis—of applying the design method to a greenway project—will depend on the thoughtful care taken at the many steps along the way. The result will be less of an outcome and more of an ongoing dialogue between what is being discovered about the workings of nature and how design and management respond to that knowledge.

Appendix: Detailed Listing of the Ecological Greenway Design Method

Stage 1: Understanding Regional Context

Overall Question

1.1. *Are there significant unprotected biological, water, recreational, or other features in the region that could be maintained or enhanced by a greenway or network of greenways?*

Guidelines to Help Answer the Overall Question and Its Subsidiary Questions

— Landscape features do not have to be of world-class significance to warrant greenway protection, but it is logical to conserve first those unprotected areas that are the most significant in the region.
— If constraints on conservation are not absolute, it may be possible to overcome them through changes in policy or through the design of the greenway.

Subsidiary questions	Possible steps to help answer the questions
1.1a. *What are the characteristics of greenways that successfully maintain or enhance natural features and processes?*	Contact the U.S. National Park Service's River, Trail, and Conservation Assistance program or the Conservation Fund's American Greenways program.
	Review earlier chapters of *Ecology of Greenways.*
	Interview designers or managers of successful greenways.

Subsidiary questions	Possible steps to help answer the questions
1.1b. *Are there significant opportunities for maintaining or enhancing **biological diversity** in the region? What are the constraints?*	Ask national, state, and local conservation and scientific specialists this question.
	Review books and topical or regional journals that describe the region's natural history and ecology.
	Determine if there are any species in the area that are listed by federal or state agencies (e.g., Natural Heritage Program) as threatened or endangered and if there are any species native to the region that are particularly sensitive to habitat fragmentation.
	Determine the extent of existing or proposed areas for the conservation of biological diversity, including movement paths, and if there are any laws that protect biological diversity.
	Determine if there are any major barriers or frequent smaller barriers to wildlife movement in the region.
	Determine popular perceptions of biodiversity issues by holding meetings for the public or for community groups especially interested in this topic.

Subsidiary questions	Possible steps to help answer the questions
1.1c. *Are there significant opportunities for maintaining or enhancing* **water resources** *in the region? What are the constraints?*	Ask national, state, and local water resources specialists this question.

Review books and journals that describe the region's hydrology, limnology, ecology, etc.

Determine if there are any streams in the area that are especially worthy of protection because of their pristine condition or because, if restored, they would have a big impact on the degraded stream network.

Approximate the range of stream orders in the region and note their likely characteristics and sensitivity to development based on the river continuum concept.

Determine the extent of existing or proposed areas for the conservation of water resources and if there are any laws that protect streams and lakes.

Determine the scope and type of threats to either the quality or quantity of water resources in the region.

Determine popular perceptions of water resource issues by holding meetings for the public or for community groups especially interested in this topic. |
| **1.1d.** *Are there significant opportunities for maintaining or enhancing* **outdoor recreation** *in the region? What are the constraints?* | Ask national, state, and local outdoor recreation specialists this question.

Review books and journals that describe the region's recreational activities.

Review state, regional, or local outdoor recreation plans that relate to the region being studied.

Determine the potential for outdoor recreation in the region.

Determine the extent of existing or proposed recreational areas, such as parks and playing fields, and if there are any laws or other programs that allow the passage of recreationists through private lands.

Determine if there are any major threats (e.g., development) to recreational activities in the region.

Determine if any potential forms of recreation have known ecological impacts.

Determine popular perceptions of recreational issues by holding meetings for the public or for community groups especially interested in this topic. |

Subsidiary questions	Possible steps to help answer the questions
1.1e. *Are there other significant opportunities for greenway development in the region? Are there any other constraints?*	Estimate the range of landscape types in the region according to the landscape modification gradient to get some idea of the type of greenway that might be possible.

Get an overview of the approximate spatial distribution of those public lands that might be suitable for conservation or recreation and the approximate ratio of such public lands to private lands in the region.

Assess the development trends in the region by talking with planning officials, realtors, developers, and others.

Research ways of designating lands for greenways, including fee-simple purchase, easement acquisition, informal cooperation, and other means. |

Overall Question

1.2. *With the knowledge gained from the contextual study, should the greenway project go forward?*

Guidelines to Help Answer the Overall Question

— The project should continue to Stage 2 for further study if there appears to be a potential role for a greenway in the region and no insurmountable constraints.

Stage 2: Selecting Project Goals and a Study Swath

Overall Question

2.1. *What are the goals of the project?*

Guidelines to Help Answer the Overall Question
and Its Subsidiary Questions

— Every greenway project should start with biological conservation, water resource protection, and recreational goals, regardless of how developed or pristine its landscape matrix. (Probably one or more of these types of goals will dominate.)
— If recreation must be excluded from a greenway because of the sensitivity of biological or water resources, the project should still have a recreational goal, one limiting human use.

Subsidiary questions	Possible steps to help answer the questions
2.1a. *Which ecological or recreational issues of the region discovered in Stage 1 should be addressed by the goals of a greenway?*	Present and explain the issues discovered in Stage 1 to appropriate community groups.

Use community participation to identify and rank key conservation goals for greenways in the region. |

155

Subsidiary questions	Possible steps to help answer the questions
2.1b. *What are workable objectives for each of the goals?*	Translate each of the broad goals into one or more specific, workable objectives.

Overall Question

2.2. *What are the key uses of the greenway?*

Guidelines to Help Answer the Overall Question and Its Subsidiary Questions

— Select as key uses the elements that will be the main beneficiaries of the greenway as described by project goals and objectives. They may be species of management concern, guilds of plants or animals, some form of human recreation such as hiking or bird watching, or some form of water resource management such as flood control or interception of pollutants in overland flow.

Subsidiary questions	Possible steps to help answer the questions
2.2a. *What will be the most important uses of the greenway?*	Review the project goals and objectives identified in the previous question.
	Rank the key uses so that in the event any of them conflict there can be a consistent mechanism for resolving the conflict.
2.2b. *What are the ecological conditions needed to maintain and enhance each use?*	Research the key uses by reviewing appropriate scientific literatures and interviewing experts to determine the criteria necessary to support the movement needs of each use.

Overall Question

2.3. Where is the most promising study swath?

Guidelines to Help Answer the Overall Question and Its Subsidiary Questions

— A promising study swath should cover a broad area that encompasses known biological, water resource, and recreation opportunities for a greenway and that has few serious obstacles to the project's goals; eliminate from study obviously inappropriate lands, including insurmountable barriers.
— Not all lands designated for conservation should be assumed to have the qualities needed to serve as nodes for a greenway; connect areas of known quality.
— An overall strategy for outlining a swath is to find an area with good greenway potential and then to draw generously a line around it on a map, including adjacent areas.
— The entire region may be taken as the study swath if there are no obvious areas to eliminate from consideration or if the goal is to produce a regional greenway network.
— Use broad-scale mapping at this stage; hand-drawn overlays may be best at this stage.

Subsidiary questions	Possible steps to help answer the questions
2.3a. *Which areas within the region have the qualities needed to serve as nodes for a greenway?*	Determine if there are habitat patches that are now separated but were once connected.
	Determine if there are lakes, ponds, or wetlands that could be protected or enhanced if they were part of the greenway.
	Determine if there are existing or proposed recreational nodes, such as parks, other greenways, or trailheads, that would benefit if connected to the greenway.
	Determine if there are areas of historic interest, of high visual quality, or of other cultural interest that might be useful parts of the greenway.
2.3b. *Which areas are already managed for biological diversity, water resource protection, or recreation?*	Review comprehensive plans, zoning maps, and land-use plans to determine locations of existing or proposed protected lands (note whether they are privately or publicly held).
	Review laws and regulations to determine any additional protection that these might provide.
2.3c. *Where are there linear landscape elements, such as abandoned rail lines or hedgerows, that might form the spine of a greenway (even though they may not connect significant nodes)?*	Locate abandoned (or soon to be abandoned) railroad rights-of-way and assess their availability.
	Locate hedgerows or other landscape features such as utilities that might be valuable elements of a greenway.
2.3d. *What areas can easily be eliminated from consideration because they present significant constraints and no opportunities for a greenway with the given goals?*	Eliminate from consideration those areas that obviously hold no promise for fulfilling the project goals or for supporting the key uses.
2.3e. *What general areas are suitable for some form of development (housing, agriculture, etc.) that might compete for land with greenways?*	Review comprehensive plans, zoning maps, and land-use plans to determine locations where development is encouraged.
	Ask land planners, realtors, and developers which broad areas are likely to be developed.

Overall Question

2.4. *With the knowledge gained to this point should the project go forward?*

Guidelines to Help Answer the Overall Question

— The project should go to Stage 3 for further study if there is a swath within which there appear to be sufficient resources to support a greenway.

Stage 3: Defining Greenway Boundaries

Overall Question

3.1. *Where within the swath is the best general alignment for the greenway?*

Guidelines to Help Answer the Overall Question

and Its Subsidiary Questions

— A good alignment for a greenway should provide high connectivity for each of the key uses.
— Redundant segments are helpful in a greenway that protects wildlife.
— Determining alignments for riparian corridors is as easy as finding where streams run; evaluating their quality is much harder.
— The steps shown here for riparian alignments are for ranking the alignments, not for finding them.
— Existing and potential trailheads should be considered as recreational nodes.
— Also include relevant landscape-scale guidelines from the sections about selecting alignments at the ends of chapters 3, 4, and 5, and see the main text of those chapters for discussion.

Subsidiary questions	Possible steps to help answer the questions
3.1a. *What are the disturbance characteristics of the swath that might affect either greenway alignment or width setting?*	Get an overview of the structure and function of the landscapes under study.
	Identify species (especially exotics) that invade disturbed areas within the study swath and that might be favored by the edge conditions that may exist along the greenway.
	Get an overview of the patterns of change common in the study swath, both due to natural as well as human causes. Especially note the range of size of disturbance patches and the likely patterns of development.

Subsidiary questions	Possible steps to help answer the questions
3.1b. *Where are the best alignments for the key biological uses?*	Research the habitat and movement criteria of the biological key users by reviewing scientific literature, interviewing experts, and investigating other sources.
	Map the landscape structure within the swath, identifying the location and quality of matrices, patches, and corridors as they appear on a vegetation map or on aerial photographs.
	Reclassify the landscape structure map (using the key-use movement criteria gained through research) to indicate the resistance to movement through the landscape for the first key biological use.
	Using the habitat criteria gained through research for the first biological key user, develop a habitat suitability map.
	Rank the zones on the habitat suitability map from highest to lowest suitability for habitat and thereby develop a habitat nodes map.
	Create separate resistance-to-movement, habitat suitability, and habitat nodes maps for each of the key biological uses.
	Identify separate greenway alignments for each biological key use by connecting nodes on the habitat nodes map by finding routes of least resistance.
3.1c. *Where are the best alignments for the key water resource uses?*	Create a map of the perennial and intermittent streams, lakes, and wetlands in the study swath.
	Determine the stream order of each stream and estimate its characteristics according to the river continuum concept.
	Note any stream confluences as special nodes.
	Estimate the water quality of the streams in the swath; use field measurements if there are no existing data.
	Estimate the sediment and nutrient flows into streams; use field measurements if there are no existing data.
	Define the regional relationships between the integrity of stream communities, the configuration of riparian vegetation, and the land uses in the region's basin.

Subsidiary questions	Possible steps to help answer the questions
3.1d. *Where are the best alignments for the key recreational uses?*	Create a map of the existing and proposed outdoor recreation areas and trails in the study swath.
	Note the regional relationships between trails and other facilities and the human populations and land uses in the study swath.
	Determine the necessary criteria of the recreational key users by reviewing recreation literature and interviewing experts and members of recreation clubs.
	Evaluate the swath based on the recreational use criteria for recreational movement potential.
	Identify and rank existing and potential recreational nodes for the first recreational key user.
	Create separate suitability-for-recreational-movement maps and recreational nodes maps for each of the recreational key users.
	Identify separate greenway alignments for each recreational key user by picking nodes on the recreational nodes map and then connecting them by finding routes for recreational movement between them.
	Walk the alignments in the field to verify the analyses and the accuracy of the data.
3.1e. *How are the best alignments to be combined into a single unified greenway system?*	Overlay all the routes for all the key uses and look for any overlap.
	Determine a configuration of routes that accommodates all the key uses and as appropriate, also includes redundant links and general connectors.
	Note the key uses intended for each node and alignment of the network.

Overall Question

3.2. *Where should the boundaries for the greenway be set?*

Guidelines to Help Answer the Overall Question and Its Subsidiary Questions

— Boundaries should be set so that they adequately buffer greenway functions from outside influences and so that sufficient area exists within the greenway to sustain the key uses.

— Also include relevant landscape-scale guidelines from the sections about setting widths at the ends of chapters 3, 4, and 5, and see the main text of those chapters for discussion.

Subsidiary questions	Possible steps to help answer the questions
3.2a. *How can widths be set locally along the greenway alignment in response to the needs of key uses?*	Review each segment (the connector between two nodes) to see which key uses are intended for that segment and then set widths so that each use's width requirements are met along the entire segment.
	Do the same until all segments have boundaries set with variable widths.
	Map property boundaries.
	Compare the boundaries set according to use needs with landownership patterns.
	Readjust the alignment if there is major conflict between the ownership patterns (and property availability) and the use-set widths. To some degree this will depend on the means to be used for securing the greenway (outright purchase, easement, informal cooperation, etc.) and the availability of any of these means for a given property.
	Field check the widths to verify the analyses and the accuracy of the data.
3.2b. *What is the priority for acquiring and implementing each segment of the greenway?*	Estimate and rank the degree of threat facing each segment of the greenway.
	Estimate the overall significance to the greenway of each segment based on the quality and significance of nodes, alignments, and widths.
	Rank each segment from high to low, with the highest segments being those that are of greatest significance and that face the greatest threat and the lowest segments being those that are of the lowest significance and facing the least threat.

Overall Question

3.3. *With the knowledge gained to this point should the project go forward?*

Guidelines to Help Answer the Overall Question

— If there are viable alignments and widths that will meet the requirements of the key uses, then the project can go forward to Stage 4.

Stage 4: Creating and Implementing Site Designs and Management Schemes

Overall Question

4.1. *What is the design program for the greenway?*

Guidelines to Help Answer the Overall Question

— Elements of the design program must not threaten the ecological integrity of the greenway or compromise functions of the key uses.
— See the relevant site-scale guidelines from the sections about preparing site designs and management plans at the ends of chapters 3, 4, and 5, and see the main text of those chapters for discussion.

Overall Question

4.2. *Where should facilities (such as trails, wildlife underpasses, bridges, etc.) be sited and how should they be implemented?*

Guidelines to Help Answer the Overall Question

— The siting of elements of the design program must not threaten the ecological integrity of the greenway or compromise functions of the key uses.
— See the relevant site-scale guidelines from the sections about preparing site designs and management plans at the ends of chapters 3, 4, and 5, and see the main text of those chapters for discussion.

Overall Question

4.3. *How should ecological restoration be accomplished where it is needed?*

Guidelines to Help Answer the Overall Question

— All degraded areas within the greenway should have their ecological integrity restored where possible. Highest priority should be given to those areas that will, if restored, remove a functional break in the greenway for one of the key uses or users.
— Restored lands should serve as demonstration areas for the owners of degraded lands outside the greenway. Such owners should be encouraged and assisted in restoring their lands since this will help support the functions of the greenway.
— See the relevant site-scale guidelines from the sections about preparing site designs and management plans at the ends of chapters 3, 4, and 5, and see the main text of those chapters for discussion.

Overall Question

4.4. *How should the greenway be managed?*

Guidelines to Help Answer the Overall Question

— Management of the greenway can be as important as or more important than design; it must sustain the greenway.
— There should be continuity from the design process to the management phase because many management concerns can be anticipated in the design process and because, if kept current, the extensive data gathered for the greenway's design can be of great help in management.
— See the relevant site-scale guidelines from the sections about preparing site designs and management plans at the ends of chapters 3, 4, and 5, and see the main text of those chapters for discussion.

References

Berger, J. J., ed. 1990. *Environmental Restoration.* Island Press, Washington, D.C.

Cairns, J., Jr. 1988. *Rehabilitating Damaged Ecosystems.* CRC Press, Boca Raton, Fla.

Forman, R. T. T., and M. Godron. 1986. *Landscape Ecology.* John Wiley and Sons, New York.

Jolley, H. E. 1969. *The Blue Ridge Parkway.* The University of Tennessee Press, Knoxville.

Jordan, W.R., III, M. E. Gilpin, and J. D. Aber. 1987. *Restoration Ecology: A Synthetic Approach to Ecological Research.* Cambridge University Press, Cambridge.

Leopold, A. 1933. *Game Management.* University of Wisconsin Press, Madison.

Little, C. E. 1990. *Greenways for America.* Johns Hopkins University Press, Baltimore.

Lyle, J. H. 1985. *Design for Human Ecosystems.* Van Nostrand Reinhold Company, New York.

Massachusetts Division of Conservation Services. 1990. Open space and recreation plan requirements. Executive Office of Environmental Affairs, Commonwealth of Massachusetts, Boston.

Pearsall, S. H., D. Durham, and D. C. Eagar. 1986. Evaluation methods in the United States. In M. B. Usher, ed., *Wildlife Conservation Evaluation,* Chapman and Hall, London.

President's Commission on Americans Outdoors. 1987. *Americans Outdoors, the Legacy, the Challenge.* Island Press, Washington, D.C.

Root, R. B. 1967. The niche exploitation pattern of the blue-gray gnatcatcher. *Ecological Monographs* 37: 317–50.

Severinghaus, W. D. 1981. Guild theory development as a mechanism for assessing environmental impact. *Environmental Management* 5: 187–90.

Shafer, C. L. 1990. *Nature Reserves: Island Theory and Conservation Practice.* Smithsonian Institution Press, Washington, D.C.

Short, H. L. 1983. Wildlife guilds in Arizona desert habitats.

U.S. Dept. of Interior, Bureau of Land Management, Service Center Tech. Note 362.

Short, H. L., and K. P. Burnham. 1982. Technique for structuring wildlife guilds to evaluate impacts on wildlife communities. U.S. Dept. of Interior, Fish and Wildlife Service Special Science Report 244, Washington, D.C.

Spirn, A. W. 1984. *The Granite Garden: Urban Nature and Human Design*. Basic Books, New York.

Starr, J., and J. Estes. 1990. *Geographic Information Systems: An Introduction*. Prentice Hall, Englewood Cliffs, N. J.

Steinitz, C. S., P. Parker, and L. Jordan. 1976. Hand-drawn overlays: Their history and prospective uses. *Landscape Architecture* 66(5): 444–55.

Thomas, J. W., R. J. Miller, C. Maser, R. G. Anderson, and B. E. Carter. 1979. Plant communities and successional stages. Pages 22–39 in J. W. Thomas, tech. ed., *Wildlife Habitats in Managed Forests: The Blue Mountains of Oregon and Washington*. USDA Forest Service, Agric. Handbook No. 553, Washington, D.C.

Tomlin, C. D. 1990. *Geographic Information Systems and Cartographic Modeling*. Prentice Hall, Englewood Cliffs, N. J.

Verner, J. 1984. The guild concept applied to management of bird populations. *Environmental Management* 8(1): 1–14.

Daniel S. Smith

Greenway Case Studies

7

Earlier chapters in this book presented scientific documentation of specific greenway functions and discussed a variety of design problems and solutions. Diverse issues were raised that relate to wildlife habitat and movement, water quality, hydrology, aesthetics, recreation, and techniques for greenway design and management. Although much remains to be learned, there is clearly a great deal of evidence to show that greenways can serve specific functions and that there are numerous ways to improve ecological integrity through greenway design.

However, examples of carefully designed, multifunctional greenways are relatively rare. Many greenways have been designed largely for recreation or scenic values. Many other conservation-oriented projects have focused on land protection without fully considering the intricacies of ecological function. There are, nonetheless, a growing number of greenway projects that systematically consider some or all of the functions outlined in earlier chapters. This chapter presents

eight such case studies from different parts of the United States.

These examples illustrate a variety of ecological issues and applied design solutions. Each case highlights at least one of the major themes of this book: wildlife conservation, water resources protection, or recreation design (Table 7.1). A few focus almost entirely on wildlife, although most cut across thematic boundaries and involve a number of related issues. Each description provides an evaluation of the design and management techniques that have been used in the particular case.

Most of these examples lack the kind of scientific documentation of ecological functions provided in earlier chapters, and several projects are still in the design or implementation phase. Evaluation provided here is based on a combination of site visits, interviews with people involved in the design or management of the greenways, and a review of literature when it exists. The detail presented here is thus somewhat variable,

Table 7.1 Eight greenway case studies and the design issues considered.

| | Thematic Focus | | |
Case Study	Wildlife	Water	Recreation
Southeastern Wisconsin Environmental Corridors	▲	▲	
Florida Wildlife Corridors	▲		
Rio Grande Valley State Park (Albuquerque, N. Mex.)	●	●	▲
Boulder Greenways (city and county of Boulder, Colo.)	▲	▲	●
Santa Monica to Santa Susana Mountains Wildlife Corridors (southern Calif.)	▲		
South Platte River Greenway Design (Brighton, Colo.)	▲	●	▲
The Woodlands New Town (Tex.)	▲	▲	●
Quabbin to Wachusett Wildlife Corridor Study (Mass.)	▲		

Note: ▲ represents a primary focus; ● represents a secondary focus.

depending on the information that was available for a particular project.

The cases were selected either because they represent innovative design techniques or because they are successful in achieving their objectives; often the cases were selected for both reasons. They provide examples of how some of the ideas in this book have already been implemented under various circumstances. As real-world applications, they offer lessons of experience for future projects.

Southeastern Wisconsin Environmental Corridors

For more than twenty years the Southeastern Wisconsin Regional Planning Commission (SEWRPC) and its constituent local governments have made systematic efforts to delineate and protect greenways, known locally as environmental corridors. The result of these efforts is an extensive network of open space that spans the continuum from urban to suburban to rural landscapes. By applying an innovative combination of land-

use regulation and land acquisition to the highest-priority corridors, the seven counties have achieved what may be the most complete regional system of greenways in North America today.

Background

The seven-county southeastern Wisconsin region covers roughly 2,700 square miles (1.7 million acres) of rolling, glacially sculpted terrain to the west of Lake Michigan. The region is largely agricultural but also includes the cities of Milwaukee, Waukesha, Kenosha, and Racine in its eastern reaches. Near the region's western borders, there are a number of substantial tracts of remnant hardwood forest. This east-to-west transition from urban to agricultural to more forested landscapes, although not uniform throughout the area, illustrates the concept of the landscape modification gradient (see chapter 2) and has a marked impact on the types of greenways that have been protected in the region.

Corridor protection in southeastern Wisconsin dates from the 1920s, when a system of parkways, designed by Charles B. Whitnall, was initiated in Milwaukee County. In the 1960s, the concept was further promoted by Professor Phillip Lewis, Jr., of the University of Wisconsin at Madison. Lewis recognized the concentration of important natural resources along waterways and ridgelines and recommended their protection by the state for both recreation and conservation (see chapter 1 for further discussion). Lewis's recommendations were adopted by the SEWRPC as part of its regional land-use plan in 1966 (Rubin and Emmerich 1981; SEWRPC 1985). Since then, corridor protection has been one of the commission's primary goals.

The Region's Greenway Types: From Urban to Rural

Figure 7.1 shows the region's extensive array of primary environmental corridors, which total 467 square miles (additional area is covered by secondary environmental

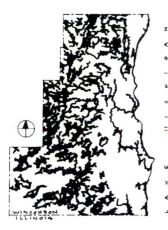

Figure 7.1 Primary environmental corridors in the seven-county southeastern Wisconsin region cover 467 square miles, or roughly 17 percent of the region. About 349 square miles (75 percent of the total corridor area) have been protected from most forms of development through land acquisition or a combination of local, state, and federal regulations. (After Southeastern Wisconsin Regional Planning Commission 1985.)

corridors; see later discussion of corridor protection). Although there is great variety within this system, the following examples from Milwaukee and Waukesha counties (Figure 7.2) give a representative flavor of the basic greenway types present in the region: urban riparian, agricultural riparian, and ridgeline.

Within Milwaukee County, three principal drainages—the Root, Menomonee, and Milwaukee rivers—as well as several smaller streams are protected with riparian greenways that generally range from a few

hundred to several thousand feet wide and serve multiple functions in this highly developed landscape. They provide habitat for native species (white-tailed deer, muskrat, gray fox, coyote, red-shouldered hawk) and in places are wide enough to harbor sensitive interior-forest bird species like acadian flycatcher, American redstart, cerulean warbler, and ovenbird. Several of these corridors include roads and thus serve as parkways for at least part of their length. Most contain walking or bike trails for recreation and commuting. The focus on riparian areas helps control floodwaters and maintain aquatic habitat. In southern Milwaukee County, where farming still persists in a few areas, the Root River is protected from sediment and fertilizer by a mostly continuous wooded buffer (Figure 7.3).

Outside of metropolitan Milwaukee, the environment grades quickly into a traditional midwestern farming landscape. Here, riparian corridors are maintained along waterways and contain naturally meandering stream channels, wetlands, and, in adjacent uplands, wooded habitat that is rare in this intensively farmed land. For instance, a greenway along the Fox

Figure 7.2 Primary environmental corridors in Waukesha and Milwaukee counties and their relationship to a landscape modification gradient from the city of Milwaukee in the east to more rural areas in the west. (After Southeastern Wisconsin Regional Planning Commission 1985.)

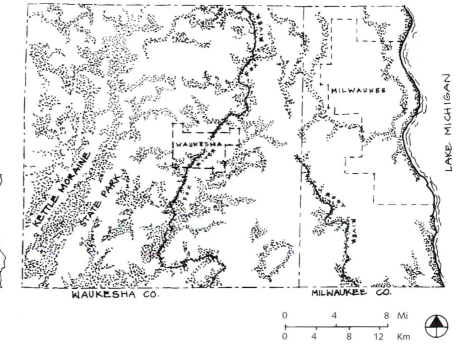

Figure 7.3   Where farming persists along the Root River in southern Milwaukee County, the river's riparian forest filters eroded soil moving downslope. (Photo by D. Smith.)

Figure 7.4   North and south of the city of Waukesha, a wooded buffer shields the Fox River from adjacent corn fields. (Photo by D. Smith.)

River, extending both north and south of the city of Waukesha helps filter out agricultural sediment and probably removes excess nutrients as well (Figure 7.4). It provides habitat for beaver, red and gray fox, coyote, mink, weasel, and white-tailed deer and probably functions as a movement pathway between larger habitat areas. Unfortunately, many species are unlikely to traverse Waukesha's urban center, where the corridor becomes a recreational park with mowed grass and a scattering of shade trees (Figure 7.5). South of Waukesha, at the Fox River Wildlife Sanctuary, artificial ponds and wetlands have been constructed (Figure 7.6). Careful vegetation management in the sanctuary has eradicated invasives like reed canary grass and purple loosestrife and has brought back blue vervain, cattails, and other native species.

In the region's far western reaches, Kettle Moraine State Forest contains an exceptional example of interlobate glacial moraine, a massive, 100-to-300-foot-high ridge of glacial till piled up between adjacent lobes of the Wisconsin glacier more than 10,000 years ago. The 19,000-acre forest stretches along the ridge for 20 miles (Figure 7.7) and includes associated wetlands along its margins. This protected area is wide enough to contain extensive interior forest. It serves

as breeding or permanent habitat for several dozen species of fish, 15 kinds of amphibians, 233 bird species, and over 40 kinds of mammals (Wisconsin Dept. of Natural Resources). The forest is connected to other, smaller natural areas nearby and thus has the potential to serve not only as a preserve but also as a reservoir of native species, helping to maintain diversity beyond its immediate boundaries.

Kettle Moraine State Forest is also an important regional center for recreation. The Ice Age National

Figure 7.5   The Fox River flows through the city of Waukesha where it is maintained as a traditional urban park and thus provides less protection for both wildlife and water than in areas outside the city. (Photo by D. Smith.)

Figure 7.6 Artificial ponds and wetlands south of Waukesha have helped restore wildlife habitat along the Fox River. Boardwalks allow people to see the wetlands close up and prevent disturbance to vegetation and wet soils. (Photo by D. Smith.)

Figure 7.7 In western Waukesha County, Kettle Moraine State Forest includes a ridgeline greenway several miles wide, surrounded by intensive agriculture. (Photo by D. Smith.)

Scenic Trail winds along 36 miles of ridgeline and connects to numerous local trails. State campgrounds provide a getaway for the nearby urban population. Recreation is also provided for throughout the rest of the region. The SEWRPC has recommended a system of seventy county and state parks and 500 miles of recreational trails within environmental corridors as part of park and open-space plans for each of the seven

counties. At present, sixty of these parks and 170 miles of trails are available for public use.

Greenway Delineation

Some of the region's greenways, including Milwaukee's parkways and Kettle Moraine State Forest, existed before the SEWRPC initiated its corridor protection program. Most, however, have been designed since 1966 by the commission.

The design process begins with a comprehensive resource inventory of each county, mapped on aerial photographs at a scale of 1"= 400'. The resulting data base resides in a geographic information system (GIS), covers all pertinent classes of natural resources including vegetation, soils, wildlife habitat, hydrology, scenic vistas, and land use, and is updated every five years. These data form the basis for corridor design and other planning activities undertaken by the commission.

Each resource type is assigned an importance value between 5 and 20, based on its relative importance as determined by consensus of the SEWRPC staff and technical advisory committees (Table 7.2). For a given portion of the region, the GIS is used to combine maps showing all of the resource types, and any area covered by at least one of these resources is marked off. Then the cumulative point value for all resources coinciding in a particular area is calculated. Any area with a point total of 10 or more is considered to have significant natural resource value. Although some isolated areas have a value of 10 or more, high-value areas usually line up along waterways and ridgelines.

This use of overlays, a variation of the method popularized by Ian McHarg (see chapters 2 and 6 for further discussion), has been a standard in ecological planning for more than twenty years. Overlays are quite effective as a means of identifying the location and pattern of important resources and combinations of resources and thus revealing the relative sensitivity of various locations to development impacts.

Still, this method has a drawback as used here in

Table 7.2 Natural resource elements inventoried by the Southeastern Wisconsin Regional Planning Commission

Natural Resource Element	Point Value
Lakes	20
River or Stream	10
Shoreland (perennial)	10
Shoreland (intermittent)	5
100-year Floodplain	3
Wet, Poorly Drained and Organic Soils	5
Wetland	10
Woodland	10
Wildlife Habitat (high-value)	10
Wildlife Habitat (medium-value)	7
Wildlife Habitat (low-value)	5
Steep Slopes (more than 20%)	7
Steep Slopes (12–19%)	5
Prairie	10
Scenic Viewpoint	5

Note: Other cultural elements, like existing park designations and historic sites, are also assigned point values ranging from 1 to 15.

Source: Rubin and Emmerich (1981).

Table 7.3 Guidelines for determining the maximum length of connecting corridors for wildlife

Acreage of Smaller Habitat Area	Maximum Length of Connecting Corridor	
	Feet	Miles
640 or more	2,640	1/2
320-639	1,760	1/3
160-319	1,320	1/4
80-159	880	1/6
40-79	660	1/8
20-39	440	1/12
5-19	220	1/24

Note: Guidelines are based on the size of the smaller of two habitat areas to be connected.

Source: Rubin and Emmerich (1981).

that it fails to consider adequately ecological process. The location and arrangement of particular types and combinations of resources are unduly favored over the functional interactions between elements of the landscape. Thus, for example, although the method will recognize a riparian corridor as significant, the method does not specifically consider the role of upland vegetation in filtering out contaminants headed for a stream. As the method has been adapted by the SEWRPC, this problem is partially compensated for by assigning a 10-point value to upland forest and to a buffer of up to 75 feet along perennial streams—but the issue of corridor width is not fully addressed. As identified by the overlay technique, riparian buffers may be too narrow to achieve their intended function (or, if water quality is the only goal, they may be unnecessarily wide). Alternately, if there is no extant upland buffer, the overlays will not highlight an area that might usefully be *restored* to a forested condition. Nor does the method consider the width or area of habitat needed for a given species or community of wildlife but only focuses on the presence or absence of significant habitat.

However, one important element of corridor function, connectivity, is specifically addressed. Obviously, this method favors the maintenance of connectivity among natural areas by focusing on linear aggregations of natural features. Further consideration of connectivity is built into the method in order to connect natural areas separated by short stretches of land that fall shy of the 10-point cutoff. The distance over which these connections are made is determined by a set of specific guidelines relating to the smaller of the two areas to be connected (Table 7.3). For instance, if the smaller of the two areas is more than 640 acres (1 square mile), a connecting zone one-half-mile long can be included in the corridor; if the area is only 100 acres in extent, the connecting zone can be no more than 880 feet (one-sixth mile) long (SEWRPC 1981).

These guidelines are based on the assumption that smaller areas will contain only small mammals and other species unlikely to travel more than short distances. Larger areas, however, support species such as deer and fox, which will roam farther in search of food, cover, or new territory. These guidelines were developed in consultation with regional experts familiar with species likely to use various-sized habitat patches. Guidelines are thus focused on the particular conditions and species of the region. However, the actual distance animals will travel will depend on the species present, the type of habitat being used or traversed, the size and location of other nearby habitat patches, adjacent land use, and other factors. Although these numbers serve as a useful guide, they lack an empirical basis and, taken alone, could lead to oversimplification of complex issues. To ensure that the guidelines are effective in individual cases, they are applied flexibly by a staff biologist at the commission.

Greenway Protection

Greenways in the region are protected through a combination of land acquisition and land-use regulation. Once an area is found to have significant resource value, the degree of protection it receives depends on its dimensions and acreage. Areas that cover more than 400 acres and are at least 2 miles long and 200 feet wide are designated as primary environmental corridors and are usually protected to a high degree by county and state governments. Areas that contain between 100 and 400 acres and are at least 1 mile long are designated as secondary environmental corridors (these corridors have no minimum width). Secondary corridors are recommended for protection by local government but are usually not protected by counties or the state. Finally, disjunct areas that exceed 5 acres and 200 feet in width are designated as isolated natural areas, which are also recommended for protection at the local level but receive no county or state protection. No designation is inviolate, but since the state and the counties are generally better able to restrict development in the corridors than are local governments, primary corridors usually receive greater protection.

Primary corridors encompass 467 square miles, or roughly 17 percent of the region (Figure 7.1). Of this

area, 147 square miles, or 31 percent of the total corridor area, have been purchased by local, county, and state governments. An additional 44 percent of primary corridors (202 square miles) that occur on private lands have been protected through local, county, and state regulations or the federal Wetlands Protection Act.

One of the more effective regulatory tools used to protect the corridors lies in the permitting process for sanitary sewer extensions. Like all planning commissions in the state, the SEWRPC is charged with maintaining an areawide water-quality management plan that designates sewer service areas and environmentally sensitive lands within those districts (in this case, sensitive lands are defined as primary environmental corridors). Before the state's Department of Natural Resources can approve a proposed sewer extension, it must determine that the extension and associated development will not intrude upon any primary corridors.

However, exceptions can be made in specific cases. Parks, outdoor recreation facilities, and low-density residential developments (with 5-acre minimum lot sizes) are sometimes considered to be compatible with corridor protection, in which case they are allowed to intrude upon corridor lands. Although these uses may in fact be benign in some cases, they may be detrimental in others. Recreation areas and low-density development may be less intrusive visually than other land uses, but they can have a major impact on wildlife by increasing edge and introducing invasive species and direct human disturbance.

It is important to note that these different levels of protection do not necessarily reflect the functional significance of the different designations. Primary corridors do contain the most important wildlife habitat in most areas, especially for interior-forest species, because they are larger and wider than secondary corridors. But many of the intermittent tributaries that make up secondary corridors are potentially quite important as filters of sediment and excess nutrients. With current policy, however, they are considerably less likely to be protected from encroaching agriculture or development. Corridors less than 100 acres in extent, 1 mile in length, and 200 feet wide receive no protection, even if they are functionally significant.

Conclusion

As noted earlier, the method used to design greenways in the region could be of more use if it focused more attention on ecological process, specifically in relation to corridor width. There is also a lack of protection for small but potentially important corridors. But these problems, both elucidated by fairly recent advances in ecological understanding and the second also rooted in limitations of landowner support, do not diminish the enormous success achieved in the region. By using state-of-the-art inventory and mapping techniques and a systematic delineation method, by providing leadership to its constituent governments, and by making the most of strong popular support, the planning commission has achieved a largely continuous and highly functional regional greenway network.

Florida Case Studies

During the last ice age, when sea level was as much as 400 feet lower than today, the peninsula that is now Florida was roughly two times its current size. It also contained a much greater diversity of life than in historic times; there were over 110 species of mammals, about twice as many as today. Many species, among them jaguar, jaguarundi, ocelot, sloths, and llamas, actually originated in South America and subsequently died back from the northern parts of their range as the climate warmed and the Floridian land mass shrank (Harris 1985).

These extinctions took place over thousands of years because of long-term climate change. Today, native species in Florida face similar threats over the course of only years or decades as the direct result of human influence. Since 1970, the number of species in the state listed as threatened or endangered has more than tripled, from 24 to 80, and another 189 species are being considered for these designations (Harris and Gallagher 1989). This trend is unmistakably associated with human activity: during the same twenty-year period, Florida's human population has jumped from 7.5 to 14 million, the number of urban acres in the state has risen from roughly 3 million to about 5 million, and the number of highway miles has grown from 80,000 to 110,000 (L. D. Harris personal communication). Automobiles and powerboats are now the leading known cause of death for all large mammals in the state, with the exception of white-tailed deer (Harris and Gallagher 1989).

As concern for Florida's rich assemblage of native wildlife has mounted, the state and federal governments, as well as private groups, have increased their efforts to preserve what remains. A number of extensive wildland systems still exist, but all are threatened by the rapid pace of development. Over the course of the past decade, an emerging goal of conservation across the state has been to maintain connectivity among natural areas by preserving key wildlife movement routes.

The following examples—the Pinhook Swamp Wildlife Corridor (also linked to the Suwannee River Corridor), the Wekiva River Greenway, and a series of wildlife underpasses along southern Florida's Interstate 75—span the state from north to south and represent some of the most important projects underway in Florida (Figure 7.8). Each of these efforts illustrates different issues for greenway design. The Pinhook Swamp is a significant natural area in its own right, but it also forms a broad linkage between large, federally owned habitats. The Wekiva River Greenway will protect habitat and link together a series of existing state holdings on the fringes of metropolitan Orlando. On the Wekiva, wildlife underpasses will also be needed to reduce the impact of heavily traveled roads. In the southern Florida example, a series of underpasses is being built to help maintain the last wild population of

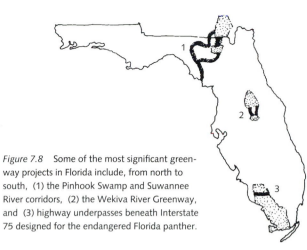

Figure 7.8 Some of the most significant green-way projects in Florida include, from north to south, (1) the Pinhook Swamp and Suwannee River corridors, (2) the Wekiva River Greenway, and (3) highway underpasses beneath Interstate 75 designed for the endangered Florida panther.

the endangered Florida panther. These underpasses have been shown to function for panther and other wide-ranging species and may prove to be an effective solution to the common problem of road kills.

Pinhook Swamp Wildlife Corridor and Suwannee River Corridor

Pinhook Swamp Wildlife Corridor

The Pinhook Swamp connects the Okefenokee National Wildlife Refuge in southeastern Georgia to Florida's Osceola National Forest (Figure 7.9). In 1988, The Nature Conservancy and the U.S. Forest Service began protecting the Pinhook as a movement corridor for wildlife.

The 400,000-acre Okefenokee National Wildlife Refuge contains the largest swamp in the southeastern United States and perhaps the richest biologically. Ten miles to the south, the Osceola National Forest contains 162,000 acres of wetlands, swamp, and pine-dominated uplands. The Pinhook Swamp, which serves as the headwaters for both the Suwannee and the Saint Marys rivers, spans the distance between these two protected areas and covers upwards of 60,000 acres. Since 1988, The Nature Conservancy has made several land purchases totaling nearly 30,000 acres in the Pinhook. These lands, which make up the core of a roughly 5-mile-wide linkage between the two larger

areas, have been resold to the Forest Service as an addition to the Osceola National Forest. These acquisitions already cover most of the distance between Osceola and the Okefenokee; The Nature Conservancy hopes eventually to purchase upwards of 70,000 acres, thus maintaining a continuous habitat area of over 600,000 acres. In addition, the new preserve will contain an ecosystem that is a major wildlife habitat and a source of clean water.

This landscape is home to black bear, white-tailed deer, the endangered red-cockaded woodpecker, and three rare plants: Catesby's lily, spoonflower, and the parrot pitcher plant (Middleton 1990). Were it to become isolated in the future, the Osceola National Forest would contain very small and thus tenuous populations of black bear and red-cockaded woodpecker (Harris 1988). In combination the Osceola, the Pinhook Swamp, and the much larger Okefenokee can accommodate considerably larger populations. However, even this combined area of 600,000 acres may not be large enough for viable, self-sustaining populations. Genetic exchange with other populations will probably be needed to ensure long-term survival (Reed Noss, personal communication). This could be achieved either through physical linkages with other habitat areas or by artificially transporting individuals from one population to another.

The Florida panther, an even more wide-ranging species, once roamed this area and may one day be reintroduced. In 1988, five panthers from Texas (members of a distinct subspecies) were released temporarily in the Okefenokee to test the potential of this habitat to support the large cats, each of which requires up to 150,000 acres of territory (Harris and Gallagher 1989). Two animals were killed by hunters, a third died of unknown causes, and the two remaining cats survived for almost a year before they were recaptured (Noss 1991). The fact that two of the five panthers were shot in less than a year suggests that limiting human access by closing unpaved roads in the refuge may be necessary for future reintroductions to succeed (Noss 1991).

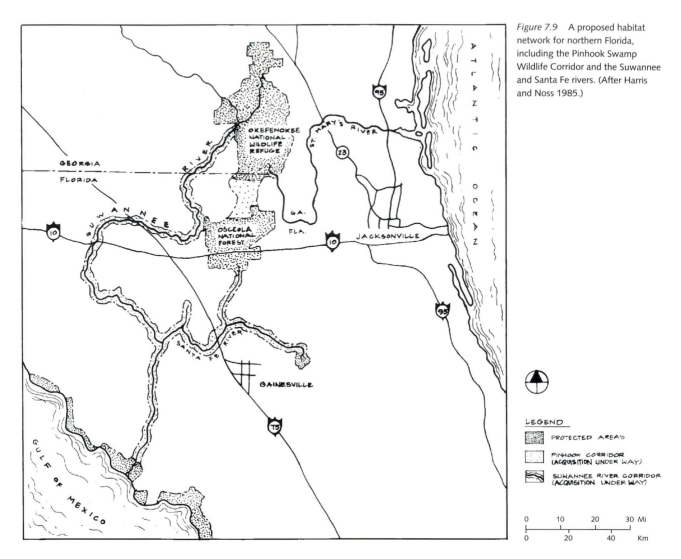

Figure 7.9 A proposed habitat network for northern Florida, including the Pinhook Swamp Wildlife Corridor and the Suwannee and Santa Fe rivers. (After Harris and Noss 1985.)

Given the very large range of Florida panthers, even the combined area of the Okefenokee-Pinhook-Osceola complex would support only a very small population (probably less than ten). But if connected to other habitats, either by corridors or by occasional trapping and transport of individuals, these reserves could become a functional component of a larger metapopulation (Noss 1991). Other possible candidates for reestablishment in this area are the whooping crane and the red wolf.

With an average width of about 5 miles, the Pinhook corridor is probably insulated enough from nearby logging or development to offer both habitat and a movement pathway for panthers or wolves. However, there may still be a need for buffer zones along the margins of the corridor, which is still relatively narrow compared to its neighboring preserves and thus more vulnerable to human intrusions. Panthers or wolves could become victims of road kills or poaching. The obverse is also a possible problem; panthers may attack and kill livestock, pets and, in very rare cases, even people, as occurred in Idaho Springs, Colorado, in 1991 (see Boulder Greenways case study). The initial protection of the Pinhook has paved the way for important reintroductions of rare animals. But, as always, design and management must remain responsive to changing conditions.

Suwannee River Corridor

Reed Noss and Larry Harris (1986) proposed that the Okefenokee-Pinhook-Osceola system become part of a more extensive habitat network extending down the Suwannee River to the Gulf of Mexico (Figure 7.9). The Suwannee is one of the last free-flowing rivers in the Southeast and runs through some of the least populated portions of Florida. The river is diverse biologically, containing many different aquatic, wetland, and upland communities and numerous rare species, including the eastern indigo snake, wood stork, American alligator, southern bald eagle, manatee, and several species of crustaceans found nowhere else in the world (Lynch 1984).

Of special concern along the Suwannee's lower reaches is the possibility of a rise in sea level caused by climate change. Because large areas of habitat near the coast are only a few feet above high tide, a small rise could inundate vast areas and force wildlife to move inland. An unobstructed pathway leading away from the coast could be crucial in the decades to come.

Determining whether connectivity can be maintained along the Suwannee's entire length would require a study of land uses along the river. This has not yet been done, nor has any particular agency committed itself to protecting the river's full length for wildlife movement. But much land has already been acquired. The Nature Conservancy and the state have purchased several natural areas along the Suwannee and its tributaries for habitat protection. To protect habitat and maintain water quality and natural flood storage, the Suwannee River Water Management District has acquired over 36,000 acres covering 94 of the river's 426 miles of frontage south of the Georgia border (frontage, measured on both sides, is equivalent to twice the river's length). The district has proposed purchasing an additional 152 miles, which would bring

the total to 246 (Suwannee River Water Management District 1992). Although significant gaps in the protected corridor remain, these efforts have already protected significant habitats, maintained connectivity along portions of the river, and helped ensure continued high water quality.

Wekiva River Greenway

Well to the southeast of the Suwannee River and just north of Orlando is the Wekiva River. Here, proposed massive subdivisions could sever the natural connectivity between a series of existing state parks and the Ocala National Forest. In 1985, the state launched a greenway initiative to protect large areas of habitat and critical movement pathways along the Wekiva and its tributaries.

Spurred by tourism and massive migration to central Florida, Orlando is one of the fastest-growing cities in the country and has become surrounded by extensive areas of suburbs, planned developments, and commercial strips. Amid this pattern of growth, the Wekiva River begins due north of the city and runs for 20 miles to the northeast where it meets the Saint Johns River.

Despite its proximity to Orlando, the Wekiva remains largely unspoiled. The river's course includes six state protected areas, totaling over 31,000 acres (Figure 7.10). So far, these state lands remain functionally connected to each other and to the 430,000-acre Ocala National Forest by privately owned habitat areas. This mixture of private, state, and federal lands makes up a sprawling mosaic of river, wetlands, and upland forest (Figure 7.11) that still harbors a robust collection of wildlife, including bobcat, river otter, gopher tortoise, and American alligator. Sherman's fox squirrel and the Florida black bear, both under consideration as federally endangered species, are also present.

In response to potential fragmentation of this area, the Florida Department of Natural Resources (DNR) has initiated a series of land purchases that will establish a two-pronged greenway between the Wekiva's

Figure 7.10 The Wekiva River Greenway (in progress), which will connect existing state parks near Orlando with the Ocala National Forest.

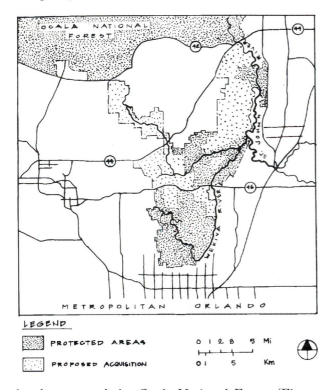

LEGEND

☐ PROTECTED AREAS

☐ PROPOSED ACQUISITION

headwaters and the Ocala National Forest (Figure 7.10). One route will extend to the northwest and include a mixture of streams, swamps, and uplands. The other route will follow the Wekiva itself to its juncture with the Saint Johns and then proceed north to the Ocala. Both routes are important for protecting riparian and upland habitat, maintaining water quality, and providing alternate movement pathways for wildlife.

The Florida black bear is the species most at risk here. The Ocala National Forest and surrounding habitats support a population of about 200 bears, and biologists estimate that about 24 of these live in the Wekiva watershed. If this southern habitat becomes isolated, it would probably not sustain such a small population for very long.

Along most of its length, the proposed greenway is at least 1 to 2 miles wide and can therefore provide substantial habitat for the bears as well as a safe movement corridor. The greenway's western prong, however, is as narrow as one-quarter mile in two places. Because this narrow width may be problematic, the DNR hopes to widen the corridor at these locations.

In addition to proposed development, animals along the Wekiva are threatened by several major roads that already bisect the area. Again, bears face the greatest peril. On average, at least 3 bears are killed by cars in the Wekiva basin each year, and the number of deaths has been growing along with increased traffic. Since the population in the basin stands at only about 24, the loss of only a few bears each year may have a significant impact.

To better understand movement patterns of bears in the area, a tracking study was undertaken along 6.5 miles of Florida Route 46 west of the Wekiva. This road segment was known to have the greatest bear mortality; 14 bears were killed there between 1980 and 1989. Tracks were monitored along a 5-foot-wide strip of exposed soil running parallel to the road (Wooding 1990). Although many animals successfully crossed at the river, others crossed at predictable locations to the west, where road kills occurred (Figure 7.12).

To allow bear and other animals to cross the road in safety, two underpasses have been proposed at the most frequently used and dangerous locations. Importantly, bear tend to cross where there is continuous cover on both sides of the road (Wooding 1990). When the underpasses are built, existing wooded corridors leading to the crossing sites will be maintained to guide animals to the underpasses. A 10-foot-high chain-link fence will be erected along the length of the road with breaks at the underpasses.

This research of bear movement was initiated in response to a proposed high-speed beltway around Orlando. The highway may eventually run roughly parallel to Route 46 and would cause even greater disruption of wildlife movement than the existing road. Wooding (1990) has suggested that maintaining sufficient connectivity for bear would require construction of an additional four underpasses at strategic locations.

Although there are no immediate plans to con-

Figure 7.11   The Wekiva River provides both rich wildlife habitat and an outstanding scenic and recreational resource on the fringes of metropolitan Orlando. (Photo by D. Smith.)

struct these underpasses, their eventual completion is likely as part of a statewide effort by the Department of Transportation to minimize conflicts between roads and wildlife (Gary Evink, personal communication). Although land protection is the first and most important element of the greenway effort, protecting the corridor's integrity from past and future road intrusions will be the second critical step.

Figure 7.12   Near the Wekiva River, collisions between bears and automobiles have become common enough to warrant cautionary signs for motorists. (Photo by D. Smith.)

Southern Florida Panther Underpasses

In southern Florida, the Department of Transportation has made an ambitious effort to provide for wildlife movement beneath a new interstate highway by constructing a series of underpasses. Without these structures, Interstate 75, which runs east to west from Naples to Miami and Fort Lauderdale, would split one of the state's largest and most important habitat areas in two. Although many species are likely to benefit from the underpasses, the critically endangered Florida panther was the project's main impetus.

A small remnant population of panthers continues to roam this part of the state. These are the only known panthers remaining in the eastern United States, and their numbers have dwindled to between thirty and fifty, an extremely low range if the species is to survive in the wild over the long term (Maehr et al. 1991). The population may have already been weakened by genetic inbreeding, as suggested by a 95 percent level of sperm infertility among males (Harris 1988). By any reckoning, these cats are in dire need of careful protection and management.

173

Areas where the panthers reside include Big Cypress National Preserve, Fakahatchee Strand State Preserve, the Florida Panther National Wildlife Refuge, portions of Everglades National Park, and surrounding private lands (Figure 7.13). The area currently occupied by panthers is slightly more than 2 million acres, almost one half of which is in private ownership. These animals are highly mobile; home ranges can be anywhere from 40,000 to 170,000 acres depending on sex and age. Young males may relocate as much as 60 miles away from their place of birth (Maehr et al. 1991). Maintaining large areas of connected habitat is obviously crucial for the panthers.

Three major roads cross through the area (Figure 7.13). Interstate 75, recently upgraded from a two-lane state road, carries by far the heaviest traffic and is the greatest obstacle for wildlife.

To allow panthers to move freely from one side of the highway to the other, a series of twenty-three underpasses, each 70 feet in width and 7 feet high, are being constructed along a 38-mile-long section of the

Figure 7.14   A wildlife underpass beneath I-75 in southern Florida. A 10-foot-high chain-link fence funnels panthers and other wildlife to the underpass, which measures 70 feet long by 7 feet high. (Photo by D. Smith.)

new road, beginning 12 miles east of the city of Naples (Figure 7.14). In addition, thirteen bridges crossing wet areas are being extended by 40 feet to allow animals to cross on adjacent dry land at these locations. A 10-foot-high chain-link fence topped with barbed wire runs along the highway between the underpasses to keep animals off the road. Maintenance of this fence may be a crucial element of the program; if holes develop in the fence, animals could enter the highway, where they might be trapped and killed.

Although the underpasses are being built at roughly one-mile intervals, their placement is not random. Crossings were identified by the location of previous road kills and by radio telemetry studies of panther movement patterns conducted by the Florida Game and Fresh Water Fish Commission.

Monitoring of animal movement through these underpasses (some of which were completed as early as 1990) has demonstrated their effectiveness. Melissa Foster, a graduate student at the University of Florida, has photographed animals moving through three of the underpasses with cameras triggered by infrared monitors. Over almost eighteen months of monitoring in 1990 and 1991, Foster's cameras recorded 837 crossings of 20 species, including 10 panther, 2 black bear, 133 bobcat, 9 alligators, and 361 white-tailed deer.

Figure 7.13   A 38-mile-long zone of Interstate 75, where underpasses permit movement of Florida panthers between protected areas.

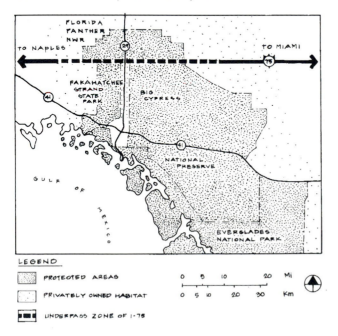

Although these underpasses are not linked with greenways, they illustrate an effective design—because of their width and openness—that can be integrated into greenway corridors. The efficacy of these underpasses, and their long-term effects on panther movement, will be further evaluated as the Florida Game and Fresh Water Fish Commission continues its radio telemetry studies.

This tracking research, which has been conducted throughout the panther's range, has also shown that panthers use a forested corridor running through private agricultural land to travel between Fakahatchee Strand State Preserve and the Corkscrew Swamp Sanctuary 10 miles to the northwest. For a mile of its length, the corridor is as little as 100 yards wide (D. Maehr, personal communication). Apparently, the relatively low impact of agriculture provides enough insulation from people to make this narrow corridor suitable for the panthers. This finding suggests that, in addition to highway underpasses, maintaining movement corridors on private land may be important to the species' survival (Maehr 1990). Although the future of the Florida panther is uncertain, pursuing these two strategies for maintaining connectivity may give the cats a push away from the brink of extinction.

Conclusion

Each of these projects may prove important to the maintenance of healthy populations and communities of wildlife at the regional level. The panther underpasses and perhaps eventually the Pinhook Swamp Corridor (if panther or red wolves are reintroduced) may be vital to the protection of endangered species. As noted in chapter 3, a statewide system of wildlife corridors and buffer zones has been proposed that would tie together many important habitat areas in the state. Various portions of this network are now being pursued by private and public organizations at the local and state levels. This network would transcend protection of populations at the regional scale and increase the likelihood that entire biotic communities could be maintained over the long term. Connecting the temperate forests of northern Florida to the subtropical woods and swamps of the Everglades might help buffer the effects of climate change on wildlife.

Implementing such a network would take many years, and the magnitude of the undertaking can hardly be overstated. As time passes and property values rise, corridor protection will become harder still. Yet, even partial implementation of the proposal could go far toward protecting Florida's wildlife. With input from the academic community, state and federal governments, and private groups, these three cases can serve as tests for the corridor concept. They may, once their effectiveness is more fully evaluated, serve as models to point the way to other efforts.

Rio Grande Valley State Park, New Mexico

The Rio Grande is born of melting snow high in the Rocky Mountains in Colorado and runs south through New Mexico before flowing on to form the border between Texas and Mexico. For most of its length, the river provides critical riparian habitat that is rare in the desert Southwest. Ironically, one of the best preserved reaches of the upper Rio Grande once it leaves the high mountains is within the city of Albuquerque, where farming and grazing, so common along the rest of the river, have been excluded from the floodplain.

The Rio Grande Valley State Park covers over 5,000 acres and is among the country's largest urban natural areas (Figure 7.15). The park possesses a wealth of regionally important resources including water, forest, and wildlife. It is also a much-used urban recreation area. Although activities like hiking, horseback riding, picnicking, and nature study are encouraged, park management ultimately gives highest priority to protecting ecological integrity, especially in sensitive and unique habitats. A holistic approach to design and

Figure 7.15 The lush riparian forest of the Rio Grande Valley State Park stands in contrast to surrounding land uses. (Photo courtesy of Albuquerque Open Space Division.)

management that includes resource inventory and mapping, minimum-impact recreation design, and ecological restoration, makes this park an instructive example for greenway design.

Background

In the arid Southwest, extensive riparian forests of native cottonwood and willow, called bosques (pronounced bos-kays), existed in the presettlement landscape within the floodplains of major perennial drainages. In contrast to the vast dry areas surrounding them, bosques host high densities of resident wildlife and migratory birds. With the advent of dams, flood control, and irrigation in the twentieth century, these forests and their associated wetlands have become increasingly rare. As the bosques have declined, they have become even more critical as oases for animals in this dry landscape.

The Rio Grande Valley State Park is one of the few remaining bosques of significant size in the region. Until the 1980s, however, the land that now comprises the park was unmanaged and suffering from neglect. Invasive plant species had taken over portions of the forest. Recreation was completely unregulated and causing ecological damage in many places. State pro-

tection was achieved in 1983, and management responsibility was assumed by the city of Albuquerque's Division of Open Space.

This ecosystem has been changed a great deal by human intervention in the twentieth century. In the 1930s, a series of flood-control and irrigation projects were completed that lowered the local water table by over 5 feet, controlled the river's channel, and reduced its overall flow. In 1939, an agreement was reached with the state of Texas for a regular annual discharge of Rio Grande water downstream. Since then, in order to reduce water loss through transpiration, a swath of 600 feet, encompassing the river and a portion of its floodplain, has been kept clear of trees (Albuquerque Parks and Recreation 1987).

These changes have seriously degraded the riparian forest. With the exception of one human-made oxbow on the west side of the river, wetlands, which are so important to the bosque's wildlife, no longer exist. Native cottonwood and black willow, which cannot reproduce without the moist soils caused by periodic flooding, are aging and are not being replaced by young trees.

Exotic species like Siberian elm and salt cedar, which have much lower value for wildlife and whose seeds germinate freely in dry soils, have taken over portions of the forest. Because their leaves have low nutritional value, these exotic species support much lower densities of native plant-eating insects, which in turn result in a smaller food supply for many native insect-eating birds. The effects of another exotic species, Russian olive, are less clear. Although Russian olive has expanded its range at the expense of native species, the fruits of this tree provide dependable food for many bird species.

Overall, the forest has less abundant and less diverse wildlife than it did a century ago. Many large species are gone, including turkey, mountain lion, and wolves. But relative to surrounding areas, the park remains highly productive as wildlife habitat. At least 130 species of birds use the forest permanently, seasonally, or during migration (Hoffman 1990). In spring and summer, the bosque has exceptionally high densities of breeding birds. Beaver, coyote, gray fox, and muskrat also reside in the park.

Recreation Design

Before its designation as a state park, many areas of the bosque were degraded because of heavy and often indiscriminate human use, including recreation, woodcutting and trash dumping. Informal trails and recreation areas crisscrossed the area with little regard for impacts to vegetation and wildlife (Figure 7.16). Woodcutting and dumping have now ceased. To maintain healthy biological communities, trails and other recreational sites are being located according to the relative sensitivity of different parts of the park to human disturbance.

Vegetation types within the park were inventoried and mapped in 1984 as the first phase of recreation design and management. Management zones were then delineated according to the habitat value of vegetation patches and their sensitivity to disturbance.

Three main factors were considered in determining patch significance: vegetative composition, patch size,

Table 7.4   Management zones within Rio Grande Valley State Park

Management Zone	Allowable Uses
Nature preserve	Education, nature observation, walking trails
Open-space conservation area	Rustic picnic sites, horse and bicycle trails
Light recreation area	Developed picnic sites, non-motorized boat access
Recreation area	Group picnic areas, developed recreation sites, access points

Note: Management zones are based on habitat value and the vulnerability of vegetation. Allowable uses are the highest-intensity recreational uses allowed in each zone.

Source: Albuquerque Parks and Recreation (1987).

and patch juxtaposition (M. Molles, personal communication). Vegetative composition was determined by both the mixture of species and the structure of vegetation. Patches with a high concentration of native species and diverse structure were considered to be especially important. Width was the most important element of patch size because wide patches contain more interior habitat and are less vulnerable to human disturbance. Juxtaposition boosted a patch's importance if high-quality patches existed nearby, thereby providing a high degree of connectivity between significant habitats. Although all three variables were considered in determining patch importance, patch size, especially width, was usually found to be the most important factor for wildlife.

Based on this analysis, four management categories were defined, each having a different recommended level of recreational use, ranging from low-impact nature trails to picnic areas and developed recreation sites (Table 7.4; Albuquerque Parks and Recreation 1987). This scheme was adopted in 1987 as part of the park's management plan and serves as a general guide for the design and management of facilities within the park. Figure 7.17 shows the delineation of the four management categories for a section of the park.

One element that might usefully have received more consideration in this procedure is evaluation of the degree of functional connectivity between high-

Figure 7.16   Recreational use of the Rio Grande Valley State Park can be quite heavy, especially along the banks of the river. Once indiscriminate, such use is now regulated according to ecological sensitivity. (Photo courtesy of Albuquerque Open Space Division.)

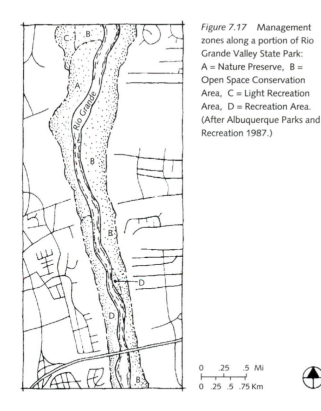

Figure 7.17 Management zones along a portion of Rio Grande Valley State Park: A = Nature Preserve, B = Open Space Conservation Area, C = Light Recreation Area, D = Recreation Area. (After Albuquerque Parks and Recreation 1987.)

0 .25 .5 Mi
0 .25 .5 .75 Km

2. Where possible, locate improvements in or near areas with existing disturbance.
3. In environmentally sensitive zones, locate trails along existing levees and ditch roads.
4. Design spur trails to the water's edge to minimize impact to sensitive shoreland areas.
5. Identify sensitive habitats where recreation will be excluded altogether.

The management zones adopted in 1987 are now being refined according to a Biophysical Land Units (BLU) planning method developed by the Bureau of Land Management (Albuquerque Office of Open Space 1990). The method calls for mapping (more detailed than in the 1984 study) of four basic features: vegetation, soil, terrain, and hydrology. In this case, several other layers of information will be added, including bird and mammal populations and habitat, human use patterns (trails, illegal camp sites, and dumping areas), adjacent land uses, and burned areas. All of these maps will be digitized into a geographic information system (GIS) and updated as conditions change over time.

These data will be analyzed with the GIS and used to find the most suitable location for trails and other facilities and to determine the types and intensities of recreation that are appropriate in various places and in different seasons. The GIS data base will also be used for monitoring long-term changes in vegetation communities.

This effort illustrates the importance of a systematic, information-oriented approach to recreation design and management. By conducting a thorough inventory of natural features and human use, by using maps and a GIS to conduct spatial analysis, and by using the results to guide recreation design, a strategy has been developed that allows people to use the park without unduly harming its unique ecosystem. Furthermore, the design is being complemented by educational programs aimed at both nature interpretation and responsible use of the park.

quality habitat patches. Considering juxtaposition in the determination of patch importance is a start, but it falls short of the need to understand and maintain connectivity along the entire length of the park. Study of wildlife movement along the corridor could be useful in determining to what degree animals will cross low-quality patches (which often receive significant human use) to reach adjacent high-quality patches. If they will not cross these areas, it might be useful to restrict use of low-quality patches that lie between more important habitats.

More recently, a series of policies have been developed to guide the future design and management of recreation. Most attention is given to the location of different uses as a means of minimizing recreational disturbance in sensitive areas:

1. Locate improvements in areas most resistant to human impact and where biological diversity and productivity will be least affected.

Ecological Restoration

In addition to protecting existing habitats, the park's managers are working to restore degraded areas. As described earlier, a major problem in the riparian forest is the lack of reproduction of native cottonwood and black willow and their replacement by less desirable, exotic species. To reverse this trend, salt cedar and Siberian elm are being cleared away in many places, and native cottonwood and willow are being reestablished in their place with pole plantings. By planting 1-to-3-three-inch diameter branches deep enough in the ground so that they are below the water table (usually 7 to 8 feet deep), the trees can be successfully regenerated. This habitat restoration is especially important in

Figure 7.18 Remaining wetlands along the Rio Grande provide rich wildlife habitat. Proposed artificial wetlands could help restore habitat diversity along the river. (Photo by D. Smith.)

areas disturbed by fire or, before the park's creation, by woodcutting, where exotics are apt to become rapidly established. It is hoped that this program will eventually restore the cottonwood-willow forest to its original state.

Artificial wetlands have been proposed as a second restoration effort. Before the river's flow was altered, natural wetlands covered extensive areas of the floodplain and supported a richer community of wildlife than is found today (Figure 7.18). Artificial wetlands could help return the bosque closer to its original condition. These wetlands have also been proposed as filters for pollution headed for the river. As in many western cities, one half of Albuquerque's water use is for lawn irrigation. The drainage from this irrigation, rich in excess nutrients from fertilizer, could be routed to series of wetland ponds where nutrients would be taken up by vegetation and eventually incorporated into organic sediments. These wetlands could also be located at the periphery of sensitive habitat areas to form a physical barrier that would keep people from entering. With this added function, the wetlands would address a full range of concerns from pollution control to habitat restoration to minimizing recreational impacts.

Conclusion

In addition to recreation design and management and habitat restoration, other programs in the park include long-term ecological monitoring and careful regulation of potentially damaging recreation events involving large numbers of people. Also important have been a thorough reevaluation of the park's management structure and a clearly stated series of goals and objectives built on a consensus of city and state agencies and park users. As always, even the most sophisticated strategies for design and management must be backed up by popular support and effective administration.

Management of the bosque is likely to be successful first because it seeks to restore native species and ecosystem processes, second because it recognizes the need to make resources available and enjoyable for people, and finally because it attempts to harmonize those two overarching goals. Implicit in this approach is an understanding of the symbiotic relationship between the city and the park. The city's residents need a place for exercise and recreation. In return they support government protection and enhancement of the bosque. The river and its forest are no longer self-maintaining as natural systems, but if properly cared for, they can continue to provide enjoyment for people and a refuge for wildlife.

Boulder Greenways, Colorado

Boulder County, Colorado, is located on the eastern edge of the Rocky Mountains and enjoys some of the most spectacular scenery in the United States, including a portion of Rocky Mountain National Park. The county, along with the city of Boulder, has a growing population, which now stands at over 200,000. To save natural areas and greenways, there are several ongoing open-space protection and management programs.

The city of Boulder acquires open lands within and outside its borders, is creating both a greenbelt surrounding the city and an urban greenway system, and is conducting stream restoration projects. The county also purchases land but is most involved in planning and growth regulation as a means of protecting both riparian and upland greenways within its jurisdiction. The Boulder County Nature Association, a private group, has proposed a countywide network of core habitat areas, wildlife corridors, and riparian corridors. The association works with private and public landowners to promote land protection and effective stewardship of natural areas within this network. All three organizations are creating greenways of different types to protect wildlife habitat and movement routes, to maintain water quality, and to provide recreational opportunities.

Background

Boulder County encompasses portions of the Great Plains and the Rocky Mountains, two of the major landscape types in North America. Where the high plains meet Colorado's Front Range in a dramatic change of elevation and biological communities, one finds a richness of wildlife characteristic of such convergences. Plains' species meet those of the mountains, and elevational gradients allow for seasonal migrations of large herds of elk and mule deer. Historically, grizzly bear, antelope, and bison roamed the area. The zone where the Rockies meet the plains was potentially "one of the most important large mammal habitats in North America" (Boulder County Nature Association 1989, 1).

With settlement of the county in the nineteenth century came many ecological changes. A dozen spe-

Figure 7.19 Boulder's greenbelt and tributary greenways, including existing municipal, county, and state lands as well as areas slated for future acquisition by the city. The greenbelt, which has a variable width, forms a nearly continuous band around the city.

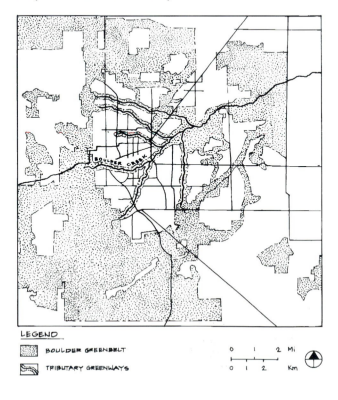

LEGEND

BOULDER GREENBELT

TRIBUTARY GREENWAYS

cies of mammals and birds are now locally extinct, and 90 percent of the county's shortgrass prairie has been lost. Bison, antelope, gray wolf, and grizzly bear are missing from this landscape, and prairie birds like short-tailed grouse and long-billed curlew are also gone. Nonetheless, a great variety of wildlife remains. All told, 78 mammal and 284 bird species are known to occur (Hallock 1990). Many species persist within only a few miles of the city limits, including elk, mountain lion, and black bear.

Both the county and city have undergone increasing development pressure in recent decades. Affected by expansion of nearby Denver and housing the major campus of the University of Colorado as well as numerous corporate and industrial facilities, the city's population jumped from 20,000 to over 90,000 between 1950 and 1970. In the face of this growth, a strong appreciation for open space among residents has been crucial in promoting open-space programs.

City of Boulder Open Space and Greenways

Boulder Greenbelt

In 1967, an open-space acquisition program was started by the city, funded by a dedicated 0.4 percent sales tax; in 1989, the tax was raised to 0.77 percent. Since its inception, the program has protected 20,000 acres of land in and around the city at a cost of $67 million. Most of the program's funds are now being used to complete acquisition of a greenbelt just outside the city's borders to limit urban sprawl, protect natural areas, and provide recreational access (Figure 7.19).

Much of this open space is leased to ranchers and farmers for livestock grazing. Unlike conventional range management, grazing is conducted on an intensive, time-limited basis to imitate the grazing cycles of native plains ungulates. By confining cattle to a relatively small area for a brief period of time, competition encourages them to eat invasive weeds like Canadian thistle, napweed, and cheatgrass, which they would probably otherwise ignore in favor of more palatable

grasses (D. Wheeler, personal communication). To prevent degradation of streamside habitat within these grazed areas, no livestock are allowed within riparian corridors or on nearby steep slopes.

Tributary Greenways Plan

In addition to this acquisition of land for the greenbelt, riparian greenways are being created within the city itself. A comprehensive greenway master plan was adopted in 1990 and is now being implemented (City of Boulder 1990; Figure 7.19). The plan outlines a framework for protecting and restoring riparian corridors of Boulder Creek and its tributaries within the city. A set of guidelines was developed for designing the greenways that covers the full span of multiple-use objectives, including water-quality improvement, flood control, habitat restoration, and recreational use.

The guidelines are adapted to riparian conditions typical of Boulder's stream and vegetation types and its urban environment. Because most of the tributaries are now channelized, the plan devotes significant attention to restoring stream channels. It specifically addresses the design of two-stage channels that can accommodate both low flows and periodic floods, as well as the restoration of alternating sequences of pools and riffles, which are crucial to a diversity of stream habitats. Restoration of native wetland, riparian, and upland vegetation is emphasized. Except in areas devoted mostly to recreation, trails are to conform to the relative sensitivity of natural features by avoiding large or fragile habitat patches and by approaching stream banks only at selected locations.

Connectivity along the greenways is specifically addressed as an important feature for wildlife movement. The guidelines also recommend making greenways as wide as possible to increase suitability for wildlife. Unfortunately, width is limited by existing development in most places, and heavy recreational use probably causes at least partial breaks in connectivity at some locations. So, although the tributary greenways are important for wildlife in this urban context, they are unlikely to include the full diversity of local species.

Much of the Boulder Creek Greenway, the program's showpiece, has already been completed. For several miles through the city center, the channel of Boulder Creek has been restored from a degraded state to a more natural condition, streamside vegetation has been restored where necessary, and recreational trails have been constructed (Figures 7.20 and 7.21).

Before restoration began, Boulder Creek had been channelized and shortened by 30 percent to speed drainage of floodwaters. Channelization had flattened out the streambed, thereby increasing sediment deposition and reducing the habitat variety created by pool-and-riffle sequences and channel meanders. Both riparian vegetation and aquatic habitat were seriously degraded. Restoration was started in the 1980s when the stream's low-flow channel was deepened to increase flow velocity and sediment transport. Stair steps and drop structures were added to produce alternating

Figure 7.20 Along much of Boulder Creek, native vegetation has been maintained or restored along the stream's edges. (Photo by D. Smith.)

pool-and-riffle sequences. Riparian vegetation, once trampled by dispersed recreation, was restored, and asphalt paths were laid down away from the stream's fragile banks. Recreationists using the paths now stay within view of the stream and encounter it periodically, but their impacts are minimized.

The width of natural vegetation within the greenway is relatively narrow where it traverses the urban center, ranging from about 10 to 50 feet beyond the stream's banks. Although terrestrial wildlife are probably limited mostly to human-adapted species, riparian vegetation has been a key factor in restoring aquatic habitat. Although trout were rare in Boulder Creek a decade ago, their population has increased substantially in recent years, and it is hoped that continued revegetation will further enhance habitat and increase food supply.

The floodplain of Boulder Creek is also being managed to retain storm water, rather than speed its flow to downstream areas as channelization had done. Along a quarter-mile section of the creek that has been prone to flood damage, forty-seven buildings have been purchased by the city. Once the buildings are removed, the entire area will be lowered by 2 to 3 feet to increase floodwater storage capacity. This action will enlarge the stream's floodplain so that it can hold some of the extra runoff now coming from impervious surfaces.

When this excavation is finished, the land will be graded and used as a developed recreation site with ball fields and a playground. Although the area will become an important community asset, it might alternatively have been designed to play a more significant ecological role. Depending on the depth of excavations, this area could either become a wetland or a substantial patch of riparian forest, both of which now cover only small areas along the creek's modified urban reaches.

All of these improvements have helped restore Boulder Creek from its earlier degraded state. On a sunny day, the greenway is a center of activity for the community. Kayakers paddle the creek, and paths are filled with bikers and walkers. The greenway provides

Figure 7.21 Since the restoration of Boulder Creek and improvement of recreational facilities, the greenway has become a center of urban recreational activity. (Photos by D. Smith.)

an oasis for urban wildlife, a flood-control mechanism, and an important resource for people.

Lower Boulder Creek Restoration

Channelization of Boulder Creek did not stop at the city limits but continued farther downstream to the east for several miles. The resulting broad, shallow streambed caused high water temperatures and excessive algal growth. Problematic in their own right, these factors caused changes in stream chemistry as well. The overabundant algae absorbed a large portion of the water's dissolved carbon dioxide to fuel photosynthesis and this in turn raised the water's pH. The combination of high temperature and pH increased

conversion of ammonia (a nitrogen compound) emanating from a sewage treatment plant to an un-ionized, toxic form subject to state water-quality regulations (Windell et al. 1991).

This nitrogen conversion was not the only problem. Water quality was degraded by non–point source contaminants as well. For years, cattle had used the creek as a water source and fed on its lush riparian vegetation. Predictably, the livestock overgrazed tree seedlings and herbaceous growth, trampled the streambanks, and accelerated erosion, causing an overall degradation of riparian and aquatic habitat. Boulder Creek also received water enriched with farm-born nutrients from irrigation drainage ditches.

By the mid-1980s, the city was faced with installing costly improvements to its sewage treatment plant in order to meet ammonia standards. Still, these improvements would only have solved part of the water-quality problem, since non–point sources would remain. Since studies suggested that a combination of stream restoration and non–point source reduction practices could complement the new plant, a demonstration project using these measures was undertaken (Windell et al. 1991).

Along 4 miles of the stream, easements of up to 125 feet on each side were donated by landowners. Restoration focused on narrowing and deepening the stream's low-flow channel to increase flow velocity. Pools, riffles, and aeration structures were created to enhance aquatic habitat and increase dissolved oxygen and carbon dioxide concentrations. Stream banks were stabilized with logs and then revegetated with willow and cottonwood cuttings to maintain bank stability and to produce shade and enhance aquatic food supplies. Cattle were fenced out of the riparian zone so that the restored banks will not be trampled.

So far, 3.5 miles of the creek have received this treatment. Along part of this length, the problem of nutrient inputs from agricultural drainage was also addressed. A drainage ditch was rerouted to flow into existing wetlands and into one artificially constructed wetland to filter out nutrients and other contaminants before water reaches the creek.

Overall, these measures are expected to reduce particulate and dissolved contaminants entering the stream, while simultaneously enhancing habitat for aquatic and terrestrial wildlife. They are also expected to help control levels of un-ionized ammonia. By speeding the flow of water, cooling it through shading, and creating an aquatic environment that will support less vegetation and thereby lower pH, it is hoped that conversion of ammonia to its toxic, un-ionized form will be reduced significantly (Windell et al. 1991).

One lingering concern is the fate of the ammonia farther downstream, where it may still be converted to the un-ionized form. Although some ammonia will be taken up by plants or become attached to soil particles, problems may arise downstream if water there is warm and has a high pH. But the project has nonetheless restored aquatic and terrestrial habitat and is likely to improve water quality substantially. Continued monitoring will eventually give a clearer picture, both at the site and downstream.

Ecological Design at the County Level

Greenway conservation in Boulder extends well beyond the city limits, where both the county government and the Boulder County Nature Association are protecting upland and riparian greenways as well as larger, nonlinear conservation areas.

County Planning and Growth Management

The county has identified significant habitat areas and elk migration corridors on private land, which are also used by deer, mountain lion, and black bear (Boulder County 1986). Elk use these corridors, mostly located along ridgelines, to move between summer pasture in the high mountains and winter range in the lower foothills and on the plains.

On occasion, herds have been observed moving through more developed areas that interrupt tradi-tional migration routes. In the fall, the animals sometimes build up on the west side of a sparsely developed area over the course of a few weeks, like water behind a dam, and then suddenly move through, usually at night, to reach winter pasture. This behavior suggests that uninterrupted corridors may not always be crucial for elk migration. However, the effects of obstacles on the herd's condition and on survival of individuals are unknown. Conflicts with people, such as automobile collisions and property damage, are also possible. Certainly if development becomes dense enough, the elk will not make their way through. Therefore, maintaining corridor integrity for elk and other large mammals is a sensible course in the face of increasing human pressure.

The county is working with private landowners to protect these upland greenways as well as several key riparian corridors. The width and alignment of corridors are based largely on traditional elk routes, natural landforms, and the extent of existing development. As is so often the case, there is no empirical evidence or even rule of thumb for designing the boundaries of these greenways. Careful studies of wildlife movement or riparian systems might help identify the most appropriate configurations. But, given the current pace of development in the county, limited financial resources are now directed toward planning and management.

To protect these corridors, the county uses several voluntary planning tools, including cooperative land-management plans, transfer of development rights, and cluster housing. Combined with negotiations between the county and developers, these tools usually lead to adequate compromises between development and conservation. Ultimately, however, the county has authority to deny approval for new construction that intrudes excessively on these ecologically significant areas.

The Boulder County Nature Association

The Boulder County Nature Association is working with private landowners, municipal and county governments, and federal agencies (U.S. Forest Service and National Park Service) to implement a broader ecosystem plan for the county (Boulder County Nature Association 1989). The plan includes critical areas identified by the county but also delineates a more extensive, connected network of open space composed of core habitat areas and connecting corridors (Figure 7.22). These areas are composed of a mosaic of private, federal (mostly Forest Service), county, and municipal holdings. The core areas include the full diversity of forest and grassland habitats within the county and are linked together with ridgetop and streamside corridors to provide for animal movement and to protect riparian habitat and water quality.

The association helps provide direction and acts as a facilitator for the owners that manage these lands. Their work is limited to cooperative efforts, such as

ecological management planning for private lands, transfer of development rights, creative development plans, fee acquisition, and encouragement of land trades to consolidate disjunct federal lands into larger units with a high degree of connectivity. Recent efforts have focused on negotiating donated conservation easements along key portions of two elk migration routes and a 2-mile segment of riparian habitat.

Conclusion

The city of Boulder's proximity to large areas of open space allows people and nature to mix to an unusual degree. A short drive west of town leads through suburbs to expansive natural areas little touched by human influence. By protecting nature in the midst of devel-

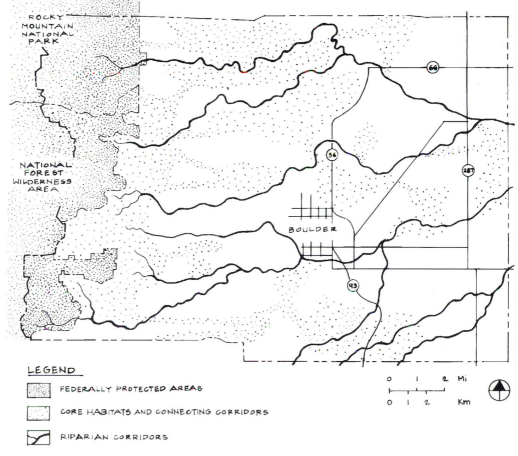

Figure 7.22 A habitat network for Boulder County, as proposed by the Boulder County Nature Association. The association works with both public and private landowners to protect and manage these areas. The county government also provides regulatory protection for the most critical elements of the network.

LEGEND

FEDERALLY PROTECTED AREAS

CORE HABITATS AND CONNECTING CORRIDORS

RIPARIAN CORRIDORS

oping areas, greenways are being used to bring nature and people still closer.

Although the advantages of this integration are many, problems can occur, sometimes unexpectedly. For instance, mountain lions, normally reclusive, have become accustomed to feeding on the abundant mule deer that congregate near the city, where forage is good and the deer are safe from hunters. There have been numerous instances of the lions killing domestic cats and dogs—tempting prey for a wild animal—and they have even threatened people on a few occasions. In nearby Idaho Springs, a jogger was killed in 1991 (Mason 1991).

Although educating people about ways to avoid such attacks can go far toward preventing such tragedies, there is no simple or complete solution. These incidents are a reminder that the distinction between open space as a recreational playground and open space as wilderness, where people are not in control, can be deceptively thin. Along with human impacts on nature, threats to people's safety should be carefully considered.

The different approaches to land protection taken by the city, the county, and the BCNA are appropriate to their organizational strengths and financial resources. The city, with funds generated by its open-space sales tax, is able to maintain an aggressive acquisition program in addition to its work in stream restoration. The county, with a smaller acquisition budget but planning authority over a large area, stresses land-use regulation and growth management. The association, having limited resources to pursue its extensive and ambitious ecosystem plan but enjoying strong landowner relationships, acts as a catalyst and facilitator for both the private and public sectors.

Yet all of these organizations have similar goals and maintain a high level of cooperation. The city and county have collaborated on land acquisition in the past, and all three agencies pursue complementary goals. The combination of public support, funding for acquisitions, effective regulatory and planning pro-

grams, and interagency cooperation goes far toward protecting an open-space system that maintains scenic beauty and ecological health.

Santa Monica Mountains to Santa Susana Mountains Wildlife Corridors, California

Development seems to spread endlessly through the Los Angeles Basin and into surrounding areas. Urban sprawl, a multitude of highways and some of the nation's worst air pollution all contribute to Los Angeles' image as a city of poor environmental quality. Yet, a major effort is underway to preserve and link together several large habitat areas north and west of the city—the Santa Monica Mountains, the Simi Hills, and the Santa Susana Mountains (Figure 7.23)—using greenways and highway underpasses. In this example,

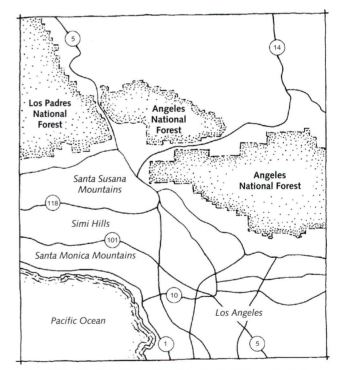

Figure 7.23 The Santa Monica Mountains, the Simi Hills and the Santa Susana Mountains bordered to the southeast by Los Angeles and to the north by national forests.

Figure 7.24 Wildlife corridors connecting the Santa Monica Mountains, the Simi Hills, and the Santa Susana Mountains. When completed, the network will tie together over 270,000 acres of habitat, which will be further connected to national forest lands to the north.

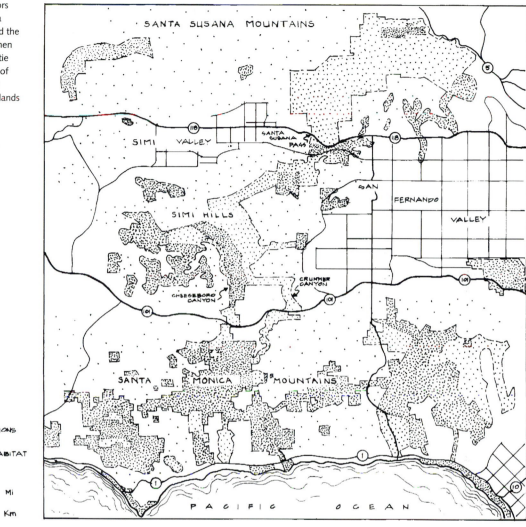

greenway design has been based on an evaluation of landscape characteristics, the needs of local wildlife species, and patterns of property ownership. Once completed, this habitat network is expected to exceed 270,000 acres (Figure 7.24), be further connected to larger habitats to the north and east, and include most of the area's native species.

Background

The Santa Monica Mountains stretch for 50 miles along the Pacific Ocean, largely within the bounds of Los Angeles County. Rising to over 3,000 feet, they define a rugged coastline and contain deep canyons and high mountain slopes with expansive stretches of dense chaparral and oak woodlands. Despite their proximity to the city, the Santa Monicas are home to many species of wildlife including mule deer, badger, coyote, bobcat, long-tailed weasel, gray fox, acorn woodpecker, and burrowing owl. Most remarkable is the continued presence of mountain lion and golden eagle.

Just to the north of the Santa Monica Mountains lie the Simi Hills, a smaller, lower range that forms a topographic link to the Santa Susana Mountains, still

187

farther north. These ranges harbor wildlife communities similar to the assemblage found in the Santa Monicas. The Santa Susanas in turn connect with much larger mountainous areas of the Los Padres and Angeles national forests to the north and east.

In earlier times, these areas formed a contiguous expanse of rugged mountain habitat, in contrast to the surrounding lowlands of the Los Angeles Basin and the San Fernando Valley. In the last several decades, as the growth of Los Angeles has spread westward, these ranges have been split apart by two major freeways and associated development (Figures 7.23 and 7.24). Core habitat areas within the Santa Monica Mountains, the Simi Hills, and the Santa Susana Mountains remain largely intact, with acreages of roughly 144,000, 32,000, and 96,000, respectively (Edelman 1990; Soulé 1989). But the movement of large mammals between these areas has been seriously inhibited by fragmentation.

In the long run, these isolated habitats are unlikely to sustain populations of wide-ranging native wildlife species (Edelman 1990; Soulé 1989). For instance, although mountain lions still exist within all three areas, their total population is estimated at only eight to twelve. To put this estimate in perspective, conservation biologists believe that populations of at least several hundred are needed for the long-term survival of most species (Shafer 1991). Although more numerous than mountain lion, bobcat, gray fox, coyote, and badger may also face localized extinction over the course of a century or more.

In hopes of reversing the trend of fragmentation, the National Park Service (which administers the Santa Monica Mountains National Recreation Area) and the Santa Monica Mountains Conservancy, a state agency, have jointly developed plans for wildlife corridors that will link the three mountain ranges together (Edelman 1990; Santa Monica Mountains Conservancy 1990). Both agencies are working to protect land within the corridors and to construct wildlife underpasses at critical freeway crossings.

Network Design

It is instructive to consider the proposed design and configuration of this network in some detail. This examination will begin in the north at the large national forests and proceed south toward the coast (Figure 7.23).

The Los Padres and Angeles national forests contain over 650,000 acres, are connected to other large mountainous habitats, and are likely to sustain populations of most species present in the region. They may thus serve as long-term reservoirs of species and genetic diversity for the smaller habitat areas to the south; the national forests can be likened to a stable anchor for the overall network. Animals moving between these vast areas and the Santa Susana Mountains do not yet encounter any insurmountable barriers. There is some concern, however, that this connectivity could be compromised in the future as development continues to spread and intensify (Edelman 1990).

Moving south from the Santa Susanas, a wildlife corridor will cross the Simi Valley Freeway (Route 118) at Santa Susana Pass and continue to the southwest for about 2 miles into the core habitat area of the Simi Hills. Lands within this greenway have been proposed for protection by the state of California. Clearly, the most critical barrier along this stretch is the six-lane freeway. Continuous heavy traffic makes this road virtually uncrossable for wildlife. Mountain lion, deer, and badger that do attempt to cross the road are often struck and killed by cars. Occasionally, animals successfully cross the freeway at a road overpass at the east end of Santa Susana Pass, but traffic and roadside development make this route far from optimal.

By coincidence, at the west end of the pass there is a tunnel beneath the freeway, originally built for equestrian use (Figure 7.25). The tunnel is 16 feet high, 16 feet wide, and 170 feet long. From either end it appears long and dark; terrain and vegetation on the other side are barely visible. The freeway has a six-foot-high chain-link fence along its length, which,

Figure 7.25 An underpass beneath the Simi Valley Freeway (Route 118) built originally for equestrian use serves as a passage for wildlife despite its cramped appearance. (Photo by D. Smith.)

together with freeway traffic, probably encourages wildlife to use the tunnel despite its cramped dimensions. To investigate the feasibility of a wildlife underpass, for local species in general and at this location in particular, a tracking study was conducted at the equestrian tunnel in 1989 and 1990 (Edelman 1990).

Dirt was spread across the middle of the tunnel, checked for tracks each week and then raked smooth again to record the next week's tracks. Over the course of two monitoring periods, totaling fifty-two weeks, several species used the tunnel regularly. There were fifty mule deer crossings, ninety-five coyote crossings and forty-two bobcat crossings. Gray fox and ringtail used the tunnel infrequently (nine and four crossings, respectively), and there were four sets of unclear tracks that may have been left by mountain lions. Despite its narrow width, the equestrian tunnel appears to be an important route for wildlife movement. It is reasonable to assume that a wider tunnel, designed specifically for wildlife, would offer an even more effective route.

Moving south into the Simi Hills, the next critical juncture begins at Cheeseboro Canyon, owned by the National Park Service, and leads south to the Ventura Freeway (Route 101) (Figure 7.26). The canyon, near-

ly a mile wide, contains a perennial stream with abundant riparian vegetation and offers a natural animal migration route. Although adjacent lands to the west will soon be developed and a major landfill lies to the southeast, the canyon should offer adequate cover and isolation even for shy, wide-ranging species.

A potential problem lies just north of Route 101, where the corridor must veer away from Cheeseboro Canyon, which extends to the southwest, and traverse a series of steep hills to the south before reaching the proposed underpass. This route, made necessary by planned development farther down the canyon, is less than ideal because animals probably prefer to travel through the riparian zone's dense cover rather than

Figure 7.26 The Ventura Freeway (Route 101) is nearly impassable for wildlife and currently blocks movement between the Simi Hills and the Santa Monica Mountains. Proposed underpasses would reestablish connectivity between the two ranges. (Photo by D. Smith.)

across the more open hills. Downstream development, however, should inhibit wildlife movement in that direction. Meanwhile, planned enhancement of the upland traverse, including artificial water sources and added plantings for cover, should improve the effectiveness of this route.

At about the middle of Cheeseboro Canyon, a second corridor will branch off to the east and then run south through Crummer Canyon to provide an alternate route for animals moving between the Simi Hills and the Santa Monicas. This corridor will provide another movement option in the event that human or natural disturbances make one of the corridors unusable.

At the southern ends of Cheeseboro and Crummer canyons, underpasses will be built beneath the Ventura Freeway. These will lead to several properties proposed for state acquisition, which will serve as a link to Malibu Creek State Park in the heart of the Santa Monica Mountains. From there, further connections will extend to the Pacific Ocean, eastward to Topanga State Park, and westward to Point Mugu State Park, all part of the Santa Monica Mountains National Recreation Area.

The basic framework of this habitat network was based on the location of existing core habitats and opportunities for protecting suitable linkages. But this sort of broadbrush design would certainly have been incomplete. A more detailed approach that considered particular species and local conditions was needed.

Before embarking on more detailed design, a study of native species of concern was undertaken, including estimates of their population sizes, territorial needs, and minimum viable populations for long-term persistence (Soulé 1990). Based in part on that study, the following guidelines were developed to maximize effectiveness for several fragmentation-sensitive indicator species, which included mule deer, mountain lion, bobcat, badger, gray fox, long-tailed weasel, and coyote (Edelman 1990, personal communication):

1. Locate movement corridors along traditional wildlife movement routes.
2. Make complex terrain with multiple movement routes a priority for inclusion. This provides alternate routes in case of human impacts or natural disturbances.
3. Seek a minimum corridor width of 1,500 feet. Across any significant distance (i.e., one-quarter mile or more), width should be even greater.
4. Ideally, locate corridors so that their edges include

steep terrain that will deter human use and development.
5. Include water sources wherever possible.
6. Make areas with structurally diverse vegetation, uncommon in this dry environment, a high priority for inclusion.
7. Include grassland and chaparral wherever possible as habitat for badger and gray fox, respectively.
8. Locate corridors as far from human activity as possible.
9. Include subcore habitat areas, or nodes, within or adjacent to corridors wherever possible to increase wildlife presence in and movement through the corridors.
10. Maximize the width of crossings of nonfreeway roads to increase the number of alternative crossing points for animals.

These guidelines focus on important points such as providing cover, water, and habitat diversity, insulating corridors from human activity, providing nodes along longer stretches of corridor, and providing multiple movement pathways. The guidelines form a strategy for determining corridor locations and boundaries based on local species and landscape variables. Of particular interest are (4), which makes use of the area's steep-sided canyons as a sort of topographic buffer zone, and (10), which recognizes that animals may learn to adapt to road barriers by crossing at safer locations, assuming they are given the opportunity to do so.

Conclusion

Although there is clearly a need for quick action to preserve what natural habitat still exists in the area, it was recognized that a solid information base together with a careful strategy for corridor design, including specific guidelines, were needed to ensure proper function of the habitat network. By applying these guidelines, along with detailed information on property ownership, to the generalized framework of corridor locations, a detailed design for land acquisition was created. With this strategy now in place, the more pragmatic work of actually implementing the network is proceeding.

Both the Santa Monica Mountains Conservancy and the National Park Service are working toward implementation through acquisition of land and conservation easements as well as strategic land trades with large landholders. State highway commission funds will be made available in coming years for construction of the freeway underpasses. Once these linkages are complete, the Santa Monica Mountains, the Simi Hills, the Santa Susana Mountains, and the national forest lands beyond will have been restored as elements of a functional, regional-scale network of wildlife habitat supporting a nearly complete native faunal assemblage. If the network functions as expected, wildlife populations should be large enough to be self-sustaining—a fairly remarkable feat in the burgeoning fringes of Los Angeles.

South Platte River, Brighton, Colorado

North of Denver, the South Platte River winds through an agricultural landscape, a mosaic of farms within which lies a sparse network of roads and towns (Figure 7.27). Near the town of Brighton, the river's floodplain, rich in gravel deposits, is scheduled to be mined over the next several decades to supply material for a new international airport, highways, and other development in the Denver area. Subdivisions are also proposed near the river to help absorb future expansion of Denver's population.

In 1988, Joan Hirschman, then a graduate student in landscape architecture at the University of Colorado at Denver, developed an innovative design for a 2-mile-long section of the river corridor near Brighton (Hirschman 1988; Hall et al. 1989). Based on landscape ecological principles, the design proposes a

Figure 7.27 Aerial view of the South Platte River and the town of Brighton, Colorado. Note the river's context in an intensively cultivated, agricultural landscape matrix.

greenway that would serve as habitat for local wildlife, a resting place for migrating birds, and a unique area for recreation, especially bird watching. Open gravel pits that will result from mining are proposed to be converted to ponds and wetland habitat. Overall, the design focuses on maintaining and restoring a diversity of habitats, enhancing connectivity between the greenway and adjacent areas, and finding new ways to integrate people and nature through a combination of recreation and education.

Background

The study area is slightly less than a mile wide on average and contains about 1,000 acres. Most of it lies within the river's floodplain. Although the river remains unchannelized, irrigation and flood-control projects upstream have had a major impact on its flow regime and in turn on riparian vegetation. The floodplain consists of a mosaic of different vegetation types; there are streamside stands of willow and cottonwood as well as patches of three varieties each of wetland and grassland (Figure 7.28).

Before flow was altered, uncontrolled floods used to shift the channel periodically and create abandoned meanders and oxbows. Willows then became estab-

Figure 7.28 Riparian habitat along the South Platte River is a mixture of wooded and open patches. (Photo by Joan Hirschman.)

lished on these wet sites. Later, once sediment had accumulated and sites were drier but rich in organic matter, willows were replaced with young cottonwood trees.

These successional patches of willow and cottonwood are critical to providing cover and food for numerous birds, especially woodpeckers and great blue herons. Although mature stands remain along the river today, they will eventually die out, and there is little regeneration of these species in new locations.

A rich variety of birds currently uses the site, including waterfowl, wading birds, woodpeckers, and songbirds. If artificial wetlands are constructed from gravel pits to increase the diversity and richness of habitat, the total number of bird species could theoretically reach 300 (Hirschman 1988). Red fox, white-tailed and mule deer, beaver, and prairie dog also use the site.

Although this river segment is mostly surrounded by agriculture, conditions upstream (to the south) are quite different. For 40 miles through Denver and its suburbs, the river has been channelized; its floodplain has been developed for urban and industrial uses in

some places and is used for intensive recreation in others. Along this stretch, the river corridor contains only small, narrow patches of natural habitat. The Brighton site is thus very important from a regional perspective (Figure 7.29). For migratory birds using the river as a flyway, it is a crucial resting place. For people, it has the potential to become an important resource on the outskirts of a major metropolitan area.

Landscape Ecology as a Conceptual Framework

Landscape ecology was used as a framework for evaluating and designing the site within a broad context, both human and ecological. In evaluating the site, lay-

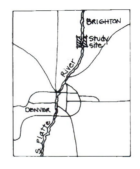

Figure 7.29 The study site and the town of Brighton in relation to the city of Denver. From a regional perspective, the site has the potential to serve as a resting place for migratory birds and as a recreation and education center for urban residents.

ers of mapped resource information were analyzed and compiled to reveal site structure, function, and patterns of change. Emphasis was placed on the need to integrate people and nature and on the implications of greenway design for ecological pattern and process at different spatial scales. The greenway was found to have potential as (1) prime habitat for local wildlife, especially birds, (2) an important stopover for migratory birds, and (3) a place for people to pursue recreation, bird watching, and environmental education. Finally, the opportunity to make connections with other natural areas nearby, particularly Barr Lake 3 miles to the southeast, and with future subdivisions adjacent to the site was stressed.

Spatial and temporal heterogeneity were found to be crucial to maintaining a diversity of birds and other wildlife. The site's location in the semiarid agricultural landscape of the Great Plains, where narrow riparian forests stand out in contrast to open land, is particularly important in this regard. Because forest-interior habitat was rare or nonexistent in the presettlement landscape, interior wildlife species are not a major concern; the design thus encourages an interspersion of wooded and open habitats that would be ill advised in a forested landscape.

Site Design

Toward the overall goal of creating a useful space for both wildlife and people, five specific objectives for site design were chosen:

1. Connect important patches with corridors to provide linkages within the site and to provide connections with other important habitats in the region.
2. Use research on patch shapes to create rich, varied areas for a high diversity of bird species and to create interesting spaces for people to enjoy.
3. Increase quantity and quality of habitat for targeted bird species, their associated guilds, and watchable birds in general.

4. Design a sequence of plantings so that patch configurations, corridors, and wildlife habitat for targeted species and guilds can be maintained over the long and short terms.
5. Design areas that are enjoyable and educational for visitors and adjacent residents. Do this in a manner that creates a balance between bird habitat requirements and people's environmental and socioeconomic needs.

As background for the design, the needs of key users of the site were reviewed, including humans and six target species of birds. The target species were western grebe, Lewis' woodpecker, common yellowthroat, yellow warbler, great blue heron, and belted kingfisher. The first four of these species are either rare or in decline locally; blue heron and kingfisher are valued as attractive species for bird-watchers. Prime habitat areas for all the target species were inventoried and mapped. Together, the six species use a wide range of habitat types in the riparian ecosystem. To make the site desirable for people, necessary elements included access points, parking, trails, education, observation blinds, a nature center, and rest rooms.

The greenway's master plan (Figure 7.30) shows the recommended shapes and configuration of gravel ponds, existing and proposed wooded areas, hiking trails, access points, and connecting corridors extending beyond the site. According to the design, gravel mining occurs mostly outside of existing prime habitat areas; some of the gravel ponds actually form new areas of important habitat. In contrast to traditional extraction that results in uniformly large, deep ponds with steep banks (an economically efficient method but inappropriate for most wildlife), the ponds are of various shapes, sizes, and depths and include numerous small coves, shallow wetlands, and islands. This design reflects research showing that these sorts of shapes, and the heterogeneity they create, typically support more diverse and more abundant wildlife, especially birds and fish (Hirschman 1988).

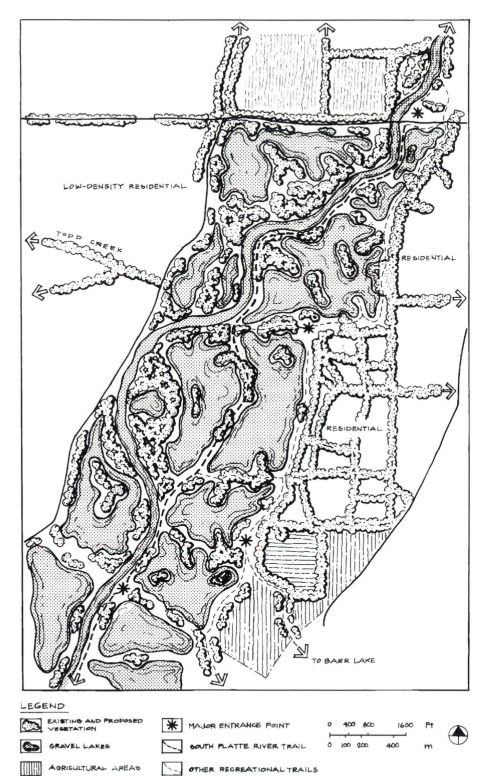

Figure 7.30 Proposed master plan for a 2-mile-long section of the South Platte River, showing the recommended configuration of gravel lakes, maintenance and restoration of native vegetation, and the extension of smaller corridors into nearby agricultural and residential areas. (Redrawn with permission from a map by Joan Hirschman.)

LOW-DENSITY RESIDENTIAL

TODD CREEK

RESIDENTIAL

RESIDENTIAL

TO BARR LAKE

LEGEND

EXISTING AND PROPOSED VEGETATION

GRAVEL LAKES

AGRICULTURAL AREAS

MAJOR ENTRANCE POINT

SOUTH PLATTE RIVER TRAIL

OTHER RECREATIONAL TRAILS

0   400   800   1600   Ft

0   100   200   400   m

Connectivity between existing prime habitat areas is retained by adjusting the location of the gravel ponds. Areas between the ponds, typically about 60 feet wide, are planted with deciduous trees to form continuous cover throughout the site. Because gravel mining may occur over the course of fifty years or more, these plantings occur in stages to create a diversity of successional stages, further enhancing heterogeneity of the site.

Where gravel ponds are less than 400 feet from the river and their banks could therefore be breached by future channel meanders, stabilization of the riverbanks with riprap or vegetation will be necessary. Where ponds are more than 400 feet from the river, the plan recommends leaving the channel in a natural state so that erosion, deposition, and resulting shifts of the stream channel can continue to occur.

The major trail in the design is a continuation of a paved trail along the South Platte Greenway, which extends south through Denver. The trail follows the eastern bank of the river except in one important habitat area adjacent to the river. This area is a remnant disturbance patch, an old river meander where a stand of cottonwood trees forms a likely site for recolonization by great blue herons, which are sensitive to human disturbance during nesting. Several unpaved trails run between the gravel ponds to the east of the river. The west side of the river, where there is no recreational access, becomes a wildlife sanctuary.

At the north end of the site, a major access point and a nature center are proposed. The center includes experimental areas of agriculture, residential landscape design, restored wetlands, and a variety of bird habitats. Educational displays help interpret these ecosystems and the landscape as a whole for visitors.

The greenway is tied to nearby areas with several narrow corridors. To the west, riparian vegetation along Todd Creek links the site with adjacent farms, which are an important food source for birds, especially in winter. A corridor is proposed along Third Creek, to connect the greenway to Barr Lake, 3 miles to the southeast. Restoration of the channelized streambed and protection of the riparian zone are proposed to make this corridor suitable as both habitat and conduit for birds. However, since the recommended width of this riparian corridor is only 80 feet, some sensitive species of birds and mammals may not benefit. Nonetheless, this connection would tie together the two most important bird habitat areas north of Denver.

Narrow corridors, 25 to 50 feet in width, also tie a proposed residential area to the greenway just north of Third Creek. Here, greater width is unnecessary, since no larger habitat areas exist within the subdivision. The wooded corridors are intended to make the development more attractive to tolerant birds and to create a sense of continuity between the settlement and the river.

Finally, the river itself ties the site to other riparian habitats. To the north, the South Platte remains in a mostly agricultural matrix, where measures similar to those proposed here could be implemented. Toward Denver, where the river corridor is channelized and industrialized, restoration could enhance connectivity and habitat.

Conclusions

Because of the design's stated emphasis on bird habitat, one element that is missing is consideration of mammals, like small predators or beaver, that could use the area but might require larger areas of habitat, wider connecting corridors, or more isolation from human influence than most birds. Future studies and design could also go beyond the objectives of this project. Impacts of the planned mining operations and subdivisions on water quality should be a key concern. Depending on the nature of nearby agriculture and suburban development, it might be possible to add elements to the design that would maximize filtration of sediment and nutrients.

The design for this 2-mile-long section of the South Platte makes effective use of landscape ecology principles. It considers processes at all scales and aims to increase spatial and temporal heterogeneity, to restore damaged areas, and to integrate people and nature. If implemented, the design would create a greenway that is highly functional in a variety of ways. By maintaining existing habitat and restoring areas that will be disturbed by mining, the greenway would become an important habitat for both resident and migratory birds. It not only would be accessible to people but through careful integration of recreational and educational facilities would increase people's enjoyment of the river and make them more aware of their own interactive role in nature. With the extension of corridors to adjacent farms, to residential areas, and to Barr Lake, the greenway would be linked to nearby communities and natural areas.

This emphasis on establishing connections with residential areas may be one of the design's most innovative features. Hirschman discusses our modern tendency to separate the natural from the artificial: "Instead of increasing contrast . . . the trend should be reversed and the influence of these natural areas extended more into and through adjacent urban, suburban, and/or agricultural lands" (Hirschman 1988, 3). This approach could be a problematic assignment in forested landscapes, where detrimental edge effects come more into play. But the concept, combined with a holistic approach to design, can go far toward promoting a more complementary relationship between people and nature.

The Woodlands, Texas

Although greenways frequently exist in urban or suburban landscapes, their design has not often been integrated into the development process itself. An exception is The Woodlands, Texas, where an 18,000-acre new town was founded in the early 1970s on the outskirts of Houston. Open space at The Woodlands includes an integrated network of greenways to provide natural drainage and flood control as well as wildlife habitat, recreation areas, and a naturalistic, wooded setting for the town.

The project was initiated by developer George Mitchell who "envisioned a city that would spring up in the midst of the woods, in harmony with the forces of nature" (Spirn 1984, 163). Toward this end, the firm of Wallace, McHarg, Roberts, and Todd (WMRT) was hired to develop an ecological development plan for the town.

The Woodlands stretches across a mosaic of pine-oak forest in the coastal plain of the Gulf of Mexico. Except where a few streams have carved their way through the land, the area is quite flat and much of it is underlain by poorly drained soils; water thus moves slowly off the site, whether through surface flow or groundwater. As will be discussed shortly, coping with this poor drainage was a major challenge for The Woodlands' designers.

An Ecological Planning Method

The planning method used by WMRT was based on both the firm's previous work and on techniques developed by Ian McHarg and his colleagues at the University of Pennsylvania's Department of Landscape Architecture and Regional Planning. In essence, the method consists of (1) ecological inventory and analysis, (2) determination of the allowable development intensity for different parts of the town based on site sensitivity and potential impacts of different types of development, and (3) development of specific guidelines for site design (WMRT 1974).

With the help of technical consultants, the designers conducted a comprehensive ecological inventory for the entire tract. The inventory included geology, groundwater and surface water hydrology, water quality, soils, vegetation, wildlife, and climate. By examining resource data, ecological process was interpreted to reveal the importance of various components and their susceptibility to development impacts.

This analysis revealed that hydrology—specifically the fate of excess runoff that would be generated by development—was a key limitation for development because of the preponderance of poorly drained soils. Traditional development strategies would have sought to move water off the site quickly by using storm drains and by channelizing streams. These actions, in turn, would have destroyed most riparian habitat, lowered the water table, reduced recharge of an underlying aquifer, decreased water quality, and caused more erratic, potentially damaging flows downstream.

It was shown that a variety of creative design solutions could be combined to preserve the area's natural drainage system and minimize disruption of the natural hydrologic regime. Solutions included retaining streams and floodplains in a natural state, concentrating development in areas with impermeable soils, and directing runoff to permeable soils, natural ponds, and artificial swales (Figure 7.31). It also became clear that preserving the natural pattern of drainage ways was key to maintaining other ecological features such as water quality, riparian vegetation, and wildlife.

The next step used a series of transparent maps from the resource inventory showing streams and floodplains, prime recharge soils, and important vegetation and wildlife habitat. Maps of these attributes—all of which were considered unsuitable for development—were sandwiched together to form a composite showing the recommended form of protected open space.

Figure 7.31 shows proposed major open space, most of which takes the form of riparian greenways along both perennial and intermittent streams. Additional open space was recommended throughout the developed areas in smaller neighborhood parks and along roads. Not all of these areas were slated to remain in a natural state, however, since parks, playgrounds, and recreational facilities were needed for residential areas. All told, the plan called for 30 percent of the site to remain in natural areas and another 14 percent of open space to be developed for recreation and other community uses.

Landscape tolerance was determined for parts of the town that were open to development. Tolerance was defined as the percentage of an area that could be

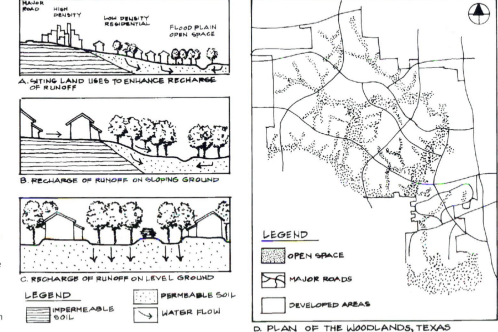

Figure 7.31 Natural drainage system for The Woodlands, including siting of development to encourage infiltration of runoff (A, B, and C) and proposed open space along perennial and intermittent streams (D). (Redrawn with permission from Spirn 1984.)

197

cleared of vegetation without unduly damaging vegetative communities and wildlife habitat or that could be covered with impermeable material without increasing the amount of runoff from the site during a typical high-frequency storm. This information was then matched with estimates of land-use intensity, the amount of clearance and coverage needed for various types and densities of development. In this way, a mosaic of allowable development intensity for areas outside the open-space network was determined that would minimize impacts to vegetation, wildlife, and hydrology. Because hydrology was the most crucial factor, concentrated development was proposed at higher elevations and on impermeable soils, areas where soil infiltration would be poor even without development.

Obviously, a certain amount of disruption to the natural environment had to be accepted if the development was to achieve other social and economic goals. For instance, planning for the *typical* high-frequency storm implicitly accepted that occasional more severe storms might not be fully accommodated by the drainage system. Economic models were employed to guide both design of the open-space system and the intensity of development, since the plan ultimately had to be economically viable for the developer.

The plan goes beyond this broad delineation of open space and allowable development intensity and includes detailed guidelines for design at the site scale. Some of the more important guidelines are summarized in Table 7.5.

Evaluation of the Master Plan and Guidelines

Together with the master plan, these guidelines are worthy of further evaluation on several counts. Maintaining natural stream channels and floodplains marks a progressive and ecologically sound approach that can be expected to work well as the core of this multipurpose network of open space. The plan's combined elements of (1) protecting floodplains, (2) concentrating development on impermeable soils where it will have

Table 7.5 Objectives and guidelines for site-scale design of The Woodlands

Objective	Guideline
Protect floodplains and stream channels in their natural states	Maintain the natural stream channel and floodplain in all drainages. Define drainage easements to protect the 25-year floodplain of all drainages. Easements will be at least 300 feet for primary drainages and 100 feet for secondary drainages. For Panther and Spring creeks, the two most important perennial streams, prohibit all development within the 50-year floodplain. Permit only minimal clearing within the 100-year floodplain: no lawns allowed, and buildings must be raised above the 100-year flood level so as not to impede floodwaters.
Retard runoff and maximize recharge to even base flow of streams	Use check dams in swales on house lots to slow flow over permeable soils to enhance recharge. Direct runoff to ponds and swales and over permeable soils with excess storage capacity.
Maintain vegetation around recharge ponds for water quality and wildlife habitat	Maintain sufficient vegetation as a buffer around ponds to ensure good water quality and habitat for wildlife. Forty percent of the pond's perimeter may be developed, but a 50-foot forested buffer must be maintained. The remaining 60 percent should have a 150-foot buffer.
Protect significant forest types	Protect and minimize clearance of pure or predominantly hardwood stands, which are less common, less tolerant of development, and better wildlife habitat than pine stands.
Protect individual trees and small stands not cleared in house lots	Maintain a buffer zone (one canopy diameter for hardwoods, one canopy radius for conifers) around each tree or stand.
Maximize aesthetics of The Woodlands through use of vegetation in site planning and design	Use native vegetation to buffer narrow front yards and to limit the artificial environment along roads.
Provide for wildlife movement	Form continuous wildlife corridors that include food, cover, and water. Major corridors should be 500 to 600 feet wide. Minor corridors should be 100 feet wide.
Buffer wildlife from disturbance by humans	Provide large areas offering diverse vegetation cover and water that are suitable as wildlife refuges. Natural areas not suited for active recreation should be selected as refuges. Major wildlife corridors should connect these natural areas. Minimize crossings of the wildlife corridors by pedestrian and vehicular movement. Keep human activity to the periphery of wildlife corridors to minimize disturbance.

Source: Adapted from WMRT (1973).

the least hydrological impact, and (3) encouraging recharge by directing drainage to areas with permeable soils and to retention ponds make up a highly effective solution to the site's hydrological constrains (Figure 7.31). Guidelines for protecting native vegetation in neighborhood parks and even individual lots enhance the plan's effectiveness by further reducing runoff and increasing infiltration. The drainage system offers financial benefits as well; when the plan was proposed, engineers estimated that it would save the developer more than $14 million compared to a more conventional system.

The plan's effectiveness, however, may be reduced by limiting the total protected width of intermittent stream corridors to 100 feet. Since the width of the stream itself is included in this figure, this width leaves a riparian buffer of less than 50 feet on each side of the stream. As is stressed in chapter 4, vegetation along intermittent drainages can be particularly important in protecting water quality because they typically make up a large proportion of the total exposed edge of the drainage network.

The Woodlands plan is farsighted in considering both wildlife habitat and the basic need of animals to move throughout the landscape. Protection of corridors for wildlife movement is explicitly included in the plan and guidelines. The guidelines also consider the impact of people and recreation on wildlife and recommend provisions to minimize this disturbance. However, the plan was created before the negative effects of edge conditions on native species were widely recognized. It thus follows the conventional wisdom of the day, noting some of the beneficial influence of forest edge without distinguishing between edge and interior species.

Although the needs of white-tailed deer were considered in recommending the width of major corridors at 600 feet, recent research suggests that this width is probably insufficient to limit invasion of exotic species that threaten forest-interior birds (Noss, chapter 3, this volume). Furthermore, the plan is not concerned with predatory mammals, the very species that would stand to benefit most from habitat connectivity but some of which may require widths greater than 600 feet. In fact, bobcat, fox, and coyote are specifically noted as undesirable species, as are certain reptiles. Many of the species considered to be desirable—cottontail rabbit, raccoon, gray squirrel, and opossum—would thrive in these narrow greenways but may not require the degree of connectivity provided, since they are well adapted to the suburban environment.

Despite these flaws, the master plan and guidelines for The Woodlands aim to preserve the oak-pine forest that spreads through the town. They effectively address ways to provide a pleasing naturalistic aesthetic with far greater local diversity and abundance of flora and fauna than would be found in a traditional development.

Implementing the Plan

More than half of The Woodlands has now been developed for both residential and commercial use. Population is expected eventually to exceed 150,000. Although many of the original plan's recommendations have been followed, others have not.

Perennial streams, the scheme's ecological backbone, have been maintained in a natural state, and a significant riparian buffer—as much as several hundred feet wide on each side—has been protected in most areas. In at least one case, however, recent construction within 100 feet of a stream infringed on riparian habitat and contributed sediment to the aquatic environment.

In another deviation from the plan, intermittent streams have been channelized, and their natural riparian vegetation has been stripped and replaced with mowed grass. Channelizing drainage ways to decrease the area of floodplains and move water off the site more quickly probably allows more house lots to be created without risking flood damage. Negative consequences of this action may include a lower water table,

Figure 7.32 A channelized intermittent stream running through a golf course at The Woodlands. Stripped of its natural vegetation, this waterway is now more susceptible to contaminants (including fertilizers) and provides virtually no habitat for native wildlife. (Photo by D. Smith.)

more uneven stream flows, reduced water quality, and a reduction in wildlife habitat and movement options. Scenic quality and recreational use of the streams are greatly reduced (Figure 7.32).

The location of high- and low-density development according to soil type and vegetation appears to have been done as planned; most roads or high-density

Figure 7.33 One of many retention ponds in The Woodlands, which increase natural storage and infiltration of storm water and provide pleasing scenery as well. (Photo by D. Smith.)

Figure 7.34 Roadside drainage is allowed to soak into the ground instead of being diverted directly to waterways, where it would contribute to heightened downstream flooding.
(Photo by D. Smith.)

development occur at higher elevations and on poorly drained soils (Spirn 1984). Natural ponds have been retained and, in some cases, enlarged to increase runoff retention and groundwater recharge (Figure 7.33). Originally, all new development made use of check dams and small retention basins to allow on-site infiltration (Figure 7.34). More recently, residential developments have been fitted with traditional storm drains because they require less maintenance than retention basins and because they are preferred aesthetically by homeowners. In this instance, more careful attention to aesthetics might have made the design more attractive. For instance, the retention basins might have been made into small areas of wetland vegetation fitted to a site's particular characteristics (M. Binford, personal communication).

Although some recommendations of the original plan have not been followed, the drainage system was clearly a success following early stages of development. After a record storm hit the area in April 1979, "nine inches of rain fell within five hours, and no house within The Woodlands flooded, although adjacent subdivisions were awash" (Spirn 1984, 166). Likewise, studies made after the first phase of development showed that downstream water quality was significantly better than below other nearby developments (Spirn 1984).

A significant portion of the planned open space has been used for development. Although the original master plan called for 44 percent of the area to be left in open space (both developed and natural), this percentage has been decreased to about 25 percent, according to promotional material for The Woodlands. One of the casualties of this reduction was an upland greenway running southwest to northeast in about the center of the town that would have linked two of the three primary drainages together. The drainages are linked farther downstream where they converge, but much upland habitat, as well as an additional option for movement, has been sacrificed.

Still, a significant portion of the town remains wooded and makes up a connected network of open space. Buffers of natural vegetation have been preserved along all major roads. Combined with regulations that strictly limit the visibility of commercial development and advertising, these roadside greenways give The Woodlands a pleasing, naturalistic appearance that is unusual for a modern suburb (Figure 7.35). Over 60 miles of paved pathways allow residents to enjoy the town's natural areas.

The vegetation also attracts many songbirds and small mammals and creates a cooler environment in the torrid east-Texas climate. But wide-ranging or sensitive species are unlikely to use these narrow corridors. If they did, the frequent road crossings would probably be a source of mortality.

Figure 7.35 Wooded roadside strips and low-key commercial development and signs help keep The Woodlands landscape pleasing to the eye and add connected habitat for edge-adapted wildlife. (Photo by D. Smith.)

Conclusion

Most of these comments regarding the effectiveness of the original plan and its implementation are based on qualitative observation. This raises an important issue for innovative projects like The Woodlands, namely, the need for ecological monitoring.

There has been no systematic monitoring at The Woodlands to help evaluate the effectiveness of the design method or its implementation. Nor is continued study or evaluation traditionally built into the design or budget of such projects; it is the exception rather than the rule. If conducted by a university or other institution with long-term follow-up capability, before-and-after monitoring of water quality and wildlife in planned developments like The Woodlands could be an invaluable source of information on which to base future designs.

Nonetheless, a useful evaluation can be made. The Woodlands has achieved many of its original goals, although it has fallen short of others. Forested corridors along roadsides and streams combined with natural vegetation laced throughout developed areas give the town an unusually pleasing aesthetic environment. In exploring The Woodlands, one feels enlivened by the sites and sounds of the remaining forest rather than pushed by relentless suburban traffic through endless commercial strips and monotonous subdivisions. Although the drainage system includes several unsightly and ecologically harmful channelized intermittent streams, it is clearly more ecologically sound than traditional drainage infrastructures because perennial streams and much of their floodplains are protected. Although native biodiversity is probably diminished because of edge effects that intrude into narrow greenways, much wildlife remains on the site, and the sounds of songbirds abound. Finally, as a new town that followed a rational, systematic, ecologically based method, The Woodlands represents an important step in the development of ecological design and an experiment from which to learn.

Quabbin to Wachusett
Wildlife Corridor Study, Massachusetts

Central Massachusetts is a largely forested region with areas of protected lands scattered through extensive areas of privately owned forest. Long interested in wildlife conservation in the area, the Massachusetts Audubon Society sponsored a series of wildlife corridor design exercises at the University of Massachusetts at Amherst in 1990. The exercises were conducted by graduate students in landscape architecture and regional planning under the direction of Professors Jack Ahern and Scott Bollens (Ahern et al. 1990). The project made use of existing data bases and a geographic information system to develop a method for greenway design and to apply the method to the central-Massachusetts landscape.

The University of Massachusetts study and the design method described in chapter 6 have common roots: both were derived in part from earlier work conducted by Paul Hellmund for the Massachusetts Audubon Society. Although chapter 6 presents a more complete and overarching method (by considering water quality and recreation), this case study represents the fullest realistic application to date of such a method.

Background

More than a hundred years ago, this part of Massachusetts, like much of New England, was mostly agricultural, having earlier been cleared of its native forest cover. In the nineteenth century, agriculture declined in importance, and abandoned land became reforested. Today, this landscape is about 80 percent forested and contains scattered roads and small towns.

Economic growth in the area is slow, and forest connectivity does not appear to be immediately threatened by development and fragmentation. But the area's proximity to Boston (about an hour's drive) suggests that this situation could change in the future. Taking a long view of potential threats to the region's wildlife suggested that careful planning during a period of relative stability could help establish a rational framework for future land protection.

The area of interest to the Massachusetts Audubon Society consists of 272,000 acres between state lands surrounding the Quabbin and Wachusett reservoirs (Figure 7.36). For the purposes of the University of Massachusetts study, a smaller target area of 38,400 acres was selected between the Quabbin Reservoir and Wachusett Mountain State Reserve (Figure 7.36). The project's main goal was to use a geographic information system to identify wildlife corridors that could link together existing protected areas. This task, guided by patterns of public and otherwise protected land, was sometimes at odds with the topographic grain of the landscape: shaped by glaciation more than 10,000 years ago, streams and ridges (both potential conduits) consistently trend south to north, as do roads (potential barriers) built along the contours of the land.

A second goal was to explore ways to integrate wildlife corridor design into the broader development process for the area. Ecological analysis of corridor options was therefore combined with consideration of development suitability and scenic resources.

The Approach

To develop specific criteria for greenway design, two fragmentation-sensitive species with fairly specific habitat requirements were chosen as indicator species: river otter and fisher. Fisher require a mixed forest of hardwood and softwood with continuous canopy. River otter require stream corridors with high water quality buffered by continuous forest and are therefore the more specialized of the two species. Since both species are predators, their presence indicates a healthy food chain at lower trophic levels. Existing cover-type data and a geographic information system were used to identify and evaluate habitat for the two species.

Potential nodes for a habitat network were identified throughout the study area by identifying areas where suitable habitat for the two species coincided with existing protected areas (Figure 7.37). Once the nodes were chosen, a series of broad swaths were

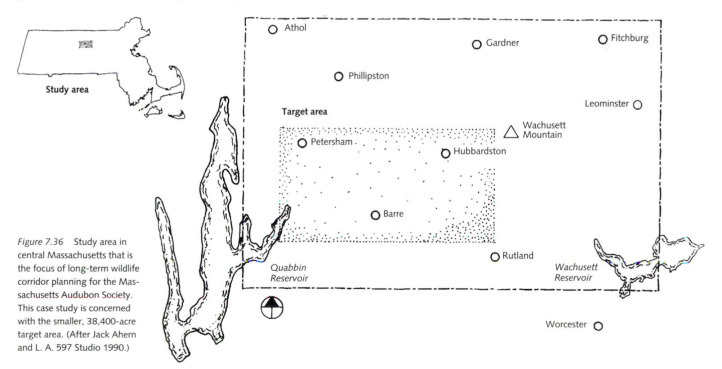

Figure 7.36 Study area in central Massachusetts that is the focus of long-term wildlife corridor planning for the Massachusetts Audubon Society. This case study is concerned with the smaller, 38,400-acre target area. (After Jack Ahern and L. A. 597 Studio 1990.)

203

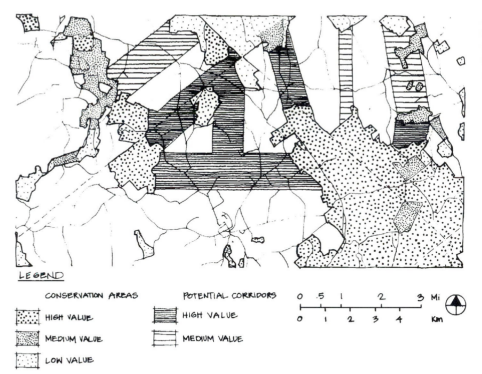

Figure 7.37 Habitat nodes (protected habitats suitable for both fisher and otter) in the target area and broad swaths capable of linking the nodes together. (After Jack Ahern and L. A. 597 Studio 1990.)

LEGEND

CONSERVATION AREAS   POTENTIAL CORRIDORS

HIGH VALUE   HIGH VALUE

MEDIUM VALUE   MEDIUM VALUE

LOW VALUE

0   .5   1   2   3 Mi

0   1   2   3   4   Km

selected that could link them together (Figure 7.37).

The study's focus was broadened to include consideration of scenic features and areas with potential for future development. Lands having development suitability (a function of soils, slope, natural hazard potential, and road access) and scenic features were located within the target area.

Next, a representative swath running east to west between the Ware River watershed, managed by the Metropolitan District Commission (a state agency), and the Massachusetts Audubon Society's Rutland Brook Sanctuary was selected for further study. (This swath appears in the center of Figure 7.37.) The scenic and development suitability information was then examined for the chosen swath. It was found that the swath did contain scenic features worthy of protection and that a wildlife corridor within the swath would probably not have a significant effect on future development, since most of the swath had fairly low development potential.

Property boundaries were also researched for the chosen swath and recorded with the GIS. Since this research and digitizing took a great deal of time, working with property information before this stage (i.e., for the entire target area) would have resulted in much wasted effort (see chapter 6 for a further discussion of this sieving technique).

Within the broad swath, specific criteria relating to habitat and movement needs of fisher and otter were used to map suitable corridors. Based on a literature review and consultations with wildlife experts, the minimum width needed for the two species was estimated at 300 feet, with an additional 50-foot buffer on each side that could be used for recreation.

In addition to width, other criteria were chosen according to two scenarios. The first scenario used wildlife habitat and movement needs as its main determinants, and the second focused on criteria that would minimize effects on private property and future development. Both scenarios emphasized the need to avoid significant movement barriers (roads and developed areas) and to provide alternate movement pathways.

Specific criteria included the following:

Wildlife Habitat and Movement Scenario

1. Select the shortest routes between habitat areas.
2. Provide interbasin linkages for otter to move between drainages.
3. Avoid barriers.
4. Establish a minimum of three routes to mitigate against future disturbance.

Least Property Impact Scenario

1. Straddle existing property lines to minimize the effects on individual parcels.
2. Connect existing protected and undevelopable lands.
3. Avoid barriers.
4. Establish a minimum of three routes to mitigate against future disturbance.

In both cases, riparian corridors (trending north to south) were known to be largely protected by state wetland and floodplain regulations; it was interbasin (upland) linkages and connection of the existing protected areas that were the main focus.

The GIS was used to locate corridors with both sets of criteria; the results of the two scenarios are shown in Figures 7.38 and 7.39. The wildlife scenario identified direct and relatively short corridors that linked drainages and the public lands together from east to west. The least property impact criteria also produced east-to-west linkages, but these corridors generally did not sever parcels of private lands and made greater use of existing public lands. How well these corridors would actually function for wildlife was not determined—this would thus be a crucial question for future research.

Because the two network configurations related so differently to property boundaries, potential suitability of land conservation techniques was considered as a final part of the study. Because the corridors designed solely according to wildlife criteria usually crossed through the middle of properties and thus disrupted other potential uses, fee-simple purchase (or variations like purchase and lease back, or bargain sales) was deemed most appropriate in this case. Corridors that straddled boundaries, however, would be easier to protect through regulatory measures like zoning or conservation restrictions because they cause less disruption to the use of private land.

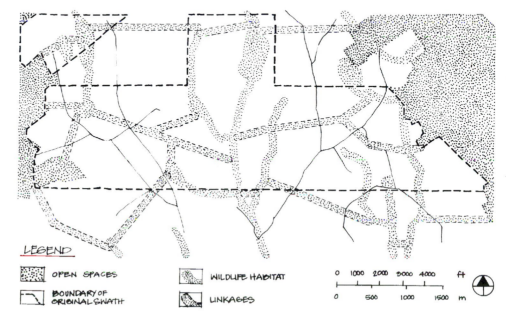

Figure 7.38 Corridor locations determined with criteria that would maximize suitability for wildlife. One of the key objectives of this scenario was to minimize interbasin travel distances for otter. (After Jack Ahern and L. A. 597 Studio 1990.)

LEGEND

OPEN SPACES

BOUNDARY OF ORIGINAL SWATH

WILDLIFE HABITAT

LINKAGES

The study does not make a final recommendation about which scenario is best but rather was intended as a preliminary exercise. For instance, the study specifically recognizes that the width criteria chosen are somewhat arbitrary and recommends a policy of adaptive management, whereby future research and monitoring could be used to further refine the method and its criteria. The overarching goal was to develop an effective design process and explore different options rather than to produce a definitive recommendation.

As is discussed in chapter 6, the use of indicator species is problematic because they sometimes fail to accurately represent the needs of entire wildlife communities. In this case, the 300-foot width deemed necessary for fisher and otter might not be enough for some other sensitive species, especially forest-interior birds.

The emphasis on ownership and development potential as part of the design process may at first seem to be a distraction from the task of designing wildlife corridors. However, recognizing and incorporating the socioeconomic context of the area contribute further to the information base upon which future land protection and policy decisions can be made. Further research

might suggest that the more direct corridors selected with the wildlife habitat and movement scenario are necessary for one or both of the two species. But, if the alternate scenario, which minimizes effects on property ownership, should prove to be effective for wildlife, its use would improve the chances of successfully implementing a corridor because land protection would be simplified and less expensive.

Conclusion

Unlike most of the case studies described in this chapter, the central-Massachusetts study was conducted in a landscape that still possesses extensive areas of connected habitat where many corridor options exist. The study is unique because it starts with few assumptions about corridor locations and proceeds systematically through different scales, locating a study area, broad swaths, and, finally, specific corridor options. Although further study of species needs, potential effects of adjacent land uses, and other factors will be needed to refine the design of particular corridors, the study provides excellent documentation of a useful method for ecological design.

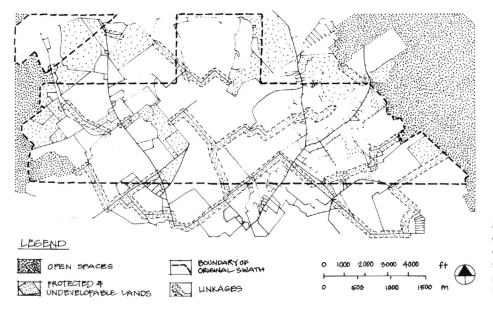

LEGEND

OPEN SPACES

PROTECTED &
UNDEVELOPABLE LANDS

BOUNDARY OF
ORIGINAL SWATH

LINKAGES

0 1000 2000 3000 4000 ft
0 500 1000 1500 m

Figure 7.39 An alternate scenario designed to minimize impacts on private ownerships. Note that the corridors straddle property lines to avoid severing private holdings. (After Jack Ahern and L. A. 597 Studio 1990.)

References

Ahern, J. and the Spring 1990 LA/RP 597 Studio. 1990. Wildlife corridor planning in central Massachusetts. In Proceedings from Selected Educational Sessions of the 1990 American Society of Landscape Architects Annual Meeting, San Diego, Calif.

Albuquerque Office of Open Space. 1990. *Bosque News* 2(2) (May/June).

Albuquerque Parks and Recreation Department. 1987. Rio Grande Valley State Park Management Plan. Albuquerque Parks and Recreation, Open Space Division.

Boulder County. 1986. Boulder County comprehensive plan: Goals, policies and maps. Boulder, Colo.

Boulder County Nature Association. 1989. An ecosystem plan for Boulder County. Unpublished manuscript.

City of Boulder. 1990. Boulder's greenways: Design guidelines. Unpublished manuscript.

Edelman, P. 1990. Critical wildlife corridor/habitat linkage areas between the Santa Susana Mountains, the Simi Hills and the Santa Monica Mountains. Unpublished paper prepared for The Nature Conservancy, San Francisco.

Hall, D., J. Hirschman, and F. Steiner. 1989. The design of nature: The use of landscape ecology in bird habitat design. In Proceedings of Council of Educators in Landscape Architecture (CELA) Annual Conference.

Hallock, D. 1990. An ecosystem plan for Boulder County, Colorado. Paper presented at the Conference on Landscape Ecology and Planning, Arizona State University, February.

Harris, L. D. 1985. Conservation corridors: A highway system for wildlife. *ENFO* 11:1–10. Florida Conservation Foundation, Winter Park.

———. 1988. Landscape linkages: The dispersal corridor approach to wildlife conservation. In Transactions of the 53d North American Wildlife and Natural Resources Conference.

Harris, L. D., and R. F. Noss. 1985. Problems in categorizing the status of species: Endangerment with the best of intentions. In Proceedings of 16th IUCN technical meeting, Madrid, Spain, November 1984.

Harris, L. D., and P. B. Gallagher. 1989. New initiatives for wildlife conservation: The need for movement corridors. Pages 11–34 in G. Mackintosh, ed., *Preserving Communities and Corridors.* Defenders of Wildlife, Washington, D.C.

Hirschman, J. 1988. Bird habitat design for people: A landscape ecological approach. Master's thesis, University of Colorado at Denver, Department of Landscape Architecture.

Hoffman, S. W. 1990. Bosque biological monitoring program: Bird population surveys in Rio Grande Valley State Park (1987–1990). Unpublished report prepared for City of Albuquerque, OpenSpace Division.

Lynch, J. M. 1984. Suwannee River Preserve Design Project. Florida Natural Areas Inventory, Tallahassee, Fla. and The Nature Conservancy, Chapel Hill, N.C.

Maehr, D. S. 1990. The Florida panther and private lands. *Conservation Biology* 4(2): 167–70.

Maehr, D. S., E. D. Land, and J. C. Roof. 1991. Florida panthers. *National Geographic Research and Exploration* 7(4): 414–31.

Mason, M. S. 1991. Lions roam in the suburbs. *Christian Science Monitor,* 26 Sept.

Middleton, H. 1989. The Pinhook: A wilderness corridor. *Nature Conservancy,* Sept./Oct.

Noss, R. F. 1991. A critical review of the U.S. Fish and Wildlife Service's proposal to establish a captive breeding population of Florida panthers, with emphasis on the population reestablishment issue. A report to the Fund for Animals. Unpublished manuscript.

Noss, R. F., and L. D. Harris. 1986. Nodes, networks and MUMs: Preserving diversity at all scales. *Environmental Management* 10(3): 299–309.

Rubin, B. P., and G. Emmerich, Jr. 1981. Refining the delineation of environmental corridors in southeastern Wisconsin. Southeastern Wisconsin Regional Planning Commission Technical Record, 4(2).

Santa Monica Mountains Conservancy. 1990. Preserving the critical link: A discussion of the wildlife corridor from the Santa Susana Mountains to the Santa Monica Mountains via the Simi Hills. Unpublished report.

Shafer, C. L. 1991. *Nature Reserves: Island Theory and Conservation Practice.* Smithsonian Institution Press, Washington D. C.

Soulé, M. 1989. U.S. Dept. of Interior-National Park Service proposed land exchange: Wildlife corridors. Unpublished report prepared for the Santa Monica Mountains National Recreation Area.

Southeastern Wisconsin Regional Planning Commission. 1985. Twenty-five years of regional planning. Waukesha, Wis.

Spirn, A. W. 1984. *The Granite Garden: Urban Nature and Human Design.* Basic Books, New York.

Suwannee River Water Management District. 1992. 1992 Land acquisition and management plan. Live Oak, Fla.

Wallace, McHarg, Roberts, and Todd. 1973. Woodlands new community: Guidelines for site planning. Unpublished report prepared for The Woodlands Development Corporation. WMRT, Philadelphia.

———. 1974. Woodlands new community: An ecological plan.

Unpublished report prepared for The Woodlands Development Corporation. WMRT, Philadelphia.

Windell, J. T., L. P. Rink, and C. Rudkin. 1991. Compatibility of stream habitat reclamation with point source and nonpoint source controls. *Water, Environment and Technology,* January.

Wisconsin Department of Natural Resources. n. d. Kettle Moraine State Forest: Southern Unit Visitor. (Interpretive park guide).

Wooding, J. 1990. Recommendations to reduce the impact of the Orlando Beltway and S.R. 46 to black bears in the Wekiva River area. Florida Game and Freshwater Fish Commission. Unpublished paper.

Case Study Acknowledgments

In addition to the references cited in the text, these case studies are based on generous assistance, information, and insight provided by the following people. Any errors are solely the author's responsibility.

Southeastern Wisconsin: Gerald H. Emmerich, Donald M. Reed, and Bruce P. Rubin

Florida: Melissa Foster, Larry Harris, Jennifer McMurtray, J. Merill Lynch, Dave Maehr, Gary Evink, and Reed Noss

Rio Grande Valley State Park: Barbara Baca, Nano Takuma, and Manuel Molles

Boulder: John Barnett, Dave Hallock, Rich Koopman, Chris Rudkin, Delani Wheeler, and Jay Windell

Santa Monica to Santa Susana mountains: Paul Edelman, Paul Rose, and Mike Williams

South Platte River: Joan Hirschman and Fritz Steiner

The Woodlands: Richard Brown and Jim Wendt

Central Massachusetts: Jack Ahern and Paul Hellmund

Paul Cawood Hellmund

Epilogue: Green Ways

Rights of Passage

Having read this book many readers may find themselves considering new ways to protect nature and even thinking differently about nature itself. One unavoidable conclusion is that the dynamics of nature can only be conserved successfully by recognizing and incorporating the inevitable change and connectedness of landscapes in what might be called green ways. But readers may reach a further and more profound conclusion, one that transcends the need for new conservation techniques, as real as that need may be. This conclusion is what Aldo Leopold saw as the need for an ethic that includes "soils, waters, plants, and animals, or collectively the land" (Leopold 1949, 204). In making decisions based on a land ethic, he believed "a thing is right when it tends to preserve the integrity, stability, and beauty of the biotic community. It is wrong when it tends otherwise" (Leopold 1949, 224–25). Landscape ecologist Richard Forman incorporates

context and change into this ethical demand: "It is unethical to consider an area in isolation from its surroundings or from its development over time" (Forman 1987, 227).

Ecologically designed greenways can help preserve the "integrity, stability, and beauty" of biotic communities when the broadest spatial and temporal perspective is brought to their design. But that same broad perspective alerts us that the natural systems discussed in this book, including the habitat and movement needs of plants and animals and the flow and filtration of water, pertain at least in some degree to *every* place on our planet.

After years of trying to make nature fit neatly and completely within set boundaries removed from people—a fit as ill conceived as square pegs in round holes—the accumulating evidence points to little success for such an approach. It is clear that isolated reserves alone will not be enough—not enough to sustain most of today's plants and animals, not enough to intercept contaminants and purify polluted waters, not enough to reduce the threats from flooding, not even enough to let a majority of people live closely with nature.

Recognizing the failure of the historical approach of creating isolated protected areas, the World Commission on Environment and Development saw a new conservation approach evolving, one they characterized as anticipate and prevent: "Altering economic and land use patterns seems to be the best long-term approach to ensuring the survival of species and ecosystems" (World Commission on Environment and Development 1987, 157).

Large numbers of people in North America and elsewhere are aware of the threats today facing tropical rain forests in Amazonia. But how many are concerned about the mundane backyard problems like the fertilizers that are running off lawns and degrading water quality in local lakes and streams? And, what about the toxic salts and oils that are ending up in the same waters after being washed from streets and driveways, or the native animal and plant species that are disappearing from North America because their habitat is shrinking and becoming isolated? Nature in need of protecting is nearer than we may have thought and more in need than we may have believed.

Today there is an ecological imperative for anyone who has anything to do with the care of land, whether as visitor, owner, designer, or manager. Ethical treatment of natural processes, including the movement of plants, animals, and water, demands a right of passage for nature, preferably through areas that have historically served as conduits but at least through suitable adjacent areas.

Recognizing and accommodating natural processes in design and planning are not new concepts. (Ian McHarg's seminal work, *Design with Nature*, was published nearly a quarter of a century ago.) But what has yet to become commonplace is the comprehensive view that obliges us to conserve connections, when appropriate, from property to property, landscape to landscape, and region to region. This view takes a broader perspective than has been permitted most designers and managers, whose actions are usually restricted by the boundaries of a single parcel at a time.

If Wildlife Flowed Like Water

Some of nature's movements through and across land are carefully protected, sometimes by law. Water is the best example of this for many obvious reasons: ignoring the movement of water can result in damage to life and property, restricting a stream's natural flow can be illegal if water rights for irrigation or drinking supply are held by others downstream, and speeding storm waters through an area can result in downstream flooding.

Few such short-term penalties, whether financial or ecological, are as apparent when wildlife movement is disrupted. There may be immediate and dire ecological consequences of human-caused changes, but since movement needs of wildlife are poorly understood, often hard to monitor, and usually ignored outside of protected lands, in most cases the impact on wildlife goes unnoticed. (Some wildlife disruptions are readily noticed, such as the semideveloped areas that partially block traditional migration routes of the elk herd in Boulder County, Colorado, as it carefully makes its way to winter pasture. See chapter 7.)

If wildlife and other elements of nature were guaranteed the right to move through landscapes in the way water requires and if the same severity of problems resulted when they could not, wildlife conservation would be radically different than it is. Every landscape would be dissected by protected movement zones—greenways.

Considerable efforts have been made over many years to protect the movement paths of one kind of wildlife—waterfowl—by preserving stopover points along flyways. Only recently have steps been taken to recognize and protect terrestrial wildlife movement corridors over large areas, such as the work described in the Boulder County, Colorado, case study (chapter 7). These efforts deal with very broad patterns of movement.

Isolated Greenways Are Not Enough

The multiple-scale approach used throughout this book and incorporated in the design method (chapter 6) is a means of looking at more than broad regional or landscape questions of connectivity. Less significant movement corridors and small streams may never be officially designated as greenways, but nonetheless they play a role in wildlife movement and water-quality protection. Considering connectivity across scales, from regions to backyards, helps identify many opportunities to protect the functions of natural systems. Official greenways have a major role to play in this protecting, but they need to be complemented with green fingers that protect waterways and maintain native connectivity. Being on private land, most of these fingers would depend on landowners' alertness to nature's needs and their willingness to preserve them. But, there could be mechanisms to help or require landowners to realize the ecological imperative of conserving such wildlife and riparian corridors.

Thus, public greenways (as well as large conserved areas) may be dedicated to maintaining and enhancing the most significant flows of animals, plants, and water, but much more enlightened thinking must come to *every* piece of land. Green fingers can follow the less significant, but still important, flows. Heavily urbanized areas will not have the same imperative as undisturbed lands, but nature exists there too and deserves recognition.

To make certain that useful connections are maintained from property to property will require greater resources and responsibility than a single landowner, designer, or manager generally has. This is a role for government and nonprofit organizations. Ongoing public and private efforts will be needed to identify and monitor the changing network of flows that needs protecting in a region. The most important areas may need official designation and legal protection, but owners of land within any part of the network should have responsibility for maintaining their link in the system. The kind of cooperation necessary from landowners will have to overcome the long-held American notion that "it's my land, I'll do with it as I please."

Worth All the Effort?

The cross-boundary characteristics of natural systems call for a perspective broader than the boundaries of a single property, even if the area is large. Movement of wildlife and protection of water resources must be examined at the scale of landscapes and regions. New agencies and organizations, or revamped old ones, will be important to meet the current all-out attack on the natural world that has reached crisis proportions.

Greenways and other forms of public open space are vitally needed, but no matter how extensive they are, they will never relieve us of our responsibility to nurture biological communities and protect water quality across all parts of the landscape. This broad-scale conservation will take the cooperation of individual citizens and property owners everywhere. Such cooperation is not gained instantly, does not result simply from legal mandate, and can only come with education. In the long run it is the growing development of what Leopold called a land ethic and ecological consciousness within each of us that will ensure the survival of natural features and processes.

There is much work to be done by many hands if we are to turn around today's ecological crisis. People who are creating ecologically effective greenways are making a contribution to this important work. But greenways are only a start. The survival of the natural world can only be assured when green ways—an ecological perspective—characterize all of our actions toward the earth.

References

Forman, R. T. T. 1987. The ethics of isolation, the spread of disturbance, and landscape ecology. Pages 213–29 in M. Turner, ed., *Landscape Heterogeneity and Disturbance.* Springer-Verlag, New York.

Leopold, A. 1949. *A Sand County Almanac.* Oxford University Press, New York.

McHarg, I. L. 1969. *Design with Nature.* Natural History Press, New York.

World Commission of Environment and Development. 1987. *Our Common Future.* Oxford University Press, Oxford.

Contributors

Michael W. Binford is a limnologist who was born and raised in Kansas. He studied at Kansas State University, Louisiana University, and Indiana University, where he received a Ph.D. in Aquatic Ecology. After working for six years at the Florida Museum of Natural History at the University of Florida, he moved to Harvard, where he now teaches landscape architects about lakes, streams, and wetlands.

Michael J. Buchenau was raised in Colorado, received his master's degree in landscape architecture from Harvard University, and is practicing landscape architecture in the Rocky Mountain region. Of special interest to Mr. Buchenau is his involvement with the Urban Ecology Group of the Denver Urban Design Forum. He is committed to site design that foremost seeks to function within broader ecological systems.

David N. Cole is a biological scientist and leader of the Wilderness Management Research Unit, part of the Intermountain Research Station, Forest Service, U.S. Department of Agriculture, in Missoula, Montana. Dr. Cole has degrees in geography from the University of California, Berkeley, and the University of Oregon. His research has focused on the ecological impacts of recreation and the management of wilderness areas.

Paul Cawood Hellmund is a landscape architect who specializes in ecological design and conservation planning. Currently he works as a private consultant in Denver, Colorado. Formerly he was an assistant professor of landscape architecture and planning at Virginia Polytechnic Institute and State University, where his research focused on cartographic modeling for solving environmental problems. For several years he worked for the U.S. National Park Service on geographic information systems projects. He received his master's degree in landscape architecture from Harvard University, where he is currently completing a Ph.D. and where he has served as an instructor.

Reed F. Noss is a consultant in ecology and conservation biology, a half-time research scientist at the University of Idaho, College of Forestry, and a research associate at Stanford University Center for Conservation Biology. He is a member of the Board of Governors of the Society for Conservation Biology, on the editorial boards for *Conservation Biology* and the *Natural Areas Journal,* and science editor for *Wild Earth* magazine. He has over sixty technical publications in ecology and conservation biology.

Daniel S. Smith lives in New Hampshire, where he is a consultant in environmental education and ecological planning and design. He previously worked for the National Park Service River and Trail Conservation Assistance Program, where he was the director of projects for the state of Maine. He holds a master's degree from the Yale School of Forestry and Environmental Studies, where he studied forest ecology and the interactions between people and their environments.

James F. Thorne is an assistant professor of landscape ecology in the Department of Landscape Architecture and Regional Planning at the University of Pennsylvania, Philadelphia. He currently sits on the Executive Council of the International Association for Landscape Ecology (IALE) as its treasurer. His research interests include landscape ecological planning, ecological restoration technology, plant competition during old-field succession, and nutrient cycling.

Index